Democracy in Hard Places

Democracy
in Hard Places

Edited by

SCOTT MAINWARING AND TAREK MASOUD

OXFORD
UNIVERSITY PRESS

OXFORD
UNIVERSITY PRESS

Oxford University Press is a department of the University of Oxford. It furthers
the University's objective of excellence in research, scholarship, and education
by publishing worldwide. Oxford is a registered trade mark of Oxford University
Press in the UK and certain other countries.

Published in the United States of America by Oxford University Press
198 Madison Avenue, New York, NY 10016, United States of America.

Library of Congress Cataloging-in-Publication Data
Names: Mainwaring, Scott, 1954– editor. | Masoud, Tarek E., editor.
Title: Democracy in hard places / [edited by] Scott Mainwaring, Tarek Masoud.
Description: New York, NY : Oxford University Press, 2022. |
Includes bibliographical references and index.
Identifiers: LCCN 2022006297 (print) | LCCN 2022006298 (ebook) |
ISBN 9780197598764 (paperback) | ISBN 9780197598757 (hardback) |
ISBN 9780197598788 (epub)
Subjects: LCSH: Democracy—Case studies. | Democratization—Case studies. |
World politics—21st century—Case studies.
Classification: LCC JC423 .D381319 2022 (print) | LCC JC423 (ebook) |
DDC 321.8—dc23/eng/20220322
LC record available at https://lccn.loc.gov/2022006297
LC ebook record available at https://lccn.loc.gov/2022006298

DOI: 10.1093/oso/9780197598757.001.0001

Contents

List of Figures

List of Tables

Acknowledgments

This book is about why democracy sometimes survives for a long time in difficult conditions. When we began planning the conference that led to the book, the COVID-19 pandemic and the January 6 insurrection at the United States Capitol would have been unthinkable to all but the most determined pessimists, but it was already a time of grave worry about the state of democracy in the world. We hope that this book not only enriches our understanding of what makes democracy in hard places possible, but also that it might inspire belief during these hard times that democracy can persist in the face of grave challenges.

The idea for this volume grew out of many conversations we had from 2016 to 2019 at Harvard University. We had neighboring offices, co-taught a course on "Getting and Keeping Democracy" in 2017 and in 2018 at Harvard's John F. Kennedy School of Government, and co-directed a program on "Democracy in Hard Places" at the Kennedy School's Ash Center for Democratic Governance and Innovation. During these years of working together, we often disagreed with one another—but in so doing, we always pushed each other to new understandings and insights. We also accrued a number of debts that we are pleased to acknowledge here.

Our first debt is to Tony Saich, the director of the Ash Center. Tony and the Center generously supported our work from the beginning. This support made possible the eponymous conference in May 2019 that gave rise to this book, and also enabled us to secure the editorial and administrative assistance necessary to bring the book to fruition. Special thanks must be rendered to Melissa D'Anello and Maureen Griffin of the Ash Center, without whom neither the conference nor the book would have happened. We also thank our assistants at the Kennedy School, Juanne Zhao and Sari Betancourt.

Our debts were not just financial and administrative, but intellectual. We, and the contributors to this volume, were fortunate to benefit from the insights of an outstanding group of commentators and participants in the May 2019 conference on Democracy in Hard Places, including Eva Bellin, Fernando Bizzarro, Melani Cammett, Timothy Colton, Steven Fish, Candelaria Garay, Frances Hagopian, Sarah Hummel, Steven Levitsky, Pia Raffler, and Deborah Yashar. We are also grateful to Harvard colleagues Daniel Ziblatt, Richard Zeckhauser, Gautam Nair, Moshik Temkin, Alex Keyssar, and Archon Fung for informal conversations that shaped our thinking about democracy and its survival. Ashutosh Varshney, the author of the chapter on India, deserves special thanks for being an invigorating intellectual presence at the Ash Center during a critical phase of this book's development.

We thank David McBride of Oxford University Press for his enthusiastic support for the project from the outset. And we record our thanks to María Victoria De Negri who, with characteristic talent and attention to detail, prepared the book for publication and compiled the index. Fernando Bizzarro provided helpful research.

Finally, Scott thanks his wonderful partner, Sue Elfin, for gracing his life. Tarek thanks his long-suffering partner, Kristin Alcorn Masoud, for tolerating his frequent failures to bring grace to hers.

The authors dedicate this book to the memory of Alfred C. Stepan, whose fingerprints are on every chapter.

Contributors

Nancy Bermeo (PhD Yale University) is currently a Nuffield Senior Research Fellow at Oxford University and a PIIRS Senior Scholar at Princeton University. She writes on the causes and consequences of political mobilization and regime change as well as the quality of democracy. Her books include an award-winning study of the breakdown of democracy titled *Ordinary People in Extraordinary Times* (Princeton University Press), and, with Deborah Yashar, *Parties, Movements and Democracy in the Developing World* (Cambridge University Press), plus *Mass Politics in Tough Times* with Larry Bartels (Oxford University Press), and *Coping with Crisis: Government Reactions to the Great Recession* with Jonas Pontusson (Russell Sage Foundation). Her latest book, *Democracy after War*, is forthcoming from Princeton University Press.

Scott Mainwaring (PhD, Stanford) is the Conley Professor of Political Science at the University of Notre Dame. His research and teaching focus on democratization, party systems, and Latin American politics. His book with Aníbal Pérez-Liñán, *Democracies and Dictatorships in Latin America: Emergence, Survival, and Fall* (Cambridge University Press, 2013) won the Best Book Prizes of the Democracy and Autocracy section of the American Political Science Association and the Political Institutions section of the Latin American Studies Association. Mainwaring was elected to the American Academy of Arts and Sciences in 2010. In April 2019, *PS: Political Science and Politics* listed him as one of the fifty most cited political scientists in the world. He served as the Jorge Paulo Lemann Professor for Brazil Studies and as faculty co-chair of the Brazil Studies program at Harvard University from 2016 to 2019.

Tarek Masoud (PhD Yale University) is the Ford Foundation Professor of Democracy and Governance at Harvard University's John F. Kennedy School of Government. He is the co-Editor of the *Journal of Democracy*, the director of the Kennedy School's Middle East Initiative, the Initiative on Democracy in Hard Places, and the co-author of, among other works, *The Arab Spring: Pathways of Repression and Reform* (Oxford University Press, 2015).

Rachel Beatty Riedl (PhD Princeton University) is the John S. Knight Professor of International Studies, Director of the Einaudi Center for International Studies, and a professor in the Department of Government at Cornell University. Her research interests include institutional development in new democracies, local governance and decentralization policy, authoritarian regime legacies, and religion and politics, with a regional focus in Africa. She is the author of award-winning *Authoritarian Origins of Democratic Party Systems in Africa* (Cambridge University Press, 2014) and co-author with Gwyneth McClendon of From Pews to *Politics: Religious Sermons and Political Participation in Africa* (Cambridge University Press, 2019). Riedl is co-host of the podcast *Ufahamu Africa*, featuring weekly episodes of news highlights and interviews about life and politics on the African continent.

Emilia Simison (MA Torcuato Di Tella University) is a PhD candidate in Political Science at the Massachusetts Institute of Technology. Her research focuses on the comparative political economy of policymaking and policy change, especially on how political institutions in democratic and authoritarian regimes shape the extent to which citizens and interest groups influence policy. Prior to MIT, she was a PhD fellow at the Argentine National Scientific and Technical Research Council (CONICET) working at Gino Germani Research Institute, and she taught at the University of Buenos Aires and Torcuato Di Tella University.

Dan Slater (PhD Emory University) is Weiser Professor of Emerging Democracies and Director of the Weiser Center for Emerging Democracies (WCED) at the University of Michigan. He specializes in the politics and history of enduring dictatorships and emerging democracies, with a regional focus on Southeast Asia. He previously served as Director of the Center for International Social Science Research (CISSR), Associate Professor in the Department of Political Science, and associate member in the Department of Sociology of the University of Chicago. He is the author of *Ordering Power: Contentious Politics and Authoritarian Leviathans in Southeast Asia* (Cambridge University Press, 2010) and co-author of *Coercive Distribution* (Cambridge University Press, 2018).

Ashutosh Varshney (PhD Massachusetts Institute of Technology) is Sol Goldman Professor of International Studies and the Social Sciences and Professor of Political Science at Brown University, where he also directs the Center for Contemporary South Asia. Previously, he taught at Harvard, Notre Dame, and the University of Michigan, Ann Arbor. His books include *Battles Half Won: India's Improbable Democracy* (Penguin Books); *Collective Violence in Indonesia* (Lynne Rienner Publishers); *Ethnic Conflict and Civic Life: Hindus and Muslims in India* (Yale University Press); *India in the Era of Economic Reforms* (with Jeffrey Sachs and Nirupam Bajpai, Oxford University Press); and *Democracy, Development, and the Countryside: Urban–Rural Struggles in India* (Cambridge University Press).

Lucan Ahmad Way (PhD University of California, Berkeley) is Professor of Political Science at the University of Toronto. Way's research focuses on democratization and authoritarianism in the former Soviet Union and the developing world. His most recent book (with Steven Levitsky), *Social Revolution and Authoritarian Durability in the Modern World* (forthcoming from Princeton University Press), provides a comparative historical explanation for the extraordinary durability of autocracies born of violent social revolution. Professor Way's solo authored book, *Pluralism by Default: Weak Autocrats and the Rise of Competitive Politics* (Johns Hopkins University Press, 2015), examines the sources of political competition in the former Soviet Union. His book *Competitive Authoritarianism: Hybrid Regimes after the Cold War* (with Steven Levitsky), was published in 2010 by Cambridge University Press. Way's work on competitive authoritarianism has been cited thousands of times and helped stimulate new and wide-ranging research into the dynamics of hybrid democratic-authoritarian rule.

Abbreviations

ADP	Agrarian Democratic Party
AEI	Alliance for European Integration
AITI	Association for the Integration of Timor in Indonesia
ANC	African National Congress
APODETI	Popular Democratic Association of Timor
ASDT	Timorese Social Democratic Association
BDPM	Bloc for a Democratic and Prosperous Moldova
BJP	Indian People's Party
BPP	European Solidarity / Petro Poroshenko Bloc
BYuT	Yulia Tymoshenko Bloc
CA	Constituent Assembly (India)
CAA	Citizenship Amendment Act
CAC	Argentine Chamber of Commerce
CDM	Electoral Bloc Democratic Convention of Moldova
CEMIDA	Center of Military Members for the Argentine Democracy
CGT	General Confederation of Labor
CNRT	National Congress for Timorese Reconstruction
CONADEP	National Commission on the Disappearance of Persons
COSATU	Congress of South African Trade Unions
CRIET	Court of Punishment of Economic Crimes and Terrorism
DPM	Democratic Party of Moldova
ECLAC	United Nations Economic Commission for Latin America and the Caribbean
ENM	United National Movement
ESMA	School of Mechanics of the Navy
EU	European Union
F-FDTL	Timor-Leste Defense Force
FALINTIL	Armed Forces for the National Liberation of Timor-Leste
FARD	Action Front for Renewal and Development
FCBE	Cowry Forces for an Emerging Benin
FPV-PJ	Front for Victory-Peronist Party
FRELIMO	Mozambique Liberation Front
FRETILIN	Revolutionary Front for an Independent Timor-Leste
FRTLI	Revolutionary Front for an Independent East Timor
GD	Georgian Dream
GDP	Gross Domestic Product
Gerindra	Great Indonesia Movement Party
GNI	Gross National Income

GNU	Government of National Unity
GOLKAR	Party of Functional Groups
IMF	International Monetary Fund
INC	Indian National Congress
JD	Janata Dal
JNP	Janata Party
KGB	Committee for State Security
KOTA	Association of Timorese Heroes
MODIN	Movement for Dignity and Independence
MPLA	Popular Movement for the Liberation of Angola
NDPU	People's Democratic Party of Ukraine
NF	People's Front
NGO	nongovernmental organization
NP	National Party
NRC	National Registry of Citizens
NU	Nahdlatul Ulama
NUNS	Our Ukraine, People's Self-Defense Bloc
OAS	Organization of American States
OIC	Organization of Islamic Cooperation
OECD	Organization for Economic Co-operation and Development
OPEC	Organization of the Petroleum Exporting Countries
PAN	National Mandate Party
PAS	Party of Action and Solidarity
PCRM	Party of Communists of the Republic of Moldova
PD	Democratic Party (Indonesia)
PD	Democratic Party (Timor-Leste)
PDAM	Agrarian Democratic Party of Moldova
PDI	Indonesian Democratic Party
PDIP	Indonesian Democratic Party of Struggle
PDM	Democratic Party of Moldova
PIL	Public Interest Litigation
PJ	Peronist Party
PKB	National Awakening Party
PKI	Indonesian Communist Party
PLDM	Liberal Democratic Party of Moldova
PLP	People's Liberation Party
PNI	Indonesian Nationalist Party
PNTL	National Police of Timor-Leste
PPP	United Development Party (Indonesia)
PPP	purchasing power parity
PR	Party of Regions
PRD	Democratic Renewal Party
PRO	Republican Proposal
PRPB	Peoples' Revolutionary Party of Benin

PSD	Social Democrat Party
PU	Progressive Union
RB	Renaissance Party of Benin
RENETIL	National Resistance of East Timorese Students
RUKH	People's Movement of Ukraine
SACP	South African Communist Party
SICONARA	Ship Technicians' Union
SJP(R)	Samajwadi Janata Party (Rashtriya)
SN	Servant of the People
SRA	Argentine Rural Society
TMC	Trinamool Congress
TRC	Truth and Reconciliation Commission
UAE	United Arab Emirates
UCEDE	Union of the Democratic Center
UCR	Radical Civic Union
UDT	Timorese Democratic Union
UIA	Argentine Industrial Union
UN	United Nations
UNAMET	United Nations Mission to East Timor
UNDERTIM	National Union of the Timorese Resistance
UNM	United National Movement
UNSD	United Nations Statistics Division
UNTAET	United Nations Transitional Administration in East Timor
UP	Uttar Pradesh
USAID	United States Agency for International Development
ZYU	For a United Ukraine!

1

Introduction

Democracy in Hard Places

Tarek Masoud and Scott Mainwaring

If recent political events have taught us anything, it is that democracy is often fragile. Throughout the world, in such places as Hungary, Poland, India, and Brazil, democratic regimes now find themselves imperiled by the rise of ultra-nationalist and populist leaders who pay a steady lip service to the will of the people while daily undermining freedom, pluralism, and the rule of law. Not even the wealthiest and most powerful of the world's democracies—the United States of America—has proven immune. The one-time "arsenal of democracy" is now sometimes held up as a candidate for democratic backsliding. In their 2018 bestseller, *How Democracies Die*, Steven Levitsky and Daniel Ziblatt testify to an "epidemic of norm breaking that now challenges our democracy" and warn of an American future in which no-holds-barred partisan warfare leads to either a perpetual state of crisis or the inauguration of a full-blown, one-party regime. As if in agreement, Freedom House now ranks the United States sixty-first out of 210 countries in terms of its level of freedom, behind much younger democracies such as the Czech Republic, Slovakia, Lithuania, Greece, Chile, and Taiwan (Freedom House, n.d.). Although we do not agree with this judgment, the Polity V project assigns the United States a score of 8 out of 10 for the year 2016, lower than its score from 1809–50 (Marshall and Jaggers 2020). And in 2015, the Economist Intelligence Unit, which maintains its own "Democracy Index," downgraded the United States to a "flawed democracy," a category re-served for countries with free and fair elections and basic civil liberties but with "problems in governance, an underdeveloped political culture and low levels of political participation" (The Economist Intelligence Unit 2020, 53).

An illustration of how much democracy has lapsed, even in places where we would not have expected it to, can be seen in Figure 1.1, which plots one hundred years of global and OECD average scores on the "liberal democracy" index compiled by the University of Gothenburg's Varieties of Democracy project (Coppedge et al. 2021). Since peaking around 2011, average scores on that index—which captures the extent of civil liberties, rule of law, judicial

Tarek Masoud and Scott Mainwaring, *Introduction* In: *Democracy in Hard Places*. Edited by: Scott Mainwaring and Tarek Masoud, Oxford University Press. © Oxford University Press 2022. DOI: 10.1093/oso/9780197598757.003.0001

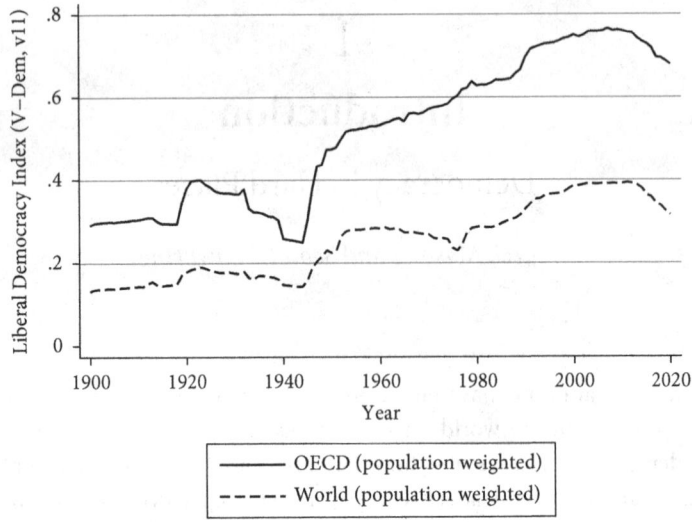

Figure 1.1. Democracy in the world, 1900–present
Source: Coppedge et al. 2021.

independence, checks on executive power, and electoral integrity—have now declined to levels not seen since the end of the Cold War, and the trend appears to point downward. "Nor," as Larry Diamond has written, "do the numbers capture the full extent of the danger." According to Diamond, "China, Russia, and their admirers are making headway with a new global narrative, hailing strongman rule—not government by the people—as the way forward in difficult times."[1] The current global pandemic threatens to make a bad situation worse, with increasing unemployment and, in many countries, shrinking GDPs fueling popular anger and testing the limits of mass and elite faith in democracy in ways that appeared to accelerate democratic regressions around the world.

These new doubts about democracy's survival in some of the world's most prosperous countries lend new relevance to studies of its survival in places less blessed by abundance. After all, if American democracy can be compromised by heightened polarization and the willingness of some political elites to undermine long-standing norms in efforts to gain electoral advantages, then democracy's persistence in large, poor, ethnically diverse countries such as India and Indonesia, with their low rates of educational attainment, rickety governing apparatuses, and frequent economic difficulties, is nothing short of miraculous. Moreover, taking stock of democracy's record across time and space, we find several such instances of democratic survival in the face of seemingly long odds. Since 1983, Argentines have held onto their democracy despite three protracted economic depressions, military mutinies, and a prior history of repeated democratic failures. In the 1990s, South Africans built one of Africa's longest-lived democracies out of the ruins of a system of white supremacy that dehumanized the great majority of citizens and pitted the races against each other. And in the early 2000s, the people of Timor-Leste erected a multi-ethnic democracy after a decades-long civil war that laid waste to countless lives and livelihoods. These cases demand our attention, both because they too face ever-present risks of democratic decay and downfall and because we may be able to derive from them lessons about how democracy can be fortified in times of challenge.

This, then, is a book about how democracy persists when all signs suggest that it should not. It puts front and center cases of what we call "democracy in hard places": countries that lack the structural factors and exist outside of the contexts that scholars have long associated with democracy's emergence and endurance. Democracies in hard places overcome underdevelopment, ethnolinguistic diversity, state weakness, and patriarchal cultural norms. They tame grasping, politically ambitious militaries; transcend influences and pressures from autocratic neighbors; and cope with polarized political parties. Without denying that democracy is easier to build and hold onto in societies that are free of such hurdles, this book asks what we can learn about strengthening democracy from those that managed to leap over them. By theorizing about democratic survival from such cases—which, in the parlance of social science, lie "off the regression line"—we capture what Michael Coppedge identifies as "the greatest potential to innovate and challenge old ways of thinking" (Coppedge 2002, 16). Are democracies in hard places the equivalent of lottery winners—dramatic exceptions to fundamental rules? Or is there something systematic that can be gleaned from such cases about how democracy can be erected and upheld around the world?

To answer these questions, this book presents nine case studies—written by leading experts in the discipline—of episodes in which democracy emerged and survived against long odds. The cases are drawn from almost every region of the world that formed part of what Samuel Huntington called the "third wave" of democracy, which began in southern Europe in the mid-1970s, spread to Latin America in the late 1970s and 1980s, and to Eastern Europe and sub-Saharan Africa in the 1990s. Six of the cases are ones of long-term democratic survival—Argentina (1983–present), Benin (1991–2019), India (1977–present), Indonesia (1999–present), South Africa (1995–present), and Timor-Leste (2002–present). The other three have more mixed democratic records—Georgia (2005–present), Moldova (1995–2005, 2010–present), and Ukraine (1995–98, 2007–14). In each case, many of the conditions conventionally associated with durable democracy were either attenuated or absent. Each case study details the constellation of obstacles to democracy faced by a given country, describes the major political actors with the potential to impact regime trajectories, and explains how the threat of democratic breakdown was staved off or averted.

Figure 1.2 plots the V-Dem "liberal democracy" scores of the cases in this book from 1974 to 2017 (the most recent year available).

Although the case studies presented in this book do not offer a unified answer to the question of how democracy survives in inauspicious conditions, readers will find in them powerful rejoinders to structural accounts of democracy's emergence and survival. This is perhaps to be expected, given that the cases were selected based on their want of democracy's hypothesized structural causes. But, as the editors of this volume, we find in the narratives of democratic survival offered in this book striking evidence of the importance of political actors, their normative beliefs, and how these beliefs shape their choices. Twenty-five years ago, Adam Przeworski and Fernando Limongi (1997, 176–77) complained that, in structural accounts of democratization, "no one does anything to bring democracy about; it is secreted by economic development and the corollary social transformations." In reality, they argued, "democracy was an outcome of actions, not just of conditions." The cases in this volume validate that observation.

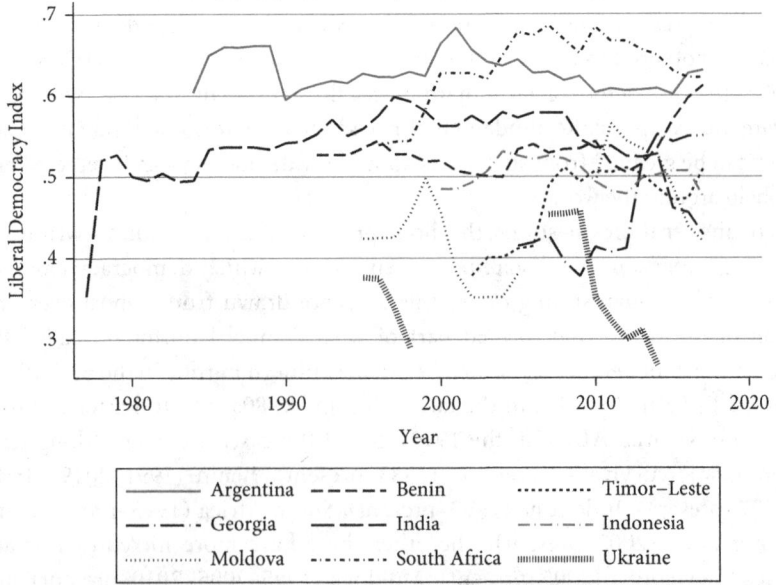

Figure 1.2. Liberal democracy scores of the nine cases in this volume, 1974–2017
Source: Coppedge et al. 2018.

Agents, Interests, and Regime Preferences

Agent-centric accounts of political phenomena have sometimes taken the form of "great person" narratives in which individual leaders operate with considerable autonomy, and in which outcomes are the result of individual decision-making. Without denying that individual leaders occasionally make a decisive difference in outcomes, this book eschews that tendency. Its focus is not on individuals but on key *collective* actors who command political resources and influence political competition (Mainwaring and Pérez-Liñán 2013, 5). These include chief executives and their ruling parties, other political parties, militaries and coercive agencies, labor unions, social movements, and civil society groups (Bermeo and Yashar 2016a). These are the agents whose preferences and choices determine whether a democracy endures, or joins the long list of democracies undone by military takeovers, *auto-golpes*, palace coups, and civil wars. Second, each chapter takes seriously the constraints under which actors operate. These constraints may take the form of structural or cultural conditions, formal institutions (such as constitutional structures or electoral rules), international actors, or other domestic actors (such as courts, militaries, or political parties). In addition to these "external" constraints, many of the chapters also highlight "internal" constraints that have hitherto received short shrift in accounts of democratic emergence and survival—in particular, the existence of deeply rooted normative commitments that shape the behavior of collective actors and take certain courses of action off the table.

Thus, if one goal of this book is to refocus the study of democratic survival from structural and external contextual conditions to the role played by political actors, another is to contribute to the debate about what drives those actors. What causes, for instance, a chief executive to forego an opportunity to expand his power at the expense of democratic legitimacy? Why would a powerful military in a fledgling democracy stick with a messy democratic system instead of answering calls to enter the fray in the name of stability? Why would an incumbent facing electoral defeat accept that defeat instead of tampering with the election or simply abrogating it outright? Assuming that democratic survival can reasonably be thought of as a function of such choices, what explains those choices?

The literature has offered two broad answers to this question. The first holds that actors' preferences over regime type are driven purely by considerations of self-interest. That is, they weigh the power and income they can expect to derive from different governing arrangements and choose accordingly. Thus, Adam Przeworski (1991) argues that democracy survives (i.e., is an equilibrium) when the losers in a particular election believe that they have enough of a chance of winning in the future to make sticking with democracy an attractive proposition.[2] Such accounts assume, as Przeworski (2019, 172) does, that "[t]he dream of all politicians is to remain forever in office and to use their tenure to do whatever they want." In this telling, political actors accept democracy and the associated constraints on power only because it serves their interests, or because they have no alternative.

The second answer to the question of why some political actors sustain democracy despite pressures to the contrary holds that self-interest or external constraints are insufficient to explain most instances of democratic persistence. In an earlier work, one of the authors of the present chapter points out that parties and movements have often upheld democratic regimes despite having plausibly better prospects outside of them: "Because actors believe in the system, they are willing to make concessions to abide by the rules of the game" (Mainwaring 1989). Without denying that actors also have instrumental goals, this alternative view locates the sources of actors' democracy-sustaining decisions in their values and normative commitments. Canonical works that share this view include Berman (1998), Bermeo (1992), Dahl (1971, 124–89), Hofstadter (1969), Lepsius (1978), Levitsky and Ziblatt (2018), Linz (1978a, 1978b), and McFaul (2002). Garrard's (2002) account of the emergence of democracy in Great Britain similarly emphasizes the acceptance of liberal values by key collective actors. Along related lines, an extensive body of literature on populism and the threat it poses to democracy hinges explicitly on populist leaders' hostility to the liberal aspects of democracy (Müller 2016b; Weyland 2020; Weyland and Madrid 2019). In short, these works conclude that democracy survives when the principal political actors who are in a position to maintain a regime or tear it down bear a preference for democracy that extends beyond self-interest and usually leads them to prioritize it over other important desiderata.[3]

The chapters in this volume take different perspectives on this issue, and this book is unlikely to resolve such a long-standing debate. At the same time, much is to be gained by placing this question firmly on the agenda for both scholars and practitioners. The urgency of understanding how political actors can be made to sustain democracy in hard places cannot be exaggerated. It derives not just from the fact that democracy around the world is under threat, but from the realization that the greatest potential for democratic expansion lies in hard places similar to the cases explored here. A recent survey by Mainwaring and Bizzarro identified 103 transitions to democracy between 1975 and 2012, many of which were in hard places, and almost half of which (46) broke down, with an average democratic duration among the breakdown cases of only eight years (Mainwaring and Bizzarro 2020). If this statistic is to be improved, scholars and practitioners must understand the factors that have enabled a small but not insignificant number of hard places to transcend the constraints of structure and achieve and maintain decent, representative government.

The remainder of this chapter proceeds as follows. First, we offer a review of some of the most important structural and contextual factors that have been hypothesized to determine a country's democratic prospects. We then identify the nine cases whose democratic trajectories this book examines, explain why we consider them hard places, and discuss how each of them fits into the book. We end the chapter with the volume's conclusions and contributions to the theory and practice of democratization.

The Effects of Context

Democracy's survival in "hard" places, and its looming retrenchment in comparatively "easy" ones, are two of the most powerful empirical rejoinders to the structural and contextual accounts of democratic transition and democratic stability. However, there is a reason those accounts became nearly hegemonic in the field of comparative democratization—they have been validated by a wealth of cross-national, statistical analyses. Accordingly, this project is predicated on the well-grounded idea that democracy is more likely to survive under some conditions than others. In this section, we discuss seven of these facilitating conditions: (1) economic development, (2) macroeconomic performance, (3) economic inequality (or, more properly, the lack thereof), (4) state capacity, (5) ethnic homogeneity, (6) democratic cultures, and (7) a pro-democratic international environment. We then introduce the cases that demonstrate the possibility for democratic survival even in the absence of some or all of these hypothesized conditions.

Of all the hypothesized enabling conditions for democracy, perhaps the one on which there is the broadest agreement is the achievement of a certain kind of prosperity, built on a shift from agriculture to industry. More than sixty years ago, Seymour Martin Lipset (1959, 75) famously found that "the average wealth, degree of industrialization and urbanization, and level of education is much higher for the more democratic countries" and concluded that "the more well-to-do a nation, the greater the chances that it will sustain democracy." In the intervening decades, scholars confirmed Lipset's initial empirical finding and offered a variety of explanations for it (Boix 2011; Boix and Stokes 2003; Epstein et al. 2006; Przeworski et al. 2000).[4] Some have argued that affluent societies are more capable of sustaining democracy because they have more educated citizenries, who are thus more rational and tolerant and less receptive to the radical ideologies and emotional appeals of would-be autocrats. For others, the correlation between economic development and democracy is largely due to the growth, in prosperous societies, of autonomous civic groups that provide citizens with the wherewithal to demand greater liberties and to deter or beat back encroachments upon them. For still others, democracy follows from development because the relative prosperity of the average citizen in a wealthy society means that economic elites possess less reason to fear expropriation if they grant or expand the franchise (Acemoglu and Robinson 2006; Boix 2003). Without development, the reasoning goes, these and other beneficial mechanisms would not operate, and political life would regress to a repressive and conflict-ridden mean. As Alemán and Yang (2011, 1143) concluded in a study of democratic transition and breakdown from 1970 to 1999, "the greatest threat to democratic survival is a low level of income."

Other scholars have noted that sustained periods of poor economic performance, in which GDP per capita either declines or stagnates, can seriously lower the probability of democratic survival (Gasiorowski 1995; Przeworski et al. 2000; Sing 2010; Svolik 2015). "Like war and revolution," Wibbels and Roberts (2010, 384) wrote, economic crises are "periods of severe disequilibria" that can "transform a political landscape in profound ways," and "shake the foundations of nations." The breakdown of Germany's Weimar Republic in 1933 is the most famous example in which widespread immiseration resulting from economic crisis contributed to the end of a democratic regime. In their study of democracy in twenty-six developing countries, Diamond, Lipset, and Linz (1987, 8) declared "it is clear that, over the long term in particular, the effectiveness of democratic regimes in satisfying people's wants heavily affects their stability" and find that the most successful democracies "have generally experienced relatively steady economic growth, which in turn has strengthened their legitimacy." It makes deductive sense that citizens would care more about economic security and less about democracy in moments of economic hardship. For this reason, Przeworski (1991, 136) argued that there were steep tradeoffs between economic reform and democracy in the post-communist countries and Latin America. Economic reforms, he wrote, "are socially costly and politically risky. . . . [T]hey hurt large social groups and evoke opposition from important political forces. And if that happens, democracy may be undermined or reforms abandoned, or both."

Yet another economic factor broadly associated with democracy's emergence and survival is the level of economic inequality. Carles Boix (2003) argues that democracy emerges when inequality decreases: "As the distribution of income becomes more equal among individuals, redistributive pressures from the poorest social sectors on the well-off voters diminish. Accordingly, the relative costs [to the wealthy] of tolerating a mass democracy decline" (Boix 2003, 10). Related arguments have been made by Lipset (1959, 83) and Acemoglu and Robinson (2006).[5] In contrast, Ansell and Samuels (2010, 1545) predict a positive relationship between democratization and rising income inequality, as democratic reforms are often demanded by "newly wealthy economic groups" that "accumulate an increasing share of national income" that they seek to defend against state predation. However, an empirical analysis by Haggard and Kaufman

(2012) of third-wave democratic transitions and reversals finds little support for the existence of a systematic relationship between inequality and democratic emergence and survival.

A fourth, non-economic structural factor sometimes identified as important to sustaining democracy is the strength of the state apparatus. At the extreme, any regime—democratic or not—that cannot maintain what Max Weber called "a monopoly over the legitimate use of violence" is unlikely to survive for long. But even states that can manage this basic, minimal function of statehood may prove unable to hang onto democracy if they lack the infrastructural power (Mann 1984) to carry out essential government functions of law enforcement, taxation, and service delivery. O'Donnell (1993) describes the danger to new democracies of "brown areas" in which state incapacity leads to a functional truncation of citizenship rights. Slater, Smith, and Nair (2014, 354) argue that democracies with ineffectual governing apparatuses quickly find themselves the objects of mass discontent and highly susceptible to military intervention: "[A]dministrative incapacity means that recurrent crises of governability will repeatedly tempt and enable military intervention to restore political stability. Meanwhile, democracy's chronic failure to 'deliver the goods' in weak-state settings will give the poor majority little reason to defend democracy against its enemies."

A fifth contextual underpinning of democratic survival identified by scholars is the presence of relative ethnic, linguistic, and religious homogeneity (Dahl 1971; Horowitz 2000; Rabushka and Shepsle 1972; Welsh 1993). Societies riven by identity-based cleavages are thought to lack the comity that helps to keep democratic competition from spilling over into bloodshed. As Arend Lijphart wrote more than forty years ago, the difficulty of "achiev[ing] and maintain[ing] stable democratic government in a plural society is a well-established proposition in political science" (1977, 1). Although recent analyses of cross-national data have attenuated the link between diversity and democratic survival (Fish and Brooks 2004; Teorell 2010), there nonetheless remain strong theoretical reasons why we might expect ethnic diversity to inhibit democratic survival. An early expression of these reasons was offered by John Stuart Mill, who, writing in the middle of the nineteenth century, declared that "free institutions are next to impossible in a country made up of different nationalities." Divided by language and culture, he reasoned, citizens in such societies eye each other with suspicion, as "one section does not know what opinions, or what instigations, are circulating in another." Instead of uniting to hold national leaders accountable and constrain their power, said Mill, the diverse citizenry's "mutual antipathies are generally much stronger than dislike of the government," which, presumably, is able to divide and conquer (Mill 1861, 289). A practitioner's corroboration of the importance of homogeneity to democracy was offered by the early twentieth-century British prime minister, Arthur Balfour, who is supposed to have said, "[O]ur whole political machinery presupposes a people so fundamentally at one that they can safely afford to bicker" (quoted in Friedrich 1939, 571). In the absence of that salutary oneness, the reasoning goes, paper stones would soon be converted into real ones. Scholars have found this danger to be particularly in a democracy's early stages, when political entrepreneurs might be most tempted to mobilize ethnic sentiments in order to acquire power (Horowitz 2000; Snyder 2000).

A sixth theorized requisite of democracy is the existence in a given society of what might be called a democratic "culture." As Welzel and Inglehart (2009) put it, "[M]ass beliefs are of critical importance for a country's chances to become and remain democratic." Perhaps not surprisingly, for many scholars, the culture most conducive to democracy is that of the Western countries in which modern forms of mass, democratic government first emerged. Thus, Almond and Verba (1963, 5), argue that a "democratic form of participatory political system requires as well a political culture consistent with it" and lament the difficulty of transferring "the political culture of the Western democratic states to the emerging nations." In his study of democratization in Britain, Garrard (2002) describes a gradual process in which previously disenfranchised groups acquired the right to participate upon their achievement of a certain level of what he calls "political fitness," defined largely in terms of their attachment to classically liberal values held among the British elite.

Democracy's early emergence and survival in Northern European countries caused some to implicate the distinctive religion of that part of the world, Protestant Christianity. Woodberry (2012, 245) notes that "by World War I every *independent*, predominantly Protestant country was a stable democracy—with the possible exception of Germany," a fact he attributes to Protestantism's emphasis on mass education and religious liberty. Other forms of Christianity, in contrast, were deemed more likely to uphold traditional, autocratic politics. For instance, Lipset (1959, 93) declared that Roman Catholicism's insistence of a monopoly on truth was at odds with democracy, "which requires, as part of its basic value system, the belief that 'good' is served best through conflict among opposing beliefs." Orthodox Christianity's hospitality to democracy has similarly been thrown into doubt (Marsh 2005), and Prodromou (2004, 62) has pointed out that "Orthodox churches often display a certain ambivalence about key elements of the pluralism that characterizes democratic regimes." If the existence today of a large number of Catholic-majority democracies appears to falsify Lipset's hypothesis, democracy continues to be weak in the Eastern Orthodox world (which is largely coterminous with the former Soviet Union).

Perhaps no religious tradition has been scrutinized for its compatibility with democracy as has Islam—a 1,400-year-old faith practiced by almost two billion people. More than 250 years ago, Montesquieu ([1748] 1900) famously argued that "a moderate government is most agreeable to the Christian religion, and a despotic government to the Mohammedan." Alexis de Tocqueville similarly thought that Islam was inimical to democracy, arguing that Islam's fusion of religion with politics meant that it could "never long predominate in a cultivated and democratic age" (quoted in Hashemi 2009, 118). More recent testimonials to this supposed incompatibility of Islam and democracy were offered by the late English historian Elie Kedourie (1994, 1), who wrote that "the idea of democracy is quite alien to the mind-set of Islam," and the American political scientist, Samuel Huntington (1991, 307), who contended that, despite containing some pro-democratic elements, "Islamic concepts of politics differ from and contradict the premises of democratic politics." Repeated cross-national studies by Fish (2002), Donno and Russett (2004), and Teorell (2010) seem to validate this skepticism, finding a robust and negative correlation between Islam and democracy, albeit one driven largely by the durable autocracies of the Muslim world's Arabic-speaking core (Stepan and Robertson 2003).[6] Although the persistence of Indonesian democracy since 1999 and Tunisia's existence as a relatively stable democracy between 2011 and 2021 could be thought to constitute rejoinders to arguments about Islam's incompatibility with democracy, the decay of previously consolidated, Muslim-majority democracies like Turkey and Mali give the hypothesis continued relevance.

A seventh contextual factor long thought to shape the possibility for democratic survival is the international environment confronting a given regime. More than fifty years ago, Rustow (1970, 348) recognized the existence of "cases where the major impulse to democratization came from the outside," although he left their analysis to scholars of international relations. Huntington (1991, 13) argued that "the occurrence and the timing of the third-wave transitions to democracy" was shaped in part by "changes in the policies of external actors, most notably the European Community, the United States, and the Soviet Union," and the "demonstration effect of transitions earlier in the third wave in stimulating and providing models for subsequent efforts at democratization." Brinks and Coppedge (2006, 464) point to the importance of superpower influence on the regime types of their clients, as well as to what they call "neighbor emulation," which they define as "a tendency for neighboring countries to converge toward a shared level of democracy or nondemocracy." In their study of democratization in Latin America, Mainwaring and Pérez-Liñán testify to the importance of neighbor influence, arguing that a "favorable regional political environment, characterized by the existence of many democracies in Latin America, increase[d] the likelihood of transitions from authoritarian rule to competitive regimes and diminishe[d] the likelihood of breakdowns of existing competitive regimes" (2013, 6). Observers of Eastern Europe, East Asia, and the Middle East have noted the ways in which regional powers exert pressures on their neighbors that lead to a kind of institutional isomorphism (Burnell 2010; Coppedge et al. 2022; Darwich 2017; Lee 2018).

Table 1.1 contains the results of a time series, cross-sectional logistic regression analysis of the correlates of democratic breakdown for the eighty-three

Table 1.1. Regression Analysis of Correlates of Democratic Breakdown

	Random effects logit			Penalized logit		
	(1)	(2)	(3)	(4)	(5)	(6)
GDP (logged)	−0.744***	−0.891*	−1.372***	−0.720***	−0.589	−0.981***
	(0.207)	(0.506)	(0.420)	(0.186)	(0.373)	(0.265)
GDP growth (%)	−5.160*	−4.045	−4.361	−5.194**	−5.193	−5.982
	(3.047)	(4.254)	(4.432)	(2.533)	(4.720)	(4.671)
Share of neighboring countries democratic	−0.755	−6.911**	−5.590*	−0.704	−4.822**	−3.583*
	(1.577)	(3.179)	(3.070)	(1.427)	(2.194)	(2.062)
Years since last transition	−0.00623	0.137*	0.116	−0.00725	0.0783*	0.0537
	(0.0310)	(0.0716)	(0.0713)	(0.0235)	(0.0457)	(0.0441)
Organization of Islamic Cooperation	−0.253	−1.967	−2.168*	−0.206	−1.228*	−1.332**
	(0.479)	(1.214)	(1.218)	(0.423)	(0.652)	(0.637)
Arab League	2.266***	4.246	5.242**	2.213***	2.845*	3.875***
	(0.822)	(3.451)	(2.524)	(0.671)	(1.474)	(1.234)
Eastern Europe	0.928*	2.262**	1.821**	0.910**	1.756**	1.353**
	(0.499)	(0.997)	(0.804)	(0.441)	(0.757)	(0.607)
Ethnic fractionalization index		−1.462			−1.209	
		(1.103)			(0.913)	
State capacity		−1.043*			−0.890*	
		(0.548)			(0.505)	
Gini index		0.0309			0.0291	
		(0.0317)			(0.0275)	
Constant	2.492*	3.838	8.066**	2.373*	1.643	5.188***
	(1.460)	(4.447)	(3.132)	(1.301)	(3.108)	(1.788)
Observations	1,675	1,026	1,026	1,675	1,026	1,026
Number of clusters (countries)	82	72	72			

Note: Cells are coefficient estimates of regression models predicting the probability of democratic breakdown in a given year. Models 1, 2, and 3 are random effects logits using Stata's xtreg command, with standard errors clustered by country. Models 4, 5, and 6 are penalized logits using the user-generated command firthlogit (Coveney 2021). Standard errors in parentheses.

$* p < .1; ** p < .05; *** p < .01$

countries that transitioned to democracy between 1974 and 2012.[7] The purpose of this exercise is to identify the factors most associated with democratic longevity and breakdown, and to subsequently calculate the breakdown risk for each of the cases in this volume. The dependent variable, democratic breakdown, is a dichotomous variable that captures a shift from electoral democracy to autocracy, measured up to 2017. Specifically, we used Mainwaring and Bizzarro's (2020) modified version of Lührmann et al.'s (2018) "Regimes of the World Dataset," which is based on the Varieties of Democracy (V-Dem) project. Lührmann et al. consider a regime minimally democratic if (1) it meets minimum standards of free and fair elections; (2) it allows for some multiparty competition; and (3) V-Dem's electoral democracy score (which ranges between 0 and 1) is at least 0.50. Mainwaring and Bizzarro modified these coding rules to exclude as either a transition or breakdown small, momentary increases above or below the 0.50 electoral democracy threshold that were followed by a quick reversion to the prior regime state. (For instance, a country whose democracy score of 0.49 jumps in one year to 0.51 before settling back down at 0.49 would not be considered to have undergone a transition followed by a breakdown.)

The key independent variables are:

- *Economic development*: This is measured as the natural log of the GDP per capita (in 2010 constant US dollars), sourced from the World Bank's World Development Indicators.
- *Economic inequality*: This is the Gini index, which measures income inequality on a scale from 0 to 1, where 1 corresponds to greatest inequality. The source for this variable is the V-Dem dataset, which in turn draws on data collected by the United Nations University's World Institute for Development Economics Research (Coppedge et al. 2018).
- *Economic growth*: This is the percentage change in GDP per capita for each country year.
- *Neighborhood effects*: This is the share of countries in each geopolitical region (post-communist, Latin America, Middle East, sub-Saharan Africa, Western Europe and North America, East Asia, Southeast Asia, South Asia, the Pacific, and the Caribbean) that score 0.5 or above on the Varieties of Democracy project's electoral democracy index.
- *Years democratic*: Calculated as the number of years since the last democratic transition.
- *Ethnic fractionalization*: This is the probability that any two randomly selected individuals from a given country in a given year will be from different ethnic groups, calculated by Drazanova (2019) from data gathered by the Composition of Religious and Ethnic Groups project at the University of Illinois at Urbana-Champaign. The index ranges (theoretically) from 0, indicating that every citizen is from the same ethnic group, to 1, where there are as many ethnic groups as individuals.
- *State capacity*: This is a measure of state infrastructural power devised by Hanson and Sigman (2013) that captures three dimensions of state capacity (extractive, administrative, and coercive). Values range from –3 to 3.

Finally, cultural and religious influences are captured with dummy variables for membership in the Organization of Islamic Cooperation (Albania, Bangladesh, Benin, Comoros, Guyana, Indonesia, Iraq, Lebanon, Libya, Maldives, Mali, Niger, Nigeria, Senegal, Sierra Leone, Suriname, Turkey, and Tunisia), the Arab League (Comoros, Iraq, Lebanon, Libya, Mauritania, and Tunisia), and for being situated in Eastern Europe (Albania, Armenia, Belarus, Bulgaria, Croatia, Czech Republic, Estonia, Georgia, Hungary, Latvia, Lithuania, Macedonia, Moldova, Poland, Romania, Russia, Serbia, Slovakia, Slovenia, and Ukraine). Summary statistics for each of these variables are presented in Table A1.1 in the appendix.

Due to missingness in the data for ethnic fractionalization, state capacity, and economic inequality, column 1 of Table 1.1 presents the results of a random effects logit without those variables included. Column 2 presents the regression results with all variables included, at the expense of losing nearly 40 percent of observations. In order to determine whether the differences in the sign, significance, and magnitudes of the coefficients in columns 1 and 2 are due to the inclusion of the additional variables in Model 2 or to the loss of observations, column 3 reports the results of a regression with only the smaller number variables in column 1 and only the smaller number of cases in column 2. Columns 4, 5, and 6 repeat the analyses in columns 1, 2, and 3 using a penalized logit estimator to account for the rarity of democratic breakdowns in the data (forty-five in 1,725 regime-years). The results of these latter regressions are substantially similar to the regressions without rare-events adjustments, although effect sizes and standard errors are generally smaller.

As expected, the relationships between democratic breakdown and GDP, GDP growth, regional regime characteristics, and state capacity are negative in most of the models—meaning that democratic breakdown is less likely in countries that are richer, growing economically, situated among other democracies, and which possess high state capacity. However, none of these variables is statistically significant across all six models reported in Table 1.1, which testifies to the uncertain relationship between structural factors and democratic survival.

Figures 1.3a through 1.3g plot the marginal effects of our key continuous predictors (GDP per capita, GDP growth, regional share of democracies, years democratic, ethnic fractionalization, state capacity, and income inequality) on the probability of democratic breakdown.[8] Figure 1.3a shows that, holding all else equal, a country whose logged GDP per capita is in the 75th percentile (approximately USD 8,500) has a 1.2 percent chance of experiencing a democratic breakdown in a given year, which is about a quarter of the probability that democracy will break down in a country whose GDP is in the 25th percentile (approximately USD 1,500). Figure 1.3b displays the effect of economic growth on the probability of democratic breakdown. A country in the 75th percentile of economic growth

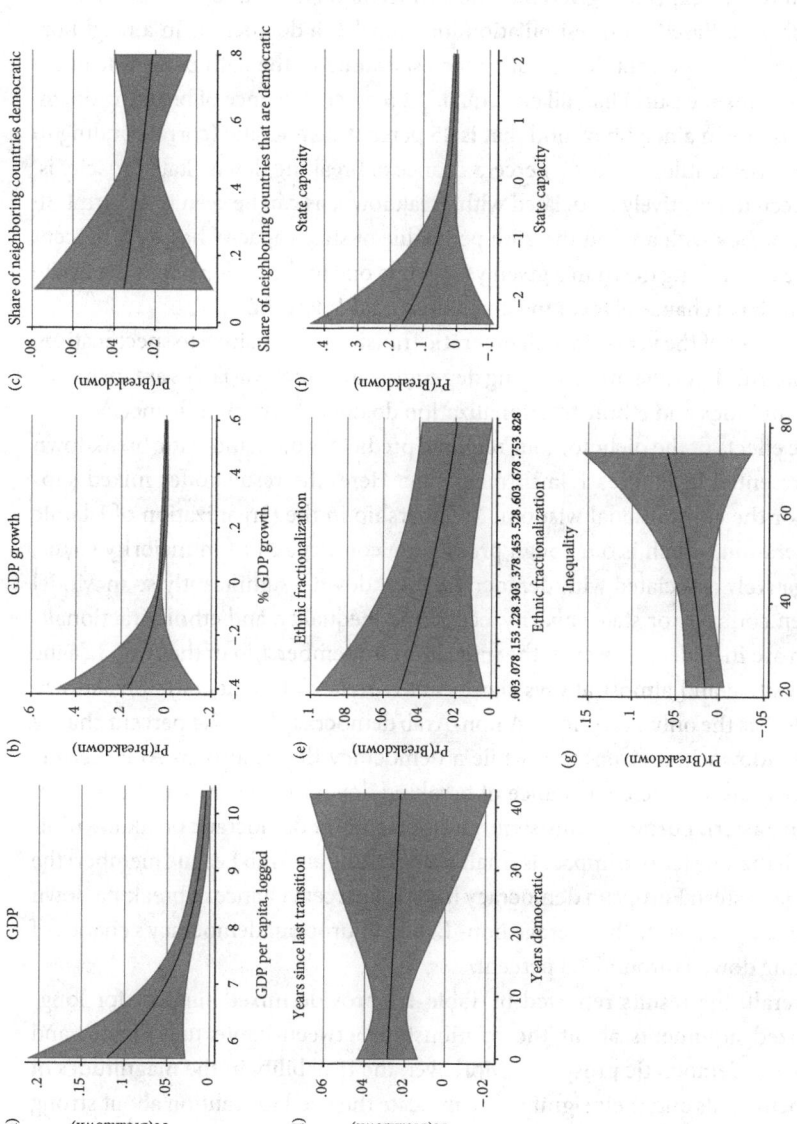

Figure 1.3. Marginal effects of continuous predictors

Sources: For (a) and (b), World Development Indicators, n.d.; for (c), (d), and (g), Coppedge et al. 2018; for (e), Drazanova 2019; and for (f), Hanson and Sigman 2013.

experiences a probability of breakdown (0.28 percent) that is ten times as small as the probability of breakdown for a country that is in the 25th growth percentile. The effect of neighbor emulation, displayed in Figure 1.3c, is relatively flat (which is to be expected, given that the coefficient on this variable is insignificant in Model 1). Based on the simulation for Model 1, a democracy in a neighborhood that is 55 percent democratic (corresponding to the 75th percentile of regions on this measure) has, all else equal, a 2.5 percent chance of breaking down, whereas one in a neighborhood that is 45 percent democratic (corresponding to the 25th percentile), has a 2.7 percent chance of breaking down. State capacity is, as expected, negatively associated with breakdown, as can be seen in Figure 1.3f. A democracy with around the 25th percentile of state capacity has a 3.2 percent chance of breaking down in a given year, while one in the 75th percentile of state capacity has a chance of breaking down of around 1 percent.

The effect of the years since democratic transition is sensitive to specification, with sign and significance changing depending on which variables are included. The Gini index and ethnic fractionalization do not achieve significance.[9]

The effects of the dichotomous regional predictors on democratic breakdown are presented in Figures 1.4a through 1.4c. Here, the results offer mixed support for the conventional wisdom. Membership in the Organization of Islamic Cooperation, which is our rough proxy for a country's Muslim majority status, is negatively associated with democratic breakdown—significantly so in Model 5 when controls for state capacity, economic inequality, and ethnic fractionalization are included. However, the indicator for membership in the Arab League is a positive and almost always significant correlate of democratic breakdown (Model 2 is the only exception). A non-Arab democracy has a 2.4 percent chance of breakdown in a given year, while a democracy that is also an Arab League member has a 17 percent chance of breaking down in a given year. Being situated in Eastern Europe is consistently a risk factor for democratic breakdown, although the substantive impact is smaller than being an Arab League member: the average Eastern European democracy has a 5.4 percent chance of breaking down in a given year, while the average non–Eastern European democracy's chance of breaking down is around 2.3 percent.

Overall, the results reported in Table 1.1 provide mixed support for long-theorized arguments about the relationship between contextual factors and countries' democratic prospects. Moreover, the instability in the magnitudes of the coefficients and their significance indicate the need for caution about strong claims about the influence of these contextual variables. The simple fact of the matter is that these variables cannot explain all of the observed variation in democratic breakdown. Thus, although the chapters that follow all clearly situate the case studies in the context of these macro variables, they also emphasize how actors have maneuvered around them to keep democracy alive despite the odds.

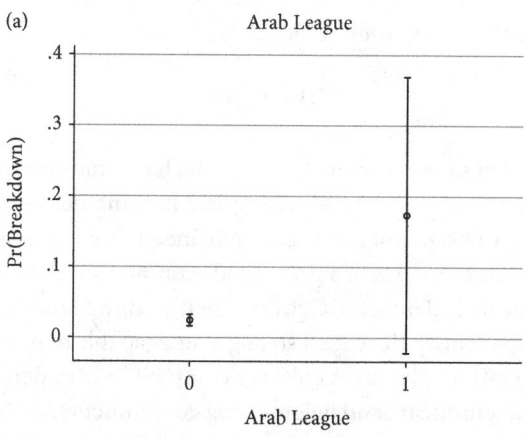

(a) Arab League

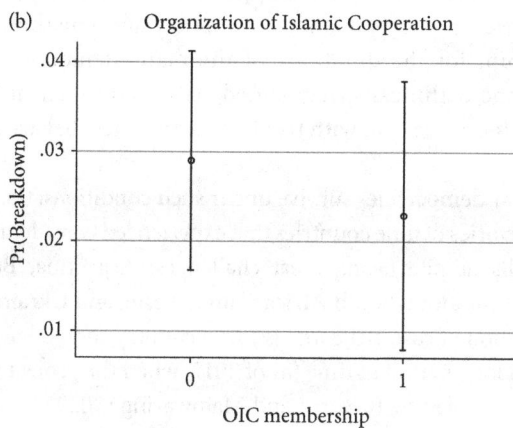

(b) Organization of Islamic Cooperation

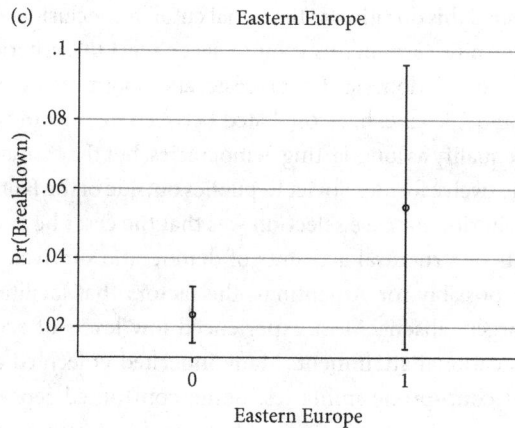

(c) Eastern Europe

Figure 1.4. Marginal effects of qualitative predictors

Note: The Organization of Islamic Cooperation includes Albania, Bangladesh, Benin, Comoros, Guyana, Indonesia, Iraq, Lebanon, Libya, Maldives, Mali, Niger, Nigeria, Senegal, Sierra Leone, Suriname, Turkey, and Tunisia; the Arab League includes Comoros, Iraq, Lebanon, Libya, Mauritania, and Tunisia; and Eastern European countries are Albania, Armenia, Belarus, Bulgaria, Croatia, Czech Republic, Estonia, Georgia, Hungary, Latvia, Lithuania, Macedonia, Moldova, Poland, Romania, Russia, Serbia, Slovakia, Slovenia, and Ukraine.

The Cases

We have identified several factors that scholars have traditionally deemed important to a country's chances of getting and keeping democracy: economic development; the absence of stark economic inequality; economic growth (or, at the very least, the absence of a prolonged economic crisis that leads to mass disillusionment with democratic government); ethnic homogeneity and the absence of deep identity cleavages; strong states capable of maintaining order and governing effectively; mass cultures compatible with democratic norms of tolerance and pluralism; and neighboring governments and foreign patrons that are themselves democratic and supportive of democratic rule. Although these factors have some explanatory power, they are nonetheless collectively unable to account for the durability of the many democracies around the world that are poor, ethnically fragmented, with traditional cultures, situated amid a sea of autocracies, and with troubled economies that are often stagnant or in crisis.

To explore how democracies survive under such conditions, the book analyzes the regime trajectories of nine countries that experienced considerable (if varying) democratic spells despite facing great challenges: Argentina, Benin, Georgia, India, Indonesia, Moldova, South Africa, Timor-Leste, and Ukraine. Two criteria guided our selection of cases. The first is that a country should have survived as a democracy for a long period of time (as of 2017, when the project was launched). Using the data compiled by Bizzarro and Mainwaring (2020), we calculated that the average duration of a third-wave democracy (as of 2017) was 12.3 years. We therefore established this duration as the initial cutoff for inclusion as a core case in the volume. Of the nine cases in this volume, seven meet this criterion: Argentina, Benin, Georgia, India, Indonesia, Timor-Leste, and South Africa. Two additional cases, Moldova and Ukraine, have oscillated between democratic and autocratic spells and do not qualify as long-lasting democracies, but they are among the most democratic of the twelve former Soviet Republics outside of the Baltics.

The second criterion for case selection was that the cases be deemed improbable by the lights of structural accounts of democratic survival. In all of these countries—save possibly for Argentina—the factors that facilitate democratic survival were largely absent. Most experienced low levels of economic development and educational attainment. Many inherited enfeebled administrative apparatuses and coup-prone militaries. Some confronted repeated economic crises. And some were located in parts of the world in which democracies were few, or were embedded in cultures and religions very different from those in which modern democracy was incubated.

Table 1.2 presents the average score for each country on each of the predictors analyzed in Table 1.1, for the entirety of the period for which it appears in the

Table 1.2. Values for Each Case on Key Independent Variables (Socioeconomic Indicators Averaged over Democratic Lifespan)

Country	GDP per capita	GDP growth (%, geometric mean)	Regional democracy share (%)	Years democratic[a]	Ethnic fractionalization	State capacity	Gini	Islamic	Arab	Eastern European
Argentina	8,511.71	1.01	55.74	34	0.13	0.20	45.88	0	0	0
Benin	726.89	2.04	41.22	26	0.77	-0.93	36.91	1	0	0
Timor-Leste	3,087.56	4.18	50.79	16	0.83	-1.42	32.5	0	0	0
Georgia	3,515.77	5.67	54.39	13	0.38	0.38	40.77	0	0	1
India	879.18	3.96	38.36	41	MISSING	-0.03	33.5	0	0	0
Indonesia	3,006.01	3.89	49.32	18	0.8	0.13	35.3	1	0	0
Moldova	1,713.23	3.29	52.16	19	0.48	-0.31	34.77	0	0	0
South Africa	6,797.02	1.31	43.81	22	0.86	0.72	59.75	0	0	1
Ukraine	2,665.59	1.69	52.97	12	0.39	-0.16	29.91	0	0	1

Sources: Coppedge et al. 2018; Drazanova 2019; Hanson and Sigman 2013; World Development Indicators, n.d.
[a] According to coding scheme in Mainwaring and Bizzarro (2020).

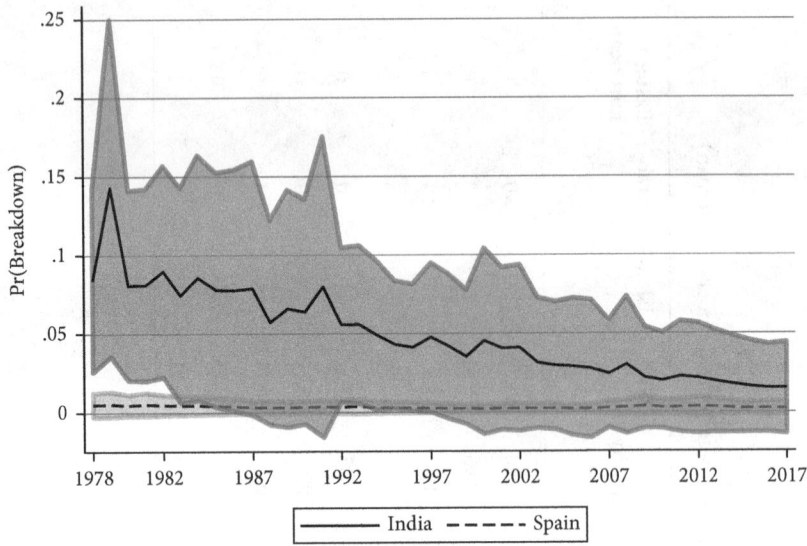

Figure 1.5. India (1978–2017), probability of democratic breakdown (benchmarked against Spain)

data. Table 1.2 highlights some of the daunting challenges the countries in this volume faced in building long-lasting democracies. Most of the countries are poor—Benin and India strikingly so. Argentina, South Africa, and Ukraine have had poor economic performance as measured by per capita GDP growth. India, Benin, and South Africa are situated in regions dominated by authoritarian regimes. Benin, Timor-Leste, India, and South Africa have great ethnic and linguistic diversity. Benin and Timor-Leste have shaky state capacity. And South Africa features some of the starkest income inequalities on the planet.

Figures 1.5 through 1.13 display the breakdown probabilities—drawn from Model 1 in Table 1.1—of each of the cases in this volume. In order to enable the reader to more easily comprehend the outsized magnitude of these (objectively small) breakdown probabilities in a given year, we include in each graph the breakdown probabilities for Spain—one of the first third-wave democracies— over the life of its democratic regime. According to these simulations, among our six cases of long-lasting democracy, India in the years just after redemocratization in 1977 faced particularly long odds. Moldova and Ukraine also had years in which the predicted odds of breakdown were vastly higher than those for Spain. For all of these cases, the probability of breakdown in any particular year was not startlingly high—although it was much higher than Spain's—but the cumulative probability of survival over the life span of these democracies ranges from poor to moderate.

The first case in the book is India, which is perhaps the quintessential democracy in a hard place, having long been identified by scholars as a stubbornly persistent rejoinder to most theories of democratization. (The annual breakdown probabilities for India, based on our model, are presented in Figure 1.5.) Poor, ethnically heterogeneous, with a caste system that seems incompatible with democracy's assumptions of formal political equality, and located in a neighborhood with precious few democracies to speak of, India seems almost entirely bereft of the things that scholars believe to be conducive to democracy. And yet, as contributor Ashutosh Varshney points out, India has been a democracy for seventy-two of the last seventy-four years. Although India has always fallen short of the liberal ideal and currently faces a populist challenge not unlike those faced by some other established democracies, it is nonetheless perhaps democracy's most remarkable success story.

Varshney's explanation for how India has eluded the democratic collapse predicted for it by most theories of democratization emphasizes the importance of the beliefs and values of that country's modern founders, and, in particular, its first prime minister, Jawaharlal Nehru. Possessed of a genuine belief in popular sovereignty, and in the equality of India's people regardless of religion, caste, or class, Nehru and his allies wrote a constitution that guaranteed the right to political organization and emphasized the inviolability of democratic procedure. But although Varshney attributes the birth of Indian democracy to the values of the country's founders, he attributes democratic persistence to the fact that India's political elites have come to see democracy as being in their interests. In particular, the proliferation of political parties at all levels of the country has ensured that "there is enough countervailing power available in the system to oppose the violation" of democratic norms and procedures. Thus, when Indira Gandhi suspended democracy in 1975 on the pretense of a national emergency, she was only able to hold the line for nineteen months, eventually giving in to pressure for new elections. Once democratic political life was resumed, Gandhi was voted out, and Indian political elites amended the constitution to make future ant-idemocratic trespasses difficult to repeat. Courts and an independent election commission have helped keep democracy intact, and the dispersion of power across India's states and union territories has given many parties a stake in preserving the regime. The story of India, then, is one of founders motivated by a commitment to democracy who created a system that eventually gave rise to a highly pluralistic federal landscape in which democracy was, until recently, by far the dominant game in town. Varshney notes, however, that the rise of the distinctly illiberal, Hindu nationalist Bharatiya Janata Party (BJP) has introduced new threats to Indian democracy, and serves as a dramatic illustration of the extent to which democracy's survival hinges on political parties' normative commitments.

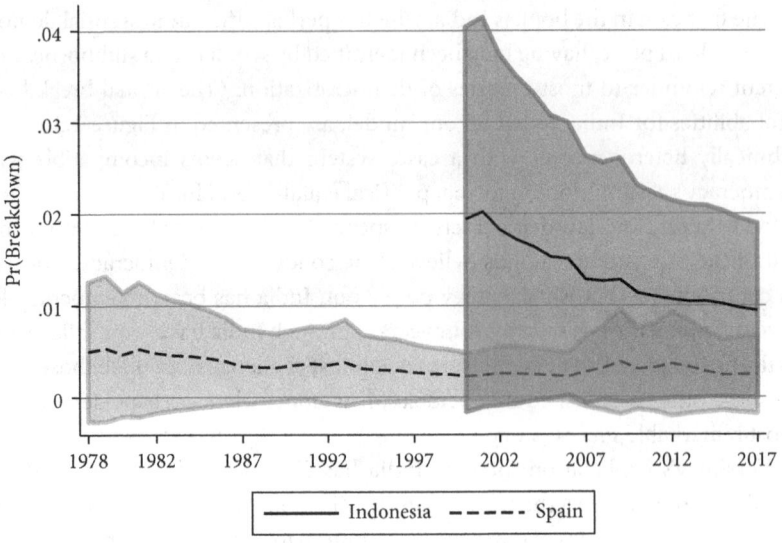

Figure 1.6. Indonesia (2000–2017), probability of democratic breakdown (benchmarked against Spain)

Indonesia, the world's third most populous democracy after India and the United States, also faced daunting challenges (see Figure 1.6 for Indonesia's predicted probabilities of democratic breakdown). That country's per capita GDP of USD 4,284 may be approximately double that of India, but it remains in the bottom half of countries. Its population of 267 million is about one fifth of India's, but Indonesians speak more than seven hundred languages, live on one thousand islands scattered across the world's largest archipelago, and mostly practice Islam, a faith that some cross-national studies of regime type find to be negatively associated with democracy. On top of all of this, Indonesia's democracy, inaugurated in 1998, came after thirty-two years of a brutal, military-backed dictatorship that had been baptized in the blood of more than half a million Indonesian communists.

Given these characteristics, argues Dan Slater, Indonesia is vulnerable to four modes of democratic collapse: a failure of the state, a military takeover, a transition to electoral authoritarianism, or the rise of a majoritarian, illiberal "democracy" in which minority rights are trampled. That Indonesia has managed to avoid these pitfalls is, he argues, a function of the legacies of the pre-authoritarian period. If the story of India is one of democratic legacies bequeathed by committed democrats, which could only briefly be undone, the story of Indonesia is one of autocrats who unwittingly erect the scaffolding that later helps to hold up (an admittedly imperfect) democratic edifice. Slater emphasizes four inheritances, three from the authoritarian period known as the New Order (1966–98). The first is an encompassing national identity that helped to instill a sense of belonging among the country's diverse peoples and to stave off ethnic polarization and secessionism. The second is the emergence of an independent, technocratic bureaucracy that would prove capable of governing even after the removal of the dictator, thus precluding the kind of administrative nonperformance that routinely sours citizens on new democracies. The third was an autocratic "ruling party" that remained intact through the transition and which kept former regime satraps invested in the new democracy by providing them with a channel for participating in it. And finally, the autocrat's strategy of dividing and ruling over the military apparatus left it without the ability to act collectively to abrogate democracy even if it had wanted to.

Slater's emphasis on how authoritarianism can structure the political landscape in ways that are later conducive to democratic survival offers a counterpoint to Varshney's emphasis on the values and beliefs of political leaders at founding moments. The differing emphases of these two contributions lay bare a key point of contention that comes up time and again in this book's narratives of democratic survival: Though most accounts in this book agree that *actors* either keep democracy alive or kill it, they differ in the extent to which they believe that their democracy-sustaining (or democracy-destroying) behaviors are the result of beliefs versus a narrowly instrumental calculation of costs and benefits.

In her analysis of democracy's emergence and survival in Benin and South Africa, contributor Rachel Riedl takes the latter position. Both countries are hard places for democracy, as evidenced by the annual breakdown probabilities

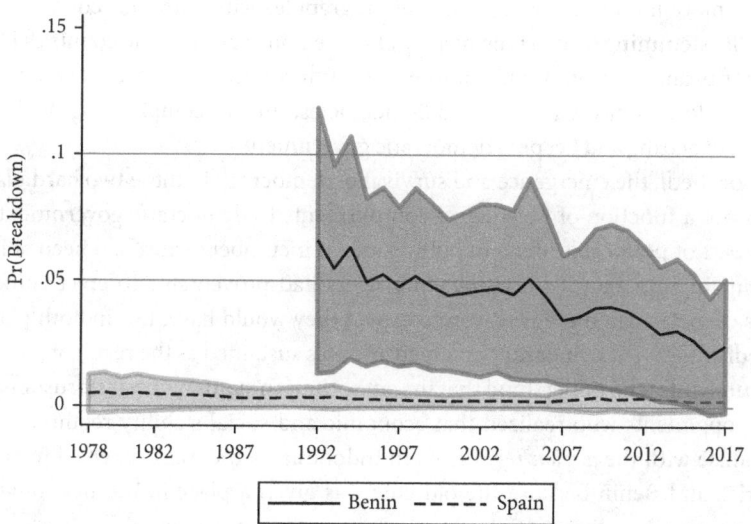

Figure 1.7. Benin (1992–2017), probability of democratic breakdown (benchmarked against Spain)

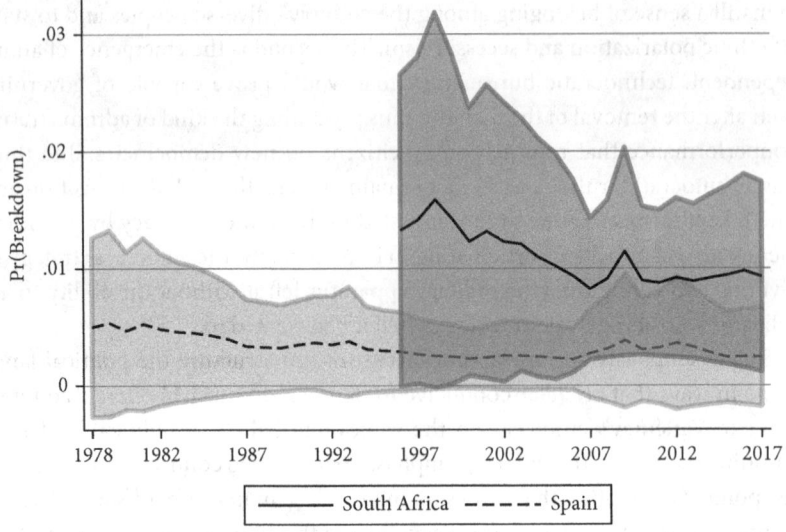

Figure 1.8. South Africa (1996–2017), probability of democratic breakdown (benchmarked against Spain)

displayed in Figures 1.7 and 1.8. Benin (Figure 1.7) is impoverished (with a current GDP per capita of USD [2010] 1,200), ethnically and religiously diverse, and plagued by low state capacity. South Africa (Figure 1.8) is more prosperous and has a more modern, effective state, but it grapples with extreme economic inequality stemming from a long history of white domination of the country's black majority and other non-white minorities. Both countries are located in a part of the world that has few long-lived democracies, further complicating the likelihood of getting and keeping democratic government.

For Riedl, the emergence and survival of democracy in these two hard places was not a function of ideological commitments to democratic government on the part of political leaders. In both places, if incumbent elites had been able to maintain autocracy, or if rising challengers had proven able to erect autocracies of their own, there is reason to expect they would have. But in both places, Riedl argues that democracy emerged and was sustained as the result of pacts by incumbents who understood that the authoritarian status quo was unsustainable and opponents who realized that economic and social stability required compromise with the *ancien régime*. As in Indonesia, democracy survived in South Africa and Benin because the old elite was given a place in the new political system and thus disincentivized from engaging in subversion.

Chapter 5, by Lucan Way, explores the fate of democracy in three of the former Soviet Republics: Georgia, Ukraine, and Moldova (breakdown probabilities

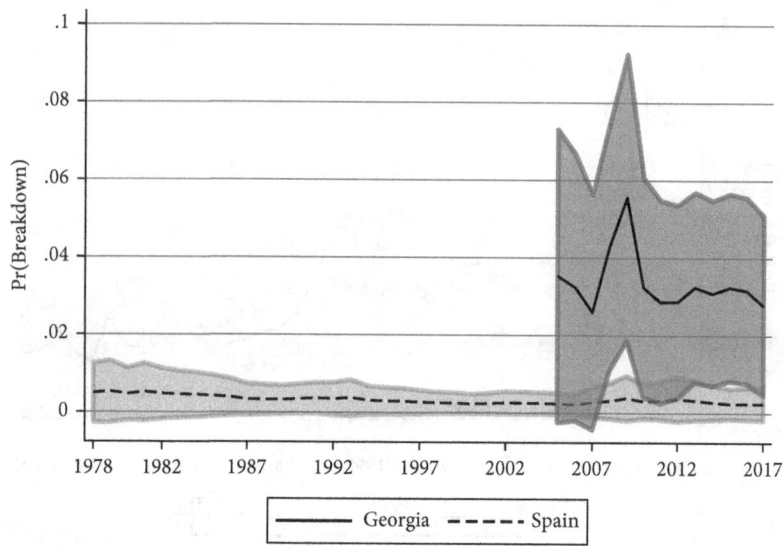

Figure 1.9. Georgia (2005–2017), probability of democratic breakdown (benchmarked against Spain)

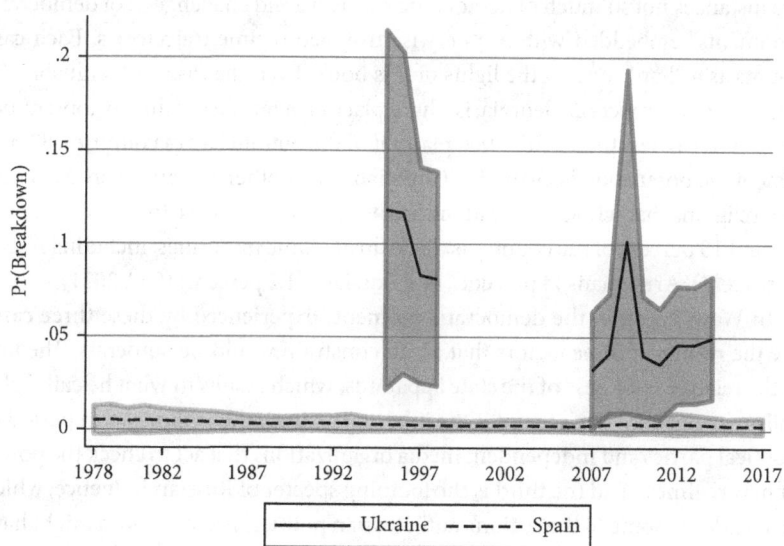

Figure 1.10. Ukraine (1995–1997, 2007–2013), probability of democratic breakdown (benchmarked against Spain)

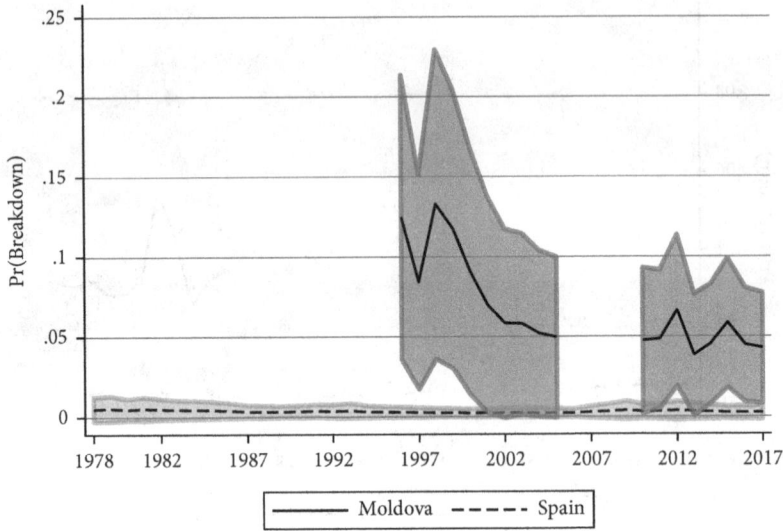

Figure 1.11. Moldova (1995–2004, 2010–2017), probability of democratic breakdown (benchmarked against Spain)

displayed in Figures 1.9, 1.10 and 1.11, respectively). According to Way, these cases are instances not so much of democratic survival amid challenge as of democratic "moments" embedded within otherwise troubled regime trajectories. Each case counts as a "hard" one by the lights of this book. Even the case with arguably the best democratic record, Georgia, is a hard place on a number of dimensions: its per capita GDP of less than USD 5,000 places it in the bottom half of countries; 83 percent of the population is Orthodox Christian and another 11 percent are Muslims, two religions that scholars have identified as being inconducive to democracy; and around 13 percent of the country is made up of ethnic minorities, including Azeris (6 percent), Armenians (4 percent), and Russians (1.2 percent) (CIA 2021).

In Way's account, the democratic moments experienced by these three cases are the results of three factors that act to constrain would-be autocrats: The first is the relative weakness of the state apparatus, which results in what he calls "pluralism by default." The second is the inheritance from the authoritarian period of political parties and independent media organizations that act to check the power of new regimes. And the third is the looming specter of Russian influence, which has rendered some of the region's anti-Russian political leaders—who might have indulged their authoritarian tendencies—receptive to external pressures to minimally uphold democracy and the rule of law in order to maintain US support.

One of the strengths of the accounts that attribute democratic survival to the constraints faced by political elites is that the origins of those constraints are relatively transparent, generally residing in conditions inherited from the authoritarian past. (Often less clear in these accounts is why the foundational democratic pacts persist over time, when they do.) In contrast, those who emphasize the importance of normative commitments to democracy often do not explain where those commitments came from. The final two chapters in this volume take this task head-on, offering accounts of democratic survival that pay close attention to the processes that convert political leaders into committed democrats.

The first of the chapters explains how democracy took root and survived in Timor-Leste, a small island nation that was occupied successively by Portugal (1702–1975) and Indonesia (1975–99), against which it fought a decades-long war of independence that claimed more than one hundred thousand lives. Of all of the cases in this volume, Timor-Leste is one of the hardest—in addition to its long history of internal war, it remains a poor country with a very weak state and a high degree of ethnolinguistic diversity. Timor-Leste's relatively high probabilities of democratic breakdown since the onset of its democracy in 2002 are displayed in Figure 1.12.

Nancy Bermeo argues that Timor-Leste's democracy has survived these challenges as a result of changes to the polity and its leaders that took place over the course of its long war for independence from Indonesia. In the waning years of the Portuguese colonial period, Timor-Leste's political and economic elite were deeply divided over their identities and their preferences for the country's future. Some wanted independence, others wanted union with Indonesia, still

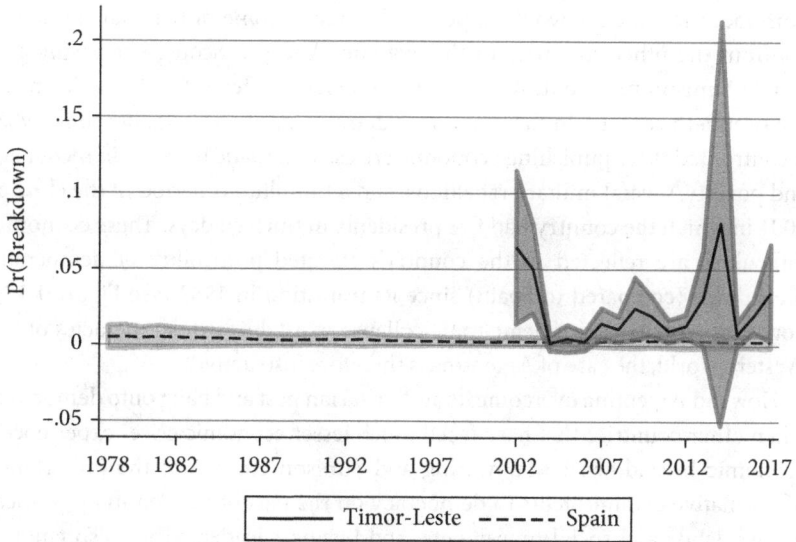

Figure 1.12. Timor-Leste (2002–2017), probability of democratic breakdown (benchmarked against Spain)

others sought union with Australia. Some were communists, others monarchists, still others Christian conservatives. These cleavages meant that Timor's political elites were unable to erect an independent government in the wake of Portugal's withdrawal in 1975, and their resulting infighting opened the door for Indonesia's invasion shortly thereafter.

However, according to Bermeo, the Indonesian occupation and the war to end it set in motion several processes that ultimately endowed Timor-Leste with the ingredients for its present democracy. First, the country's anti-democratic political and economic elites were so brutalized by the occupation that they either disappeared from the scene or gave themselves over to a new, democratic mindset. Second, the independence struggle forged a unified and inclusive national identity among the people of Timor-Leste, enabling them to overcome the ethnic and ideological cleavages that had contributed to their prior vulnerability to Indonesian aggression. Third, the war gave rise to a number of political leaders with good reputations and large constituencies who could convert their renown into votes, resulting in a post-independence political landscape that was pluralistic rather than dominated by a single group. Fourth, and finally, the exigencies of the national struggle had forced the militias to coalesce into a national army divorced from any one political party and subordinate to the authority of democratically elected leaders.

If Timor-Leste is one of the hardest places for democracy explored in this volume, the final case study, of Argentina, might appear at first glance to be the easiest. With the highest per capita GDP among our cases, a relatively capable state, limited ethnic fragmentation, and, by the 1990s, a mostly favorable neighborhood, that country would appear to be free of some of the challenges that confront the other countries in this volume. And yet, Scott Mainwaring and Emilia Simison point out, Argentina's democracy suffered five breakdowns in the twentieth century. In the years since democracy was re-established in 1983, it confronted three punishing economic crises, a dramatic increase in inequality and poverty, several military rebellions, and a tumultuous period in the close of 2001 in which the country had five presidents in thirteen days. These economic difficulties are reflected in the country's elevated probability of democratic breakdown (compared to Spain) since its transition in 1983 (see Figure 1.13). For those worried about democratic collapse in established democracies of the Western world, the case of Argentina is therefore instructive.

How did Argentina overcome its authoritarian past and hang onto democracy when other countries that have faced much lesser economic crises experienced economic breakdowns? Mainwaring and Simison emphasize the importance of normative commitments to democracy on the part of the country's political parties, labor and social movements, and business leaders. They also emphasize the policy moderation of all key actors—a profound contrast to the situation during the country's previous democratic experience of 1973–76. And like Bermeo, they identify the source of these normative commitments and the shift

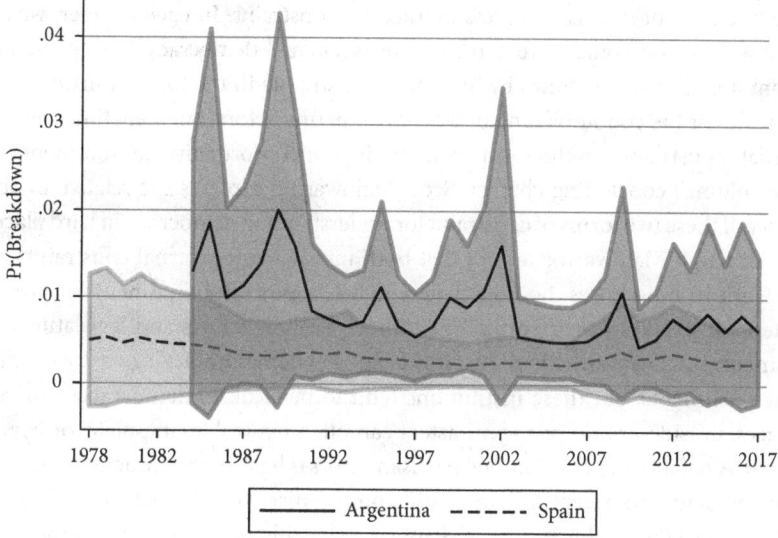

Figure 1.13. Argentina (1984–2017), probability of democratic breakdown (benchmarked against Spain)

to policy moderation: Argentina's experience with a brutal and inept military dictatorship from 1976 to 1983. According to Mainwaring and Simison, those years were so catastrophic for Argentina, marked by "torture, 'disappearances,' a reckless and failed war," and repression of labor unions and political parties, that political leaders across the political spectrum came to value democracy. They acted to uphold the democratic system even during severe economic downturns, hyperinflation, sharp increases in inequality, and dramatic increases in poverty and unemployment. Thus, when groups of officers engaged in military rebellions during a particularly difficult period for the Argentine economy, masses and elites were unified in rejecting them. As Guillermo O'Donnell (1986, 15) wrote thirty-six years ago when assessing the prospects of Latin American democracies that had recently emerged out of brutal autocratic regimes, "Largely as a consequence of the painful learning induced by the failures of those regimes and their unprecedented repression and violence, most political and cultural forces of any weight now attribute high intrinsic value to the achievement and consolidation of political democracy."

The Importance of Normative Commitments

Each of these chapters demonstrates powerfully that actors matter, but not in the manner assumed by naïve voluntaristic accounts. It is not the case that democracy is made and kept by great leaders bound only by their skills and passions.

Democratic survival is a process marked by constraint. In each chapter, we see that actors who could have abrogated or weakened democracy were prevented from doing so—sometimes by "external" constraints in the form of institutional shackles or the countervailing power of competing actors, but sometimes by "internal" constraints, in the form of deeply ingrained normative commitments. In the volume's concluding chapter, Scott Mainwaring explores the relative importance of these two forms of constraint for understanding democracy in hard places.

Although Mainwaring argues that both internal and external constraints are at work in most cases, he nonetheless makes a powerful argument for greater attention to the former. Formal institutions such as courts and legislatures do sometimes constrain rulers, helping keep democracy intact against executive encroachments, but these institutions tend to be weak in democracies in hard places; presidents and prime ministers can often control, manipulate, or bypass them. A balance of power among partisan actors is helpful to democratic survival, forcing actors to accept a democratic compromise. But the balances of power that lead to the establishment of democracy usually do not persist. In the cases in this volume, the African National Congress has enjoyed unassailable electoral hegemony since 1994. In Benin, Georgia, India, and South Africa, parties sometimes won landslide electoral victories. They had the opportunity to steamroll the opposition, and yet, they refrained from doing so (until 2018 in Benin).

In short, the external constraints highlighted by the literature are likely neither necessary nor sufficient for democratic survival. The preferences of actors over regime type matter. Some actors value the rights and procedures that are defining features of democracy. These clearly help to sustain democracy. At the other end of the spectrum are committed authoritarians who believe that different forms of dictatorship—communism, fascism, theocracy, populist illiberal democracy—are the normative ideal. These actors weaken democracy. Likewise, radical actors who demand wholesale revisions of the status quo—or who defend the status quo at all costs—raise the stakes of a democratic game and contribute to the possibility of democratic breakdown.

Surveying the cases in the volume, Mainwaring finds evidence for the importance of normative commitments to democracy across the cases. Using data from the Varieties of Party Identity and Organization (V-Party) project, he shows that none of the cases of democratic survival in our sample featured highly illiberal political parties for the period when they were undeniably democratic. The emergence of highly illiberal parties (such as the BJP in India) do not so much constitute a rejoinder to the notion that normative commitments matter as a clear warning of heightened risk of democratic breakdown (as seen in Benin in 2019, Moldova in 2001 and 2009, and Ukraine in 2010).

But if normative commitments matter, where do they come from? According to Mainwaring, they do not simply emerge from thin air or the biographical details of particular leaders. The collective actors who can make or break democracy—and political parties in particular—develop programmatic commitments to regime type that they inculcate into members and militants and which often prove durable over time—just as other programmatic commitments do (Berman 1998). In the case of Argentine parties, this commitment to democracy emerged as part of a process of repudiating an authoritarian past. In the case of India's Congress Party, the commitment to democracy and liberal ideals was shaped by an anti-colonial struggle that had at its center the liberal ideals of individual rights and freedom from domination. In Timor-Leste, the commitment to democracy took shape under the shadow of Indonesian occupation and a bloody civil war. There is every reason to expect commitments forged in this manner to endure. Though we would not go as far as Berman (1998, 207) to say that ideational motivations are so powerful as to render "political actors . . . insensitive to changes in their environment and relatively unconcerned with 'cost-benefit' calculations," we do believe that collective actors' normative commitments to democracy, once formed, constitute important "internal" constraints on their behavior. In some instances, these internal constraints can prove as important as the counterbalancing power of competitors or the shackles of institutions.[10]

Conclusion

We opened this book with testimonials to the peril in which democracy finds itself around the world, including—and perhaps especially—in wealthy countries where it was once thought impregnable. The possibility of democratic collapse where we least expected it has added new urgency to the age-old inquiry into how democracy, once attained, can be made to last. This book argues that scholars and practitioners interested in this question can learn much from democratic survivals that were as unexpected as the democratic erosions currently feared in some corners of the developed world. Just as social scientists long believed that well-established, Western, educated, industrialized, and rich democracies were immortal, so too did they assign little chance of democracy to countries that lacked these characteristics. And yet, in defiance of decades of social science wisdom, over the course of the last half-century, many countries that were bereft of the hypothesized enabling conditions for democracy not only got it but kept it, year after year after year. What is the secret of democratic longevity in such hard places? What has enabled countries such as India, Indonesia, and South Africa to hang onto democratic government despite poverty, inequality, and ethnic fragmentation? How did Timor-Leste forge a durable democracy out of the ruins of civil war? How did Argentina manage to overcome an authoritarian past and keep democracy alive despite repeated economic depressions? This book brings these and other unlikely cases of democratic survival front and center in an effort to derive lessons about what makes democracy stick, especially during moments of tumult and crisis.

Structure is not a prison. As the cases in this book demonstrate, Rustow (1970) was correct when he observed that there are no background conditions whose presence is absolutely necessary for democracy to emerge and survive. Instead, democracy is made and upheld by collective political actors—parties, executives, movements, militaries—that must make difficult choices structured not just by country-level factors and international contexts, but also by their own normative commitments. Presidents facing electoral defeat may abide by the results or use their control over the instruments of power to distort or ignore them entirely. Military officers chafing under economic hardship can either respect incumbents or throw them out. Opposition parties observing mass discontent with a regime can either wait until the next election or go "knocking on the barracks door" (Stepan 1988, 128). The latter outcomes are more likely in "hard" places than in "easy" ones, but, as the cases in this volume demonstrate, they are not predetermined. If the accounts that follow demonstrate that democratic potential exists in places that dominant structural theories would consign to authoritarianism, so too do they demonstrate that nowhere should its continued existence be taken for granted. If this volume is to make any contribution to the global fight to preserve democracy, it is to emphasize for readers that democracy is nowhere assured and nowhere doomed, but rather lives or dies depending on what political actors believe and do.

Notes

1. Diamond, Larry. 2019. "The Global Crisis of Democracy." *The Wall Street Journal*, May 17, 2019, https://www.wsj.com/articles/the-global-crisis-of-democracy-11558105463.
2. In a later contribution, Przeworski (2005, 266–67) finds that the prospects of future electoral victory "are neither sufficient nor necessary for democracy to survive." In poor countries, he argues, the income gain from ruling as a dictator might outweigh the income gain to be had from winning democratic elections, while the cost of being a loser in both circumstances is the same. In rich countries, in contrast, it may be better to be a perpetual loser under a democratic system than to risk being a loser under an authoritarian one.
3. Przeworski (2005, 265) admits that actors may have a "preference for democracy, independently of income," but he argues that this would only operate at high levels of income (i.e., not in "hard places). He writes, "as the marginal utility of consumption declines, the preference for democracy (or against dictatorship) overwhelms the eventual consumption gain from becoming a dictator."
4. An important exception to this widely shared finding is Acemoglu et al. (2008).
5. As Ansell and Samuels (2010, 1544) note, Boix (2003) and Acemoglu and Robinson (2006) offer different predictions about the *level* of income inequality that is most conducive to democratization, but the logic of their arguments is similar.

6. Andrew March (2011) offers an alternative perspective on Islam's compatibility with democracy, and particularly what he calls "liberal citizenship."

7. For exact details of coding democratic transitions and breakdowns, see Mainwaring and Bizzarro (2020, 1561, note 3).

8. All marginal effects are calculated using the results in column 1 of Table 1.1, except for the marginal effects of ethnic fractionalization, the Gini index, and state capacity, which are calculated based on the results in column 2.

9. Although non-significant, the negative correlation between ethnic diversity and democratic breakdown runs contrary to expectations. It is premature to speculate about the cause of a correlation that has yet to be consistently demonstrated, but it could suggest that social diversity renders it harder for single parties or groups to monopolize power and transform competitive regimes into autocratic ones. This does not mean that the conventional wisdom—which sees ethnic diversity as a challenge to democracy—is wrong, only that the difficulty that diversity poses could be in getting democracy, and not in keeping it.

10. In their book, *Costly Democracy: Peacebuilding and Democratization After War*, Zurcher et al. (2013) find that the success of democratization after civil wars hinges in part on the extent to which political actors "demand" democracy, which can stem from a combination of self-interest and normative belief.

Appendix

Table A1.1 Summary Statistics

Variable	Obs.	Mean	Std. Dev.	Min.	Max.
Breakdown	1,731	0.026	0.159	0	1
GDP (logged)	1,682	8.249	1.135	5.777	10.383
GDP growth	1,675	0.023	0.046	−0.407	0.599
Share of neighboring countries democratic	1,731	0.513	0.127	0.103	0.794
Years since last transition	1,731	12.270	8.953	0	42
Organization of Islamic Cooperation	1,731	0.162	0.369	0	1
Arab League	1,731	0.020	0.141	0	1
Eastern Europe	1,731	0.224	0.417	0	1
Ethnic fractionalization index	1,588	0.436	0.253	0.003	0.889
State capacity	1,118	0.209	0.791	−2.377	2.015
Gini index	1,656	41.567	10.267	21.2	74.3

2

India's Democratic Longevity and Its Troubled Trajectory

Ashutosh Varshney

At the core of this chapter lies a paradox.[*] On one hand, India is the longest lasting democracy of the developing world; on the other hand, since 2014 a democratic decline has unquestionably set in. In their recent reports, the two most widely read annual assessments of democracy worldwide, by Freedom House and the V-Dem Institute, have noted India's democratic retrogression in no uncertain terms. Freedom House now calls India only "partly free," and the V-Dem Institute says India has become an "electoral autocracy" (Freedom House 2021b; V-Dem Institute 2021). Whether or not we find these terms precise, India's democratic diminution is not in doubt. With the rise of Narendra Modi to power, the world's biggest democracy has entered a manifestly shaky period. But how should we conceptually map the shakiness? My basic claim in this chapter is that India after 2014 is not a case of democratic collapse but one of democratic erosion or democratic backsliding.[1] I will use the latter two terms interchangeably.

The analytical task of this chapter is twofold. What explains India's democratic longevity? And how might one explain the recent downward trajectory? My attempt here is to provide an integrated argument, which seeks to answer both questions. But before the argument is presented and to anchor the detailed discussion, it seems fitting to present a brief overview of India's democratic record. For most democratic theorists, competitive elections are a necessary condition for the functioning of a democracy. "No elections, no democracy" is a theoretical dictum of widespread acceptability. So let us begin with India's electoral record.

Since independence in 1947, India has held 17 national and 389 state elections. Power has changed hands eight times in the national capital and tens of times at the state level. The latter phenomenon is by now so common that political scientists have stopped counting state-level government turnovers. Until 1992–93, the third tier of government—at the town and village level—was the only unelected tier, but a constitutional amendment finally filled that gap, too. Since the mid-1990s, roughly three million local legislators have been elected every five years. Other than a twenty-one-month period of nationwide authoritarianism (June 1975–March 1977) and a few electoral suspensions in areas of

Ashutosh Varshney, *India's Democratic Longevity and Its Troubled Trajectory* In: *Democracy in Hard Places*.
Edited by: Scott Mainwaring and Tarek Masoud, Oxford University Press. © Oxford University Press 2022.
DOI: 10.1093/oso/9780197598757.003.0002

unrest and insurgency, elections have decided who will rule India and its states and, after 1992–93, its local governments as well. This has been true even in the period of democratic backsliding since 2014. Several democratic institutions have been challenged, causing the erosion, but the integrity of elections has not been undermined.

Indeed, the idea that competitive elections are the only way to form governments has been the institutionalized political commonsense of the country. Such institutionalization means that for a long time now, no major political actor or organization has proposed a non-electoral way of coming to power. The question of whether there is more to democracy than elections has remained unsettled and contested, but there is no doubt that competitive elections have formed the core of India's democratic imagination. It is hard to predict whether the electoral core of democracy will remain unimpaired in the coming years, but as of now, despite the ongoing democratic erosion, the electoral principle remains intact. Modi may not have lost nationally since 2014, but he has lost a number of state elections, which include states that are, politically and economically, extremely significant. A Trump-like campaign, questioning election integrity in the face of defeat, something not uncommon in many parts of the world, has not been launched.

In the mid-1960s, Barrington Moore was among the first to note India's democratic credentials: "[A]s a political species, [India] does belong to the modern world. At the time of Nehru's death in 1964, political democracy had existed for seventeen years. If imperfect, the democracy was no mere sham. . . . Political democracy may seem strange in both an Asian setting and one without an industrial revolution" (Moore 1966, 314). Roughly half a decade later, in what has become a foundational text of democratic theory, Robert Dahl identified India as "a deviant case . . . indeed a polyarchy" (Dahl 1971, 68–69). About two decades later Dahl was even more emphatic, calling India "a leading contemporary exception" to democratic theory (Dahl 1989, 253). Finally, after a little over another decade, Adam Przeworski et al. (2000, 87) argued that in their 1950–90 international dataset, India's democratic longevity was the most surprising: "The odds against democracy in India were extremely high."[2]

A fairly substantial body of literature has sought to explain why India stayed democratic for so long in a theoretically counterintuitive setting (Chhibber 2014; Kohli 2001; Kothari 1970b; Moore 1966; Varshney 1998, 2013; Weiner 1989). In this chapter, I engage the comparative or theoretical literature of a more recent vintage, as well as probe the new datasets that measure democracy worldwide.

I advance two arguments. First, seeking a reexamination of how democratic India has been, I draw a distinction between India as an electoral democracy and India as a liberal democracy. Using political theory, India's political history, and the V-Dem dataset (Coppedge et al. 2021), I argue that India's electoral record is considerably better than its performance as a liberal democracy. India has, on the whole, been electorally vibrant, but its democracy has substantial liberal deficits. Under the twice-elected Modi regime (2014–present), these deficits have widened quite alarmingly. Substantially eroding civil freedoms, minority rights, and institutional constraints on executive power, these deficits have primarily affected the liberal side of democracy, not the electoral side.[3] In my argument below, I will call competitive elections a minimal democratic requirement, while proposing that a fuller, or deeper, democracy also constrains governments between elections—by guaranteeing civil freedoms, protecting minority rights, and viewing executive authority as institutionally checked and delimited. India's recent democratic erosion is about the latter, not about the former, meaning that India remains electorally democratic but it has rolled back the democratic deepening that was under way for decades.

Second, for explaining democratic longevity, my argument concentrates on the primacy of *elite choices*, not on the *structural or cultural determinants* of democratic longevity that several democratic theorists have privileged, though not all. My focus on elites is divided into three parts: (1) the founding moment and the formative period of democracy, (2) the period since the only nation-wide collapse of democracy (1975–77) until 2014; and (3) the period of erosion, though not collapse, since the rise of Modi (2014–present). In the first period, I demonstrate how elite *values* played a big role in institutionalizing democracy. In the second period, I argue that while values explain the behavior of a segment of elites, especially those who led some of the constitutionally given independent institutions of oversight, such as the Supreme Court and the Election Commission, a large section of political elites developed serious *interests* in the persistence of democracy. The bedrock of values that launched the democratic experiment acquired a serious core of interests. While dealing with the recent democratic decline under Modi, I return to the explanatory salience of elite values. Modi's values, and those in power with him in Delhi, privilege Hindu nationalism, or Hindu supremacy, over what India's Constitution says, especially with respect to citizen freedoms, religious equality, and minority rights. Right through, such elite choices, framed as values or interests, dominate my explanation of democratic persistence, not structural or cultural determinants.

Though I find the formative period hugely significant and analyze it in considerable detail, it is clearly not enough to leave the explanation at such strong beginnings. Founding moments do not last forever; elite generations change and their values evolve; and norms that got institutionalized can be broken, as happened during India's Emergency (1975–77) and might happen again.[4] Origins and persistence are analytically distinct, and need to be separately accounted for.

In the discussion below, using primarily the V-Dem dataset, I first examine India's democratic record, both over time and as compared to other countries. Next, I analyze in detail the inadequacies of structural and cultural explanations and, conversely, the superiority of elite-centric analytical accounts. I then turn my gaze toward India's democratic institutionalization in the early years of independence, dealing next with the return of a vigorous democracy (1977–2014) after the Emergency breakdown, and turning finally to the erosion of democracy with the rise of Modi after 2014. The concluding remarks recapitulate the argument.

What the Statistics Say

The V-Dem dataset (Coppedge et al. 2021) has five democracy indices: electoral, liberal, participatory, deliberative, and egalitarian. Of these, following standard democratic theory, I stick to the first two: the electoral (for V-Dem, that means free and fair elections, freedom of expression, and freedom of association[5]), and the liberal (which covers, in addition to electoral democracy, individual and minority rights, and constraints on the executive, both legislative and judicial).

India's Democracy over Time

Figure 2.1 presents India's electoral and liberal indices since 1950. The electoral index hovers around 0.7 for most of the period since then, with the exception of the 1975–77 Emergency and the recent decline. The liberal index is consistently below the electoral index, mostly staying between 0.5 and 0.6, with a lowering in the two periods noted above: 1975–77 and in recent years.

India's democratic record, thus, is marked by a consistent gap between the electoral and liberal dimensions of democracy. It might be suggested that this is not a specific ailment of Indian democracy. Rather, because of the way V-Dem measures the two scores and the more stringent requirements of a liberal democracy, the electoral–liberal hiatus is a general predicament of democracies. That is indeed true, but the gap is more pronounced in India. For the period 1950–2019, Figure 2.2 plots the decadal moving average of India's electoral–liberal hiatus against similar averages from some of the major world regions (Latin America and the Caribbean, Asia-Pacific, and Western Europe and North America) as well as the world at large. Compared to other regional and the world averages, India's gap is consistently larger, except for Latin America and the Caribbean since the decade of 1990–99.[6]

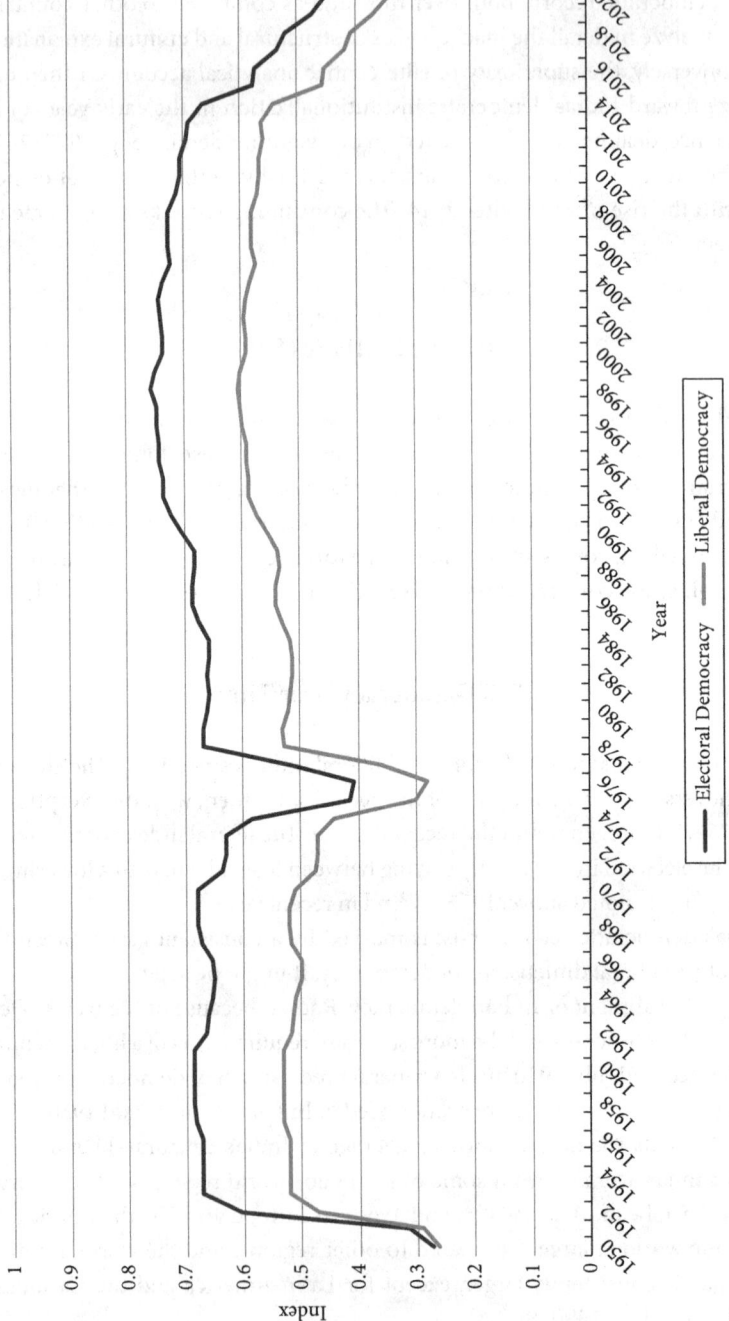

Figure 2.1. Electoral and liberal democracy index, India 1950–2020

Source: Coppedge et al. 2021

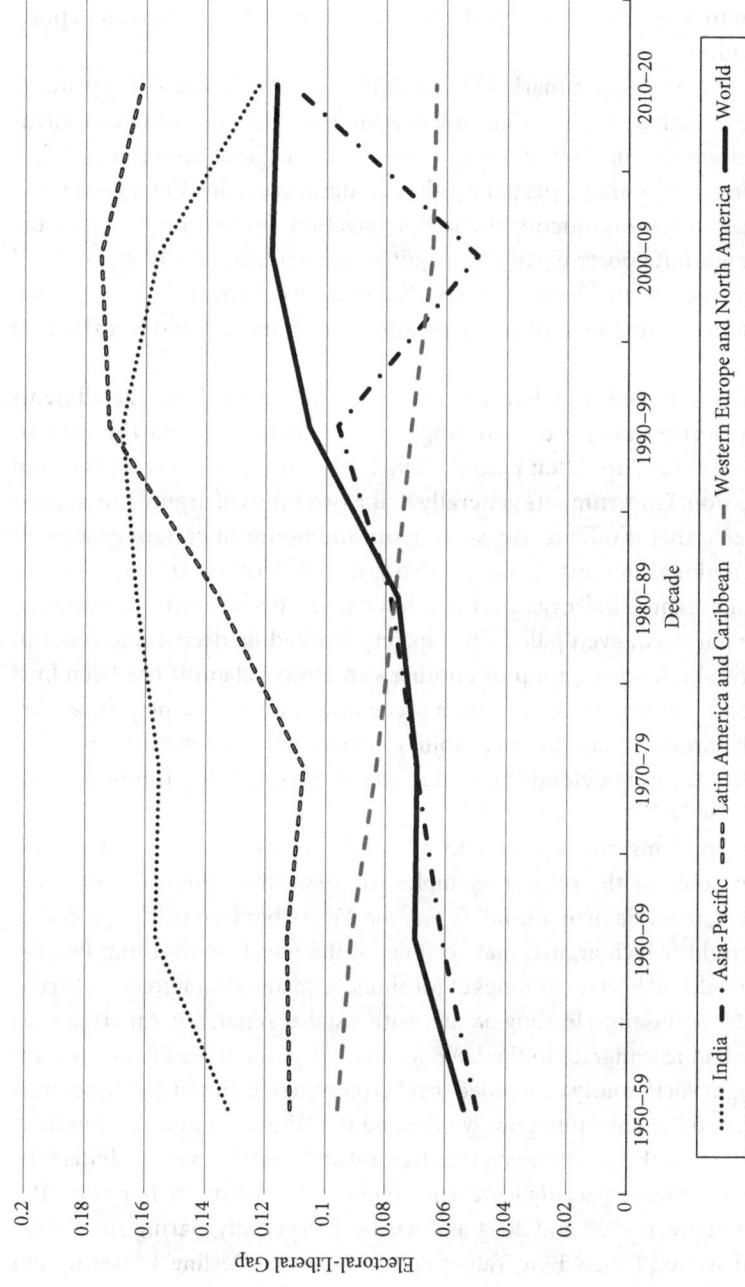

Figure 2.2. The electoral-liberal democracy gap—decadal comparison
Source: Coppedge et al. 2021

The legal foundations of India's liberal deficits are explored later (in the section entitled "New Elite Values and Democratic Decline"). Here it might be pertinent to note some typical patterns that have repeatedly emerged in post-British India.

Political parties are remarkably free at the time of elections. They are, of course, prohibited from inciting violence. Short of that, they can make virtually any argument in election campaigns.[7] Elections have been free and fair, and their verdicts are respected by all including, crucially, the incumbents. There have been arguments about how election finance might favor the incumbents, but poorer parties have quite often won, especially at state level but also at the national level.[8] A party's riches have not always helped, though it is undeniable that incumbents typically have an upper hand in garnering resources.

The election-time freedoms, however, coexist with their curtailments between elections. Once the winning party or coalition forms the government, restrictions are often placed on civil liberties, especially on freedom of expression. Governments generally make two kinds of arguments against free speech: that it offends the sentiments and honor of certain groups, or it hurts national interest. On these two grounds, writers, artists, students, and nongovernmental organizations have often been legally or administratively harassed, even jailed. In a society marked by deep-rooted ascriptive hierarchies, some group or another can always claim it has been hurt by a speech, an article, a cartoon, a piece of art, a novel, a play, or a film. When the argument about group injury or national interest enters politics, governments rarely defend the writer, the intellectual, the filmmaker, the artist, or the NGO.

These problems are common to all kinds of governments and parties. Consider some of the biggest examples. In 1988, the Congress Party government banned Salman Rushdie's *Satanic Verses* because of the protest of Muslim right, which argued that sections of the novel, by insulting Prophet Mohammed, had hurt the feelings of Muslims. Also under Congress Party rule, the late M. F. Husain, a leading painter with a stellar reputation for artistic excellence, had to emigrate to the UAE for the last years of his life because the Hindu right vociferously contended that his paintings of Hindu goddesses were obscene, and the obscenity gravely offended the Hindu community. But there is no doubt that the gulf between the electoral and liberal aspects of Indian democracy becomes especially wide when Hindu nationalists are in power. This was true between 1998 and 2004 and has been especially glaring since 2014. The final section ("New Elite Values and Democratic Decline") takes up this matter in detail.

More International Comparisons

Let us now turn to some more cross-regional and cross-country comparisons. On the electoral democracy index, Figure 2.3 compares India's performance with the following averages: for the world, for Western Europe and North America, for Asia-Pacific, and for Latin America and the Caribbean (Latin America hereafter). Generally speaking, after independence, India's index has only been lower than the average for Western Europe and North America, and higher than the average for the world, Asia-Pacific, and Latin America, including the period after the early 1980s, when democracy returned to Latin America. However, there is one set of exceptions worth noting.[9] After remaining ahead for all of the post-1950 period, India's index in more recent years has dipped below Latin America's—and has even fallen lower than the world average.

Figure 2.4 reproduces the preceding exercise on the liberal democracy index. The similarities with the electoral democracy comparison are evident. India's liberal democracy index, with no exceptions, is lower than that for Western Europe and North America. But, as above, it is on the whole higher than the indices for Latin America and Asia-Pacific. And, as was true for electoral democracy, India's recent performance as a liberal democracy turns out to be worse than that of Latin America. Indeed, its descent below the world average is also noticeable.

Figures 2.5 and 2.6 draw the comparison differently. Instead of comparing India to regions, they place India's indices against the well-known examples of democratic longevity in the Global South. Costa Rica and Botswana are often cited as the longest-surviving democracies in Latin America and sub-Saharan Africa; and Przeworski et al. (2000) also list Jamaica, Mauritius, and Papua New Guinea in the same category from their 1950–90 dataset.[10] Figure 2.5 compares all of these countries on the electoral democracy index: Costa Rica ranks consistently higher than India since 1950 and Mauritius after its independence in the late 1960s. Figure 2.6 compares their liberal democracy scores. Relative to India, Costa Rica again scores higher since 1950, and Mauritius and Botswana since the late 1960s. Also, India drops precipitously in more recent times.

In summary, the following inferences can be drawn from the empirical investigation above. First, India performs better as an electoral democracy than as a liberal democracy. Second, until recently, compared to regional averages, the electoral and liberal vigor of India's democracy has been generally behind only Western Europe and North America. Third, inter-country comparisons show that Costa Rica has been consistently ahead since 1950, Mauritius does unexceptionably better since its independence, and democracy in Botswana, too, displays greater liberalism in the last six decades. Finally, if Przeworski et al. are right and India is still a very hard place for democracy—arguably more so than

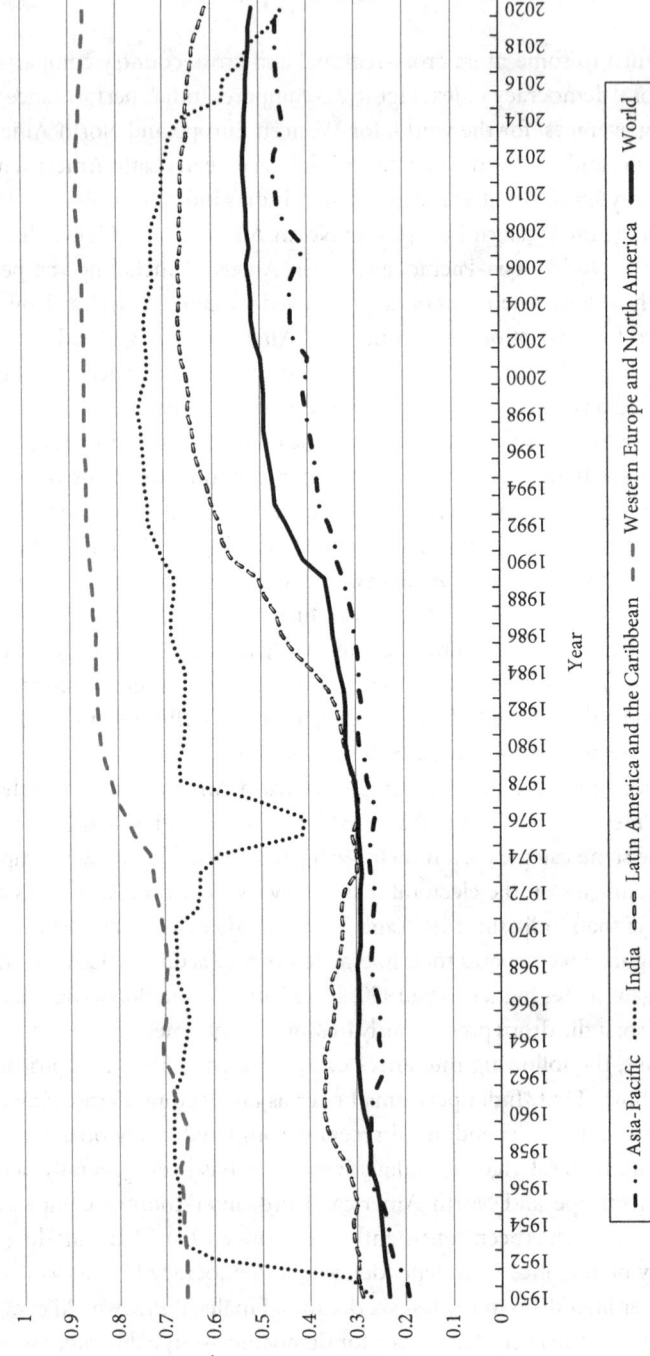

Figure 2.3. Electoral democracy index: India and some world regions, 1950–2020

Source: Coppedge et al. 2021

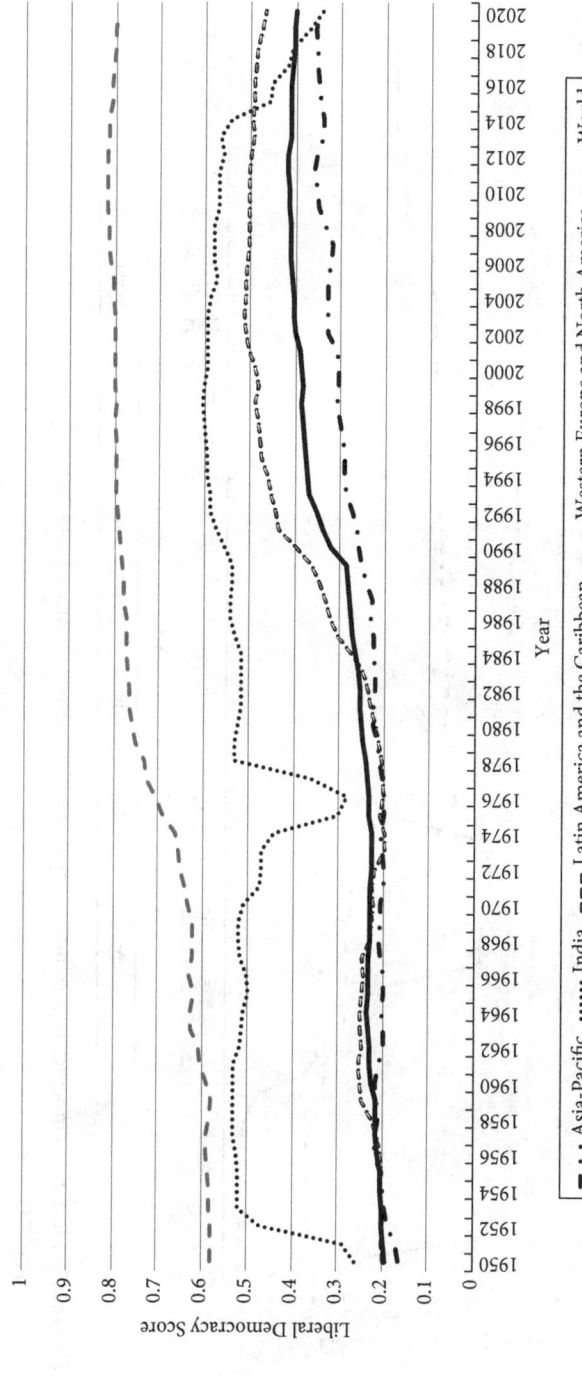

Figure 2.4. Liberal democracy index: India and some world regions, 1950–2020

Source: Coppedge et al. 2021

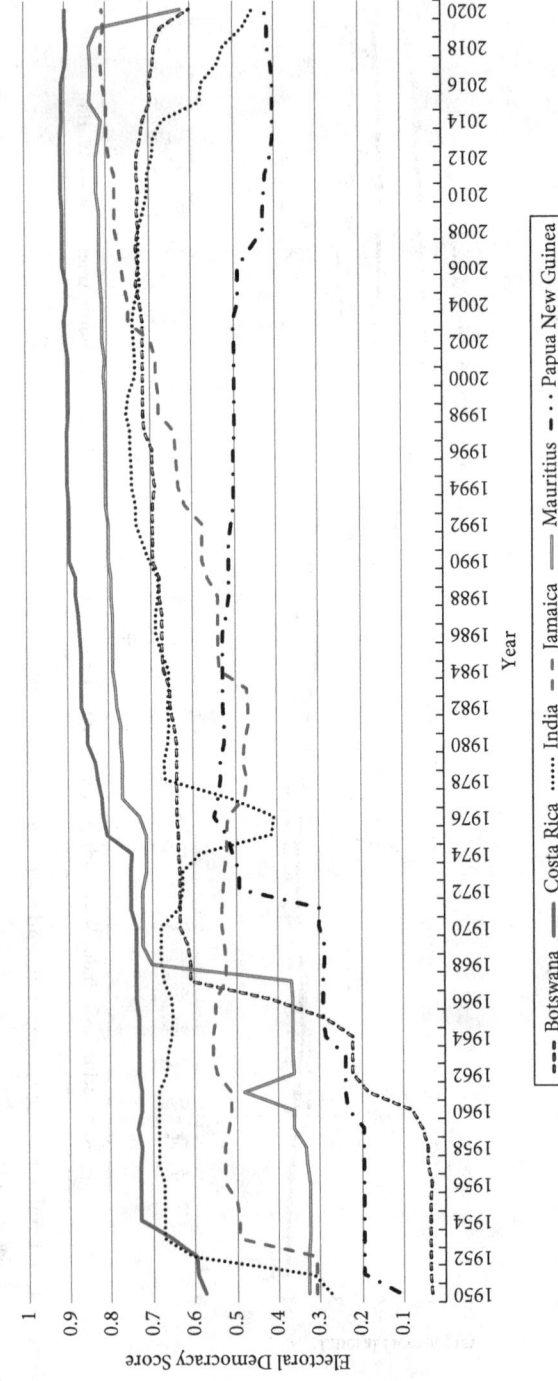

Figure 2.5. Electoral democracy index: India compared with selected countries, 1950–2020

Source: Coppedge et al. 2021

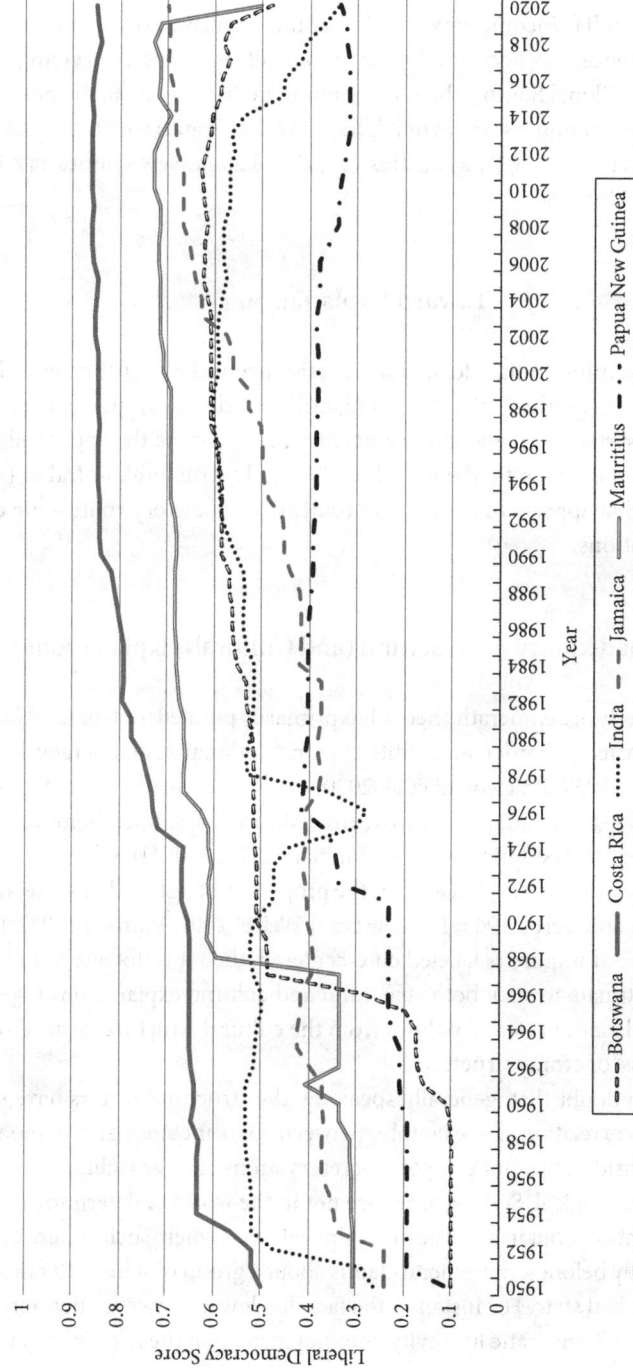

Figure 2.6. Liberal democracy index: India compared with selected countries, 1950–2020

Source: Coppedge et al. 2021

Botswana, Costa Rica, Jamaica, Mauritius, and Papua New Guinea—it can only be so because India's income, given their income-intensive explanation of democratic persistence, has been the lowest among all the longest-surviving democracies of the Global South, which turns out to be true. In 2020, the per capita incomes of these countries (in current US$) were: Botswana ($6,405), Costa Rica ($12,141), Jamaica ($4,664), Mauritius ($8,627), Papua New Guinea ($2,757), and India ($1,928).[11]

Toward Explanation

Let us now examine India's democratic persistence in light of the larger literature on democracy, theoretical and comparative. I divide up the explanations into two blocs: structural and elite-centered. I first examine the applicability of the mainstream democratic theory, which is mainly structural, to India. I then move on to what appears to be more a promising explanatory route—the elite-based explanations.

The Inadequacy of Structural (and Cultural) Explanations

A very large body of democratic theory has primarily pointed to structural factors that make it easier, or harder, for countries to institutionalize democracy: level of income (Lipset 1959; Przeworski et al. 2000), level of inequality (Acemoglu and Robinson 2006; Boix 2003), class structure (Moore 1966; Rueschemeyer et al. 1992), and degree of ethnic diversity (Lijphart 1977; Mill [1864] 1975). Some other scholars locate the explanation in the properties of political or societal culture (Almond and Verba 1963; Inglehart and Welzel 2007; Putnam 1993). If the alternative line of inquiry is labeled elite-centered, then it is not altogether analytically illegitimate to stick both structural and cultural explanations together. The latter explanations derive politics from the cultural structure, instead of the economy, class, or ethnic structure.

There is no doubt that, generally speaking, the structural factors have some validity. The correlation, for example, between high incomes and democratic survival is considerable. But two sorts of reservations emerge right away. One is simply epistemological. So long as we are not in the world of deterministic law-like generalizations, but in a stochastic realm, which is where social science theorizing normally belongs, the general claims about a group of states will not apply to each individual state. For instance, the fact that low incomes are not normally connected with democratic longevity does not mean that the relationship would operate in each country. The statistical outliers will obviously not be on the trend line. This distinction between what may be true at a group level, but not at an individual level, can easily be applied to India.

Przeworski et al. (2000) argue that income correctly predicted the type of regime in 77.5 percent of the cases (Przeworski et al. 2000, 79). But it also means that in 22.5 percent of the cases, the relationship did not hold. India clearly belongs to this latter, smaller category. It had been a low-income country until roughly 2005, graduating to a middle-income category after that,[12] but a low per capita income did not undermine its democracy.

Similarly, Acemoglu and Robinson (2006) may well be correct in stating that "democracy has the best chance to emerge in societies with middle levels of inequality" (37), and that neither in egalitarian nor low-inequality societies (such as Singapore), nor for that matter in highly unequal societies (such as Sierra Leone), can democracies stabilize themselves. But they quickly add that this prediction "about inter-group inequality may not translate into statements about standard measures of inequality and income distribution (e.g., the labor share or the Gini coefficient)" (36–37). Given the statistical untranslatability of their concept of inequality, it is hard to know whether India's income Gini coefficient, estimated to be between 0.35 and 0.45 since independence, is low, middling, or high. But even if it is middling, in which case Acemoglu and Robinson could say India supports their theory, it is not clear why India's huge caste disparities should count for less than its middling income inequalities. In Britain or Latin America, class realities might have made universal franchise a means of obtaining the "right to a good coat . . . a good hat . . . a good roof . . . [and] a good dinner" (24), but in India, securing dignity from the daily insults of the caste system might well have been a larger impulse, as some have argued (Mehta 2003; Varshney 2000; Weiner 2001). Consider how the lower-caste Ezahavas were treated until the first three decades of the twentieth century.

> They were not allowed to walk on public roads. . . . They were Hindus, but they could not enter temples. While their pigs and cattles [sic] could frequent the premises of temples, they were not allowed to go even there. Ezhavas could not use public wells or public places. . . .
>
> An Ezhava should keep himself, at least thirty-six feet away from a Namboodiri Brahmin and twelve feet away from a Nair. . . . He must address a caste Hindu man, as Thampuran (My Lord) and woman as Thampurati (My Lady).. . . . He must stand before a caste Hindu in awe and reverence, assuming a humble posture. He should never dress himself up like a caste Hindu; never construct a house on the upper class model. . . . [T]he woemen [sic] folk of the community . . . were required, young and old, to appear before caste Hindus, always "topless." (Rajendran 1974, 23–24)

In conditions like this, lasting for centuries, the struggle of lower castes in India has been, first, for dignity and for being treated as human beings, and only later for higher income equality (Chakrabarti 2019). Indeed, lower castes, given their large numbers, have used India's democracy to press somewhat successfully for conditions of dignity; their success at income improvements have not been as great (Chauchard 2017; Jensenius 2017; Varshney 2000).

Let us now turn to the arguments based on class structure. If Barrington Moore (1966) is right about the "no bourgeois, no democracy" theoretical principle, or if it is generally true that the rise of middle classes moderates distributional struggles between the rich and the poor (Acemoglu and Robinson 2006), thereby making greater structural room for democracy than would be true otherwise, then it is noteworthy that India's middle class was minuscule at the time of independence, perhaps no more than 4–5 percent of the population, and it is only after the great economic turnaround over the last three decades that India has developed a substantial middle class, now widely believed to be about a third of the country. Yet democracy kept functioning even before the 1990s economic reforms increased the size of the middle class.

Political culture and ethnic diversity as explanatory factors run into similar difficulties. The political culture argument, both in its earlier (Almond and Verba 1963) and later forms (Inglehart and Welzel 2007; Putnam 1993), concentrates on the fit between certain enduring social or cultural characteristics and the type of polity. On the whole, it is argued that a more egalitarian social structure generates civic culture, or horizontal social capital, which makes democracy work. India's caste system, the defining feature of Indian social structure for centuries, is the antithesis of equality. It has viewed human beings, and the caste groups to which they belong, as fundamentally unequal. Along with racial stratification, the hierarchical caste system has been termed a prototypical form of vertical social order (Horowitz 1985; Varshney 2012). Such verticality has generally ruled out the idea and experience of human equality. In rural India, the caste system is more entrenched than in the cities, but even as late as 2011, India was 68 percent rural and as much as 83 percent in 1951. The hierarchies of the caste system have not prevented democracy from working in India.[13]

The argument that ethnic diversity is an unfavorable condition for democracy goes back to John Stuart Mill. Mill's original argument took the following form:

> Free institutions are next to impossible in a country made up of different nationalities. Among a people without fellow-feeling, *especially if they read and speak different languages*, the united public opinion, necessary to the working of representative government, cannot exist. (Mill [1864] 1975, 384; emphasis mine)

Thus, multiple languages, according to Mill, would make the creation of a nation highly improbable. A superordinate loyalty to a national center is necessary, or free institutions would simply fracture societies and thereby undermine democracy itself. Arend Lijphart (1977) developed a creative solution to the problem Mill posed by arguing that democracy in multiethnic societies was actually possible if it took a consociational, not a liberal, form.

India has undoubtedly departed from Mill's expectations. The country has fifteen languages spoken by more than ten million each, yet democracy was not stymied by a multi-linguistic society. Interregional communication across the nation has been possible because India developed a three-language formula for its school education, allowing citizens in different parts of the country to understand each other. As a result of the education policy, India's literates became bilingual or trilingual.[14] Moreover, multiple languages notwithstanding, India has managed to generate considerable loyalty to the national center, something Mill considered virtually impossible (Stepan, Linz, and Yadav 2011).

If Mill's apprehension has not come true, how does India measure up to Lijphart's reasoning about ethnic diversities and democracy? Two responses can be given. The first is strictly formal. In a formal or literal sense, India defies Lijphart's consociational model. Its liberal deficits notwithstanding, India has mostly been a liberal democracy, not a consociational one.[15] *Individuals, rather than groups, have been the fundamental unit of political representation.* Indeed, during the break-up of British India in 1947, a serious consociational argument was made in mainstream politics. In a consociational style, the Muslim League, which led the Pakistan movement, demanded that it be recognized as the only political party representing the Muslims of India, and that there also be a fixed share of legislative, administrative, and judicial seats reserved for Muslims.[16] The Congress Party, leading the independence movement, chose to take the risk of partition rather than accept the Muslim League's consociational demands to alter the fundamental nature of the polity. It went for a type of democratic polity, in which the individual would be the fundamental unit of political arrangements (Khosla 2020), with no political organization acting as a "sole spokesman" for any community, and no fixed religious quotas in the institutions of governance.[17] It argued in favor of an open interparty competition for each community's votes. And there would be no grand coalitions or minority vetoes. *Minority rights*—for education and religious personal laws for marriage, divorce, property inheritance, and so forth—would be constitutionally granted, but no *minority quotas* in government, parliament, or civil service would be permitted.

The second answer, however, is more about political practices that depart from the liberal model of individual-based representation and give India some power-sharing features. The two most important are federalism and caste-based reservations. India's federalism is linguistic, in that all major linguistic groups have a state of their own in the federation. And the lowest castes in the Hindu hierarchy have guaranteed representation in legislatures as well as bureaucracies, in proportion to their weight in the population.

But neither of these features makes India a power-sharing democracy in a consociational sense. First, federalism is linguistically based, not religious. For over a century, if not more, religion has been the greatest fault line of Indian politics. Consociational polities are typically formed around the deepest cleavage patterns, but independent India rejected power-sharing on the basis of religion. Instead, it conceded power-sharing on linguistic lines. Second, the caste-based reservations were primarily for legislatures and civil services, not for the executives and cabinets, which is where most power resides.[18]

Bringing Political Elites In

If structural accounts are not fully adequate, where do we go next? Agent-centric explanations have been the standard alternative path to follow. In the main, the agents that carry democratic politics include elites and political organizations, especially political parties, and those related to movements. These are also often—and rightly—labeled as political, as opposed to structural, factors.

Some of this analytic spirit is evident in two relatively recent works on democracy. Mainwaring and Pérez-Liñán (2013) write:

> Political actors, not structures or cultures, determine outcomes, even though structures and cultures affect the formation and preferences of actors. We view presidents and organizations such as parties, unions, business associations, the military, and organized movements as the most important actors. . . .
>
> We emphasize the role of political factors that help political regimes survive or lead them to fail. By "political factors" we refer specifically to the impact actors' normative preferences about democracy and dictatorship . . . exercised. . . . We counterpose an emphasis on these political factors to analyses that argue that the survival or displacement of regimes depends largely on structural factors such as the level of development, the class structure, or income inequalities, or on mass political culture. (Mainwaring and Pérez-Liñán 2013, 5)

Ziblatt (2017) also points to the importance of elites. After noting that the three most widely cited accounts of democratizations have concentrated on (1) the level of economic development, (2) the emergence of a middle class, and (3) the demands of the working class for greater rights and a larger share of power, he favors the elite-centric account of O'Donnell and Schmitter (1986):

If elites can be made secure with regard to their future wealth, status, and power as democratization unfolds, . . . critical portions of the elite will become reluctant but essential democrats. On the other hand, if elites remain insecure, politically fragmented, and fearful of major loses [sic] in their future, then they will support and even lead counterrevolution, creating a historic record of unsettled democratization. (Ziblatt 2017, 16)

Stating further—and rightly—that "a country's political regime is not simply a mirror of its economy" (17), Ziblatt concentrates on political parties as actors, arguing that "it is crucial to elevate political parties, the 'political carriers' of organized interests, to the status of a variable that shapes democratization" (20).

This line of reasoning invites a serious examination of what the political elites want and why. But we still have an important larger issue left to consider: should we focus on elite *values* or elite *interests*? It is not clear if we can answer this question generally, theoretically, or in the abstract. It may be an empirical, not a theoretical, matter.

Ziblatt's elite-centered argument is strictly about interests. European materials show, he argues, that if the incumbent elites, customarily represented by conservative parties, came to the view that democratization would hurt their power or wealth, they impeded its evolution, and whether or not that brought democratization to a halt at its moment of inception, democracy over the medium to long run stumbled as, for example, in pre-1945 Germany. A cooptation of conservative parties—and thereby the interests of traditional elites—augured best for a smooth democratic trajectory, as in post-1832 Britain.

Central to this argument is the idea of a clash between incumbent elites and emerging elites, each represented by a different political party, and a compromise between the two as the foundation of democratic stability. Whatever the relevance of this argument for Western Europe in the nineteenth century, its applicability to post-colonial democracies of the twentieth century is not straightforward. Colonialism accounts for the greatest political difference between nineteenth-century Europe and the European colonies in the tropics. Generally absent in the colonizing Europe, anticolonialism was a big political sentiment in the colonies. The latter gave political parties and groups fighting for independence extraordinary legitimacy. Local elites allied with the colonial masters, however socially powerful, were eventually no match for the anticolonial organizations and parties.

Furthermore, the colonial powers, even those that were democratic like Britain, argued that the colonies were unfit for democracy (see Mehta 1999; Mill [1864] 1975). As a result, in a late colonial setting, the biggest adversary of democracy was often the colonial power, not the conservative landlord pitted against a democracy-carrying middle class or the bourgeoisie, as in nineteenth-century

Europe. In countries like Pakistan, which came about as a result of a separatist, not an anticolonial, movement, feudal landlords could still be viewed as the incumbent elites, who had to assess their interests in an incipient democracy, as Tudor (2013) has argued. But where colonial departure was not accompanied by the colony's partition, the colonial rulers were, more often than not, the greatest political force opposed to democracy.[19]

Let us nonetheless suppose that the indigenous princes and landlords, key allies of the British, can be viewed as incumbent elites in India by virtue of their association with the colonial rulers. In Britain, as Ziblatt shows, the Conservative Party represented their interests and it had the power to block democratization, unless concessions were made by emerging elites. In India, conservative parties did emerge to protect the landlords in the late colonial period, but generally speaking the emerging elites squarely defeated them in the provincial elections.[20] Those who did not participate in the independence movement simply had no effective political space to be counted as powerful political actors. The Congress Party attacked landlordism as early as 1936–37, renewing the assault after independence, when it was firmly in control of state power.[21]

But there is a sense in which the claim that, for democracy to evolve smoothly, it is necessary to accommodate the interests of incumbent elites can be made for India as well. First, after independence, when the Congress Party enacted a land reform program, aimed at crushing landlord power, the landlords began to operate at a regional, vernacular level. As Weiner (1967) showed, the landlords penetrated the district and provincial levels of the Congress Party as party members, and managed to block land reforms with varying degrees of success in different states. In an India which was 83 percent rural at the time of independence, the Congress Party needed the landlords to expand its organizational presence in the countryside, as it is the landlords who were locally influential, not the peasantry, which was dependent on them for a whole variety of economic and social reasons and, therefore, quite powerless (Herring 1982). Basically, there emerged a contradiction between the political imperatives of party building and the economic policy goals of land redistribution and tenancy reforms (Varshney 1995). And once the landlords were inside the party, they could begin to impede the implementation of land reforms. Thus, conservative parties representing landlord interests might not have risen in a big way, as in Western Europe, but a functionally equivalent political form—penetration of the ruling party at lower levels—emerged to protect landlord interests.[22]

But these messy equations emerged later, not at the time of India's democratic commencement. Moreover, they affected the lower political levels. The decision to democratize was taken at the summit of the polity, which was firmly in the hands of the emerging, not incumbent, elites.[23] It is the emerging elites who devised India's democratic constitution. And in the vigorous debates of the

Constituent Assembly (CA), lasting nearly three years, one sees enough evidence of arguments based on values, not any recognizable display of interests.

One could, of course, say that the distinction between elite values and elite interests was only theoretical at the time of independence, given the Congress Party's hegemony. It could afford to talk in terms of values, for the party could not possibly visualize losing power. Establishing a democracy, therefore, could not conceivably hurt.

To be sure, it was not easy for the Congress Party to envisage a defeat at the hands of the opposition in the very near future, but a constitution is a statement about the enduring properties of a polity, not a device for short-term power distribution. Accepting the idea of elections meant that the party could lose them in the future. Indeed, powerful opposition parties had already appeared in South India. And within ten years of independence, the Congress Party would lose the state of Kerala to the opposition parties there (and another ten years later, it would be defeated in many other states).

Interests attached to democracy did emerge later at higher levels of polity. But at its inception, the tenor of debates about democracy do not provide evidence of interests. That is why it is important to draw a distinction between the origins of democracy in India, and its persistence. The former was heavily based in elite values, and the latter in a combination of values as well as interests, as we shall note later (see the section, "Democracy's Second Innings and the Birth of Elite Interests").

The Emergence of Democracy and Elite Values

India's post-independence elites began their political education in 1920, not at the time of independence in 1947. The former was the so-called Gandhian turning point in India's freedom movement, when the Congress Party, which led the movement, turned toward mass politics. Under Gandhi's leadership, it stopped being a lawyer's club, making legal arguments with the British in the Queen's English. Instead, it started mobilizing the vernacular masses against colonial power. The mass-based movement lasted nearly three decades before independence came. What were the values the movement promoted and the elites imbibed? How did those values shape the creation of democracy?

Let me first examine the elite views about elections and universal franchise. I will provide evidence with respect to (1) the entire class of political elites, where it is available. Where it is not, I will concentrate on (2) the ruling Congress Party, which lost elections in only one state in the first two decades of independence (but started losing in several states thereafter), and (3) Jawaharlal Nehru, India's Prime Minister from 1947 through his death in 1964, the winner of three consecutive national elections—in 1952, 1957, and 1962—and the preeminent political figure of the first seventeen years of Indian independence. He did not always win policy or institutional struggles, but his stamp on the evolution of the democratic structure is beyond doubt. I will, therefore, combine three kinds of arguments: those at the level of all political elites in general, those dealing with the ruling Congress Party, and those covering the very summit of political leadership.

Universal Franchise

After nearly two hundred years of British rule, India's literacy rate at independence was a mere 17 percent. More than half of the country was below the poverty line (Ahmed and Varshney 2012).[24] The vastly poor and illiterate masses were in no position to demand democracy. Yet Indian elites committed themselves to universal franchise. Indeed, the commitment was made by the independence movement as early as 1928, the same year as universal franchise came to Britain.[25]

In the last decades of British rule, starting in 1921, Indians were allowed to vote, but franchise had three limiting aspects. First, voting was not a right but a privilege available on the basis of income, literacy, and landownership. Second, the first arena of voting was local government and, beginning in 1937, it was also extended to provincial assemblies. Before the British left in 1947, India had had two provincial elections, in 1937 and 1946. But at no point until their departure was the central legislature or government elected. Moreover, the highest British officials of the land could veto the legislation of provincial assemblies and executive acts of provincial governments. Finally, the electorate numbered thirty million in 1946, roughly 15 percent of the total adult population, but the entire country did not constitute a voting college. Rather, somewhat like what came to be called consociational democracy later, the British viewed India as a polity based on communities, not individuals. In particular, the electorate was divided on the basis of religion, with separate electorates for minorities. In such "separate constituencies," only the minorities could vote and only members of minority communities could run for office. Functional representation was also added to this legislative scheme. Some legislative seats were reserved for trade unions, business groups, the princely states, and so on.[26]

The freedom movement sought a radical overhauling of this institutional framework. One has to accept the great twentieth-century premise, argued Nehru, that "each person should be treated as having an equal political and social value" (Nehru 1942, 67). This became the defining statement about independent

India's universal franchise. It did not promise economic equality, only political equality. But that was enough to make the case that gender, income, property ownership, literacy, caste, religion, language, and tribe could not be the basis for allocation of voting rights. For decisions on who would rule India, voting was essential and all citizens had the right to vote. Nehru never gave up his belief in elections as the only way to determine which party will govern every five years. "Elections were an essential and inseparable part of the democratic process and there was no . . . doing away with them" (Nehru 1946, 53). He would also argue later: "Our democracy is a tender plant which has to be nourished with wisdom and care and which requires a great deal of understanding of its real processes and its discipline."[27]

Nehru, of course, was not alone. In 1945, an important committee of the Congress Party argued against those who thought that the poor and unedu-cated voters would make too many mistakes and would not be able to use the right to vote wisely and well. Although the voter's "judgement may be faulty, his reasoning inaccurate and his support of a candidate not infrequently de-termined by considerations removed from a high sense of democracy, he is yet no better or worse than the average voter in many parts of Europe where adult franchise has been in force for some time" (Sapru Committee Report, cited in Austin 1966, 147).

Nor was the sentiment confined to the Congress Party. In the early years of independence, the most important institutional site for India's political elites was the Constituent Assembly, which worked for over three years, from late 1946 to late 1949, to draft India's Constitution, a document that has survived until today. Consisting of 299 members, the Constituent Assembly was elected by provin-cial assemblies, and though most members were from the Congress Party, it also had several members whose ideology was different and who later became great critics of the ruling party. The latter group included some Hindu nationalists,[28] as well as the famous Dalit leader, B. R. Ambedkar, who was made the head of the Constitution drafting committee.[29] A Dalit leader, a bitter critic of Gandhi, thus became a father of India's Constitution. Ambedkar made a famous argu-ment about why even literacy was not a condition for franchise which, he argued, had to be universal.

> Those who insist on literacy as a test and insist upon making it a condition precedent to enfranchisement, in my opinion, commit two mistakes. Their first mistake consists in their belief that an illiterate person is necessarily an unintelligent person. . . . Their second mistake lies in supposing that literacy necessarily imports a higher level of intelligence or knowledge than what the illiterate possesses. (Ambedkar's presentation to the Simon Commission, 1928, reproduced in Jaffrelot and Kumar 2018, 34)[30]

The claim here was not that the illiterate people should not be educated; only that illiteracy and intelligence are analytically separable, and even the illiterate understood their interests. The chair of the Constitution Drafting Committee and his firm voice mattered.

There were undoubtedly some voices of dissent. Some members continued to favor voting restrictions, especially those based on literacy. A member pleaded: "For the first ten years, just limit this right of voting to literate people .. . . Otherwise, in my humble opinion, these elections will be a great farce. . . . My submission is that . . . we should have the provision of literacy" (Lok Sabha Secretariat 1949a).

But such views were few and far between. They could not win the day. With an overwhelming majority, across the political spectrum, the Assembly embraced universal adult franchise. The reasons for support were not identical,[31] but the support was nearly unanimous. And the final conclusion was unmistakably clear. "The Assembly . . . adopted the principle of adult franchise . . . with an abundant faith in the common man . . . and in the full belief that the introduction of democratic government on the basis of adult suffrage will . . . promote the well-being . . . of the common man" (Lok Sabha Secretariat 1949b).

As a consequence, India's electorate expanded from 30 million in 1946 to 173 million in 1951–52. The first elections, based on universal franchise, took four months, starting in October 1951 and concluding in February 1952. They were the biggest election exercise in history.[32] Two more elections were held before Nehru's death (1964)—in 1957 and 1962. The idea of elections as the only way to come to power deepened, becoming political common sense. The Congress Party could have used Nehru's death (and later a war with Pakistan in 1965) to suspend the idea of elections and announce that it was in power for the foreseeable future, if not in perpetuity. No arguments of this kind appeared in the political sphere. After Nehru's death, the fourth general elections, covering national parliament and all state assemblies, took place in 1967. The Congress Party did not lose power at the national level, but it was defeated in several states. It bowed out wherever it was defeated. It is only in 1975 that the deepening institutionalization was ruptured. This is discussed below.

Democracy's Second Innings and the Birth of Elite Interests

In June 1975, Indira Gandhi, prime minister since 1967, declared a state of emergency and suspended democracy. It was a brief interlude, lasting twenty-one months.

Two analytical questions are relevant concerning the 1975–77 rupture. Why did a break, however short, come about? And what was done to keep democracy alive after the break? The first question is about the conditions under which democratic institutionalization crumbled, the second about its return. Paradoxically, in both, the Constitution played an important role. But it was not the only factor. The Constitution, an expression of elite values to begin with, started engaging elite interests in the mid-1970s and after.

Faced with a movement against her government, which had been under way for some time and was invigorated further when a High Court nullified her election victory on the grounds that her campaign expenses exceeded the ceiling prescribed by law, Indira Gandhi threw out democracy altogether in June 1975. Her regime arrested over 110,000 opposition leaders and activists, inaugurated the doctrine of the executive supremacy in lawmaking, curbed the power of judicial oversight, imposed press censorship, abrogated citizens' right to free speech and assembly, and allowed detention without trial.[33] All of this was done using Article 352 of India's Constitution, which allowed suspension of routine democratic processes if "a grave emergency exists whereby the security of India is threatened by internal disturbances." In other words, the Emergency was anti-democratic, but not unconstitutional. A Supreme Court judgment later, for all practical purposes, certified its constitutionality, when the Court said that detention without trial and a lack of judicial scrutiny of the executive and legislature were justified in a state of emergency.[34]

Eighteen months later, in January 1977, Indira Gandhi announced new elections, releasing jailed leaders and activists and restoring citizen and press freedoms. She was seeking to re-legitimize her rule. The best available hypothesis for why she did so suggests that even she found it hard to devise non-electoral arguments for continuance in power (Weiner 1989). She lost the elections, which were supposed to bolster political legitimacy, and bowed out after defeat, instead of canceling election results as an all-powerful head of government, something that has happened in many countries.[35] In March 1977, the first non–Congress Party government was formed in Delhi. (Since then, seven more non–Congress Party coalitions have run the national government.)

As a new government took charge, one of its most important activities was to ensure that the Constitution was not used to proclaim an internal Emergency again. *This was no longer a question of values alone.* Given that virtually all new cabinet ministers and their umpteen colleagues were jailed during the Emergency, it was in the interests of the newly empowered elites to amend the Constitution in such a way that a suspension of democracy in the future would become inordinately difficult and they would not be jailed for political reasons. The 43rd and 44th Constitutional Amendments sought to achieve this purpose. "Armed rebellion" replaced "internal disturbance" as the basis for declaring an Emergency which, from then on, would also require not just the recommendation of the prime minister to the president, the titular head in a parliamentary system, but also the written advice of the cabinet, and would have to be endorsed by a two-thirds majority in parliament within a month of the proclamation. Moreover, the extension of an Emergency beyond six months would also require parliamentary approval, not simply executive wish. Finally, the power of the judiciary to investigate and judge the constitutionality of parliamentary legislation and executive decrees was restored.

If it was in the interest of Indira Gandhi and her colleagues in 1975 to use the Constitution to disable democracy, it was now in the interest of the new rulers and their parties to make democracy's suspension awfully difficult. "No Emergency ever again" was the political motto. The constitutional amendments, aimed at averting that eventuality, have stayed until now.

Indeed, India's Constitution has not been overturned at all, only amended from time to time. The Constitution has become an institutional bedrock of India's democracy. For India's democracy to end, the Constitution would have to be terminated, or radically amended to restore at least two ideas of the Emergency: executive supremacy unrestrained by judicial scrutiny, and detention without trial.

India's overall constitutional stability leads to two questions. Why has the Constitution not been overturned, only amended? And through which institutions does the Constitution maintain its centrality? Just because the Constitution exists does not mean that it can exert political power. Constitutions have repeatedly broken down, or been overthrown, in the developing world, which includes India's neighborhood (Pakistan, Bangladesh, Sri Lanka).[36]

Here, the fact that India consistently pursued a parliamentary system appears to have come to its democratic rescue. Accumulating comparative evidence makes this point clearer than ever before. In a widely read study, Stepan and Skach (1993) surveyed all democracies between 1979 and 1989. The world had forty-three consolidated democracies in this period, of which as many as thirty-four were parliamentary and only five were presidential. After analysis, they concluded that there was a "much stronger correlation between democratic consolidation and . . . parliamentarism than democratic consolidation and . . . presidentialism" (Stepan and Skach 1993, 5).

A more recent study, by Przeworski (2019), comes to a similar conclusion, though it approaches the question of longevity via its opposite: brittleness. Between 1918 and 2008, of the forty-four consolidated parliamentary democracies, only six fell, which gives us a mortality rate of 1 in 7.3. In the same period, there were twenty-six consolidated presidential democracies, of which seven fell, which yields a mortality rate of 1 in 3.7. That is twice as high as for consolidated parliamentary systems. "The weakness of presidential systems," concludes Przeworski, "is manifest" (Przeworski 2019, 35).[37]

Presidential democracies have both repeatedly broken down and often suspended constitutions. Corrales (2018) notes that since the early 1980s alone, when democracy returned to Latin America, there have been twenty-four attempts to elect Constituent Assemblies, all aimed at rewriting the entire constitution; eleven were successful, thirteen were aborted.

There is a good deal of literature on why parliamentary democracies and their constitutions are more durable.[38] The details of the literature need not detain us here, except to note a major recurring theme especially relevant to India. Being a parliamentary system, which organically connects the executive and the legislature, India has never witnessed politically crippling stalemates between the two separately elected summits of institutional power in a presidential system: the president and congress. Such institutional paralyses, it is argued, have led to more frequent democratic breakdowns in presidential systems. India's adoption of a parliamentary system and its ability to resist the temptation for a presidential conversion of its polity appear to have a lot to do with its constitutional as well as democratic longevity.

Of course, in and of themselves, constitutions do not act. To make their presence felt in active politics, constitutions require actors and institutions to stand up and extend fighting support. It is necessary to understand who these agents of constitutional and democratic stability were, and why.

Three kinds of actors have played this role in Indian democracy, especially after its awkward turn in 1975–77. First, armed with two constitutional amendments described above (43rd and 44th), which restored its power of judicial review, the judiciary acquired new teeth in the post-Emergency era. If the courts in the past assertively exercised judicial scrutiny of the executive and the legislature, those elected to power would often choose the method of constitutional amendment, or parliamentary supermajorities, to overturn unpalatable judgments. However, after the executive excesses of the Emergency and their electoral rebuff, the political space for an executive pushback declined for many years thereafter and the elected elites did not think it advisable to push back against the judges.[39]

In particular, the judiciary added two new forms of scrutiny for checking executive and legislative power. First, Public Interest Litigation (PIL) was institutionally promoted. In conventional citizen–government interactions in a democracy, the standard notion of *locus standi* allows only those aggrieved—by executive or legislative action—to challenge the injury in a court. This requirement often works to the disadvantage of the poor and the marginalized because they either might not have the resources to reach courts directly, or might not even know that courts could invalidate government action. By allowing individuals or organizations to argue on behalf of those who can't afford litigation or are unaware of its possibilities, PIL made a huge intervention into the democratic political process, repeatedly pushing governments on behalf of the citizenry. This practice took off in the early 1980s.[40]

Second, in arenas of national life, where no prior laws existed, the judiciary adopted a quasi-lawmaking role, or initiated court-supervised executive action. Using this new mode of intervention, the judiciary issued to the governments guidelines on how to deal with sexual harassment in the workplace, on the rights of sexual minorities and slum dwellers, and on a whole host of environmental matters, including air and river pollution, forests, and wildlife.

Polls repeatedly showed in the 1990s and 2000s that the courts were more popular than parliaments, assemblies, and political parties (Krishnaswamy and Swaminathan 2019). This situation may not last forever, as the relationship between the judiciary on one hand and the executive/legislature on the other tends to be more pendulum-like than static in democratic polities. But it is important to note that the popularity of courts lasted long enough in India for the judiciary to check executives and legislatures on behalf of the citizenry, or what has sometimes been presented as national interest. While the independence of the judiciary might have come under a cloud since the rise of Modi, as analyzed in the next section, its power in the three-and-a-half decades after the Emergency unquestionably increased. The term "judicial sovereignty" was used to describe the power of courts after the 1990s (Mehta 2007).

The Election Commission is the second institution which started taking its power seriously. Unlike the US and perhaps several other polities, India's Election Commission is set up by the Constitution as an independent institution. The Election Commissioners are appointed by the executive for a fixed term, which can't be altered by governmental changes. The primary responsibility of the Election Commission is to conduct free and fair elections, which includes preparation of election rolls, registration of political parties and election contestants, watching election campaigns, checking voter intimidation, and supervising the behavior of election officials. As McMillan (2010) has argued, the Election Commission has gone through three phases in its evolution: a phase of confident establishment during the first elections under Nehru (1947–64), a phase of subservient quiescence under Indira Gandhi (1967–84), and a phase of assertive activism after the late 1980s. Modi's rise may have raised some doubts about the continuing independence of this institution, too, but there is no denying the fact that it has maintained the integrity of the election process for very long.

The quiescence of the middle period, listed above, was because Indira Gandhi exercised fearsome power, and the constitutionally independent institutions were either unwilling or unable to stand up to her. This included both the judiciary and the Election Commission. And the activism of the last period was driven by two interconnected factors, both leading to the greater consolidation of the idea that free and fair elections were the only device for coming to power and forming governments.

The first factor was the end of Congress Party hegemony and the emergence of a fluid party system, leading to coalition governments, which lacked the overwhelming power of an Indira Gandhi. And the second factor was the continued popularity of the Election Commission, repeatedly evident in polls. Generally speaking, the Election Commission and the judiciary kept receiving the highest trust rating in polls during the 1990s and 2000s (de Souza, Palshikar, and Yadav 2008). As a result, much like the judiciary, the Election Commission also felt bold enough to discipline both election officials whose behavior it deemed unfair and prejudiced and politicians whose campaign violated the legal canons, or widely accepted norms. When it suspected voting fraud, it also "countermanded" elections in some constituencies, ordering re-polls. Like the courts, the assertive behavior of the Election Commission may also not last forever, but the assertion has lasted long enough to generate strong citizen faith in the freedom and fairness of elections. For decades now, no significant challenges to the election verdicts have been launched, and the incumbents who lose elections routinely bow out.

A third set of actors, in addition to the courts and the Election Commission, is simply the political parties. So many parties have been in power since the early 1980s, mostly at the state level but also in Delhi, that serious stakes in the persistence of democracy have been created. Parties not in power in Delhi have sometimes run half of the state governments. As a result, if the ruling party at the center—and sometimes at the state level, too—egregiously breaks democratic norms, countervailing power is, in principle, available in the system to oppose the violation and seek to correct it, substantially if not wholly. Parties mobilize citizens for mass protests, launch court challenges, and mount press campaigns. This does not always, or fully, prevent the abuse of political power or eliminate predatory governmental conduct, but the generally available balance of power means that either the excesses can be reduced in frequency or their severity can be checked. All political parties swear by the Constitution, and use that as a resource to challenge governmental excesses.

More important for our purposes, democracy could not easily be suspended, for it would constitute the kind of executive excess that would touch off legal challenges by political parties and countermobilization sponsored by them. Democracy's suspension would hurt the interests of simply too many elites, and they have so far had power in the system to hit back.

Another way of conceptualizing this phenomenon is to say is that by giving a taste of power to a large number of political parties, *federalism in effect has become a mainstay of democracy*. Democracy would potentially be under a serious threat if the same party ruled in Delhi and all states, unless the party was committed to democratic values, not to perpetuation in power by hook or by crook. A multiplicity of parties in governments, at the center and states, creates countervailing power in the polity, if not an exact balance of power. As argued in the following section, federalism has become a real problem for Modi's desire for greater control of the polity; for a collapse of India's democracy, if not its erosion, federalism would also have to come apart.

New Elite Values and Democratic Decline: Modi and Hindu Nationalism

In its 2021 report, Freedom House announced: "India, the world's most populous democracy, dropped from Free to partly Free status" (2021, 2). And putting its finger on the heart of the matter, it attributed the decline to the Hindu nationalist ideology of Narendra Modi, India's prime minister since May 2014, who has won two straight national elections, in 2014 and 2019. "Under Modi, India appears to have abandoned its potential to serve as a global democratic leader, elevating narrow Hindu nationalist interests at the expense of its founding values of inclusion and equal rights for all" (Freedom House 2021b, 8).

V-Dem Institute's 2021 report went further. Instead of calling India "partly free," it concluded that India in 2020 had become an "electoral autocracy" (V-Dem Institute 2021, 6). Its judgment is based on two criteria. First, "the overall freedom and fairness of elections . . . was hard hit" (20). And second, the "diminishing of freedom of expression, the media, and civil society have gone the furthest. The Indian government rarely, if ever, used to exercise censorship . . . before Modi became Prime Minister" (20). Hungary and Turkey, it adds, "became (electoral) autocracies in 2018 and 2014 respectively, and India now joins their ranks" (20).

V-Dem Institute is right about the second factor—the attack on freedom of expression, media, and civil society—but wrong about the first, namely, the corrosion of free and fair elections. Even under Modi, elections continue to be competitive. Ironically, a remarkable piece of evidence came just a few weeks after the publication of the V-Dem report in March 2021.

In West Bengal, Tamil Nadu, Kerala, and Assam, state elections took place. The BJP in general and Modi in particular fought very hard. They lost all states except Assam, but did not challenge the results. West Bengal was especially important. It is the third largest state of India; its historical significance is beyond doubt; and of all states, Modi campaigned most vigorously there, leaving Delhi twenty times in the space of roughly six weeks to address election rallies. When the results came, a regional party under a political archrival had clearly defeated the BJP. Instead of questioning the integrity of election results, Modi conceded defeat.

To be sure, we can't predict whether Modi's acceptance of election results will continue to mark his conduct in the future as well. Moreover, some of Modi's appointees to the Election Commission, the body that not only conducts the elections but also certifies the results, continue to be civil servants, who have been close to Modi, serving him at various points in his political career. But that, in and of itself, is not a violation of democratic principles. Partisanship routinely accompanies democracy, parliamentary or presidential. It is the use of partisanship to undermine the basic processes, or the fundamental principles, of democracy that would constitute an unacceptable violation. If Modi's appointees to the Election Commission were to overturn the results of an election, or deprive voters opposed to Modi of their franchise, then it would be legitimate to claim that the fundamental tenets of an electoral democracy were transgressed.

But that has not happened yet. Modi and his party, the BJP, not only won the national elections of 2014 and 2019, widely viewed as free and fair, but what is even more critical for democratic theory, they also lost key state elections before the 2019 national victory and after. But the Modi government has not used its power, in a constitutionally unauthorized way, to annul any of the state elections.

To say that India is not an electoral democracy is therefore an overstretched claim. Instead, the best description would be that the electoral aspects of democracy notwithstanding, the basic structure of a liberal democracy, comprising freedom of expression, independence of civil society, and minority rights, is under severe erosion. The liberal deficits, though always present in India's democratic record, have widened to an alarming degree.[41] And that is because of the nature of the ideology that animates the Modi regime. The ideology of Hindu nationalism departs from India's constitutional values in two significant ways, each hurting the liberal aspects of democracy.

First, for Hindu nationalists, India is a Hindu nation, an idea the Constitution does not endorse. Demographically, Hindus are roughly 80 percent of the nation and Muslims, at just a little over 14 percent, are the largest minority. Given India's history, Muslims are a special object of Hindu nationalist ire. The Hindu nationalists have always viewed the Muslim community, with a few individual exceptions, as insufficiently patriotic, or even entirely disloyal to India. Hence their dictum that the Muslims should not have the same rights as the Hindus, who are the "original people" of India and must be accorded cultural and political primacy.[42] In its conception of the post-independence political order, India's Constituent Assembly (1947–50) did not even come close to the notion of Hindu primacy. The Constitution is rooted in the idea of religious equality and equal rights for all citizens. If anything, it gives religious minorities manifest protections from the possible emergence of a majoritarian impulse in the polity, by guaranteeing a right to the maintenance of their religion as well as culture, including language and educational institutions, supported by state grants if necessary.[43]

Second, a muscular form of nationalism also accompanies the rise of Hindu nationalists in power. This kind of nationalism threatens not only the minorities but also the dissenting citizenry in general. According to Hindu nationalists, liberal freedoms can't build a strong nation; only national discipline and obedience to the state can. Modi has argued that citizen duties must be accorded preference over citizen rights (Modi 2019), whereas the liberals and leftists, according to Hindu nationalists, tend to celebrate only individual freedoms and minority rights, thereby sapping national strength, unity, and resolve. According to a popular Hindu nationalist discursive trope, heavily promoted by the Modi government, many liberals are "anti-nationals," who should be punished by the coercive arm of the state. Unrestrained argumentative freedoms cannot be granted to citizens and civil society groups, except perhaps at the time of elections. Nation-building ought to replace the idea of citizen freedoms, once elections are over. Aimed at taming citizen dissent, such state-supported discourse leads to an explicit or implicit attack on the institutions that cannot perform their legitimate roles without political and intellectual freedoms—courts, universities, civil society, and the press. It also privileges vigilante action if the vigilante groups seek to implement the governmental vision and harass dissenters.

India's great political paradox is that although the constitution does not permit abridgement of the rights of religious minorities, the push against civil liberties does have a constitutional anchorage that Hindu nationalists can, and do, exploit. While universal adult franchise attracted near consensus among the political elites in the Constituent Assembly, civil liberties—a cornerstone of liberal if not electoral democracy—did not. Most of the early independence elites did not want unconstrained civil freedoms for the citizenry. According to Article 19 of the Constitution, "libel, slander, contempt of court, . . . decency or morality . . . [and] security" specified limits on freedom of speech. And the First Amendment, going further, stated that civil liberties should not prevent the government from making any laws that restrict such liberties "in the interests of the security of the State, friendly relations with foreign States, public order, etc." Suspension of civil liberties at a time of emergency was also constitutionally allowed.

In other words, the idea of liberal deficits was written into the Constitution. Some governments have interpreted the restrictions on freedoms more liberally than others; others have simply viewed them more restrictively, including a use of such restrictions for targeting critics on grounds of public order or national security. Courts have intervened, but not always in defense of citizens. Courts cannot violate the constitutionally enshrined restrictions; they can only interpret whether governments have applied them properly in a given case, if the violation is brought to litigation. For all practical purposes, the extent of permissible freedom in India has depended on the nature of the ruling party/governments. Since the Hindu nationalist construction of freedoms is highly restrictive and courts have only occasionally nullified the abridgement of freedoms, India's liberal deficits have increased under Modi. The kind of power and independence the courts exercised during 1977–2014 has been on the wane.

From Ideology to Action

The impact of Hindu nationalism on statecraft has evolved in two phases. The first phase concerned the everyday practices of the state; and the second phase has been about formal enactment of restrictive laws.

Under the first Modi government, India saw a new form of communal violence—lynching. The data show a spike in lynchings after 2014, with Muslims as the main target (Basu 2021). The perpetrators were often not caught by the police. Modi maintained silence on lynchings, and when he did speak, the comments were perfunctory. As if this were not enough, Modi also appointed Yogi Adityanath to the highest office of India's biggest state—as chief minister of Uttar Pradesh (UP), a state equal to Brazil in population. Before this high-level appointment, Adityanath, head of a Hindu religious order, had also created a large vigilante organization known for its anti-Muslim mob campaigns.

The ostensible aim of lynchings is to prevent beef eating and to stop young Muslim men from marrying Hindu women, even if their relationships are voluntary. But the underlying aim is quite clear. Lynchings are basically aimed at producing a political order premised upon the idea of Hindu primacy and relegation of Muslims to secondary citizenship. In BJP-ruled states, the police hardly catch the lynchers and if they do, the prosecutorial cases have been weak. Several BJP politicians have openly supported lynchers (Varshney 2019c, 75–76).

Since the return of Modi with a larger parliamentary majority in May 2019, this project has acquired a serious legal dimension as well. The BJP's parliamentary numbers can now allow the party to underwrite new legislation. Of the various pieces of legislation, the three that are most threatening to liberal democracy bear attention.

Among the first legislative acts of the second Modi government was the amendment of the laws related to terrorism and "public safety." The government now has the power to designate any individual as a terrorist (based on writings, speeches, even possession of certain kinds of literature), and the room for judicial appeals against such detentions has been substantially reduced. A similar legal dictum applies to preventive detention on grounds of public safety. Essentially, with these laws, imprisonment for political dissent is perfectly possible, something not practiced on a significant scale since the Emergency but increasingly being practiced now.[44]

The change in laws about Kashmir was the second major legislative act. India is an asymmetric federation and compared to the other states, the Constitution had given Kashmir, the only Muslim-majority state of the country, greater autonomy and powers. In August 2019, consequent upon the passing of legislation introduced by the BJP in parliament, Kashmir lost its status as a state and was brought directly under Delhi's rule. And using the public safety act passed a few weeks earlier and summarized above, hundreds of Kashmiri politicians and activists were thrown into jail. In addition, civil liberties were suspended, making citizen protest illegal. What happened in Kashmir was a replica of the 1975–77 Emergency, but in one state, not nationwide.[45] The jailed political leaders have mostly been released, but they spent time in jail just for being critics of the Modi regime.

The third and final piece of legislation was an amendment to the nation's citizenship law, originally framed in 1955. Called the Citizenship Amendment Act (CAA), the new law provides fast-track citizenship to the members of "persecuted minorities," who entered India before December 31, 2014, from Pakistan, Bangladesh, and Afghanistan. The law not only specifies these three countries but also lists communities it designates as persecuted minorities: Hindus, Sikhs, Buddhists, Jains, Parsis, and Christians. *It leaves out only one community: Muslim immigrants*. India's original 1955 citizenship law drew no religious distinction between Muslims and others.

The Minister for Home Affairs, second in command after Modi, also announced that a National Registry of Citizens (NRC) would be created as a sequel to the CAA. In principle, using CAA, the NRC can render virtually stateless a large number of Muslims, if they don't have the documents acceptable to the government for citizenship, even if they were born in India and have lived in the country for decades.[46] As the CAA was passed and the NRC was announced as a future move, nationwide protests, mostly peaceful, broke out for three months, continuing until the Covid-19 pandemic stopped large groups from getting together and protesting. Shaken by the strength and breadth of protests, the Modi government has said it will not implement the NRC. But one can't really be sure that the idea will not come back at a future date.

Three other points ought to be noted, two institutional, a third conceptual. First, of the principal institutional mainstays of democracy after Indira Gandhi's Emergency (see the previous section, "Democracy's Second Innings and the Birth of Elite Interests"), the judiciary appears to be buckling under executive pressure. Normally shrouded in secrecy, the executive's push against the judiciary became public when four of the most senior judges of the Supreme Court gave an account of the pressures applied by the Modi government.[47] The signs of the emerging subservience of the Supreme Court are too prevalent to be missed. The legality of preventive mass arrests in Kashmir and the constitutionality of Kashmir's diminished status have been challenged in the Supreme Court. But even the *habeas corpus* cases, normally an object of instant hearing, are still to be fully heard, let alone judged. Though some of the courts have taken the Modi government to task for its decisions, those are generally lower down in the judicial hierarchy, and can be overruled by the highest court in Delhi. It is the behavior of the apex court, the Supreme Court, that is causing great anxiety in liberal circles. The idea of executive and/or legislative sovereignty, relatively unconstrained by judicial scrutiny, appears to have made a substantial comeback.

However, the role of federalism—and this is the second institutional point—as a check on the power of the central executive remains substantial. Virtually all non-BJP state governments took a clear stand against the CAA and NRC, publicly announcing their intention not to implement them in their respective states. Modi's government's withdrawal of the NRC proposal may have a great deal to do with the realities of federalism. The Modi regime has sought to truncate the power and authority of state governments, often interfering in their domains, but non-BJP governments have continued to push back.

Let me finally turn to a tricky conceptual matter. Modi's government's anti-Muslim legislative moves, both in the form of the CAA and the change in Kashmir's status, were part of the BJP's 2019 election manifesto that guided the party's election campaign. Though in the voting data it is hard to parse out how many citizens voted in favor of these specific measures in comparison to the other issues in the campaign, the Modi regime can claim, as it has, that the change in Kashmir's status and the amendment in citizenship laws were both electorally approved.[48] An apparently electorally legitimated attack on the liberal aspects of the polity has thus been launched, deepening the electoral–liberal gap.

If the national majority votes even more clearly for Hindu nationalism in the future and the state governments, one by one, fall to the BJP in state-level victories, it is politically possible to launch an attack on the Constitution, amend its basic commitment to religious equality, and turn Muslims legally into second-class citizens. It will be an electorally approved collapse of liberal democracy. That is what Hindu nationalist leaders would ideally desire, for it would show mass support, or citizen imprimatur, for their deeply held values. India has not approached that point yet. And it may not.

Conclusion

By way of conclusion, let me recapitulate the main arguments of this chapter. First, India's record as an electoral democracy is far better than its record as a liberal democracy. Electoral vitality coexists with liberal deficits. This is in part due to a founding ambiguity in India's Constitution. The Constitution vigorously supports the idea of universal franchise, but by making citizen freedoms subject to considerations of public order, not simply national security, the Constitution has installed a weaker notion of civil liberties. The ruling governmental regimes have basically determined how liberally, or restrictively, the idea of civil liberties would be interpreted and executed. The courts have not been a consistently strong exponent of civil freedoms.

Second, my argument about India's democratic longevity has centered on elite choices, not structural conditions. Elite choices, in turn, are a composite of two different aspects: values and interests. Reflected in the Constitution, values of the first generation of political elites accounted for the early institutionalization of democracy. However, elite values alone do not explain India's democratic longevity, as substantial elite interests over the last few decades have come to be associated with democracy. Power is no longer the monopoly of one party, and a variety of parties hold power at different levels of the polity. The multiplicity of parties and elites with a stake in power contribute to democratic perseverance. Those parties and political actors who would be hurt by the suspension of democracy have tended to fight for their interests.

Third, the electoral–liberal gap widens when Hindu nationalists come to power, as is true today. This happens because Hindu nationalists privilege Hindu supremacy over the protection of minority rights and liberal freedoms. The longer the Hindu nationalists remain in power, the weaker will India become as a liberal democracy. But whether it will also cease to be an electoral democracy remains uncertain.

Notes

* For comments on an earlier draft, I am grateful to Nancy Bermeo, Jennifer Bussell, Niraja Jayal, Madhav Khosla, Sudhir Krishnaswamy, Pratap Mehta, Vishnu Pad, Dan Slater, Arun Thiruvengadam, Steven Wilkinson, Deborah Yashar, and especially Scott Mainwaring and Tarek Masoud. Bhanu Joshi's research assistance is highly appreciated.
1. Further explanations of these terms are available in Haggard and Kaufmann (2020) and Levitsky and Ziblatt (2018).
2. It should, however, be noted that Przeworski et al.'s conception of democracy relies on only one of Dahl's two criteria. It is only about contestation, not participation (2000, 34–35).

3. It is noteworthy that for a democracy theorist like Przeworski, such deficits do not constitute a democratic disqualification so long as the criterion of competitive elections is satisfied. And for him, governmental turnovers are a key indicator of electoral competitiveness. The basic intuition here is that a non-democratic system would not allow incumbents to lose power, even if elections went against them.

4. Also relevant, in a comparative sense, is the fall of democracy in Chile (1932–73), Uruguay (1942–73), and Venezuela (1958–2000s). While 1932, 1942, and 1958 were not founding moments for these countries, as 1947 was for India, there was a collapse of democracy after decades of existence.

5. On the inclusion of freedom of expression and association under electoral, as opposed to liberal, democracy, see my comment in note 41.

6. Why Latin America and the Caribbean developed such a large gap after 1990–99 is interesting, but it need not detain us here. My focus is on India.

7. In the 2019 campaign for national elections, one of the key slogans of the opposition Congress Party was that Prime Minister Modi was a "thief." The leader of the opposition Congress Party believed that though Modi fought the 2014 elections on an anti-corruption platform, a defense deal he struck in France, after coming to power, unmistakably revealed corruption. The campaign went on for months. No one from the Congress Party was arrested during the campaign.

8. At the national level, the winners were poorer in 1977, 1989, 1996, 1998, and 2004. At the state level, the numbers are much greater, including the widely noted 2021 elections in West Bengal. A state-level party, Trinamool Congress (TMC), defeated the BJP, which outspent its opponents by a huge margin but lost decisively.

9. One more exception is for some years between the early 1950s and early 1960s, when India's index exceeded that for Western Europe and North America. Greater disaggregation of V-Dem data, not presented graphically here, shows that North America pulls the average down in those years. While the indices for Canada and the US are consistently higher than those for India, following the United Nations Statistics Division (UNSD) methodology, V-Dem also includes in the region of North America: Bermuda, Greenland, Saint Pierre, and Miquelon and Antarctica. It is not clear that Greenland should be counted separately because it is not an independent country. And Bermuda gained independence only in 1995. Because of these complications, it is perhaps not advisable to make too much out of India having a higher index than Western Europe and North America.

10. Two things should be added here. First, as noted earlier, for their definition of democracy, Przeworski et al. (2000) do not use the full Dahlian measures, concentrating only on contestation (not on participation, let alone the liberal freedoms). Second, their exceptional list also includes Belize, Solomon Islands, and Vanuatu. For ease of exposition, I only pick four from their exceptional list: Jamaica, Mauritius, Papua New Guinea, and India.

11. These numbers are based on the World Bank's open data site (data.worldbank.org). In principle, one should also look at per capita incomes at an earlier point. The World Bank gives us the following numbers at current prices for 1960: Botswana ($58), Costa Rica ($381), Jamaica ($429), Papua New Guinea ($115), and India ($81). Only

Botswana had a lower GDP per capita then, which should, in principle, complicate the assessment of Przeworski et al. The 1960 income statistics are not available for Mauritius.

12. The World Bank's middle income category ranges from a per capita annual income of $1,026–$12,375 (at 2018 prices). India entered the lower middle-income category in 2005. China had done so roughly a decade earlier.

13. The classics on how democracy and caste could coexist are still relevant. See Rudolph and Rudolph (1967) and Kothari (1970a).

14. In government schools, where a lot of Indians have been educated, pupils would be taught in their mother tongue and would additionally learn Hindi and English. Depending on the resources of a state, two languages were definitely taught virtually all over India, and attempts for a third were also made.

15. Lijphart (1996), however, argues that India is a consociational democracy, a claim not accepted by India specialists. The most systematic critique has come from Wilkinson, who flatly argues that "Lijphart miscodes post-independence India as consociational" (2004, 154).

16. Wilkinson (2004) argues that pre-independence India was consociational.

17. The quotas that were instituted were caste-based, not religious.

18. Lijphart (1999) puts India in the middle of thirty democracies in terms of the propensity to form coalition governments. Coalitions per se should not be viewed as a core feature of consociationalism. A key question is: do coalitions mirror the diverse groups in society? Only in recent years have India's coalition governments at the national level incorporated a lot of lower caste politicians. The upper castes have always had more ministers in the cabinet than their weight in the population.

19. Sri Lanka may be among the few exceptions. Its universal franchise was born in 1931, when the British were still the rulers.

20. The exception was the province of Punjab, where the Unionist Party triumphed in 1937. Elsewhere, the parties representing landlords could not win provincial elections.

21. In the 1950s, too, a party representing the interests of the propertied emerged. Called the Swatantra Party, it fought elections. But it played no role at the time of Constitution making in the 1940s, when democratic institutions were put in place. Moreover, it ceased to be a force after two elections. It could not successfully fight against the Congress Party, the institutional carrier of anticolonial nationalist sentiment.

22. In the case of the indigenous princes, the accommodation of interests worked differently. The British had sovereign powers over the entire country, but they left Indian princes to administer their own territories, constituting a third of India. The Congress Party steadfastly opposed the power and authority of the princes, but offered them an olive branch: a government-funded allowance to the princes, called privy purse, would be granted in return for the formal accession of their territories to independent India. Almost all princes accepted the arrangement, and those very few who did not were militarily crushed. Privy purses were a small compensation for the authority and

powers to tax that the princes lost, but they understood that the winds of change and legitimacy were with the Congress Party.

23. In her comparison of India and Pakistan after 1947, Tudor (2013) also argues that power was in the hands of middle-class leaders in India, not the landlords, a class that dominated western Pakistan.

24. Poverty rates were more reliably calculated after 1961.

25. The commitment was made by the Nehru Committee (1928), which worked, among other things, on the kind of polity India should have.

26. The legislature was split into "no less than thirteen communal and functional compartments for whose representatives seats were reserved" (Austin 1966, 144).

27. Nehru's letter to chief ministers, March 21, 1951. Quoted in Khosla 2014, 115.

28. Syama Prasad Mukherji was among the most prominent Hindu nationalists to be a member of the Constituent Assembly, as was the Communist politician Somnath Lahiri. Congress Party members, however, were roughly 80 percent of the Assembly.

29. Ambedkar was not only the most educated Dalit in history until then, but also the most educated leader across the entire political spectrum. His first PhD, combining law and political theory, was from Columbia University, and the second, in economics, from the London School of Economics.

30. Ambedkar made this argument as early as the late 1920s, an argument he never changed.

31. See the summary of the debate in Austin (1966, 46–49).

32. Here is a description of the scale of the exercise: "At stake were 4,500 seats—about 500 for Parliament and the rest for the provincial assemblies. Some 224,000 polling booths were constructed and equipped with two million secret ballot boxes, requiring 8,200 tons of steel. To type and collate the electoral rolls by constituencies, 16,500 clerks were appointed on six-month contracts. About 180,000 reams of paper were used for printing the rolls. To supervise the voting, 56,000 presiding officers were chosen. They were aided by 280,000 lesser staff members; and 224,000 policemen were put on duty to stop violence and intimidation" (Guha 2007, 144). In addition, Shani (2018) gives a detailed account of how the huge electoral rolls were prepared, and how the elections took place.

33. All of this was primarily done though the 42nd Constitutional Amendment, passed without the presence of most opposition leaders in parliament. Prakash (2018) provides a detailed account of the Emergency.

34. This was the 4–1 decision of the Supreme Court in *ADM Jabalpur v. Shivkant Shukla*.

35. She did bounce back in the next elections in 1980, but she obviously did not know that in 1977, when she lost.

36. The divergent constitutional histories of Pakistan and India are perhaps worth noting. Carved out from the same British colony which also led to the birth of independent India, Pakistan has witnessed three constitutions since its birth. Indeed, it could not finalize a constitution for the first decade of its existence, by which time India not only had a constitution in place, but also had conducted two national and many state elections. See Tudor (2013).

37. For how he defines "consolidated democracies," see Przeworski (2019, 29–32).
38. See especially Linz (1990), but also the critique of Linz by Mainwaring and Shugart (1997).
39. Rajamani and Sengupta (2010) compare the pre- and post-emergency history of judicial review.
40. For more details, see Divan (2016).
41. Based on V-Dem measurements, Figure 2.2 (in the first section of this chapter) does not show the widening gap between the electoral and liberal dimensions since 2014. It suggests India's decline on both fronts. Moreover, the descent looks symmetrical. It turns out that this symmetrical decline is, in fact, an artifact of the way V-Dem measures electoral and liberal democracy. V-Dem's electoral democracy score is not simply based on Robert Dahl's two minimal criteria—contestation and participation—which are widely viewed as the best ways to measure the electoral core of modern democracy. V-Dem's electoral score also includes "freedom of expression . . . and association" (Coppedge et al. 2020a, 35). And its liberal democracy index, in addition to the electoral democracy, takes note of "the importance of protecting individual and minority rights" (Coppedge et al. 2020a, 43). The concept of liberalism in modern liberal theory certainly includes individual and minority rights, but also freedom of expression and association (Ryan 2012). It is unclear how to conceptually separate freedom of expression from individual civil rights. Similarly, to include freedom of association under electoral democracy raises conceptual awkwardness, for it includes both freedom to form and operate political parties and freedom for non-party civil society organizations. An electoral democracy may privilege freedom for political parties over freedom for civil society, as has become true of India under Modi. Generally speaking, if a democracy provides freedoms both to parties and to civil society, it is a deeper democracy, or a deeper polyarchy, as Dahl would put it, but it is best to stick to a minimal notion of electoral democracy and a more comprehensive notion of liberal democracy.
42. For details, see Varshney 2002, 2013, 2019b.
43. See Agnes 2016; Reddy 2016.
44. The V-Dem reports it as follows: "The Modi-led government in India has used laws on sedition, defamation, and counterterrorism to silence critics. For example, over 7,000 people have been charged with sedition after the BJP assumed power and most of the accused are critics of the ruling party" (V-Dem 2021, 20).
45. For more details, see Mehta 2019.
46. For a definitive analysis of the original citizenship law, see Jayal (2013). For details of the new changes, see Varshney (2019a).
47. This is discussed at some length in Varshney 2019b.
48. See the analyses in Varshney (2019c) and Jaffrelot and Vernier (2020).

3

The Politics of Permanent Pitfalls

Historical Inheritances and Indonesia's Democratic Survival

Dan Slater

To be a new democracy is to be confronted by a plethora of pitfalls. When democracy is born in a "hard place" (Chapter 1, this volume), these pitfalls are especially deep and dauntingly numerous. These risks are especially acute during democracy's fragile first days, when nobody knows for certain how the new system is going to work, how their rivals are going to behave, and whether they will be able to thrive under an unfamiliar and fluid set of rules (Lupu and Riedl 2013).

This does not mean that democracy's many pitfalls simply disappear over time. If widespread processes of democratic backsliding and erosion across the world throughout the difficult decade of the 2010s have taught us anything, it is that the classic notion of democratic consolidation—democratic systems gradually becoming bulletproof against autocratic actors and impulses, especially once they reach some magical threshold of economic development—has always been a complacent conceit at best, and a dangerous illusion at worst.

Casting aside the idea that democracy can ever truly consolidate, I argue in this chapter that democratic survival entails navigating a *politics of permanent pitfalls*. I argue further that, to be adequately understood, this politics must always be placed in historical perspective, grounded deeply within the case where democracy is struggling to take root and survive. My argument is not that historical forces matter more than proximate factors—or pivotal actors—for democratic survival. It is that any account of democratic survival which ignores historical forces specific to the country in question is necessarily—in fact woefully—incomplete.

The same can be said for any account that fails to distinguish, conceptually and theoretically, among the myriad ways that democracy can backslide and break down. Merely historicizing any country's relative democratic success with piles and piles of historical material is insufficient as well. What is needed is not just historicizing, and not just theorizing, but *historically theorizing* democratic

Dan Slater, *The Politics of Permanent Pitfalls* In: *Democracy in Hard Places*. Edited by: Scott Mainwaring and Tarek Masoud, Oxford University Press. © Oxford University Press 2022. DOI: 10.1093/oso/9780197598757.003.0003 survival. This requires, in turn, *aligning the inheritances a country possesses with the pitfalls it confronts.* We cannot even know which pitfalls pose the greatest threat to democracy in a particular country in the first place unless we first know how historical inheritances have made some pitfalls more ominous and permanent than others.

This chapter focuses on Indonesia: one of the very hardest places, and thus one of the biggest surprises, of any case where democracy has arisen and, for the most part, succeeded in the first two decades of the twenty-first century. How have Indonesia's historical inheritances helped it survive the politics of permanent pitfalls, at least thus far?

My argument centers on two historical inheritances Indonesia enjoyed when transitioning to democracy, in what appeared to be the hardest imaginable circumstances, in 1998–99: (1) *egalitarian nationalism* inherited from before the authoritarian period, and (2) *institutional strengths* inherited from the authoritarian period itself. I argue that these two historical inheritances help explain why Indonesian democracy has succeeded to the considerable extent that it has, because of how they align with four major pitfalls that new democracies so often confront: (1) state failure, (2) military takeover, (3) electoral authoritarianism, and (4) illiberal democracy.

My definitions of these concepts draw directly from their standard usage in the field. State failure simply means a collapse of central authority so severe that a country becomes better described as anarchic than either democratic or autocratic. Military takeover simply means the seizure of direct power by men in uniform, as transpired in February 2021 in Myanmar. The more subtle and significant distinctions lie between electoral authoritarianism (Schedler 2013) and illiberal democracy (Zakaria 1997). Most pithily put, electoral authoritarianism sees a dominant ruling group doing whatever it takes *to win elections*, while illiberal democracy sees a dominant chief executive doing whatever they want *after winning elections* (Slater 2018a).

All four of these threats pose permanent pitfalls to democracy, especially in a challenging context like Indonesia. Not all pitfalls represent equivalent threats in any particular case, or even in general, across the world, however. I argue that, of all four pitfalls, *illiberal democracy is the hardest to eliminate, because it is the easiest for a single irresponsible elected politician to bring about.* Mainwaring and Masoud are absolutely right to argue in this volume's introduction that democracies survive or collapse through the concrete actions of leading politicians, and not just as a reflection of underlying structural conditions. The key point here is that one aspiring autocratic actor can inflict illiberal democracy on a country after gaining executive power. Building electoral authoritarianism requires a level of elite collective action and institutional engineering that practicing illiberal democracy does not.

This does not mean that illiberal democrats can rule without considerable public support and elite compliance. No chief executive is an island. What it means is that electing a single illiberal democratic leader—a Bolsonaro, a Duterte, a Trump—can be sufficient to propel a country into a bout of illiberal democracy, but not to establish a system of electoral authoritarianism. Actors are absolutely critical in shaping regime outcomes; but they can push democracy more easily into some pitfalls than others.

Like so many countries—perhaps even all countries—Indonesia has not entirely escaped, and can likely never entirely escape, the pitfall of illiberal democracy. Whether Indonesia will avoid succumbing to an illiberal democratic fate depends largely on whether its deep but increasingly distant inheritance of egalitarian nationalism can withstand the challenges of those who would undermine and undo it.[1] Indeed, it has been Indonesia's lingering vulnerability to illiberal democracy that explains the recent softening in the country's democracy ratings. But it is vital to appreciate that the other three main threats to democracy—state failure, military takeover, and electoral authoritarianism—have all been successfully evaded. Those critical escapes are likely to continue, and these are no mean accomplishments.

In the following section I detail why Indonesia qualifies as a hard place for democratization. It was not just the country's underlying features, but also the disastrous environment in which democratic transition occurred, that should illustrate why Indonesia's democratic success was emphatically against the odds. The subsequent two sections explain why the *egalitarian nationalism* that arose during Indonesia's fierce independence struggle and the *institutional strengths* that emerged under Suharto's authoritarian New Order regime (1966–98) have given Indonesia a set of historical inheritances that have helped it beat those long odds. The chapter's fourth section distinguishes four common pitfalls that new democracies face—state failure, military takeover, electoral authoritarianism, and illiberal democracy—and details how Indonesia's historical inheritances have served as resources for avoiding each of those pitfalls.[2] I pay particular attention to the significance of egalitarian nationalism in fending off the massive threat of right-wing populist-authoritarianism that Indonesia confronted in the presidential elections of both 2014 and 2019. The conclusion remarks on the enduring and even endemic danger of illiberal democracy—the most permanent of pitfalls—not just in Indonesia but across the democratic world.

Indonesia as a Hard Place

There are at least seven reasons in the comparative politics literature why a country might be considered a hard place for democracy to emerge and thrive: (1) economic underdevelopment, (2) economic crisis, (3) ethnoreligious polarization, (4) Muslim majority, (5) large population, (6) authoritarian neighborhood, and (7) national disunity. Without arguing that all of these factors are *indeed* barriers to democratization, the fact remains that they are commonly *seen* as barriers, and that as of 1998 Indonesia arguably confronted *all seven of them*— some of them in spades.

We should begin with the obvious. Indonesia is the fourth most populous country (factor #5) and has the largest Muslim population in the world (factor #4). To the extent that democracy correlates with countries where both the total population and the Muslim population are smaller—weakly defensible causal claims but persistently robust correlations nonetheless—Indonesia democratized with a double demographic difficulty. Southeast Asia has also always been a predominantly authoritarian regional neighborhood (factor #6), with a supermajority of countries being stably authoritarian rather than even intermittently democratic. As of 1998, when Indonesia commenced its democratic transition, only the Philippines and Thailand qualified as electoral democracies in Southeast Asia, and neither could even remotely be said to be the kind of model democracies that might provide a positive demonstration effect. Although Indonesia's close relations with the United States, as forged during the Suharto era, arguably made democratization more likely both to arise and endure, there were certainly no regional tailwinds aiding Indonesia's regime transition—especially when one adopts a wider regional lens and considers the growing influence of China along Asia's Pacific rim. Indonesia also clearly confronted the stiff headwinds of national disunity (factor #7), as the restive provinces of Aceh, East Timor, and West Papua all credibly threatened to use their new democratic rights to separate from the Indonesian republic. In the case of East Timor, this separation indeed occurred, first through the peaceful means of a referendum, and then violently as the Indonesian military and its local militias exacted a horrible price on the East Timorese for decisively rejecting Jakarta's harsh embrace.[3]

The first three barriers mentioned above require a bit of deeper discussion. Especially complicated is the question of ethnoreligious polarization (factor #3). To be sure, Indonesia is one of the most ethnically, linguistically, and religiously diverse countries in the world. The country has no shortage of cleavages that have manifested into conflict at one time or another, including Muslim and non-Muslim, Javanese and non-Javanese, "indigenous" (*pribumi*) and "Chinese," and, at the local level, all manner of tensions between majority and minority ethnic groups (Slater 2015). Yet, ironically, Indonesia's sheer number of identity cleavages makes it difficult for any single point of friction to combust into national flames. Horowitz (2013) has gone so far as to argue that Indonesia's complex cleavage structure is more of a benefit for democracy and stability than a threat. Perhaps the most judicious way to put it is that Indonesia's riotous diversity presents both challenges and opportunities for crafting a stable democratic and pluralistic order. But surely the fact that Indonesia lacks the relative ethnic homogeneity of a Japan or South Korea makes it more of a "hard place" for democracy than it would otherwise be.

This brings us to the first two theorized hindrances to democratization mentioned above: economic underdevelopment (factor #1) and economic crisis (factor #2). The latter is especially significant in the Indonesian case. Among all the countries that have democratized since the third wave began in the 1970s, none has done so amid more dramatically worsening economic conditions than Indonesia. As Figure 3.1 indicates, the drop in economic growth rates from the start of the Asian financial crisis in 1997 until its bottom in 1999 was truly precipitous. This plunge in real economic output was paralleled in the financial sector, where Indonesia's currency (the rupiah, or Rp) plummeted from over Rp2000/$ to under Rp13000/$ in a matter of weeks, and the private banking sector utterly collapsed under the weight of its dollar-denominated debts. To the extent that democratizing during economic crisis produces rockier outcomes than democratizing in good economic times (Haggard and Kaufman 1995), the conditions surrounding Indonesia's democratic transition could hardly have been less auspicious.

Yet this is not to say that Indonesia democratized without any economic strengths to its name. As Figure 3.2 indicates, Indonesia's fall was so dramatic in

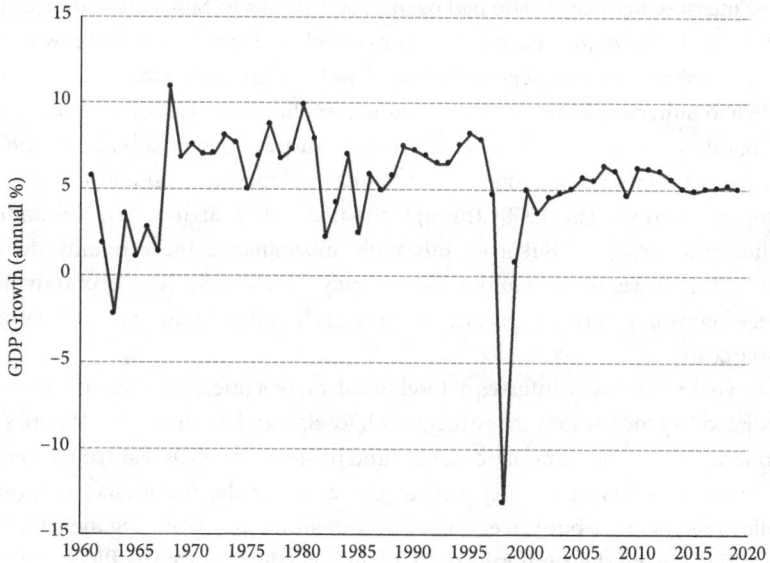

Figure 3.1. Indonesian economic growth rates, 1961–2019
Source: World Development Indicators n.d. (indicator: NY.GDP.MKTP.KD.ZG)

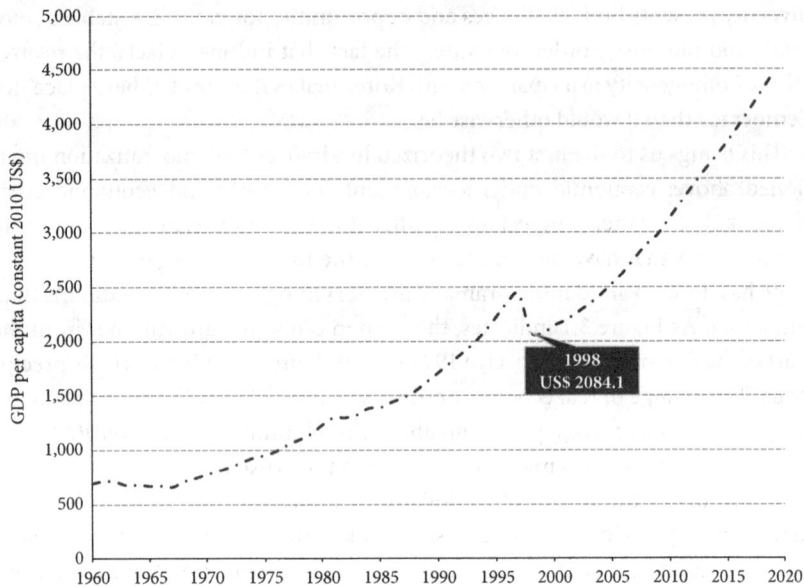

Figure 3.2. Indonesian economic development levels, 1960–2019
Source: World Development Indicators n.d. (indicator: NY.GDP.PCAP.KD)

large measure because its rise had been so stratospheric. Suharto's authoritarian rule from 1966–98 may have been an era of colossal corruption, but it was also unmistakably an extended period of rapid and sustained growth.

When Suharto seized power in a counterrevolutionary bloodbath against the Indonesian Communist Party (PKI) and its suspected sympathizers in 1965–66, the country was an economic basket case. Hyperinflation and hunger ran rampant from the late 1950s through the mid-1960s, as Indonesia's founding father and president, Sukarno, miserably mismanaged the economy during the country's years of "Guided Democracy" (1959–65). The economy was overwhelmingly agricultural and far from self-sufficient in rice, the nation's staple crop.

By virtue of massive influxes of foreign aid, oil revenue, and economic reforms designed to generate new investment both foreign and domestic, the Indonesian economy had made a dramatic turnaround by the mid-1970s. Far from catering to urban dwellers at the expense of the countryside, Indonesia's economic policymakers made both rice self-sufficiency and family planning their highest priorities, easing the rural misery that had helped galvanize the PKI's rise into one of the largest communist parties in the world. Economic growth then spiked considerably in the 1980s, after the US-Japan Plaza Accords strengthened the yen and sent avalanches of Japanese foreign direct investment into Indonesia and its low-wage industrializing neighbors.

The upshot was that by the late 1990s, Indonesia's GDP per capita had surpassed $2,000 (constant 2010 US$; World Development Indicators, n.d.), and urban areas were increasingly filled with educated middle-class citizens who resented the Suharto regime's astonishing corruption and rankled under its smothering blanket of authoritarian controls. It would be from these urban middle-class sectors that the bulk of protesters would come as the Suharto regime floundered in the face of financial meltdown.

Suharto would step down peacefully and constitutionally in May 1998, handing over power to his handpicked Vice President B. J. Habibie. Under continuing pressure from Jakarta's civil society, Habibie would quickly take the lead to remove authoritarian controls and accelerate Indonesia's electoral timetable to schedule free and fair parliamentary elections in June 1999. By the time Habibie was removed in a parliamentary vote and a new democratically constituted government was installed in October 1999, Indonesia's democratic transition could be said to be complete.

In the pages that follow, much more will be said about the strengths and weaknesses of Indonesian democracy. For now, it is simply essential to establish that Indonesia has, indeed, remained a democracy by standard global measures from 1999 until the present day. As Figure 3.3 indicates, Indonesia's democracy score shot upward with the transition of the late 1990s, improved still further in the first decade of the 2000s (even as Southeast Asia's other electoral democracies, the Philippines and Thailand, suffered either serious backsliding or outright collapse), and softened only slightly throughout the 2010s.

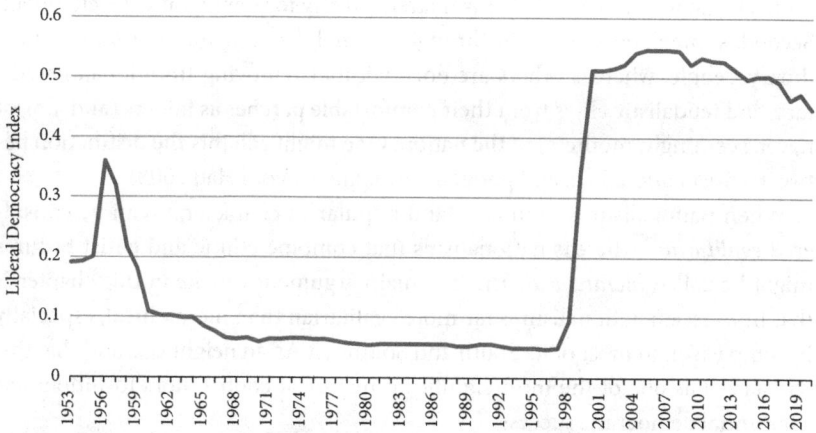

Figure 3.3. Indonesia's liberal democracy score over time, 1953–2019
Source: Coppedge et al. 2021

As I discuss below, it has been Indonesia's lingering vulnerability to illiberal democracy that explains the softness in the country's democracy rating. The other three main threats to a young democracy in a hard place like Indonesia— state failure, military takeover, and electoral authoritarianism—have been successfully evaded, at least thus far. To help us understand why, the next two sections explore the two sources of historical inherited strengths—(1) egalitarian nationalism, and (2) authoritarian institutional development—that underpin Indonesia's surprising democratic survival and impressive levels of democratic success.

Egalitarian Nationalism

Nationalism has a bad rap in liberal circles, and not without reason. Treating the nation as a higher priority than more universal values can lead to harmfully prideful behaviors abroad and dangerously prejudicial actions at home. For present purposes, the critical point is that nationalism is often deployed against ethnic and religious minorities, defining them as second-class citizens undeserving of the full liberal protections that are supposed to accompany democracy as it is substantively understood. For democracy to thrive, it may seem, nationalism needs to be tamed.

Yet nationalism comes in many different varieties, and not all of them work at cross-purposes to democratic development. Two main distinctions are important.[4] First, the national political community can be defined in more inclusive terms or exclusive terms when it comes to ascriptive identities such as ethnicity and religion. As scholars have long argued, nationalism can be more civic or more ethnic in character, and this matters greatly for democratic development. Second, some nations are built through the mobilization and lionization of ordinary people, whereas others are born without removing traditional, hereditary, and feudalistic elites from their comfortable perches as fathers (and almost never, seemingly, mothers) of the nation. One might call this the distinction between elitist nationalism and popular nationalism (Vom Hau 2008).

When nationalism is both civic and popular in character, it can be considered *egalitarian*, whereas nationalisms that combine ethnic and elitist features might be called *hierarchical*. The first main argument I make in this chapter is that Indonesian nationalism is far more egalitarian than hierarchical, especially in comparison to most of its South and Southeast Asian neighbors, and that this has served as one of the most significant historical contributors to Indonesia's substantial democratic success.

Indonesia's egalitarian nationalism was a product of its revolutionary path to independence in 1949. As by far the most significant and valuable colony in the

Dutch empire, Indonesia was not going to gain its freedom without a fight. If India was the jewel in Britain's crown, Indonesia was Holland's entire diamond-encrusted tiara. So when World War II ended and Japan surrendered to the Allies after its four-year reign over Indonesia, the Dutch returned to the scene with every intention of staying for good.

What followed was a bloody and brutal battle for independence, known simply in Indonesian nationalist lore as *perjuangan*: struggle. The most prominent figure in this struggle was Sukarno, a charismatic, polyglottal orator who had been inspiring popular mobilization against the Dutch, across every imaginable social divide, for decades. Sukarno's consistent message was that Marxists, Muslims, and nationalists could all unite, and indeed must unite, for Indonesia to expel the Dutch. All good things would follow from ending colonialism.

Sukarno spent much of the prewar period in a colonial prison for expressing these ideas and mobilizing them as the leading founder of the Indonesian Nationalist Party, or PNI. Japan's conquest of Indonesia was a godsend for Sukarno and the nationalist movement he led, since Japan aimed to rule with the collaboration of popular anti-Dutch nationalists rather than traditional pro-Dutch collaborators. They even went so far as to mobilize an entirely new Indonesian army dedicated to national self-defense.

Under Japanese rule, egalitarian nationalists like Sukarno shared power, not prison cells. That left them in an ideal position to lead the violent popular struggle for independence against the returning Dutch, and to make their ideals the founding principles of the newborn republic.

These nationalist ideals were neither exclusionary nor elitist. In both its civilian and military wings, Indonesia's nationalist movement was led by figures lacking hereditary status or any other kind of hierarchical standing above common people, also known as the *rakyat*, a word that gained mythic nationalist power rivaling both *perjuangan* (struggle) and *merdeka* (independence). Perhaps even more significantly, Indonesia's leading nationalists fended off efforts to define the nation in religious terms, either by making the majority religion of Islam a recognized national religion or by mandating that Muslims must follow Islamic law. Although Indonesia would not be defined as a secular nation, like India, the state would maintain at least a formal equidistance from all of the country's major religions. According to the official national philosophy of *Pancasila*, belief in a single God is mandatory, but the practice of any particular faith is not.

Egalitarian nationalism does not ensure democracy—no single causal factor does, including economic development—but it does help secure it and sustain it. When dictators become too corrupt, popular nationalism helps instill the sense of popular sovereignty that draws crowds into the streets to topple them. When forces of ethnic or religious intolerance attack minorities in ways that are incompatible with substantive democracy, civic nationalism provides a set of narratives, laws, and practices that can help defend disfavored groups against those who would menacingly reduce a diverse *demos* to a narrow *ethnos* (Mann 2004).

To be sure, types of nationalism are ideal types, and no nation is ever defined in entirely egalitarian or hierarchical fashion. Equally importantly, the triumph of egalitarian nationalism at the moment of independence does not eliminate those favoring more hierarchical visions of the nation from the political scene. Initial battles to *define* the nation in egalitarian terms evolve into ongoing battles to *defend* the nation from those who refuse to accept that all citizens—regardless of ethnicity or religion—should have the same rights and equal political status. Indonesia's egalitarian nationalism is far from pristine, and it is even further from unchallenged, as we will explore below, when discussing the presidential elections of 2014 and 2019 (in the section titled "Avoiding Four Pitfalls"). Yet it provides an enduring resource for democratic development and defense that almost all of Indonesia's neighbors sorely lack.

Authoritarian Institutional Development

Every democracy in the world relies, to some degree, on features that first developed before that country became a democracy. Perhaps a vibrant urban middle class emerged during authoritarian times. Maybe a smoothly functioning legal system was built by a colonizer with nothing but authoritarian intentions. Sometimes a sense of national self-consciousness, solidarity, and social capital emerges in the very process of collectively defying a tyrant, whether homegrown or foreign in origin. Widespread literacy might have first emerged through religious instruction when a country was still ruled by a precolonial dynasty.

Of most importance for our discussion here, sometimes authoritarian regimes build institutions that a democracy can inherit and turn to purposes of democratic stability, even if that was by no means the original intent of those institutions' creators. Institutional development under Suharto's authoritarian regime was especially impressive in two domains, both of which ultimately paid surprising and unintended dividends for democratic stability.

The first was state capacity. The Dutch colonial state had been world-renowned for its governing effectiveness—albeit overwhelmingly for repressive and extractive purposes—but this institutional inheritance was largely squandered during Indonesia's first two decades of independence (Anderson 1983). Once an authoritative executor of commands across the vast archipelago, Indonesia's inherited postcolonial bureaucracy found itself starved of resources and bereft of operational autonomy during the hyper-mobilized years of revolution, parliamentary democracy, and Sukarno's "Guided Democracy." Sukarno profoundly mistrusted political parties, but he respected bureaucrats even less. By the time Sukarno was toppled in the confusion of conspiracy, communism, and *coup d'état* that ripped the country apart in 1965–66, the Indonesian state was in no position to govern, and there was scarcely a functioning private economy to govern in any event.

The tide turned dramatically with Suharto's takeover. In the transition's first phase, anti-communist elements in the Indonesian military, led by Suharto and allied closely with Islamic civil society, unleashed a horrific bloodbath against the Communist PKI and its suspected sympathizers. Hundreds of thousands died; millions were traumatized. It was upon this mountain of corpses—and it would be a disservice to those lost souls to call it anything less—that Suharto's "New Order" would originally be built. Yet with the truly enormous and epically tragic exceptions of the PKI and, after the mid-1970s, East Timor, the Suharto regime governed less through deadly repression than through smothering coercion and sweeping cooptation. The anti-communist mass killings were not the exception that proved the rule; they were the exception that established New Order rule.

It was only through the wholesale reconstruction and revamping of the Indonesian state that the Suharto regime became as stable—even, for long stretches, boringly stable—as it was. The military was the political heart of the New Order, but it was by no means its organizational entirety. For starters, Suharto invested massive new resources in the bureaucracy, at first thanks to the revenue floods of Western foreign aid and the OPEC oil boom, and later by virtue of the booming revenues that restored economic growth and foreign direct investment made possible. Military officers were typically given a variety of leading positions in government ministries, but this was more to ensure the political loyalty of the bureaucracy than to install full-blown military governance. Bureaucrats were generally entrusted and empowered to govern, in areas ranging from family planning to rice self-sufficiency to managing price volatility in vital basic commodities. Considering that bureaucrats overwhelmingly supported the New Order as a bulwark against communism and as a welcome source of developmental and technocratic energy—in addition to the obvious risks of openly associating either with communist or Sukarnoist ideology—Suharto need not have worried that bureaucrats needed terribly much military oversight to do the regime's bidding.

The upshot of the state-building that unfolded during the three decades of the New Order was a highly impressive track record of economic growth and a remarkable run of relative political stability (Smith 2007). To be sure, both growth and stability were fueled by colossal corruption that ultimately helped bring the Suharto regime down in the 1997–98 Asian financial crisis. Yet the fact remains that a Leviathan quite capable of governing was one of the Suharto regime's most important byproducts. As we discuss in the following section, this has helped Indonesian democracy avoid the pitfalls of state failure and military takeover, especially.

The second critical domain for institutional development under Suharto's New Order was that of political parties. Since the regime had such widespread support across the political spectrum—a spectrum newly and violently shorn of its left wing—it did not fear a return to highly controlled electoral and party politics within the first decade of its founding. Although it was a military regime, it commanded tremendous civilian support. Party development and electoral politics provided these supportive civilians with routes to influence and largesse, even under the suffocating coercive blanket of New Order rule.

Most significantly, Suharto quickly supported the building of a regime-supporting political party called Golkar. The party's name reveals both its origins and its governing purpose. Short for "*golongan karya*" (functional groups), Golkar was a political vehicle constructed from the wide variety of conservative political organizations that arose to counter the radical leftist mass mobilization of Sukarno and the PKI during the early to mid-1960s. In formal terms, Golkar was not a political party but an umbrella organization—symbolically, a hovering *banyan* tree—under which all these political organizations could shelter and coalesce. This made it easier for Suharto to mandate that all Indonesian civil servants become Golkar members, since the organization was more like a bureaucratic superministry than a partisan vehicle in formal terms. Yet in practice, Golkar would compete in national elections every five years against the two parties that the regime permitted to form—the Islamic PPP and the nationalist PDI—and crush them. In essence, the state apparatus itself assumed the electoral role of a political party, without surrendering any of the powers or resources it held by virtue of being Indonesia's ultimate sovereign authority.

By both hook and crook, Golkar commanded overwhelming electoral support from the New Order's founding election of 1971 until its final election of 1997. Unlike the many pure military regimes and single-party regimes that transitioned to democracy after the Cold War with no recent electoral experience, Indonesia became a democracy in 1999 with a firmly established electoral system already in place. Party competition had been tightly governed, but it had not been absent. Moderate and conservative politicians knew that elections were something they could continue to win, at impressive levels if not at the landslide levels of the authoritarian era, even after full democratic competition was installed. Golkar was the only political party with an established presence at the local level across the entire Indonesian archipelago.

The economic crisis and surrounding corruption that felled Suharto in the mass protests of 1998 left Golkar weakened but by no means destroyed. For all the uncertainty that surrounded Indonesia's democratic transition in 1998–99, regularized democratic procedures quickly served more as a source of stability than of instability amid the general tumult. The stoutness of the Golkar-led party system that had been built under the Suharto regime was critical to the surprising democratic stability that followed it.

At the end of the day, institutions matter because they provide predictability. Given the extreme unpredictability of politics during times of democratic transition in "hard places"—especially when that transition is sparked by a severe crisis—it is enormously helpful for a young democracy's stability to have functioning party and state institutions. The sad fact is that when new democracies do not inherit such strong institutions from the authoritarian period, complete with many of the unseemly personnel who commanded them, they either try to build them from scratch under the most unpropitious of circumstances, or simply try to make democracy function without them. Indonesia democratized with a heavy institutional inheritance, but not an entirely burdensome one.

Avoiding Four Pitfalls

Explaining democratic success requires thorough and systematic attention to the variety of ways that democracies can fail. At least four distinct pitfalls tend to confront new democracies, and Indonesia has been no exception. A new democracy can experience (1) *state failure*, if governance fails and either the country falls apart in civil war or separatism, or ruling elites take extreme authoritarian measures to prevent such outcomes from arising. It can also fall through (2) *military takeover*, if men in fatigues refuse to accept the hindrances that democratic politics presents. In less extreme but increasingly common scenarios, democracy can backslide into (3) *electoral authoritarianism*, if politicians start doing whatever they want to win elections, or (4) *illiberal democracy*, if they start doing whatever they want after winning them. Put otherwise, electoral authoritarians target their coercion against opposition parties seeking to topple them through the ballot box; illiberal democrats take coercive aim at minorities, critics, and protesters who refuse to accept quietly and quiescently their majoritarian mandate.

In light of the arguments offered in this chapter, how have Indonesia's inheritances of egalitarian nationalism and institutional strength helped the country avoid wrecking on these multiple sharp shoals? And why does illiberal democracy continue to present the pitfall into which Indonesian democracy remains likeliest to plunge?

State failure loomed especially large as a potential outcome during Indonesia's tumultuous transition years. The provinces of East Timor, Aceh, and West Papua all presented credible separatist claims. Ethnic and religious violence erupted in various parts of the archipelago, most notably in the eastern Indonesian districts of Ambon, Maluku, and Poso. Riots against Indonesia's ethnic Chinese minority hit as close to home as Jakarta itself. Islamist terrorism delivered repeated blows, most infamously in Bali. Leading country experts quite seriously asked whether the Republic could endure without the military holding it all together by force. Less than a decade removed from the collapse of the Soviet Union and Yugoslavia, the notion that powerholders in Jakarta would fail to keep the country intact and minimally governable was far from far-fetched.

Inheritances of strong nationalism and a strong state proved up to these challenges, however. Remarkably in hindsight—and even in real time—East Timor was permitted to exit Indonesia by popular referendum, though pro-integration militias long backed by the Indonesian military inflicted a horrible price on East Timor's people for so choosing. Not only was it remarkable that East Timor was allowed to secede; equally remarkable was the lack of separatist sentiment in other parts of the archipelago which, like East Timor, had sizable Christian majorities. Even as Christian communities feared eradication in the deadly religious conflicts that erupted in demographically divided districts like Ambon and Maluku, no wider push for Christian separation and self-determination gathered steam. In part, this was because national politicians invoked the pluralistic version of nationalism, embodied by the concept of *Pancasila*, in their condemnations of religious violence. Christians might not have been made to feel at home in certain areas, but their rightful place in the Indonesian nation was never seriously questioned.

The Indonesian state also came decisively to the rescue of the country's founding "unity in diversity" ideal. Steeled by over three decades of military rule, the Indonesian military and security services were quickly deployed to conflict zones across the archipelago, and they restored peace in surprisingly short order. A national policy of decentralization also allowed divided provinces to split, making local ethnoreligious conflicts less intractable. Islamist terrorism was also effectively snuffed out by highly professionalized intelligence services. In sum, state failure was avoided because the Indonesian nation was inclusive enough and the Indonesian state was capable enough to prevent the Republic from violently unraveling.

While the Indonesian military was strong enough to help keep the country together, it did not use this strength to reassume direct control of the political system. Herein lay perhaps the biggest surprise of Indonesian democratization. During the years preceding Suharto's fall, the overwhelming consensus among Indonesia-watchers was that his New Order would be followed by some variety of collective military rule.

Yet this did not come to pass. The first reason was because Suharto had increasingly personalized, factionalized, and to some extent Islamicized the military during his final years in power. This left the Indonesian military as the country's most powerful actor, but not a highly cohesive actor, as Suharto exited the scene in the face of cascading mass protests and elite defections. Of particular importance was the intense factional rivalry between Suharto's son-in-law, Prabowo Subianto, who commanded the military's strategic units in and around Jakarta, and the national head of the military, Wiranto. Prabowo proved ready and willing to unleash violence as a way of justifying martial law and his own assumption of dictatorial powers—much as his father-in-law had done in 1965. Wiranto and other professional soldiers saw Prabowo as an up-jumped opportunist who was a scourge on the military rather than a savior of national stability. It was more important to Wiranto and his ilk to restrain Prabowo and restore military unity during crisis times than it was either to keep Suharto in power or to salvage the military's leading governance role.

This is not to say the military simply stepped aside. For the first five years of Indonesian democracy, the military retained a sizable proportion of appointed parliamentary seats, and prominent military officers played a major role in electoral politics. Indeed, Indonesia's first directly elected president, Susilo Bambang Yudhoyono (2004–14), was one of the top military officials of the late Suharto era. Yet the military surrendered its parliamentary seats with nary a fuss in the constitutional revisions that followed democratization in plenty of time for the 2004 national elections.

The best explanation for why the military did so lies in Indonesia's institutional inheritance. Electoral support in 1999 and 2004 did not flow to former radical opponents of the New Order or to proponents of root-and-branch military reform, but to conservative and moderate parties and politicians with deep experience in Indonesia's military-led political system. Of particular importance was the continued leading role played by Golkar, which has remained one of Indonesia's top electoral performers and has consistently secured leading roles for itself in governing coalitions and cabinets. Although a colorful cornucopia of new parties has emerged during Indonesia's twenty-plus years of democracy, most of them derive their leadership from former leading figures of Golkar. And although PDI and PPP were designed to be mere shadow parties under Suharto's New Order, their post-authoritarian incarnations have thrived. To the considerable extent that the military can continue to rely on familiar moderate politicians with deep New Order roots, there is simply no manifest reason for military men to dominate the civilian arena.

Besides avoiding the fates of state failure and military takeover, Indonesian democracy has not backslid into electoral authoritarianism. This arises when one party or political leader gains majoritarian control through elections, then uses that control to stifle opposition and competition for the country's top political posts. The main reason Indonesia has been at least relatively immune to electoral authoritarianism is its sheer scale and diversity, combined with the role of egalitarian nationalism in ensuring that Indonesia's vast array of ethnic and religious communities enjoy a rightful role to play in national political life.

Golkar was unable to maintain the kind of majority support that could have allowed it to rebuild the electoral authoritarianism of the New Order era. Electoral support in 1999 flowed to the party vehicles of egalitarian nationalism: the PDIP representing Indonesia's Sukarnoist, pluralist, *Pancasila* ideological stream; the PKB channeling the world's largest Islamic social organization, the Nahdlatul Ulama (NU); and PAN as the main vehicle for another massive Islamic group, the Muhammadiyah. All of these parties had roots in the ideological developments of the nationalist struggle and had maintained much of their vibrancy during the New Order.

If any party had early prospects of capturing majority electoral support, and at least potentially imposing electoral authoritarianism from that perch, it was PDIP. Led by Sukarno's daughter, Megawati Sukarnoputri, PDIP secured over 33 percent of the 1999 parliamentary vote. Yet the robustness of Islamic parties as well as the continued kingmaking role of Golkar ensured that Megawati was brought into sweeping power-sharing arrangements rather than being allowed to rule alone after she was elevated to the presidency in 2001. In terms of institutional inheritance, perhaps the most vital point is that Golkar proved strong enough to help stabilize democracy in tandem with other leading moderate parties, but far too weak to impose a new electoral authoritarian regime on its own (Slater and Wong 2018).

Social complexity and diversity may be a permanent challenge to democracy, as scholars have long recognized (Rustow 1970). Less appreciated is the fact that it also complicates the task of any would-be electoral autocrat trying to assemble a winning coalition across cavernous spatial and demographic divides. Suharto brought pluralists, Islamists, Javanese, and non-Javanese into his ruling authoritarian coalition by force, with a significant assist from the binding agent of a widely perceived communist threat. Assembling a winning electoral majority without significant recourse to coercion is a more enormous political task in a land of "multipolar fluidity" (Horowitz 2013) like Indonesia than in a country where electoral appeals to a single religion or ethnicity can conflagrate nationwide without hitting any firewalls.

And yet electoral majorities *must* be assembled democratically, every five years, in direct presidential elections. This fully democratic process could carve a path to electoral authoritarianism in Indonesia, *if and only if* a majority coalition solidifies over time behind a president who lacks commitment to upholding the fairness of the electoral system. With Indonesia's two-term limit on presidents, this task is complicated, but not impossible. The question then becomes: has there been any prospect in Indonesia of a freely elected president not only ignoring institutions of horizontal constraint and abusing critics and minorities (i.e., illiberal democracy: more on which below), but also assembling a steady majority coalition dedicated to tipping the electoral playing field in its favor and keeping a minority opposition coalition out of office in perpetuity?[5]

Without question, the clearest threat to establish electoral authoritarianism in Indonesia in such a fashion has arisen via the reemergence of Prabowo Subianto and his populist party vehicle, Gerindra. After being dishonorably discharged from the military and spending a spell overseas burnishing his economic fortunes if not his political reputation, Prabowo returned to the scene and attempted to win (in other words, buy) the chairmanship of Golkar. Defeated in that effort, Prabowo founded Gerindra and garnered a spot as Megawati's running mate for the vice presidency in 2009. The Megawati-Prabowo team was trounced in President Yudhoyono's landslide re-election. Prabowo then rose to the top of the ticket in both 2014 and 2019, standing as one of the two presidential candidates in both contests. Both times Prabowo would face off against former Jakarta Governor Joko Widodo (Jokowi), a member of PDIP and a seeming stalwart of Indonesia's pluralist, *Pancasila* tradition.

The stage was set, both in 2014 and 2019, for the onset of electoral authoritarianism. All it would require was a Prabowo victory. To understand why, it is essential to understand how party coalitions work in Indonesia. Despite the country's "multipolar fluidity" (Horowitz 2013)—or perhaps in some respects because of it—presidential elections are always followed by the construction of vast, supermajority coalitions transcending most if not all key identity divides (Slater 2018b). When PDIP leader Megawati was president from 2001 to 2004, every party except a tiny Islamic party joined her government. When retired general Yudhoyono was president from 2004 to 2014, every single party except PDIP shared power. If Prabowo had won in either 2014 or 2019, this coalitional arrangement surely would have been reproduced. Even though Gerindra would not have majority support on its own, every party except PDIP would have backed Prabowo after he won the presidency. This would have given him the sweeping legislative majority necessary to attack Indonesia's voting system and keep the lone remaining opposition party, PDIP, out of power by means foul rather than fair.

Indonesia's political elites were thus in no position to stop a Prabowo-led march into electoral authoritarianism. But Indonesia's voters were. And in both 2014 and 2019, Prabowo was soundly defeated by Jokowi, by approximately a 55–45 percent margin. It is impossible to say with absolute certainty whether Prabowo would have attempted to undermine Indonesian democracy to the point that it would be better considered electoral authoritarian, or would have succeeded at doing so. What is certain is that he has simply lacked the numbers—more specifically, *the voters*—to give it a try. Indonesian democracy has thus passed its sternest tests by defeating a likely aspiring authoritarian at the ballot box, rather than desperately trying to restrain him after he has gained presidential powers.

This leaves illiberal democracy as the main lingering threat to Indonesian democracy. Whereas electoral authoritarianism would see an elected leader stifling political opposition, illiberal democracy in Indonesia would most likely see him attacking religious minorities as second-class citizens. The very diversity that *tempers* the threat of electoral authoritarianism, as just discussed, simultaneously and permanently *tempts* opportunistic politicians to become illiberal democrats.

It is here that egalitarian nationalism has mattered most, and must continue to hold the line against those who would undermine it. In both the 2014 and 2019 presidential campaigns, Prabowo began assembling an alliance of conservative Muslim forces for his battles against the PDIP and Jokowi. This pattern had already begun to emerge in the 2004 and 2009 campaigns, when Yudhoyono curried favor with conservative Islamists in his successful efforts to trounce Megawati and her more pluralist electoral coalitions. Yet Prabowo raised the religious sectarianism to another level. This increasing religious polarization showed its greatest effect in 2017 when ethnic Chinese Jakarta Governor Basuki Tjahaja Purnama, popularly known as Ahok—the folksy and plain-spoken running mate for Jokowi in his 2012 gubernatorial campaign—was defeated in his re-election campaign and subsequently imprisoned for insulting Islam in the wake of massive protests to bring him to justice for doing so. The defeat and imprisonment of Ahok sent chills down the spine of every believer in Indonesia's ethnic and religious pluralism. The looming question in the wake of Ahok's jailing was whether the Islamic mass movement that arose to bring him down would then succeed in 2019 by doing the same to Jokowi, removing a president from power who hews to pluralist nationalism rather than Islamism.

Jokowi prevailed in that contest, but only by tilting further in the direction of illiberal democracy than his pluralist backers preferred. Most importantly, Jokowi replaced old Golkar stalwart Jusuf Kalla as his running mate, instead selecting a deeply conservative Islamic leader from the NU, Ma'ruf Amin, to become his new vice president. The clear goal was to inoculate himself from religious attacks without squandering his overwhelming support among pluralist nationalists. Although the Islamist rhetoric was even stronger in 2019 than in 2014, it was almost surely more muted than it would have been if Jokowi had not protected his Islamic flank as he did with his controversial choice of running mate.

The best analytical post mortem on the 2019 elections makes the pluralist foundations of Jokowi's big re-election win abundantly clear (Pepinsky 2019). In the starkest terms, Jokowi's victory was an enormous win for non-Muslims and their continued status as full citizens in the Indonesian nation. Jokowi's stupendous advantage over Prabowo among non-Muslims became even more pronounced in 2019 than in 2014. In Bali, where the population is predominantly Hindu, Jokowi secured over 90 percent of the vote. Yet in a country that is predominantly Muslim, non-Muslims can be no foundation for outright victory. It was instead Jokowi's sharply expanded support among largely rural Muslim voters in Central and East Java that carried the day. The main difference between the 2019 and 2014 votes was that Jokowi gained overwhelming support from followers of the NU, especially in Central and East Java, after basically splitting the NU vote with Prabowo in the 2014 campaign.

It is not hard to perceive how legacies of egalitarian nationalism helped make this democratically fortuitous result possible. Any particular election result may be highly contingent, and candidate-specific characteristics indeed help explain why Indonesia defeated illiberalism at the ballot box in 2019 while India did not (Slater and Tudor 2019). Yet if Indonesian nationalism did not make substantial room for non-Muslims, it is hard to imagine how the pivotal PDIP-NU electoral alliance could even have formed in the first place. The popular character of Indonesian nationalism was also on full display in the country's record turnout in the 2019 vote: nearly 82 percent, spiking from an already impressive voter turnout of just under 70 percent in 2014. It is thus clear that Jokowi was able to tap into Indonesia's deep reservoirs of egalitarian nationalism—a nationalism in which Islam may play a major role, but the *rakyat* play the leading role—to save both his own presidency and, arguably, Indonesia's democracy from its avatar of illiberalism, Prabowo.

Yet Jokowi himself has been increasingly tempted since his re-election to deepen his own illiberal practices in turn. When urban protests erupted before Jokowi's second inauguration over bills passed by parliament that would gut Indonesia's independent anti-corruption commission, remove environmental regulations on the mining industry, and restrict certain forms of political dissent, the newly re-elected president unleashed police repression and internet controls not seen since Indonesia democratized. This was not an electoral authoritarian gaining a stranglehold on national power for himself and his ruling party by restricting his electoral opponents. These were the actions of an illiberal democrat, backed by the legitimacy of an emphatic double-electoral mandate, using the full force of the state apparatus against society at large when it challenges and speaks out against the political designs he shares with the broad swath of Indonesia's political elite. By subsequently inviting Prabowo himself to serve as his defense minister, Jokowi signaled with abundant clarity that his second term would be defined by the pursuit of economic development and political stability, not the continued defense of democracy. That job is once again being left to Indonesia's civil society, armed with an egalitarian nationalist spirit that provides a strong defense, but by no means an unbreakable guardrail, against the ravages of illiberal democracy.

Conclusion

Indonesia does not stand alone in the crosshairs of illiberalism. Anywhere there are minorities to be scapegoated, dissidents to be intimidated, or liberal institutions of constraint (e.g., parliaments, courts, anti-corruption commissions) to be steamrolled, elected politicians will be tempted to gin up popular support by doing so. The sad fact of the matter is that illiberal measures are not only painfully easy for abusive leaders to impose—they are also often painfully popular among a winning plurality of voters. The electoral side of democracy can mobilize the power of the many against democracy's liberal side. Our canonical theorists *realized* the possibility that democracy might undermine liberalism; sadly, more and more contemporary countries appear to be literally *realizing* this fate.

This is by no means a concern exclusive to Indonesia, where, more than in many places, the electoral majority has rejected the most illiberal options on offer. Illiberal forces in Indonesia are clearly on the rise, but not yet fully in the ascendant. In this respect, Indonesia looks very much like the main trendline in the rest of the world. As fine-grained data from V-Dem show, electoral aspects of democracy have continued to improve around the world over the past decade. Yet over the exact same period, the key liberal features of democracy—specifically freedoms of expression and association—are quite vividly under global attack (Ding and Slater 2021; Luhrmann and Lindberg 2019).

It is not only through extremist Islamic pressures to restrict Indonesians' pluralistic freedoms that illiberal democracy could tighten its grip. In a provocative inversion of the conventional notion that religious pluralism bolsters democracy, Fealy (2021) argues that Jokowi's coercive turn against radical Islamic groups, strongly backed by Jokowi's allies in the military, marks the rise of "repressive pluralism" in Indonesia. In this scenario, religious pluralism does not serve as a wellspring of democracy but as a rationale for pluralism's most avid defenders to impose authoritarian measures, at least ostensibly to protect it.

It is not hard to see parallels for where this could lead. Containing Islamic civil society has provided a ready pretext for military domination in cases like contemporary Egypt and Kemalist-era Turkey. Even in Indonesia itself, one might see the Suharto regime as a military-led dictatorship that was nearly as concerned with bridling Islamists as communists. Indonesia does not seem primed to fall into the pitfall of outright military takeover, for reasons discussed above. Yet its military could easily become a leading player in an illiberal democratic arrangement in which either political Islam is in the ascendancy and minorities are increasingly repressed, or political Islam is in the elected government's crosshairs and it is Indonesia's religious majority that is increasingly repressed.

This contrarian take on pluralism only reinforces this chapter's argument that illiberal democracy represents the most likely pitfall into which Indonesia might fully fall. Indonesia is already worrisomely trending in an illiberal direction, but it is still much further removed from an electoral authoritarian outcome, and a much further cry from either military takeover or state failure, likely as both of those might have seemed two decades ago. Any adequate theory of democratic backsliding should distinguish among all these competing democratic risks. Ironically, the same diversity that gives illiberal democrats a target-rich environment in which to hunt also makes it much harder for any one leader or party to gain a stranglehold on electoral authoritarian power. If democracy keeps backsliding in Indonesia, we can expect illiberal democracy to tighten its clutches first, particularly though the power aggrandizement of a domineering president. Collective actors supporting either electoral authoritarianism or a full-blown military takeover would then be waiting in the wings, sharpening their talons.

Notes

1. Indonesia has thus far fended off the challenge of exclusive, hierarchical nationalism to its inclusive, egalitarian nationalist inheritance more successfully than India, for example (Slater and Tudor 2019).
2. A fifth pitfall in Indonesia that I have discussed elsewhere at length (perhaps for some readers, *ad nauseum*), what we might call elite collusion, is better considered a threat to democratic quality than survival. If elite collusion is to lead to outright democratic breakdown, it would need to do so through one of the other pitfalls discussed here. Elite collusion at the levels Indonesia has experienced—through party cartelization via promiscuous power sharing among ideologically diverse political parties (Slater 2018b)—is also considerably rarer than the other four pitfalls, making it less essential for a conceptually and theoretically oriented intervention such as this.
3. East Timor's secession gave birth to the new republic of Timor-Leste, discussed in Nancy Bermeo's contribution to this volume (Chapter 6).
4. This paragraph and its broader argument draw on my collaborative work with Maya Tudor of Oxford University (Tudor and Slater 2016, 2020).
5. A brief comparison to democratic backsliding in the Philippines is informative. Rodrigo Duterte is a consummate illiberal democrat, ruling in whatever manner he sees fit. He also enjoys almost universal support among the political elite. But whether he can parlay that support into assembling a coalition that undermines electoral fairness and keeps either himself, his daughter, or some other close ally in Malacanang Palace for more than just his single five-year term—thus crossing the boundary to electoral authoritarianism—remains to be seen.

4

Africa's Democratic Outliers

Success amid Challenges in Benin and South Africa

Rachel Beatty Riedl

Sub-Saharan Africa arguably poses some of the most challenging conditions for democratic emergence and survival. According to our existing theories, this is due to a number of structural conditions: low levels of economic development and industrialization; regions of natural resource extraction; increasing levels of inequality between political-economic elites and the masses; low levels of state capacity related to colonial and neocolonial predation and post-independence challenges to broadcast power; and multilinguistic, multiracial, multiethnic, and multireligious populations. Yet three decades of democratic endurance in significant, key cases suggest that the continent has much to teach us about how democracies continue despite extremely challenging conditions. This chapter explores two very different cases—South Africa and Benin—with highly diverse challenges and yet strikingly similar pathways to the establishment and maintenance of democracy against all odds. In both countries, extreme political, economic, and ideological crises made incumbent elites perceive the need to concede their prior mandate for dominant control. Reactions against an intolerable past allowed new types of strategic alignments to be realized between economic elites, security agents, ruling parties, and opposition elites. Transition-era bargains for inclusive access to the state, security, political representation and economic dominance resulted in a concession for democracy as a system of political inclusion and bounded uncertainty. In these cases, opposition elites realized significant benefits to stability and order that could be had with including the old regime in the new ruling coalition. Despite the challenges of a racially or ethnically cleaved society in South Africa and Benin, the democratic bargain was *maintained* through self-interested and embattled incumbents staring down the precipice and opting for institutional compromise given the infeasibility of maintaining the status quo *and* opposition elites' preferences for maintaining economic and social order that they could inherit when allowing the incumbent some enduring role.

Democratic survival was sustained for as long as self-interested economic and political elites saw the cost of institutional inclusion and bounded

Rachel Beatty Riedl, *Africa's Democratic Outliers* In: *Democracy in Hard Places*. Edited by: Scott Mainwaring and Tarek Masoud, Oxford University Press. © Oxford University Press 2022. DOI: 10.1093/oso/9780197598757.003.0004 political turnover as lower than the cost of potential insecurity (economic, political, and personal) and zero-sum exclusion from the elite sphere of influence. Incumbent presidents of all ideological persuasions have been held back from executive aggrandizement and personal impunity by the collection of counter-elites enforcing inclusive, informal, power-sharing models of heterogeneous elite access to power. In South Africa, inclusive, informal power-sharing has meant the gradual reformulation of the African National Congress (ANC) leadership and accommodating internal factions; a growing and diverse political opposition; and maintaining the buy-in of the apartheid-era economic and political elite in the regime system. In Benin, informal power-sharing has been achieved through the fluidity of the party system with inclusive bandwagoning around independent candidates elected president, and it has been funded by a state-aligned economic elite. When that balance of power became too concentrated—when economic and political power rested in one central figure in Benin, President Talon—the counter-elite were no longer able to contain the executive impulses to ravage democratic freedoms and political opposition.

In sum, the tenable democratic compromise survives for as long as the counter-elite are sufficiently diverse to raise the costs of democratic defection, stemming from opposition political elites, economic elites, security forces, workers, unions, media, and civil society leaders. Balancing against incumbent overreach does not occur solely among opposition political parties; rather, opposition parties' ability to compete is a direct result of the commitment to democracy as the tenable compromise from all sides, in the absence of strong institutional protections. Institutional design at the moment of transition helped establish a framework for the endurance of such a tenable compromise. But institutions alone cannot explain three decades of democratic survival, especially when constitutional change has occurred so rapidly and extensively in the region, undermining protections such as term limits and civic liberties. The institutional framework follows the democratic bargain, and helps to maintain the equilibrium for as long as the evolving political and economic distribution of power can be managed within it.

The Puzzle of Democracies in Hard Places in Africa

African democracies present a real puzzle to most theories of democratization and endurance. According to our existing theories of democratic origin and endurance, they are exceptionally unlikely to endure due to a number of structural conditions: low levels of economic development and industrialization; pockets of natural resource extraction; low levels of state capacity related to colonial predation and postcolonial challenges in nation-building; and multilinguistic, multiracial, multiethnic, and multireligious populations.

Yet the third wave of democratization swelled across Africa in the early 1990s, producing a set of political transformations that moved the vast majority of countries from military and single-party regimes to multiparty regimes, with varying degrees of associated liberalization. This vast political shift to multipartism was due to a combination of two interrelated factors (Englebert 2002; Herbst 2001; Riedl 2014; Young 2012). First, the accumulating consequences of the politics of economic crisis (van de Walle 2001) and long-term economic stagnation of the 1970s and 1980s created tensions within the ruling party in some cases, the disenchantment of civil servants and police and military officers who were not getting paid, and the growing frustration of the domestic population over the lack of development and public services. This contributed to real pressures for reform from within, and the potential for destabilizing protests, particularly in the capital cities (Bates 1984). Second, the end of the Cold War, the defeat of the Soviet Union, and the associated changing priorities in international aid created external pressures for economic and political reform to maintain foreign assistance and promoted the model of capitalist multipartism for contemporary political organization. The ascendancy of the "West" and the neoliberal order meant that ruling parties or opposition elites that had previously identified as Marxist-Leninist or received financial support from the Soviet Union were particularly at pains to internally restructure and make new external alliances. The collapse of the USSR had profound reverberations within African ruling parties.[1] The geopolitical changes catalyzed experimentation with alternative models for maintaining power, such as new forms of competitive authoritarianism (Levitsky and Way 2010). Thus, the move to multipartism was part and parcel of the shift from Cold War–era single-party rule toward attempted new models of hegemonic control or various types of reform. This world-historical moment created a stimulus for political change, a move to multipartism, and the potential for a democratic transition. But it did not in any way guarantee enduring democracy (Bratton and van de Walle 1997; Levitsky and Way 2010; Lynch and Crawford 2011; Young 2012).

Given that the institutional changes to implement multiparty elections across the continent had a variety of outcomes (Figure 4.1), there are empirical and theoretical gains in understanding *where and when democracy was maintained against the odds*. Two particular pathways led to democratic endurance. The first, authoritarian-led democratization, was possible where incumbent ruling parties had sufficient mobilizational, coercive, and/or material strength to manage the transition on their own terms, shape the institutional landscape according to their preferences, learn to lose, and reap the benefits of institutionalized

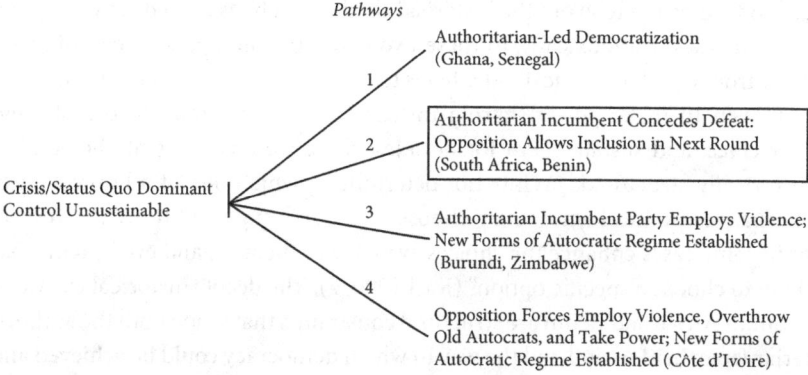

Figure 4.1. Regime transition pathways

competition and alternation (Riedl 2014; Riedl et al. 2020). In Africa, Ghana and Senegal exemplify this pathway.

This chapter focuses on an alternative pathway for democratic endurance, when the authoritarian incumbent must exit power at the transition and the incoming leaders pursue a strategic institutional inclusivity. In this pathway, the authoritarian incumbent lacks the capacity to remain at the helm in the new system, yet the rising opposition constructs a system that purposefully includes remnants of the old order and guarantees continued access to political and material power resources (Riedl 2018). This is the case for Benin and South Africa, wherein groundbreaking and previously unthinkable transitions ousted the old regime and empowered a set of transition leaders, who constructed a new institutional system and yet carved out inclusions based on a perceived need for *consensus rule* to carry the country forward.

These transitions appear more revolutionary and more precarious, because the old order is dismantled and a new process of negotiation and inclusion takes place. The transformation requires uncertainty about the nature of the new compromises. New actors construct the democratic rules of the game. Yet, in those countries that successfully maintain democracy, the new participatory coalition allows the ousted incumbents to maintain a role, or to repurpose themselves in new form that allows collusive power-sharing. The high political uncertainty surrounding crisis-wracked transitions to democracy encourages party elites to cope by sharing power and forging institutions to guarantee state access across the country's most salient political cleavages (Slater and Simmons 2013). While not in control of the transition, outgoing authoritarian incumbents find safeguards for access and representation in the new system's institutional crafting. The rising opposition—the transition leaders—realize the benefits of including the authoritarian incumbents both to help stabilize the new regime economically and to avoid the historical shadow of chaos from deep ethnic and racial divides. Paradoxically, in these two cases, the omnipresent fear of instability from racial or ethnic divides helps to forge a new inclusive coalition.

Driven to make power-sharing institutions to accommodate the old and new elites, and sustain them for decades, these were contingent choices, but historically structured. "While not determining which one of a limited set of alternatives political actors may choose, . . . 'confining conditions' . . . restrict or in some cases enhance the choices available to them . . . and even predispose them to choose a specific option" (Karl 1990, 7). The deeply historical cleavages in South Africa and Benin are structural constraints that shape both the authoritarian/apartheid period and the way in which democracy could be achieved and maintained through compromise with old and new political elites. The repudiation of the past regime created both a commitment to a new system as well as a deconcentrated, diversified set of political and economic actors to be included in its aggregation. Importantly, no single ascendant group was sufficiently powerful to *perceive* its interests in dominating the political field—a commitment to democratic endurance was born as a solution to managing conflict between an outgoing but economically resourced elite and an incoming and internally factious elite.

Certainly, deep racial or ethnic divides do not generally augur for inclusive coalitions. In pathways 3 and 4, authoritarian incumbents or opposition members employ violence and limit participation, political rights, and civil liberties, and new forms of autocracy are established (Adejumobi 2000). But given these varied outcomes, and that democracy was never prone to begin or continue over time under these challenging conditions, the grave risk and historical weight of racial/ethnic instability in Benin and South Africa helped drive rising opposition to realize the strategic value of including the former authoritarian incumbents in the new participatory, representative, and consensus-based political order.

South Africa and Benin established enduring democracy due to the interaction of three contextual factors that catalyzed and maintained the inclusive coalition. First, it was precisely the *extreme political, economic, and ideological crisis* that made elites willing to *concede their claims for hegemonic control and use their incumbency to bargain for inclusion and benefits in the next system.* These regimes were on the brink of revolutionary overthrow, civil war, and/or state collapse, yet they had not crossed the threshold. They retained a structural position to negotiate, to concede with benefits. Incumbents became acutely aware that they and the system that upheld them could not endure as it was. Instead, they settled for a way out of the impasse and a system of electoral competition with formal and informal guarantees that would protect their economic and physical security and their ability to continue to be elite in the future, albeit without the possibility of dominance.

Second, the *historical experience* of instability, violence, and political chaos associated with racial (in South Africa) and ethnic (in Benin) *divisions* created incentives for the rising opposition to prioritize security, governmentality (Bayart 1989), and inclusive institutions in order to maintain a state that they could rule over. This bargain for security at the height of a looming crisis included broad power-sharing mechanisms, and citizens, political elites, economic elites, and previously divided security forces all had a stake in supporting the new system.

Third, *significant redistribution was off the political agenda*, and this agreement among outgoing and incoming elites allowed the inclusive power-sharing pact to endure. This argument at first glance seems to support the idea that democratic transitions are most likely to occur when the costs of repression become greater than the costs of inclusion, because authoritarian incumbents cannot maintain themselves at the helm (Acemoglu and Robinson 2006; Boix 2003).[2] However, as with many democratic bargains, the demands for political reform and representation did *not* entail a redistribution of economic power, and certainly not to the masses. The democratic bargain included an *enlarged* political and economic elite class; increased macro security, state functionality, and reduced external and internal barriers to accumulation; and instituted elections as a mechanism for expressing, channeling, and ultimately limiting citizen discontent. In these cases, democracy is an institutional guarantee of the power-sharing bargain among elite representatives of social groups defined by ethnicity or race, not a class-based redistribution settlement.

Democratic Survival

So how did democracies survive against the odds? For thirty years in South Africa and Benin, the compromise of inclusion among contesting elites—crafted under duress, but institutionalized as durable power-sharing and rule through consensus—facilitated democratic endurance. In South Africa, consensus rule meant a commitment to maintaining white capital, and representation through national Proportional Representation and elements of federal rule through provincial autonomy. In Benin, consensus rule meant low barriers to entry for political parties and candidates so that the former ruling-party members could reconstitute in new ways, as well as constitutional and legislative protections to require full agreement of all representatives before further changes could be made to the system.

The economic, political, and social challenges they faced made them some of the most unlikely to achieve stable democracy at the moment of multiparty reform, and yet the role of incumbent elites conceding to partial inclusion and insurgent opposition's strategic power-sharing facilitated meaningful and lasting democratic rule. The bounded uncertainty and rotation of elites—with little actual exclusion and manageable turnover of the top post—was deemed to be a lower cost than the potential risks of physical insecurity, economic disruptions due to strikes and protests, and full political exile. The all-or-nothing, zero-sum stakes of the authoritarian era ceded to an expanded circle of all ideological persuasions. While no one single economic or political opponent would be strong enough to hold executive aggrandizement and presidential impunity at bay, the coalitional weight of heterogeneous economic and political elites in both countries was sufficient to serve as a counterforce to successive attempts by presidents in Benin (Mathieu Kérékou, Boni Yayi) and South Africa (Jacob Zuma) to stay in power and/or avoid accountability through increasing dominance.

Democratic survival in these cases demonstrates the interaction between agentic and institutional approaches. Certainly lacking the structural foundations for democracy, South African and Beninese heterogeneous elites (economic and political, outgoing and incoming) each perceived a strategic opportunity to maintain a democratic regime as a limited informal power-sharing agreement. In doing so, they limited threats from below for greater redistribution and state services, suppressing social movement pressures for economic and public service dividends by providing elite inclusion across the diverse spectrum of representation provided by democracy. By maintaining representatives of the old apartheid regime in the system in South Africa, and politicians associated with the failed authoritarian single party in Benin, both countries avoided civic conflict and limited physical insecurity to elite rulers, while also limiting potential for protest and economic disruption through the inclusive channels of democratic representation. This system maintained various degrees of political power to the elite class; private property was maintained in South Africa, and lucrative deals were made to control the port authority for economic elites in Benin. To create further incentives to maintain this strategic equilibrium, and recognizing its fragility, elites crafted institutions to help lock in mechanisms of inclusive power-sharing.

Benin and South Africa today each face distinct challenges in democratic endurance. In South Africa, the challenge to democracy stems from a rise in radicalism, a willingness to consider non-democratic forms of rule linked directly to a legitimacy gap, and growing perceptions of corruption (de Jager and Steenekamp 2019). These democratic deficits are represented by a slide in the V-Dem Liberal Democracy Index from its height in 2007 at 0.68 to a score of 0.57 in 2019, but they are not severe enough to question the democratic compromise at the elite level (Coppedge et al. 2020b). In Benin, the breakdown of the inclusive power-sharing pact in 2019 stems from the overconcentration of economic and political power in a single player—the current president, Patrice Talon. Talon's calculation to further centralize all resources in his "empire" and dramatically limit opposition reflects a new calculation—that inclusive power-sharing and the grand coalitions of the past are no longer necessary or preferable to maintain order, stability, and governmentality in Benin. His dangerous politics of excluding the opposition have led to dramatic democratic backsliding (Freedom House [2020a] estimates a 13-point slide in Benin's 2019 score compared with 2018; V-Dem Liberal Democracy Index shows a decline from a high in 2017 at 0.63 to 0.46 in 2019 [Coppedge et al. 2020b]). But Talon's calculations may prove the previous democratic transition strategy correct in the end: without inclusive power-sharing, Benin teeters on the edge of political violence and a return to its ethno-regional paralysis of the post-independence years.

Case Selection: Benin and South Africa as Africa's Democratic Outliers

This analysis focuses on two deeply divergent cases with shared general challenges: Benin and South Africa. At one level, they are both "hard places" for democracy to take root, in ways that resemble many countries across Africa and globally, as described in this volume. The extreme challenges include a highly diverse, multiethnic citizenry, challenges of state capacity in the periphery, and relative levels of underdevelopment of a large section of the population. Colonial legacies of arbitrary borders created states with little national cohesion and then were administered by divide-and-rule tactics to further separate the population (Lang 2009) and extraction to benefit the political class (Mamdani 2018). Power was highly centralized in the executive, with few checks (van de Walle 2003). But Benin and South Africa each confronted unique challenges to establishing democracy as well.

In Benin, the post-independence history of tripartite ethno-regional divisions and deadlock contributed to extreme political instability, with six coups and as many government breakdowns and new constitutions in the first twelve years (Decalo 2018; Magnusson 2001). The underlying ethno-regional fragmentation and an equally divisive economic and social disparity between north and south created a perpetual crisis. Benin was temporarily stabilized with the final military takeover by Mathieu Kérékou in 1972, and the transformation to a nominal Marxist-Leninist single-party regime, buttressed by the military. The coercive power of the state was put to use as a threat to society and individuals through the suppression of political and civic activities, arbitrary arrest and torture, suppression of local religious and cultural practices, and generalized assaults on property rights (Challenor 1970; Ronen 1975). This combination of fragmented society and coercive military/personalist/single-party rule did not provide an institutional foundation for successful democracy (Banégas 2003, 2014).

Equally critical, Benin's economic conditions did not provide fertile ground for a flourishing democracy. In 1990, the country ranked near the bottom of global levels of development, at a level of $1,230 GNI per capita, PPP (current international $, World Development Indicators, n.d.) and was facing massive public debt. In addition, it was reeling from the latest oil-price decline shock in the 1980s, in which neighboring Nigeria sharply contracted its demand for informal trade, the main source of sustenance for much of Benin's population (Magnusson and Clark 2005), resulting in significant economic decline (Figure 4.2). The state economy was a classic rentier state, in which material benefits are closely related with access to political power, and maintaining power is therefore necessary for one's economic condition (Bierschenk 2009). "By the late 1980s the government was bankrupt, the banking system was looted, paychecks were months in arrears, and the civil service was on strike. The state virtually collapsed. By any historical or economic standard, Benin was a poor prospect for democracy" (Magnusson 2001, 218). Mired in weakness and instability, with the specter of past ethno-regional cleavages, Benin's challenges were daunting.

In contrast, in South Africa, the headwinds to establish a peaceful democracy were relatively different, and largely distinct to the racialized legacies of the

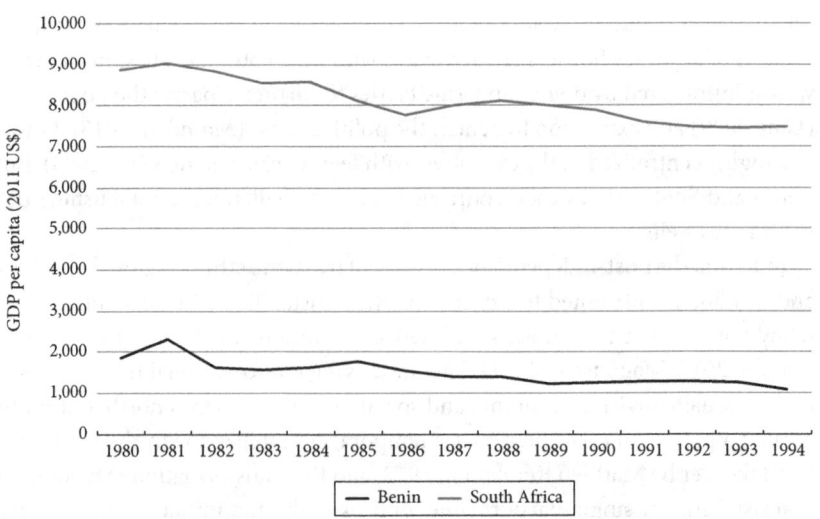

Figure 4.2. Pre-transition economic decline in South Africa and Benin, 1980–1994

Source: Coppedge et al. 2020b

apartheid system and competitive oligarchy. Whereas Benin lacked an institutional basis of multiparty competition, but had mobilized—even demanded—full participation under the single-party regime, South Africa had established vibrant multiparty democratic competition and institutional mechanisms for the transfer of power within an extremely limited portion of the population (Heribert and Moodley 1993, 20; Southall 2001, 22; Thiel and Mattes 1998, 101). This difference highlights Dahl's (1973) paradigmatic differentiation between pathways of limited participation with high competition and those which had high levels of participation but limited competition.

Rather than democracy, most external analysts and many internal players were preparing for the prospects of violent revolution in the late 1980s, and "very few predicted the possibility of a soft landing for apartheid" (Herbst 2003, 107). Even after the founding post-apartheid elections in 1994, many thought democracy was not possible, arguing that "South Africa lacks the social requisites associated with the consolidation of liberal democracies: broad-based economic development and national homogeneity" (Giliomee 1995, 84). Others recognized that despite the Truth and Reconciliation Commission's attempt to deal with apartheid-era justice claims, the police and justice system's systemic racism was a barrier to overcome in the transition to democracy (Shaw 1997). Many feared extreme polarization following the negotiated settlement, as the centrist compromise would be unable to contain the stratification of the goals of black and white South Africans (O'Flaherty 1992).

South Africa's economy was established and relatively strong on the continent, with large corporations diversified across various sectors (Nathan 2004, 5), providing overall significantly higher levels of development at $6,180 GNI per capita, PPP (current international $) in 1990 (World Development Indicators, n.d.). Far from a "failed state," South Africa was effectively integrated into the global economy and had a manageable debt (Habib and Padayachee 2000, 247). Yet the country was also facing significant economic decline throughout the 1980s (Figure 4.2). The economic implosion was due, in large part, to rising international sanctions against the apartheid regime, levied on South African companies, and decreasing investor confidence in the face of rising domestic political turbulence, which made the status quo unsustainable (Giliomee 1995, 89; van Wyk 2005, 53).[3] And the extreme levels of inequality meant that the vast majority of the population was both economically impoverished and politically disenfranchised. South Africa's economy was completely dependent upon white capital. The Gini Index value in 1993, prior to the transition, was 59.3, one of the highest in the world (World Development Indicators, n.d.). This concentrated distribution created major challenges for democratization, because the white minority feared total personal insecurity and economic appropriation with the loss of political power. And many within the black majority recognized the need for economic stability but also faced strong demands for reorienting the economy to address the structural apartheid of labor and capital control. Rising domestic protests created disruption in the supply of labor and productivity at the macro level and increased costs of state monopolization of force. This economic instability was both a challenge and a catalyst for the elite compromise necessary for democratic reform. The vastly unequal distribution of wealth suggested the huge risks the ruling apartheid regime faced from democratization, yet the increasing sanctions and domestic pressure made the existing political and economic situation untenable.

Crucially, despite the vast differences in economic distribution and social cleavages, in both countries it was not possible for the ruling party to maintain hegemonic political control. The fiscal pressures created splits within the ruling classes. In South Africa, the white ruling class had important differences between the British and Afrikaner populations, with the Afrikaners generally supporting a "Nationalist Unity" agenda for apartheid, although this cohesion was precarious even within the Afrikaner population (Lieberman 2003; Welsh 2009). Whites who were more oriented toward external markets, and British with foreign passports which guaranteed them an exit option, moved toward regime transformation prior to the Afrikaners. Benin's fiscal crisis meant that civil servants, police, and other elements of the security apparatus were not getting paid, and these agents of the state started to turn against the ruling party. These economic pressures on the elite were coupled with massive discontent and rising protests from the population for reform. Both South Africa and Benin were facing political, economic, and ideological crises, and stakeholders on all sides sought reforms to allow macro political stability, a new ideological foundation for rule, and the foundations to regenerate economic opportunity. These were not regimes that could rely on state control of natural resources; instead, there were demands from all sides for a functional state and political reforms to facilitate future economic stability and growth.

Today, both South Africa and Benin represent incredibly divergent modes of democratic durability. Benin's democracy has produced four executive power transitions of individual and political party, demonstrating high levels of volatility, competitiveness, and participation. During the past three decades following the transition, Benin ranks solidly in V-Dem's Liberal Democracy Index, given the highly competitive political landscape and political rights and civil liberties accorded through 2018 (Figure 4.3). The institutional separation of powers, and in particular the autonomy of the courts, the role of civil society in mobilizing against democratic threats, and the dizzyingly fluid playing field of candidates indicate high levels of contestation and participation on the part of the elites and citizens alike. According to 2016–18 Afrobarometer data (Round 7), 80 percent of the population rejects single-party rule, and 72 percent say that

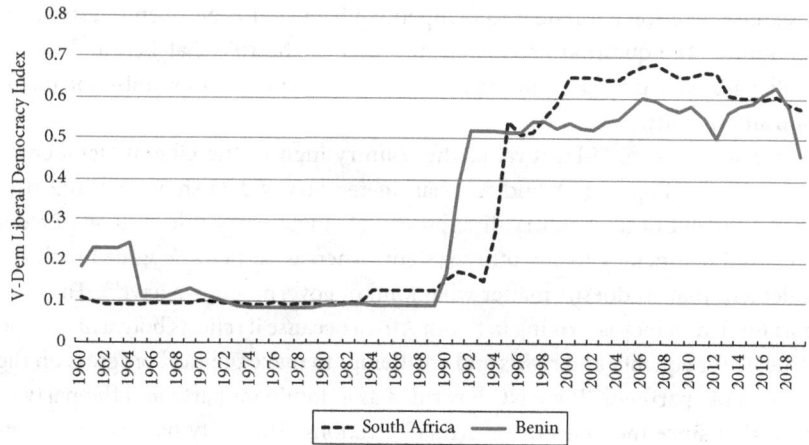

Figure 4.3. V-Dem liberal democracy index rankings in South Africa and Benin, 1960–2019

Source: Coppedge et al. 2020b

democracy is preferable to any other form of government (only 13 percent think "it doesn't matter what kind of government we have"). Of course, the fluidity of the democratic playing field creates challenges for accountability, but citizens had the ability to vote for an array of candidates and sanction those that were not performing, creating extremely high levels of turnover in the National Assembly (at times, over 70 percent).

Benin's recent democratic backsliding in 2019–20 marks an attempt to end the consensus rule and inclusive coalition that sustained democracy over the prior period. As economic and political power became overly concentrated in the executive, the current president has endeavored to cut out opposition (Preuss 2019). Because President Talon himself was a major funder of a diversity of political parties in prior governments, and mobilized the civil society movements against earlier constitutional changes and potential term limit challenges, his strategic role in maintaining a fluid and rotating political elite field was critical. When, however, his economic interests (and particularly his control over the lucrative port) were threatened by his erstwhile ally, President Boni Yayi, Talon recalculated that his economic dominance and security *required* direct political control, rather than indirect proxies. Once Talon assumed the presidency, the combined force of the political opposition and economic competitors was largely insufficient to contain his crackdowns on civil liberties and political rights. The diffusion of economic and political resources helped Benin's fragile democratic equilibrium maintain against all odds, but with Talon's ascension to executive control, there are few checks on his dominance. Whether the threat of political instability will force a return to competitive inclusion is an open question for the future. The question itself is an indicator of the role that Benin's historic challenges have played in undergirding the democratic compromise for inclusion and stability.

In South Africa, V-Dem ranks the country high in the Liberal Democracy Index (0.57) (Figure 4.3), and Afrobarometer survey data show that in 2016–18, 62 percent of the country disapproved of single-party rule, and 54 percent preferred democracy to any other system (whereas 25 percent agreed with the statement that "it doesn't matter what kind of government we have"). The support for democracy is striking in South Africa because it reflects both a liberation struggle for equality and rights and an attempt to make political progress on the legacies of apartheid. The ANC has ruled as a dominant party and the party of liberation since the first post-apartheid elections. The party has also seen significant internal rotation with five separate presidents elected. The strength and social rootedness of the ANC have provided stability to the democracy, allowing institutional bargains of inclusiveness to be worked out in practice. But the lack of party alternation in the executive has also limited accountability and opposition voice. The strength of the ANC undermines the constitutional separation of powers and the accountability of the executive to the electorate (Seekings 2009). Yet the formal procedures of representative democracy remain deeply significant for a range of social group interests to be expressed and for transformation to occur over time.

Forging and Maintaining Democracy

The question both Benin and South Africa faced as they began to embark on reforms was the degree to which the former autocratic rulers (and the identity groups they represented) could concede power while maintaining institutional guarantees for representation, economic security, and continued political veto and agenda-setting powers. Unlike many expectations and fears of majority rule and massive appropriation, the ruling elite found that moving to democracy did not entail a full concession of power. Rather, democracy entailed new strategic bargains over including the former elite and mapping out rules of the game that would protect certain perquisites. The road to increasing participation in South Africa and contestation in Benin was paved with negotiations around the preservation of formal and informal access to the political center. Institutional foundations (federalism in South Africa) and informal practices (of the vast majority political parties bandwagoning into the presidential coalition in Benin) were crafted to provide inclusion for the former political elites and the groups they represented along with the ethnically diverse newcomers.

Crisis, Cleavage, and (No) Redistribution as Context

Democracy was never a foregone conclusion, much less its endurance. In both countries, civil war loomed large and political violence was omnipresent. Society was highly mobilized for reform through domestic riots. Political inclusion and competition—democracy—was the first core priority. For some, democracy was an end in itself. There were absolutely ideological believers who have been committed to maintaining a democratic polity: Nelson Mandela in South Africa and Nicéphore Soglo in Benin stand out as identifying democratic principles as the necessary solution for their respective countries' peace and harmony. For others, democracy was a means to an acceptable end of economic and physical security and partial political representation rather than full. Particularly for outgoing economic, political, and security elites, their changed positionality and strategic reassessment through crisis and repudiation of the past was what allowed for a democratic bargain to be struck and maintained.

In South Africa, economic empowerment was tightly intertwined with political rights and the end of the apartheid system. Claims for redistribution and reshaping a structurally unequal economic system were central, but they were also balanced by a pragmatic agenda to stabilize white-owned capital and harness it to the benefit of all citizens (Emery 2006). Among the apartheid white ruling class, the critical shift was from hegemonic political control to institutional guarantees for political overrepresentation and economic ownership. The new constitution adopted a form of federal governance that provides protection for the economic elite from maximal redistributive taxation (Inman and Rubinfeld 2012a). Among the black majority of the national liberation movement, the key shift was from revolution to democratic participation, legal equality, and reconciliation. Negotiations struck a crucial balance between advocating for their position and making concessions. In doing so, they alleviated white fears (e.g., the ANC specifically ensured whites of their jobs, pensions, and farmland) while also maintaining black support for the transition (Welsh 1994, 222–23). While not addressing inequality, the system improved the economic welfare of both the white minority and the black majority, contributing to the enduring support for democracy.

In Benin, economic crisis meant that the ruling elites also gave up their claims to hegemonic control. In 1990, mass mobilizations and protests forced the ruling party to accept pressures for reform. They held a National Conference as a way to negotiate the crisis, which was meant to give voice to all sectors of society, to vent their frustrations. The goal was to increase temporary participation and voice among stakeholders throughout the country, and re-emerge in control. The opposition declared their own sovereignty, but they too made limited demands. They allowed the sitting president to maintain his position as head of state. They prioritized political foundations of constitutionalism, democratic contestation, and social participation over any questions of redistribution. Group claims were not made on the basis of class but on the basis of regional, ethnic, or associational representation.

In sum, political-social-economic-ideological crises provided a foundation for far-reaching reforms and for the crafting of democracy. The nondemocratic ruling elite needed to be in a structurally untenable position; the pro-regime coalition was cracking from within under pressure. But these conditions were far from sufficient. In many other cases across the continent, these conditions proved ripe for civil conflict and new forms of authoritarian rule. In both South Africa and Benin, recent history and the threat of political instability cleaved along ethno-regional or racial lines upped the ante of costs and benefits of competition over power. Given the high probability of disorder, the insurgent opposition had a strategic use for maintaining and including the declining ruling elite in some form. Whether for economic stability and potential future growth in South Africa or for sociopolitical stability in Benin, the old guard was maintained in inclusive institutional guarantees. This avoided destructive conflict and allowed democratic provisions of electoral representation as an institutional fix. Political channels for participation and representation (and therefore economic protections *against* democratic theory of drastic redistribution through expropriation) were critical to democracy's founding and endurance.

South African Negotiated Compromise

Apartheid's long history in South Africa set the stage for a deep institutional and social cleavage that had to be addressed in order to achieve durable democracy.[4] The increasing violence and social, political, and economic disorder throughout the 1970s and 1980s created high animosity and distrust between the governing elite and the mobilized black majority, but it also laid bare the stark reality that a solution could not be zero-sum (Nathan 2004, 3–4). For South Africa to avoid civil war and implosion, incumbents and opposition increasingly realized, however painfully and against their ideological preferences, that a negotiation of some kind would have to take place. By 1979 the South African government was producing reports about labor laws and worker segregation that ultimately viewed apartheid as unworkable, due to the increasing migration of blacks into "core areas" (white South Africa) (Wiehahn Commission 1979; cited in Herbst 2003, 100).[5] Throughout the 1980s, white-led reform was carried out largely by Afrikaner nationalists in power, with the objective to *avoid* the "creation of a multiracial government, but [ensure] the preservation of effective White control" (CIA memorandum, January 1981; quoted in Herbst 2003, 101).[6] There was widespread recognition that Blacks, Coloreds, and Asians recognized the intention of these reforms, further fueling tactics of protest and township riots between 1984 and 1986, and labor union strikes to exert pressures on the government. An emerging opposition within the Afrikaner National Party in favor of more substantive changes lacked influence in the party itself or in Parliament, but began to create divides within the party as well as the broader community. President Botha sought to maintain apartheid and was ideologically against an integrated government. Yet structural forces pushed negotiations along without him; economic discussions began in the business sector between white business leaders and the ANC, along with academics and other professionals. Ahead of the political leadership, they sought to refine business strategy, regain a quiescent labor force, and increase cooperation internally and externally (Marais and Davies 2015).[7] Estimates of the state's capacity to exert sufficient coercive force meant that they were capable of avoiding democracy: "Pretoria's economic, political, and military resources are sufficient to avert the collapse of the white regime" (CIA Special National Intelligence Estimate, August 1985; quoted in Herbst 2003, 102).[8] So while the costs of repression were mounting internally, the regime had capacity to maintain apartheid through coercive force, yet many began to see the imperative of change in one way or another. Botha's stroke in 1989 led to change in the leadership of the National Party (NP), and F. W. de Klerk's rise signaled less of an ideological shift than a recognition that, given the growing unrest in South Africa, "a clear departure from the policies of the past— one way or another—was needed" (O'Brien 2017, 627).

De Klerk is emblematic of the structural position of the white ruling class— embattled and facing the need to reform, but with a wealth of resources at his disposal to negotiate in the interests of his constituency's enduring power. De Klerk rose to the leadership of the National Party and then state presidency in 1989, known simultaneously as a strategic reformer and for his conservative attitude. His past ministry positions suggested that he "did not decide to negotiate an end to apartheid because of a lifelong commitment to liberty and equality. Rather, he understood that economic decline and a changing international climate meant that the situation he inherited was unsustainable. . . . [He] came to realize that in such a context, his best chance of protecting the interests of his supporters was to lead, rather than to resist, change" (Cheeseman 2015, 108). Yet there was much to constrain him in imagining a democratic future in South Africa. He said that "change would take place without endangering the 'values and achievements of communities and individuals of the past and our dreams and future plans'" (Giliomee 1995, 94). De Klerk tried to play down the significance of changes in order to "reassure his white constituency that the change underway was not all that threatening" (Saunders 2009, 162).

An important structural change coincided with the transition from Botha to De Klerk and contributed to the end of apartheid and the enduring democratic compromise of South Africa: the dissolution of the USSR and the fall of communism as a defining threat on the international stage. Without Soviet support for the ANC, the Frontline States (a coalition of African states committed to ending apartheid and white minority rule) exerted more pressure on the ANC to negotiate instead of using violence (Rantete and Giliomee 1992, 527). The fall of the USSR did not change the ANC's ultimate goals or leadership, but it did change their tactics away from violent confrontation and oriented them toward compromise. De Klerk also admitted that the collapse of communism in Eastern Europe opened up the possibility for substantive negotiations with the ANC, as Botha, and to a lesser degree De Klerk, saw serious negotiations with a communist movement to be unacceptable, as the South African government sought to align itself with the Western world (Rantete and Giliomee 1992, 518–19). When the ANC was receiving significant funding and militant support from the USSR, was made up of an important segment of Communist Party members, and was championing "drastic agrarian reform, widespread nationalization of key conglomerates and ministries, and radical improvements in the conditions and standards of living for the working people," the West was hesitant to pledge full support behind the ANC (Habib, Pillay, and Desai 1998, 103; see also Habib 1995). However, with the fall of communism, the ANC lost their main source of support and was essentially forced to embrace neoliberal free-market principles and shun more radical state interventions (van Wyk 2005, 150). South Africa's established business elite furthered negotiations in this wake, making the costs of a radical interventionist economic program appear even higher and more impractical (van Wyk 2005, 151). The increasing contact and communication between white business leaders, NP moderates, and ANC leadership became crucial to building trust between the main negotiators. The Western and Southern Africa regional orbit of multiparty systems and elections in the early 1990s further paved the road for an inclusive, negotiated transition, rather than a radical agenda and zero-sum confrontation (Nathan 2004, 2).

The ANC's experience as a virtual government in exile for multiple decades—operating from neighboring Tanzania and Zambia—was also key to its ability to envision an institutional bargain that would absorb the majority of white apartheid elites. This extended governance, experience over time, created a flexible internal organization capable of integrating a variety of homeland-based political parties and civic bodies established during the years of ANC exile, returning soldiers, and varied types of liberation bureaucrats returning to play a role in the transition and newly established democratic government.

The strength of domestic opposition to apartheid, and notably the ANC revolutionary anti-apartheid movement, sought full participation and citizenship rights as primary objectives of reform. The anti-apartheid movement was highly mobilized, internationally connected, and ideologically oriented to end white minority rule (Cheeseman 2015, 106). But the ANC itself was also internally divided, with different factions representing varied visions of a post-apartheid world and the means to achieve it, and different views about the value of liberal, multiracial democracy. The South African Communist Party (SACP) had a considerable degree of influence, particularly within the military wing of the ANC, and maintained its insurrectionary predisposition. The Congress of South African Trade Unions (COSATU) also maintained a historic alliance with the ANC and, through their strike capacity, furthered the strategic and economic case for a democratic resolution. Breakaway factions such as the Pan-Africanist Congress supported a more radical African racial identity. Nelson Mandela was a key leader, strategically and symbolically. He combined the urgency and necessity of liberation with the recognition of the structural constraints that must be addressed to achieve it. Mandela and his co-patriots in exile (Oliver Tambo, President of the ANC, Thabo Mbeki, Jacob Zumba) began a negotiation that evolved in relation to the declining position of the white minority's perceived ability to benefit from the status quo. ANC leaders pursuing this negotiation identified the structural inequalities that had contributed to four decades of impasse, and ultimately *accepted* the contradictions that overcoming the stalemate would entail in maintaining the incumbent elite politically and economically, and committed their side to a negotiated settlement (Welsh 2009). By the late 1980s the ANC leadership was strategically and coherently planning for a post-apartheid liberal democracy, and they presented this plan as a cautious move toward a negotiated settlement. ANC leaders like Thabo Mbeki, the head of the ANC's directorate of international affairs in exile, and Mandela, from prison, began a series of meetings with senior government officials and cabinet ministers to begin to craft an institutional blueprint for an inclusive settlement that could be acceptable to the white ruling regime.

The ANC's position, and their ability to negotiate for compromise, was shaped by the structure of society. On one level, the pre-apartheid model of social consensus seeking was crucial to inform a shared model of democracy and legitimate the negotiation process that led to democratic elections, the negotiation strategy of the ANC, and the settlement that emerged from it (Nash 2002, 253). Mandela's transformation of this consensus-seeking social order "legitimated the ANC's role as interpreter of the African consensus on the basis of the sacrifices of its leaders" (ibid., 253). On another level, the apartheid organization of society was made up of "sectors"—youth, women, business, labor, political parties, religious and sporting bodies, and the like—each with a distinctive role to play. This idea emerged from the organizational needs of the struggle against apartheid when repressive conditions prevented them from mobilizing directly around political demands. It was now used to "insulate the leadership of the liberation movement from critical questioning" and thus allowed them to seek compromise and negotiation (ibid., 253). Mandela explained to the Consultative Business Movement with white economic elites, in May 1990, that "Both of us, you representing the business world and we a political movement, must deliver. The critical questions are whether we can in fact act together and whether it is possible for either one of us to deliver, if we cannot and will not cooperate" (CBM 1997, 57–58). In calling upon business, and in turn labor, youth, students, women, etc., to act within the limits of a "national consensus," the question of the basis of that consensus could be removed from sight (CBM 1997, 58, 65, 66). "In effect, the 'tribal elders' of South African capitalism were gathered together in a consensus that could only be 'democratic' on the basis of capitalism" (Nash 2002, 253). White South African business elites played a decisive role as midwives and sustainers of democracy— just as they had been the staunchest allies of the oppressive apartheid regime— because they sought to create a new political and economic climate to protect and maximize the gains accrued in a highly uncompetitive economy (Makgetla and Shapiro 2016).

This consensus was maintained during the transition's negotiated settlement process (the Convention for a Democratic South Africa and the subsequent Multi-Party Negotiation Process) and throughout the continuing decades of democratic endurance. In overcoming the possibility of revolution, the inclusive model of democracy formed the ideological contradictions of the new South Africa. At the outset of the institutional negotiations, preferences were extremely varied: "the reformists among the regime camp, particularly the government... favoured some form of power-sharing model to provide statutory guarantees for the rights of minorities, while the hardliners in the regime camp . . . favoured federalism and some form of self-determination respectively in order to protect the interests of at least some cultural groups. Moderates in the anti-regime camp, such as the ANC, favoured majority rule as the best model, but the anti-regime radicals . . . favoured black domination. These were the first preferences of the various actors," but through negotiation these were moderated to compromise over institutionalized power-sharing (Seo 2008, 452). Negotiations broke down many times over the government's preference for power-sharing and the ANC's preference for majoritarianism, and in these instances international mediation played a role in overcoming the deadlock (ibid., 452). The threat from incumbent hardlines, opposition radicals, and the further escalation of violence also provided structural incentives to find compromise, establish an interim government of national unity, and institutionalize power-sharing. Ultimately, the institutional foundations of guaranteed representation, land and wealth protections, and judicial independence provided both sides with more confidence that a negotiated settlement could produce a lasting outcome and, therefore, represented a viable path forward (Cheeseman 2015).

This commitment is institutionalized formally through a two-tier version of proportional representation (PR) (Barkan 1995). Under the South African electoral system, two hundred seats in the National Assembly are allocated on the basis of the party vote nationwide, and two hundred are allocated on the basis of the party vote in each of nine regions. This version of PR has resulted in each party's gaining a proportion of seats that is virtually identical to its percentage of the total vote, with the largest parties guaranteed participation in the government proportionate to their vote, and thus, proportionate to white representation in society when voting along racial lines.

The negotiated settlement also institutionalized power-sharing in other formal ways: the parties agreed to a Government of National Unity (GNU) for the first five years after elections, and the interim Constitution provided for a series of power-sharing arrangements. It entailed that any political party securing a minimum of 5 percent of the national vote would be guaranteed a cabinet post, and any party which secured at least 20 percent of the national vote was entitled to nominate a deputy president of the republic (Booysen and Masterson 2009).

Similar power-sharing arrangements exist at the provincial level, and the semiautonomy guarantees regional strongholds to the white minority, such as the Western Cape. "The federal elements eventually built into the 1993 and 1996 Constitutions . . . and the state that emerged . . . should be seen as a negotiated compromise, rather than the product of a single clear vision," and dispersed power among three spheres of government (national, provincial, and local) to articulate certain principles of cooperative government (Steytler 2005). The provincial boundaries were explicitly negotiated to assure the white (NP) and black (Inkatha Freedom Party representing the rural blacks of the historic Zulu nation) political minorities control over public resources and policies in at least one province each (Inman and Rubinfeld 2012b).

The federal system was critical to institutionalizing power-sharing and guaranteeing non-redistribution over time, at the heart of democratic endurance. The form of federal governance established in the constitution provides "protection for the economic elite from maximal redistributive taxation. Appropriately structured, federal governance creates a 'hostage game' in which the majority central government controls the tax rate but elite run province(s) control the provision of important redistributive services to a significant fraction of lower income households" (Inman and Rubinfeld 2012b). The federal governance structure therefore provided sufficient protection to the economic elite to support democracy, and it has contributed to overall gains in the economic well-being and quality of life, including access to services, as well as the rise of a new black middle class, further reinforcing the economic and political interdependence of the society (Munyeka 2014; Southall 2018; Wieczorek 2012). The basic institutions of capital markets, private banking system, and contract law were well established *and maintained* through this negotiated process, providing an economic basis for neoliberal reforms to be rapidly and successfully enacted (Bratton and Landsberg 1998).[9]

The consensus model requires the majority to sacrifice in the cause of building and maintaining a democratic system, but it preserves the role of capital and the power of incumbent elites in the process. It informs the "real relationships of power behind the facade of formal democratic procedures. In its many institutional embodiments. . . it calls upon the oppressed majority, in particular, to sacrifice in the cause of building a new society" (Nash 2002, 254). This consensus preserves the role of the chief intact—from Mandela to Mbeki to Zuma to Ramaphosa—and is based upon ties of solidarity in the common struggle of apartheid for the black majority, and the elite consensus on power-sharing and lack of redistribution.

The consensus model has also been embodied in the country's approach to justice, through the Truth and Reconciliation Commission's non-retribution, reconciliation paradigm. The Truth and Reconciliation Commission sought to address both victims and perpetrators; justice would be restorative, not criminal, to provide amnesty and reparations. This approach individualized the process, reducing apartheid from a relationship between the state and the entire community to one between the state and individuals (Mamdani 2002). Similarly, the establishment of a constitution and Constitutional Court that was legitimate in the eyes of most South Africans was crucial to achieving successful democratic endurance. This legitimacy had to be based upon the freedoms equally applied across all members of society and the limitations it placed upon abuse of authority—equally capable of restraining the incoming ANC as the outgoing NP (Klug 2008).

As this model has continued over time, and through various presidencies, some have argued that the continuation of the initial mandate to share representative power undergirds the unity, stability, and, ultimately, democracy in South Africa. For example, the Government of National Unity was designed to provide ministerial posts to the new opposition (the NP and its allies); Mandela and Mbeki continued the practice, despite being under no obligation to do so (Nathan 2004, 4–5), in order to maintain the precious balance between capital and state. The opposition NP eventually decided to disengage from this practice in order to more effectively differentiate in electoral competition, but it took up the practice of appointing a Shadow Cabinet to operate in parallel in order to hold the national executive to account, oppose problematic legislation, and propose credible alternatives before Parliament.

The vibrancy and maintenance of South Africa's democracy will likely not be threatened by the racial cleavage that obstructed its origins. If anything, the emerging threat to democratic endurance is from within the ANC, frustration with their corruption, and their dominant hold on power. Of course, the ANC's dominance *is* fundamentally linked to its legitimacy as liberators of the country, providing human rights and freedom through the end of apartheid (Booysen 2014). And their inability to address redistribution has given rise to the more radical Economic Freedom Fighters, whose platform advocates for extensive nationalization of industry. The opposition's evolution into a more multiracial party, the Democratic Alliance, suggests the evolution of a stable competitive landscape. And the ANC's ability to undertake internal reform, including leadership change and accountability measures, suggests another positive indicator for continued democratic endurance in South Africa. These elements continue to be based on the institutionalized premise of non-retribution, reconciliation, power-sharing, and representation that make up South Africa's enduring democracy.

The stability that democracy provided was part of the glue that keeps it maintained. Emerging from the precipice of economic and political upheaval, South Africa's inclusive bargain highlighted the gains to be shared by a new, broader elite class and the societies that support them. Yet this bargain also took off of the table a political revolution and socioeconomic restructuring. Democracy's bargain formally *avoided* massive redistribution. More radical members of the trade unions, the ANC, and the Communist Party were frustrated by this settlement. But, in South Africa's enduring democracy, they continue to contest and push the boundaries of that bargain. Indeed, the compromise of South Africa's democratic founding maintains in the shared interests of elites, the interdependence of labor and capital, and of incumbents and opposition, to prioritize stability, macroeconomic growth, and human rights and democratic participation as the fruits of liberation.

Inclusive Coalitions in Benin

Benin's ruling elites were not worried about expropriation in the way that those in South Africa were. In Benin, as in most of sub-Saharan Africa in the late 1980s, private markets and avoiding tax capacity were not the main sources of elite accumulation. Calls for a democratic transition were not about the transfer of resources from an elite group to the masses. Rather, political elites and their associates became economic elites by controlling access to state resources;[10] maintaining access to the state was the core concern.

In Benin, ruling elites and citizens were worried about a more immediate and generalized breakdown of the political and economic system as the country faced a gripping crisis. And whereas South Africa's compromise of mediated demands gave whites overrepresentation in the political sphere through formal institutions, in Benin the inclusive coalition was largely informal but was buttressed by lower barriers to entry for new coalitions of recycled and ascendant elites. The ruling party was dismantled, and the former ruling party elites dispersed into new and highly fluid constellations.

Much like in South Africa, the key players included the ruling party, forced by its changing economic and political situation to grapple with reform, a rising and diverse set of opposition elites (some who had been abroad during the authoritarian period), and a broad array of civil society actors including union representatives, religious groups, youth associations, market women, and so on, who helped to agitate for change and demand inclusive reforms. International actors were similarly but minimally involved in that they no longer condoned the ruling party's authoritarian hold on power and began to restrict funds (in Benin through withheld foreign aid, rather than the sanctions imposed on South Africa), and in doing so contributed to a transition toward multipartism but did not require the ruling party to lose power or to create a level playing field. As will be discussed comparatively in the following section, the international influence at the time was one of several factors that contributed to the shifting perceptions of the ruling party's diminished ability to sustain itself and increased the party's openness to consider negotiated reform, as well as opposition's sense of possibility to establish a new order during the transition, but this democratic inclusion had to be sustained by domestic actors throughout the subsequent decades in order for democracy to endure (Gazibo 2005, 2013).

As the economic, political, and ideological crisis of Benin's ruling Marxist-Leninist party mounted along with the financial bankruptcy of the state in 1989, the authoritarian incumbents employed a tactic that had successfully been used previously to quell social unrest and build consensus around the party's path forward: a National Conference. In February 1990, the ruling *Parti de la Révolution Populaire du Bénin* (PRPB) called together an assembly of delegates that was deliberately meant to be representative of all social, religious, professional, and political interest groups whose aim was ostensibly to chart the course forward in support of the current regime (Nwajiaku 1994). Yet, on the second day, this National Conference declared itself sovereign, proclaiming that all its decisions would be legal and binding. This severed the control of the ruling party from directly determining the institutional order of the new political system. Surprisingly, the military and ruling party elites accepted the decision and continued to participate, largely because the bankruptcy of the state meant that the status quo was not sustainable, and this process deliberately did not exclude them entirely (Nzouankeu 1993).

The Conference put in place, through negotiations with all participants including the military and representatives of the previous government, a constitutional order and electoral institutions to usher in a competitive democracy. The National Conference itself disbanded the sitting PRPB government but did not banish its powerholders from the table in crafting the new order. The inclusivity of the democratic bargain was premised on this foundation: "With the outcome of any election uncertain at best, those who were likely to compete for power [and have informal channels of access to it] found incentives to create a system that would not guarantee absolute power to the elected but rather limit their rivals' ability to monopolize the regime" (Magnusson and Clark 2005, 559). The goal of the legislative branch with low barriers to entry was to avoid ethno-regional political dominance, by ensuring that parties and candidates representing different regions of the country would all be included, no regionally based party would be excluded, and access to resources and power would be distributed widely.

The trajectory of President Kérékou is also illustrative in this regard. As the head of the ruling party and president, Kérékou oversaw the financial decline and bankruptcy of the state. And the bankruptcy diminished the president's networks of his former patrimonial base, such that both the ruling party and the military were simultaneously more autonomous from the president and weakened in their overall capacity vis-à-vis the population and potential counter-elites. The National Conference was conceived as way to build conciliatory support to end the political and economic deadlock. When the body declared itself sovereign, Kérékou lacked the support of the international community, the military, and the loyalty of his core party elite as well as the civil administration of the state. Therefore, he had no choice but to accept the declaration. While the ruling party was dismantled, the President was maintained as a figurehead and allowed to stay on in his official capacity. This inclusivity was central to the fragmented, discombobulated ruling elite's acceptance of the new democratic system. The president was assured a role in the proceedings, there was reconciliation rather than retribution, and the ruling party was able to break up into new constellations and be incorporated into new party configurations to continue to vie for power.

Regarding this process of new rule formation in the National Conference, "it is almost certainly a mistake to equate these with the greater *democratic* proclivities of groups" represented (Nwajiaku 1994, 431). The crisis and resulting political reformulation provided an opportunity for new associational groups to form and a new arena for battles between the leaders of the fading ancien régime and counter-elites who used the new political space to legitimize their claims to power. Some actors were committed to democracy in their ideology, while others were using the new structures to contest for power. Rising opposition elites were instrumental in using the political reformulation to ensure their inclusion into new power dispensations in the future and setting rules that would ensure their future ability to compete and collude in that space (Banégas 2003). Low barriers to entry for party formation and competition was one key element of the new democratic order to facilitate inclusive bargaining of elite recirculation under new party organizations (Riedl 2014).

Therefore, even at the point of the National Conference, democracy was not the obvious outcome. President Kérékou's maintenance as a figurehead and ability to compete in the founding multiparty elections was critical to reassuring the security forces and northern region that their interests would not be excluded in the new regime. The military's relative weakness due to the state's bankruptcy was also a key factor in allowing the National Conference to proceed to elections. The military did not prop up the incumbent regime, nor were they sufficiently coherent and organized to install a temporary military regime to guide the transition period and overly influence the outcome. Benin's National Conference was inclusive of the military, but neither they nor the PRPB elites were dominant. They were sufficiently assuaged that their past transgressions would not be prosecuted. And though the ruling party was conceding hegemonic control, it was assured future access to power, and therefore, partial control. Democratic elections and rules were the formal guarantees of this bargain, and they allowed agreement on access and partial control.

Rising opposition elites included members of the legal establishment, business representatives, and ex-patriots returning to the scene. In Benin, contrary to South Africa, the opposition itself was not coherent or well formed from years of liberation organization. The opposition elites in Benin were themselves fluid and uncertain about their relationships to one another, and their individual relationships to future structures of power (Diop 2006; Riedl 2014). This, too, shaped the entire delegation's preferences for inclusivity and participation of all past and future political entities.

Their principal concern was to avoid the chaotic turmoil and crippling ethno-regional divisions that had plagued the country following independence. To do so, they sought to maintain President Kérékou as a figurehead, and they allowed him and other members of the defunct PRPB to compete in the founding multiparty elections as independent candidates and under new party labels. In shaping the new system, the emphasis was on inclusivity, consensus, representation of all forces of the nation, and achieving a stable regime system that could address the deep crisis the country was facing (Nzouankeu 1993). The instability of the moment created incentives to ensure that all could participate in the new political system, and to avoid shutting out a particular group. The National Conference dialogues, the rising opposition elites, and the resulting institutions were based on the premise that stability and recovery could best be achieved through broad participation and inclusion. Opposition activists in exile were given amnesty, and they returned to the country to "put the past behind us and build the future. Everybody realized that we almost ended up in a civil war, and that we had someone at the head of the country who realized that and adapted his method in favor of peace, and that's what counted" (author translation).[11] A nonpartisan bishop who was respected for his neutrality and consensus-seeking was selected by the Conference to preside over the agenda. This priority shaped the institutional formation of political party registration, electoral code, and the constitutional court that would help stabilize democracy over the next three decades.

Benin's democracy has endured, in large part, because the contestations over elite access and ascension to power are waged as electoral, democratic, and constitutional mobilization (Gisselquist 2008). The challenges have been many, with the most extreme tests hinging on whether incumbent presidents would accept defeat (after a re-election loss) or leave office after their second terms (in accordance with term limits), and whether defeated challengers would accept electoral results. The combination of domestic mobilization, elite power-sharing through pre- and post-electoral bandwagon coalitions around the executive, and electoral and judicial institutions maintained democracy through an explicit focus on *inclusion* and *consensus*.

One of the informal mechanisms of successful inclusivity in Benin is the electoral and political practice of grand coalition bandwagoning among almost all candidates, parties, and representatives in the National Assembly, around the president. The practice began with Nicéphore Soglo's presidency (1991–96) but was expanded greatly when he was defeated by the returning "chameleon" Kérékou (nicknamed for his ability to reconfigure himself to the new democratic environment) in 1996 (Banégas 2003). Soglo built up a traditional political party apparatus, the Renaissance Party of Benin (RB), and a coalition of six additional parties in the National Assembly organized around supporting his ruling party supporters—but also an opposition set of parties. Kérékou ran as an independent candidate, and his victory in 1996 was followed by a massive reorientation of party alignments for the 1999 National Assembly elections. While the RB maintained the plurality of seats (twenty-seven out of eighty-three), many of the remaining fragmented party landscape joined in a presidential bandwagon to support the new President Kérékou. This also provided autonomy for some of the MPs and party leaders who sought to contest future presidential contests as independents or on their own party labels. In the 2003 National Assembly elections, the Presidential Movement coalition won a total of fifty-two of the eighty-three seats, then composed of eight parties. This pattern continued with successive presidents, giving maximum flexibility to the inclusive bargain of limited power-sharing that has served as a mechanism of democratic continuity in Benin.

Low barriers to entry for parties and candidates to compete in elections have also contributed to Benin's democratic endurance through ensuring access to political power to all regions and groups across the country. The proliferation of candidates and parties, and overall fluidity in the political party landscape, has encouraged grand coalitions by avoiding stark opposition camps, allowing shifting allegiances, and ensuring that former authoritarian ruling party members could be regenerated into new, viable elected representatives. No matter what region or background, political elites could align with successive presidents and have access to power.

In institutional terms, the National Conference prioritized the principle of participation and wanted all groups to be easily represented—therefore, both forming a party and running for election as an independent were facilitated through the electoral code and political party charter (Riedl 2014). The resulting proliferation and fluidity of parties and independents further contributed to the bandwagoning tendencies, as party labels and distinctions had little meaning; party elites were free to ride the coattails of the presidential movement. In doing so, they maintained access to state resources and supported the ongoing democratic project institutionally because they were not cut out entirely.

The self-prescribed autonomy Benin's Constitutional Court has from the executive branch, combined with a democratic political culture among the elite, which stems from the tradition established by the aforementioned National Conference, has allowed for the Constitutional Court to greatly contribute to democratic endurance (Bockelie 2013; Magnusson 2001). The court has undergirded Benin's democratic tradition since the transition to democratic rule by giving citizens a channel through which they can file complaints, increasing political transparency (Gisselquist 2008). The courts greatly heightened their legitimacy during the critical 1994 budget crisis and the 2006 elections. During the 1994 budget crisis, which emerged as a result of an executive–legislative dispute, the Constitutional Court stepped in and resolved the conflict, which marked the first time in Benin's postcolonial history that a constitutional authority supplanted the military as the arbitrator of institutional disputes.[12] The courts also played a crucial role in the 2006 elections, which marked the first time that a sitting president had to abide by a term limit. The courts, along with Electoral Commission, established key procedures that would be followed for the elections and that effectively managed the debates surrounding the constitutional age limit and term limits to be upheld.

Critically, the Constitutional Court upheld the principle of *consensus* by striking down a Constitutional reform that had passed the National Assembly, declaring that though it had passed the necessary numerical threshold of votes, because it did not have the support of all opposition deputies, it did not truly respect social consensus. The Court's action was perceived as a democratic check on the legislative dominance of the presidential majority, upholding the principles of the National Conference of consensus and supporting the mass mobilization of the public to safeguard the constitution from change (Ologou 2017). This key moment for Benin's democracy reinforced the values of inclusion and the necessity of broad-based agreement to enact any institutional change. By establishing their legitimacy, the courts were able to provide an alternative to political strife. Citizens connected their protests and defense of the Constitution with the Court's decision. This affirmed public trust in the judicial branch, and the sense of agency of the general population in protecting the nation's democratic tradition.

The citizens' mobilization and victory represent a form of continuity of the principles of the National Conference itself. Participation and consensus were embedded at the mass level, because the Conference itself included many social representatives. Domestic mobilization has been important in times of democratic challenge in Benin, particularly around questions of constitutional reform and presidential term limits. Benin's constitution has been safeguarded by domestic protests to defend the consensus principle and to maintain term limits. After former authoritarian leader and reformed democrat President Kérékou was elected and governed from 1996 to 2006, he considered whether to try to amend the Constitution to allow a third term run. But a mass mobilization campaign—supported financially and organizationally by opposition elites—rallied around a "Don't Touch My Constitution" campaign in the streets and markets. Ultimately, Kérékou did not proceed with any formal attempt to change the constitution or otherwise delay elections, and the 2006 elections marked Benin's third democratic alternation in power to outsider candidate Boni Yayi. President Yayi again tested the question of flexible term limits in 2016, and the Constitutional Court maintained its vigilance. President Yayi also built an inclusive coalition by integrating ministers and public servants from across the regional divisions of the country into his administration. The elite bargain of inclusivity, limiting hegemonic control, and allowing alternation has been tested at the bounds but maintained by the relative dispersion of economic and political power and the role of popular mobilization, supported by counter-elites and channeled through institutions designed to limit and check these tendencies.

Since President Talon was democratically elected in 2016, demonstrating yet another successful executive turnover in Benin, the model of inclusive power-sharing through grand coalitions has been attacked and undermined. Talon's control of power and resources in the economic sphere (the "King of Cotton," Talon controls the majority of Benin's key export crop as well as management over the port's import-export revenue) facilitated his centralization of the political sphere as well. He previously served as the financial backer of the plethora of parties and candidates, and contributed to their fluidity. Once he decided to enter the political sphere himself, there was no longer a need to support other political candidates to assure his economic interests, and his goal became to concentrate power and serve as a chief executive for the country. Talon has instituted a series of political reforms that break down the previous foundations of democratic endurance, including new appointees to the Constitutional Court,[13] a new political party registration code that has barred opposition parties from participating in elections (notably beginning with the 2019 legislative elections), and the creation of an anticorruption court, the Court of Punishment of Economic Crimes and Terrorism (CRIET), which is widely accused of being politicized to attack the president's political opponents (Freedom House 2020a). These reforms raise red flags for democratic governance, human rights, and effective accountability.

Talon's more extreme exclusion of key political players in Benin *has severed the compact of collusive power-sharing that undergirded Benin's democratic model since the transition to multiparty competition.* The basis of the National Conference provided a strong institutional foundation to maintain democratic governance by prioritizing widespread access to state power, broad-based representation, and political party fluidity to regenerate expired autocrats. But the even more important legacy of the National Conference process was to create an inclusive coalitional model of access to state resources and power among a variety of regional and sectoral interest groups. Presidents Nicéphore Soglo (1991–96) and Mathieu Kérékou (1996–2006) allowed broad bandwagon coalitions to form around them in the National Assembly and in their administrative appointments. Boni Yayi (2006–16) maintained the practice with some targeted closure, and Patrice Talon's aggressive exclusion marks the end of this compact, which previously facilitated political alternation and democratic endurance. The consequences of this closure include increased political instability at the elite level, protests and citizen–state clashes, degradation of democratic institutions to serve political centralization and autocratic ends, and diminished mechanisms of accountability and inclusion for citizens across the country.

International Powers and Normative Commitments to Democracy: Alternative Arguments

Two common perceptions of democratization and endurance in sub-Saharan Africa in general, and South Africa and Benin in particular, relate to the role of international support for democracy and the role of committed democratic ideologues.

As the analytic narratives of South Africa and Benin make clear, international pressure intensified the existing domestic crisis—adding to the financial pressures of the apartheid ruling class and the fiscal bankruptcy of the Beninese state. This pressure made it likely that incumbents would stare down the precipice and realize the need for a change to the status quo. In South Africa, international factors were significant to democratization itself in two distinct ways. First, the dissolution of the Soviet Union and the end of the Cold War meant the ANC was no longer a communist threat, and therefore was a viable negotiating partner in Western eyes, as well as to the domestic ruling party. The ANC had to shift their own strategy to be more procapitalist and promarket; they tempered their means (violence) and ends (reduced their focus on redistribution and adapted to a more neoliberal orientation). The transition mentality coming out of Eastern Europe with the end of the Cold War also reshaped political leadership within the National Party and the type of negotiated settlements the party might be willing to consider in response to the rising threat of democratic majoritarianism (Saunders 2009). Second, foreign aid following the transition helped buttress the new inclusive power-sharing coalition, with a massive inflow to expand public services to the general population. These factors influenced the structural constraints and opportunities that both the authoritarian incumbents and rising opposition faced before and after the transition, but they did not predetermine the content of the negotiations or necessitate their survival.

Similarly in Benin, the international context created external and internal pressures for economic and political reform that pushed the authoritarian incumbent to face the need for some kind of transition (with the dissolution of Soviet support), but it was not determinative of the outcome. Neighboring examples in Togo, Burkina Faso, and Côte d'Ivoire make clear that a transition to multiparty elections without ceding power and some neoliberal economic reform was enough to satisfy Western donors (Gazibo 2013). French involvement in the transition in its former colony created conflicts of interest with the Beninese population, as French pressures for the transition process to unfold in a controlled manner seemed designed to guarantee the authoritarian incumbent's maintained position (Nwajiaku 1994). Yet France did push for economic and political reform in Benin, because President Kérékou had been more isolated from Western development assistance over the past decade, and France withheld funds earmarked for relief of the economic crisis until the National Conference was held (Seely 2009). Following the transition, USAID and other Western donors have largely focused aid on the health and education sector, because they could take for granted the self-sustaining democratic foundations Benin developed (McMahon 2002). As in South Africa, Benin's public service sector has benefited from these donor relations, which indirectly has helped to maintain the inclusive coalition at the political elite level. But the rapid autocratic decline that President Talon invoked demonstrates how little influence donor calls for maintaining democracy have in the face of domestic will to centralize power. The bargain that sustained Benin's democracy for decades was one of domestic inclusion.

The role of democratic ideologues plays a similar role to international aid in South Africa and Benin: facilitating the conditions that make a democratic bargain possible but not guaranteeing its success or endurance. In South Africa, Nelson Mandela's iconic status is legendary. His role as a broker in the negotiating process was crucial to forging consensus. But Mandela was released from prison and allowed to participate in negotiations because of the changing structural conditions that forced the incumbent party to reckon with their uncertain futures. Mandela came to the helm of the ANC with a centrist position because of the changing structural conditions that brought together the labor union, the Communist Party, and the militant "Spear of the Nation" wing to cohere behind a negotiated transition process. Mandela was part of a movement that shaped his own ideology and strategy over time, as well as those of his oppressors. And the movement, and the institutions forged through compromise, continue to *sustain* South Africa's democracy through party leadership changes and generational changes.

In Benin, there was no parallel movement, as the fluidity of the transition came out of diverse groups representing different sectors of society. And there was no parallel symbolic figurehead; neutral interventions were sought by nonpartisan lawyers and religious leaders to steer the dialogue and help craft the new institutional foundations. In Benin, many of the key players were not committed democratic ideologues, given the representation allotted to the former ruling party and military elites. They were often self-interested and embattled elites staring down the precipice and opting for institutional compromise given the infeasibility of maintaining the status quo. The fact that democratically oriented meditators could play a key role was a consequence of once hegemonic elites, and their opponents for power, attempting an institutional reform after prior decades of recalcitrance and rising conflict. Successive presidents flirted with democratic abrogation, particularly Kérékou and Yayi both considering constitutional changes and third terms, but the fluid alliance of economic and political supporters with their ability to mobilize civil society protests, made these men reconsider their strategic course of action and cede power to the next elected executive.

Conclusion

The cases of Benin and South Africa defy scientific predictions regarding the emergence and durability of democracy because of the barriers to achieving simultaneous stability, accountable competition, and inclusion in states that were never crafted on that premise. The bandwagon model in Benin and the dominance of the ANC coalition in coordination with remnants of the ancient apartheid regime in South Africa provide guarantees for representation, and mitigate against hegemonic control. This represents the coordination among different factions within the broader society, and the shared interests provide a foundation for continuing the democratic bargain.

The surprising relative success of these two countries lies in their shared ambition to avoid economic redistribution and retributive justice but rather to seek reconciliation and an integrated political future. Ruling elites were forced to reckon with their declining ability to maintain hegemonic control. In the face of potential civil war (revolutionary, ethnic) or a military insurrection and replacement with the next authoritarian regime, the ruling political class sought to ensure protections, partial political influence, and their ability to continue accumulation. The strength of the South African institutional environment provided a foundation for that negotiation, and the National Conference in Benin swept the old ruling party out but allowed them to reenter in new forms.

The critical factors thus include institutions that facilitated moderation and provided the opportunity for negotiation and inclusion, such as the party organization of the ANC, the selection of proportional representation to allow multiple representatives in South Africa, and the National Conference model and political party charter in Benin. The successful outcome meant installing a viable multiparty competition by virtue of the "institutionally oriented" strategies that political elites deployed across the transition to share power. The return of certain former politicians, and political parties, shaped the politics reducing the uncertainty of competition, a factor that has reinforced the institutionalization of power.

Moreover, these transitions and their enduring institutions interact through a historical process at a particular moment of world-historical time (of ideological and material pressures for multiparty liberal democracy) and in relation to a set of structural factors that determines the distribution of social and economic power within highly cleaved societies. In Benin and South Africa, uniquely, these allowed a preference for partial control rather than hegemonic control. The expanded set of political elites facilitated economic accumulation among broader constituencies, political stability, and increased physical security. In large part, it was the depth of the past cleavages and fear of how they could otherwise unfold that made this bargain more valuable and sustainable.

Notes

1. The legacy of anti-colonial liberation movements and post-independence nationalist models created deep ideological, organizational, and strategic ties to the Soviet Union across parts of the continent.
2. Or, more generally, as the ruling class becomes increasingly incapable of repressing the discontent and demands for inclusion.
3. As the economic situation in South Africa grew dire in the 1980s, the predominantly white and wealthy business owners realized that some form of negotiated settlement with the opposition would be necessary in order to create an environment that was favorable once again for businesses (Marais and Davies 2015, 4–6).
4. Apartheid was officially instated in South Africa in 1948, when the Afrikaner-based National Party (NP) won political power.
5. Bureau of Intelligence Research, *South African Labor and the Wiehahn Reforms*, report no. 1290, December 12, 1979, NSA Archives, p. 12.
6. Director of Central Intelligence, "South Africa: The Politics of Racial Reform." Interagency Intelligence Memorandum, January 1981, p. 2.
7. Crucially, the fact that the ANC push for majoritarian rule was *not* focused on expropriation or complete exclusion of the NP and white minority more generally, and their increasingly conciliatory approach, fostered the deep splits within the white ruling coalition, between the British and Afrikaners, and even within the Afrikaner support for apartheid. The pressures created by sanctions and the rising mobilization of the liberation movement meant that it was becoming unsustainable for the ruling party to maintain its hegemonic political control, and this forced discussion of reforms. Once reforms were on the table, increasing splits within the ruling party and popular protest expressing discontent pushed an increasing number of citizens to mobilize against the regime.
8. Director of Central Intelligence, "Prospects for South Africa: Stability, Reform and Violence," Special National Intelligence Estimate, SNIE 73.2–85, August 1985, p. 3.
9. The removal of sanctions and accompanying increased flexibility in production, increased human resources development, and increased involvement of employees in managerial decision-making stand out as drivers of economic growth and stability that accompanied the post-apartheid years.
10. For example, the para-statals, contracts, licensing decisions, and commercial networks that controlled profitable informal trade were main drivers of economic opportunity (Adjaho 1992; Chabi 1993).
11. Judicaël Zohoun, "Me. Robert Dossou apprécie les acquis et les avancées." [Mr. Robert Dossou appreciates the gains and advances.] *24 Heures au Bénin*, February 24, 2020, https://www.24haubenin.info/?Me-Robert-Dossou-apprecie-les-acquis-et-les-avancees.
12. Throughout the first term of the democratically elected president, Nicéphore Soglo, multiple institutional crises plagued the regime. An environment of uncertainty was created by arms theft and low-level military discontents as well as political confrontations between the president and the National Assembly and an assertive

new Constitutional Court (Magnusson and Clark 2005). The military, crucially, did *not* intervene in these disputes. The Constitutional Court emerged as a legitimate and respected public institution, one that helped minimize the centralizing tendencies of executive power and the potential overreach of the National Assembly, and ultimately forced mediation.

13. In 2018, Talon made his personal lawyer, Joseph Djogbénou, President of the Constitutional Court and has in general greatly imposed his influence on the Court, thus reducing the Court's objectivity (Kohnert and Preuss 2019; Stroh 2018).

5

Georgia, Moldova, and Ukraine

Democratic Moments in the Former Soviet Union

Lucan Ahmad Way

After the collapse of the Soviet Union in 1991, post-Soviet countries[1] confronted extraordinarily inhospitable conditions for democratic development. Totalitarian rule had decimated all independent civil society that might challenge state power and left post-Soviet countries without powerful or autonomous private sectors. Furthermore, in contrast to post-communist states in Central Europe and the Baltics, post-Soviet states were never given an opportunity to join the European Union—a fact that deprived elites in those countries of critical incentives to democratize. Partly as a result, the region failed to produce a single stable democracy. Regime types ranged from quasi-totalitarianism (such as in Turkmenistan), to classic authoritarianism (such as in Russia and Azerbaijan), to the competitive authoritarianism we observe in such countries as Armenia and Kyrgyzstan.

Nevertheless, an exclusive focus on the region's record of democratic failure obscures important cases of democracy in hard places. Even in such inhospitable terrain, certain countries have managed to attain democracy—albeit for a relatively short period of time. This chapter focuses on "democratic moments," a term I use to describe cases in which democracy (or something very close to it) emerges but remains unconsolidated and short-lived.[2] During these democratic periods, countries host free and fair elections, allow the existence of free media, and (very often) witness peaceful turnovers of power via the ballot box. Examples include Georgia in the 2010s; Moldova in the 1990s and 2010s; and Ukraine in the early 1990s, late 2000s, and late 2010s.

A comparison of Georgia, Moldova, and Ukraine suggests that "democratic moments" in hard places are a product of three mechanisms: First, authoritarian weakness results in the establishment of "pluralism by default." In such cases, pluralism emerges not from a particularly strong civil society, powerful institutions, or democratically minded leaders but instead from weak control over the coercive apparatus and underdeveloped ruling parties. Would-be autocrats have been unable to rely on armed forces to repress opposition, or to use ruling parties to keep allies in line. A second factor is the persistence of media and political

Lucan Ahmad Way, *Georgia, Moldova, and Ukraine* In: *Democracy in Hard Places*. Edited by: Scott Mainwaring and Tarek Masoud, Oxford University Press. © Oxford University Press 2022. DOI: 10.1093/oso/9780197598757.003.0005 parties from the prior authoritarian period. Although these institutions once provided key support for authoritarian rule in the previous regime, they may help uphold fledgling democratic moments by creating checks on the new regime. Finally, a third factor—Russian influence—has had both negative and positive effects on democracy. On one hand, President Vladimir Putin has actively promoted autocratic behavior of pro-Russian leaders in these countries, and threats from Russia have sometimes encouraged media restrictions. At the same time, Russian presence in the region has made anti-Russian leaders in these countries highly susceptible to even mild international democratizing pressure. While international pressure was much less powerful and consistent in the post-Soviet region than in Central Europe, it nonetheless encouraged the emergence of democratic moments by preventing certain power-holders from indulging in the most serious abuses of democratic norms. Overall, these three factors have promoted often very real but unstable democratic development.

In the following section, I discuss the obstacles facing democracy in the former Soviet Union and explicate the three factors described above. Then, I explore how these factors worked to produce democratic moments in Georgia, Moldova, and Ukraine—the three most democratic countries in the former Soviet Union. Both Moldova and Ukraine experienced periods of genuinely democratic rule in the post–Cold War era. While Georgia failed to fully democratize, the government maintained democratic contestation.

The Former Soviet Union as a Hard Place

In the 1990s, many observers assumed that the twelve newly independent states were well on their way to democracy.[3] However, seventy years of communist rule had generated highly unfavorable conditions for democracy. The Soviet totalitarian system undermined democratic development by politicizing the state bureaucracy and preventing the emergence of any economic or political forces outside of state control. In contrast to authoritarian regimes elsewhere, in which an authoritarian executive coexisted with a relatively autonomous private sector, Soviet totalitarian rule had maintained direct control over the economy and almost all aspect of people's lives. Until the late 1980s, economic activity—from large industrial plants to street cafes—was directed by a vast party-state bureaucracy.

The Party prohibited the emergence of *any* political organization or activity outside regime control. Independent parties, trade unions, or even nonpolitical associations such as sports leagues or chess clubs were strictly forbidden. Independent political initiative was strongly discouraged, even if it was in ostensible support of the regime. Thus, when a thirteen-year-old Marina Morozova, a friend of the author, gathered four of her friends to protest American nuclear weapons in front of the United States embassy in Moscow in the summer of 1978, this endeavor was met with tremendous suspicion by Soviet authorities. A KGB officer who questioned the girls explained, "Today, you are organizing a protest against the United States. But tomorrow you could protest against the Party!" These characteristics of the Soviet system meant that the twelve independent states emerged in 1992 without any established political or economic organizations or networks that could challenge the government.

Simultaneously, the pervasive partisan penetration of state institutions such as the courts and police meant that such institutions were highly vulnerable to manipulation in the post-Soviet era. As a result, new governments faced relatively few institutional obstacles in using tax authorities and coercive and regulatory agencies as weapons to put down opposition. In the decades after 1991, tax officials, for example, targeted opposition politicians and businesses with audits and fines not applied to friendly forces.

Finally, post-Soviet countries confronted relatively weak external democratizing pressures. In contrast to their Central European counterparts, autocrats in the former Soviet Union met with softer and more sporadic external demands for democratic change (Kopstein and Reilly 2000; Levitsky and Way 2010; Levitz and Pop-Eleches 2010). Most importantly, not a single post-Soviet country was given the opportunity to join the European Union, which emerged in the 1990s as one of history's most effective democracy promoters (Vachudova 2005). Aid was only loosely tied to democracy and, where pressure was applied, it was often half-hearted.[4] As a result, autocrats did not face any kind of clear incentive to refrain from abuse.

Such conditions contributed to the overwhelming failure of democracy in the region. In 2019, seven of twelve post-Soviet countries were ranked by Freedom House as "not free," while the rest were labeled "partly free." The only post-Soviet country ever to have been ranked as "Free" by Freedom House was Ukraine between 2005 and 2009. Of the seventy-six executive elections held in the former Soviet Union between 1991 and 2019, only eight have resulted in the peaceful democratic transfer of power to opposition forces (Freedom House 2019a).[5]

Democratic Moments in the Former Soviet Union

This litany of failure nonetheless conceals important democratic successes in the region. In addition to Ukraine, two other countries—Georgia and Moldova—experienced democracy or something very close to it after the Cold War. During democratic moments, elections were generally free, fair, and competitive; all adults had suffrage; there were few if any violations of freedom of speech, press, and association; and power was held by elected officials rather than by non-elected "tutelary" authorities (e.g., militaries, monarchies, or religious bodies) (Dahl 1971). At the same time, democracy was not consolidated: leaders regularly tried to abuse their power and change the fundamental rules of the game. Democracy was not regularized or taken for granted and was often short-lived. Nonetheless, the emergence of genuine democracy in such inhospitable terrain cries out for explanation.

Georgia, Moldova, and Ukraine represent the three most democratic countries in the former Soviet Union according to V-Dem (Coppedge et al. 2021). Detailed case study analysis (see Way 2015) suggests that significant democratic moments emerged in Georgia in the mid- and late 2010s; in Moldova in the 1990s and again in the 2010s; and in Ukraine in the early 1990s, late 2000s, and finally after 2014. While this description of regime evolution does not precisely match V-Dem's scorings over time, it represents the author's best assessment based on a detailed analysis of the cases.[6]

First, Moldova quickly transitioned to democracy after the Soviet collapse and witnessed peaceful democratic turnovers in 1996 and 2001. However, the election of the Communist Party of Moldova in 2001 led to a clear slide into competitive authoritarianism after the government began a generalized assault on media freedom. Following the ouster of the Communists in 2009, the country witnessed a resurgence of democracy and peaceful democratic turnovers in 2016 and 2020.

Next, Ukraine came very close to democracy in the early 1990s but witnessed backsliding in the late 1990s. It then experienced a clear democratic moment following an electoral revolution in 2004 (the Orange Revolution) that resulted in the election of Viktor Yushchenko. Under Yushchenko (2005–2010), Ukraine was a full democracy: there were no serious assaults on media or other violations of civil liberties, the opposition was given the fullest freedom to organize, and in 2010 Yushchenko left office after a completely free and fair election that saw the democratic election of Viktor Yanukovych. The democratic moment ended after Yanukovych jailed opposition leaders and undermined media freedom. But after Yanukovych's ouster in 2014, the country again came close to democracy and witnessed a peaceful democratic turnover in 2019.

Finally, Georgia, which experienced total state breakdown in the early 1990s and had weaker conditions for democracy than either Moldova or Ukraine, experienced a particularly surprising democratic moment in the early 2010s. In 2013, the country experienced its first peaceful and democratic turnover when President Mikheil Saakashvili left power in favor of the Georgian Dream coalition. From 2013 until 2020, Georgian Dream governed in a relatively democratic manner. The opposition was allowed to mobilize and the quality of elections improved over time. However, in early 2021, the government arrested the main opposition leader, marking a sharp turn toward greater authoritarianism.

Where Do Democratic Moments Come From?

What explains the emergence of democratic moments? How are countries able to overcome inhospitable conditions to become democratic—even for a relatively short period of time? One possibility is that these cases emerge out of completely stochastic or random variation. For example, such periods might result from the unpredictable and idiosyncratic appearance of democratically minded leaders who act in democracy-sustaining ways despite incentives to the contrary.[7] Yet, there are two reasons to doubt this explanation in the post-Soviet context. First, it is hard to argue that democratic moments are randomly distributed across the former Soviet Union—which is what we would expect if a stochastic factor such as leadership were involved. Most obviously, no post-Soviet country with access to significant natural resources experienced a democratic moment (Bellin 2004, 2012).[8] All five post-Soviet cases that rely heavily on natural resources— Azerbaijan, Kazakhstan, Russia, Turkmenistan, and Uzbekistan—ultimately created quite stable and closed authoritarian regimes.[9] (At the same time, as we will see below, the transition between democracy and competitive authoritarianism within Georgia, Moldova, and Ukraine *was* arguably more contingent.) Second, leaders during democratic moments were not especially democratic, and they engaged in repeated efforts to abuse democratic norms. This chapter contends that democratic moments emerge less from these random sources of variation and more from the systematic contextual factors of authoritarian weakness, the persistence of old regime political forces, and geopolitical vulnerability. I discuss each of these in turn.

Authoritarian Weakness

As I have argued elsewhere (Way 2015), democratic moments often result not from the strength of democrats but from the weakness of would-be autocrats. In such cases, autocrats have been too enfeebled to monopolize political control, steal elections, repress opposition, or keep allies in line—resulting in a dynamic and genuinely competitive political environment. In particular, I highlight two forms of authoritarian weakness that lead to "pluralism by default" that undergirds democratic moments in the former Soviet Union: weak ruling parties and authoritarian state apparatuses.

Authoritarian regimes with well-established ruling parties have historically been seen as more durable than military or other types of nondemocratic regimes (Brownlee 2007; Geddes 1999; Huntington 1968; Magaloni 2006, 2008; Svolik 2012). In turn, weak and poorly institutionalized ruling parties often promote more dynamic political competition. Party weakness—defined by the absence of a single, well-institutionalized party structure[10]—facilitates pluralism by encouraging elite defection to the opposition. Indeed, many opposition leaders in the former Soviet Union—Leonid Kuchma and Viktor Yushchenko in Ukraine, Mikheil Saakashvili in Georgia, Petru Lucinschi in Moldova—emerged out of previous governments that were not governed by a single party.

Party weakness was particularly endemic in the post-Soviet context because the Soviet collapse had resulted in the widespread destruction of older party structures. Fearful that the Communist Party would undermine Perestroika reforms, Gorbachev, as the Party's leader, dismantled key party institutions and hampered efforts by lower-level officials to defend party power in the face of the first competitive elections in 1989 and 1990 (Way 2015, chap. 2). Furthermore, the Party was widely blamed for the Soviet Union's disastrous economic condition in the late 1980s and early 1990s. Thus, after the failed coup of August 1991, the Party was banned in a number of new states, including Georgia, Moldova, and Ukraine. In Ukraine, for example, party cells were dissolved and officials suddenly looked on party membership as a "contagious disease."[11] In some parts of the former Soviet Union where party-state institutions remained relatively intact or where leaders benefited from easy natural resource rents (e.g., Turkmenistan, Kazakhstan, Russia, Azerbaijan), officials were quickly able to adapt. But in other cases, such as Georgia, Kyrgyzstan, Moldova, and Ukraine, which lacked such resources and witnessed significant breakdown of older institutions, leaders had a much harder time reorienting and consolidating control.

Similarly, democratic moments may occur when authoritarian state power—defined as the willingness and capacity of repressive and other state agencies to support incumbent power—is limited.[12] An extensive and cohesive coercive apparatus is necessary to enable rulers to monitor, intimidate, and suppress potential sources of opposition, and to manipulate elections. In another era, an absence of such instruments might well have led to a military or civilian coup. But in the post–Cold War era, coups are much rarer, and when they do occur, they have most often been followed by democratic elections (Marinov and Goemans 2013). In cases of weak repressive capacity, leaders have faced difficulties carrying out *any* large-scale coordinated authoritarian action and have therefore been vulnerable to even weak opposition challenges. Excepting those cases in which weakness has led to a breakdown in social order, weak coercive capacity has often provided key political opportunities for opposition mobilization and often underlies "people power."[13] This was the case in both Ukraine and

Moldova in the 1990s, when chronically underfunded coercive apparatuses with large wage arrears proved unable and unwilling to control challengers to incumbent autocrats, resulting in political openings that lasted for several years.

To be clear, even weak autocrats can engage in sporadic harassment of the opposition. Pluralism by default certainly does not guarantee democracy. The transition between democracy and competitive authoritarianism was sometimes quite contingent. However, by hampering efforts to consistently suppress opposition and prevent elite defection, party and state weakness makes it much harder for leaders to eliminate political competition—thereby generating frequent political openings and propitious conditions for democratic moments.

Persistence of Old Regime Forces

Next, I argue that the persistence of old regime political forces—in particular, political parties and media—may facilitate democratization. The survival of old regime parties and press can create checks on the power of new governments. James Loxton (2018, 28–29) has argued that former authoritarian ruling parties can contribute to party system institutionalization by anchoring one side of the regime cleavage. The checks imposed by autocratic successor parties and institutions are particularly important in the post-Soviet context, where leaders have faced few organized challenges to their rule. The total disintegration of old regime organizations undermines democracy by depriving the opposition of potentially powerful tools to challenge the new government. For example, in Georgia, the successive and complete destruction of old regime forces in 1991, 1992, and 2003 left new governments with a freer hand to abuse power. Political forces that might have provided democratic challenges to new governments in elections or via opposition media were absent. By contrast, in Ukraine in the late 2000s and Georgia in the 2010s, the persistence of media and parties from the previous government created checks on government power—thereby bolstering pluralism.

Vulnerability to External Pressure

Finally, the post-Soviet space is uniquely shaped by the regional dominance of Russian autocracy. In fact, all three countries covered here suffered Russian military intervention. Many existing accounts emphasize the ways in which Russian presence promotes autocracy in the region by strengthening pro-Russian authoritarian forces such as Leonid Kuchma and Viktor Yanukovych in Ukraine and the Communist Party in Moldova. At the same time, when explicitly anti-Russian forces have come to power, Russia has *undermined* efforts to consolidate authoritarian control by financing opposition forces and making incumbents the targets of Russian-generated opposition propaganda (Way 2016). Hostility from Russia has also enhanced dependence on Western support—thereby strengthening the impact of Western democracy promotion. Georgia, Moldova, and Ukraine have all been highly dependent on Western aid in the face of Russian military aggression. External vulnerability made these countries more susceptible to Western democratizing pressure. Such pressure was much weaker and more sporadic than that created by the European Union in Central Europe (Levitsky and Way 2010), but could still generate democratic moments. Most significantly, in Georgia in 2013, such pressure created conditions for the country's first peaceful democratic turnover in power. Overall, the contradictory impact of Russian hostility has likely enhanced regime instability in these countries.

In the next section, I describe how the mechanisms described above produced democratic moments in Moldova, Ukraine, and Georgia. All three countries emerged out of at least a half-century of totalitarian rule, with relatively weak civil societies and state apparatuses vulnerable to partisan capture and manipulation. Yet each enjoyed extended periods of political competition that, while not consolidated, was real and often genuinely democratic. I find that these democratic moments emerged from different configurations of the causes described above. In Georgia, Moldova, and Ukraine, weak ruling parties were unable to erect new authoritarian regimes. In Ukraine and Georgia, a major obstacle to the incumbent's potentially authoritarian designs was posed by the persistence of parties and media associated with the prior regime. In Georgia, democratization was further aided by its vulnerability to international democratizing pressure, which imposed limits on how far incumbents could go to cement power.

Moldova

While Moldova had weak democratic prerequisites, it experienced two democratic moments—in the 1990s and again in the 2010s—that were driven to an important extent by authoritarian state and ruling party weakness. A poverty-stricken, rural country with no serious Soviet-era dissident movement or pre-Soviet democratic history, Moldova lacked any qualities scholars would associate with democratic success when it became independent in 1991 (Crowther 1991, 184; Way 2015). Moldova was beset by ethno-linguistic tensions between a Moldovan-speaking west and Russophone east. In 1989, Moldovans took to the streets to protest Soviet-era Russification policies, with the result that Moldovan was made the official state language. This, in turn, sparked opposition among Russian speakers in the east, and a small-scale civil war ensued for several months in 1992. In short, at independence, Moldova was not a likely candidate for democracy.

Yet, Moldova in the 1990s experienced full democracy. Civil liberties were respected. Media were free and the opposition was allowed to mobilize. While President Mircea Snegur passed a draconian law in 1991 that prohibited criticism of the president, the law was never enforced (FBIS 1992). In fact, in presidential elections five years later, government media tended to be biased *against* the incumbent Snegur (ODIHR 1996, 5). When Snegur lost that election to Speaker of the Parliament Petru Lucinschi, there were no allegations of ballot stuffing or other serious violations, and a peaceful transfer of power ensued. Lucinschi in turn lost the presidency in 2001 in free and fair elections that "met international standards for democratic elections" (ODIHR 2001, 1).

The rapid emergence of democracy in such an inhospitable context can, to an important extent, be understood as the product of state and ruling party weakness. First, the Moldovan state lacked serious coercive capacity. In the early 1990s, the country's armed forces consisted of "lightly armed" and underpaid policemen, a "hastily assembled" army, and nationalist volunteers with farm implements who were mobilized to fight separatists in the east during the brief civil war of 1992.[14] Discipline was also compromised by large-scale wage arrears and pervasive low morale (King 2000, 192–93; March and Herd 2006, 365). The ruling party was similarly weak. As in other post-Soviet countries, the Communist Party completely disintegrated after the failed Soviet coup of August 1991, which in turn led to the collapse of the Soviet Union. In the early 1990s, old Communist forces attempted to regroup into the Agrarian Democratic Party (ADP), a loose, nonideological alliance of state farm directors that initially supported President Snegur (Socor 1992).[15] The ADP, described as a "collection of regional fiefdoms and personal cliques," lacked a developed organization or political identity and failed to survive beyond a single election in 1994.[16] In 1994, the party captured 56 of 104 seats in parliament but began to fragment within just over a year. In the 1998 parliamentary elections, the ADP won no seats in parliament and promptly disappeared. A strong ruling party also failed to emerge during the administration of President Lucinschi (1997–2001). Fearing the rise of a competitor, Lucinschi sought to prevent the institutionalization of any single political faction and ruled without the support of any party.[17]

The 1996 presidential election pitted three former supporters of the ADP against one another: Snegur, Prime Minister Andre Sangheli, and parliamentary speaker Petru Lucinschi. (Moldova was a semi-presidential system between 1991 and 2001 in which the president was considered most powerful.) By 1995, the state was torn asunder by a tug-of-war between these "three whales,"[18] who each sought to use "their" part of the state against the others. This resulted, first, in highly contested control over the already-weak coercive apparatus, which made it hard for any single side to use force to obtain control. Simultaneously, the head of the state media, Adrian Usatii, whom Snegur had appointed in 1989, had a falling out with Snegur in 1995 and openly backed Lucinschi in the 1996 election.[19] As a result, *even as an incumbent,* Snegur received generally negative coverage on state television—the only television to reach many rural areas (ODIHR 1996, 7). Snegur also faced significant difficulties controlling local governments—a fact that largely precluded serious vote fraud. In the end, Snegur lost to Lucinschi 46 percent to 54 percent.

A former Soviet Politburo member adept at backroom politics, Lucinschi (1997–2001) was seemingly well placed to monopolize political control. His allies gained increasing control of parliament. Just after his election, many ADP deputies went over to the president,[20] and a pro-presidential coalition, the Bloc for a Democratic and Prosperous Moldova (BDPM), gained a substantial number of seats in elections in 1998.[21] Allies of the president constituted 61 of 101 seats in the legislature. On April 21, Lucinschi's close ally, Dumitru Diacov, who had worked with him since 1995, was elected speaker of parliament.[22] Observers widely expected Lucinschi to dominate the legislature (Roper 2001, 6).

Yet coalition weakness fundamentally undermined Lucinschi's efforts to concentrate political power. The problem was *not* that Lucinschi lacked sufficient allies in the legislature but that, in the absence of a single well-institutionalized party, the president quickly lost control over the supporters he had. Fearing the rise of a competitor to his power, Lucinschi engaged in divide-and-rule tactics, seeking to disperse his support across a wide range of political organizations and prevent the concentration of power in any single group.[23] Thus, while the BDPM had been created as a pro-presidential coalition, Lucinschi openly promoted a number of competing groupings and independent deputies in the 1998 parliamentary elections—a fact that alienated many of his allies and undermined the electoral chances of the coalition.[24] Lucinschi's behavior may have been motivated by a rational desire not to tie his political fortunes to a new group that was uncertain to succeed; but his actions contributed to the perception that he was a "bad-payer of political bills."[25]

As a result, despite his strong starting point, Lucinschi was unable to concentrate political power. To begin with, the legislature deprived the president of control over the media. When state television began to attack deputies deemed critical of the president, parliament fired the head of state media and reduced the president's formal role in choosing his successor.[26] Subsequently, control over different parts of the government media complex was distributed among different parliamentary factions—which promoted pluralism in the media.[27]

Most critically, Lucinschi's efforts to strengthen presidential rule were overturned by those closest to him. Beginning in February 1999, Lucinschi proposed to dramatically increase the power of the president.[28] In response to severe opposition from the legislature, including Diacov and the BDPM (which, ironically, had run on a platform of *strengthening* presidential power), Lucinschi organized a national referendum, which garnered majority support but failed to attract sufficient turnout to make it binding (Crowther 2007, 276). While Lucinschi actively sought Western support, the Venice Commission, a European advisory body on constitutional law, concluded that the proposed changes were "contrary to European democratic principles."[29] The president's former allies, in fact, began a campaign to eliminate the directly elected presidency altogether. Diacov was not especially supportive of the parliamentary system, but he considered Lucinschi to be "totally unreliable" and concluded that strengthening parliamentary power was the only way to defeat him.[30] In 2001, Moldova became a parliamentary republic in which a president was elected by the legislature.

What explains Lucinschi's self-destructive failure to build a party? His mistakes cannot be attributed to political inexperience. A former member of the Soviet Politburo and former first secretary of the Soviet Communist Party of Moldova, Lucinschi was among the most seasoned politicians in Moldova. When the Soviet Union collapsed, he adroitly pivoted away from the Communist Party, which was banned in 1991, and quickly reemerged as the speaker of the Moldovan Parliament. However, his abandonment of the Party was a double-edged sword. In the immediate aftermath of the collapse, it allowed him to quickly regain authority amid widespread anti-communism. However, in the medium term, it left him without an organized base of support and with no ideology and few organizational networks to build a new one. While not impossible, building a new party in such a context was highly challenging. Like Boris Yeltsin in Russia and Ukraine's Kravchuk, who also retained power by rejecting the Soviet Communist Party, Lucinschi confronted a bit of a catch-22 in the 1990s. On one hand, new political forces were too weak to rely on. On the other hand, efforts to diversify allies away from these forces often alienated existing supporters. As a result, Lucinschi, like other leaders during that time, chose initially to rely on his own personal power rather than invest in party building. The result was pluralism by default.

The importance of ruling party weakness in facilitating pluralism is further evidenced by Moldova's regime trajectory after the 2001 elections that resulted in a sizable victory (71 of 101 seats) by a much better organized Communist Party of Moldova. Banned in 1991, the Communist Party had been revived in 1993 from the remnants of the old Soviet party by second-tier Soviet-era leaders who embraced party symbols and ideology. As a result, they were able to quickly rebuild a relatively robust party organization and maintained strong discipline under the leadership of Vladimir Voronin. While parliamentary rule is typically associated with greater democracy, it allowed Voronin and the party to rule with virtually no checks on their power. During the party's tenure in power, most policy decisions were made outside the legislature by the party hierarchy. In turn, the rise of the Communists led to a notable decline in civil liberties and media freedom. State-run television was censored and grew increasingly biased, and independent talk shows were taken off the air (ODIHR 2005, 1; Way 2002, 131). The Communist Party also was also much more effective than Snegur had been at monopolizing control over the state in the 2005 and 2009 elections. As a result, Moldova's democratic moment was decisively brought to an end.

However, democracy reemerged in 2009 when the Communists were over-thrown in the wake of post-election protests in April. The election left the Party just *one vote* shy of the sixty-one votes needed to elect a president. Due in part to a highly polarized atmosphere created by protest violence, the loose coalition of opposition parties was remarkably able to deprive the Communists of that single vote, and new elections were held.[31] After repeat elections in July, the op-position cobbled together a coalition government—the Alliance for European Integration (AEI)—consisting of the four non-communist parties.

In turn, the AEI was in a much weaker position than the Communists to mo-nopolize political control. As a fluid coalition of relatively equal political groups, the AEI was extremely weak by the metrics used here. The parties were "partners in a coalition" but also "political competitors" (Popescu 2012, 43). After taking power, the AEI rapidly "decomposed into mutually hostile camps" (Socor 2013). The regime incorporated strong "internal checks and balances" that made it nearly impossible for any one faction to monopolize control (Popescu 2012, 43). As in the 1990s, competing parties infiltrated different ministries and parliamen-tary committees—which created an enormous amount of default competition within the state and regime (Wilson 2013, 2).

As a result, Moldova opened up significantly. While deep antagonism to the Communist Party allowed the coalition partners to unite in banning the pro-Communist NIT TV, state-run media became more pluralist and the govern-ment was no longer sufficiently unified to impose a single editorial line.[32] Journalists no longer faced repeated harassment, and media felt free to air programs critical of the government. Media coverage was balanced and reflected a diversity of views in parliamentary elections in 2010, 2014, and 2019, as well as in presidential elections in 2016 and 2020 (held after Moldova returned to a semi-presidential system).[33] In addition, the coalitional character of the govern-ment made it nearly impossible for any single group to control the legislature. Competition among coalition partners created a highly rapacious and competi-tive political system in which leaders and parties repeatedly shifted alliances and corruption was rampant. In the spring of 2013, Prime Minister Vlad Filat, from the Liberal Democratic Party, came into open conflict with the Democrats, an-other member of the coalition. In the end, Filat was forced to resign and was replaced by Iurie Leancă in May 2013. The AEI was dissolved in favor of a new

"Pro European Coalition." Between July 2009 and early 2021, the presidency was controlled by five different politicians from different parties. During the period of parliamentary rule that lasted until 2016, three presidents were elected by the legislature: Mihai Ghimpu of the Liberal Party (2009–2010), Marian Lupu of the Democrats (2010–12), and the independent Nicolae Timofti (2012–16). In 2016, the country returned to semi-presidentialism and Igor Dodon of the Socialists became president (2016–2020)—although Prime Minister Pavel Filip's Democratic Party of Moldova (PDM) was widely considered to be the ruling party until 2019.[34] In 2016, Dodon beat Maia Sandu of the pro-European Party of Action and Solidarity and won the presidency in a close popular election. Then, in 2020, Sandu defeated Dodon in free and fair elections. When this chapter was written, Moldova could be considered a democracy.

Ukraine

Ukraine illustrates how party weakness and the persistence of old regime political institutions may foster democratic moments. Like Moldova, Ukraine suffered from a weak civil society and has been riven by identity conflicts since becoming independent in 1991. In the wake of the failed Soviet coup of August 1991, Leonid Kravchuk, a former chief of ideology in Soviet Ukraine, rode a wave of anti-communism by destroying the Communist Party and pushing for the destruction of the Soviet state. Such moves allowed Kravchuk to survive the Soviet collapse but meant that he came to power without any organized base of support.

Lacking a strong state and *any* political party, Kravchuk in 1991–94 was unable to control the legislature despite the fact that it was dominated by a nominal ally, Ivan Pliushch. In 1992, Pliushch orchestrated the firing of a prime minister loyal to Kravchuk, replacing him with Leonid Kuchma, the head of a missile factory in eastern Ukraine who had no ties to Kravchuk.[35] After a wave of strikes in eastern Ukraine in 1993, Kravchuk was forced to call early elections. Kravchuk then changed his mind and decided to postpone elections and suppress parliament. However, he was forced to relent after heads of the police and security forces refused to go along (Kravchuk 2002, 227–28). Simultaneously, Kravchuk's weak control over regional governments undermined efforts to manipulate the election process, and Kravchuk's own appointees often directly undermined the president during the election and supported Kuchma (FBIS 1994; Kravchuk 2002, 230). As a result, Kravchuk lost power to Kuchma, who promised closer ties to Russia.

The country descended into competitive authoritarianism under President Leonid Kuchma (1994–2004). Under Kuchma, the government engaged in systematic ballot stuffing, threats from government officials, and violence to ensure victory. In the runup to the 2004 presidential elections, in which Kuchma planned to install his chosen successor, Viktor Yanukovych, his regime poisoned the main opposition leader, Viktor Yushchenko—permanently disfiguring his face. However, efforts to steal the 2004 election sparked large-scale protests and an electoral revolution that led to Yushchenko's victory.

In 2005, Ukraine became a democracy. Under Yushchenko, the media was unconstrained, and the opposition had total freedom to mobilize. Elections were consistently free and fair and did not suffer from serious fraud (ODIHR 2006, 2007, 2010). In 2010, Yushchenko left office in a peaceful, democratic transition of power to Viktor Yanukovych, who then put an end to Ukraine's democratic moment.

Given that the rise and fall of democracy directly coincided with Yushchenko's tenure, it is tempting to argue that Ukraine's democratic moment was a product of Yushchenko's commitment to democracy. A closer look however, casts doubt on this idea. When Yushchenko came to power, he immediately tried to attack the financial bases of opposition forces—efforts that initially convinced Yanukovych's main backer to flee the country (Kudelia and Kuzio 2014). Yushchenko also fired fourteen thousand civil servants for lack of loyalty to the new regime and used a controversial interpretation of the constitution to shut down parliament and call for early elections.[36] It is thus difficult to claim that Yushchenko was committed to pluralism.

While we can never know if even greater commitment to authoritarianism might somehow have allowed Yushchenko to consolidate power, we *do* know that he faced significantly greater challenges to his authority from within his own coalition than did either Kuchma before him or Yanukovych after him (see below). Indeed, Yushchenko was backed by an extraordinarily weak coalition within a coalition. "Our Ukraine" was a coalition of ten parties that ruled with Yulia Tymoshenko's *Batkyvshina* party. Before coming to power, Yushchenko created a relatively equal alliance with Tymoshenko, who agreed in the summer of 2004 to sit out the presidential election in exchange for her appointment as prime minister. Competition between Tymoshenko and Yushchenko greatly hampered the latter's efforts to concentrate power, preventing him in particular from firing judges and packing the courts with regime loyalists.[37] As a result, Yushchenko found it impossible to gain the necessary support in the Constitutional Court to increase presidential powers (Trochev 2011). Divisions in the coalition also critically undermined Yushchenko's capacity to use the state to manipulate elections in his favor. Competition among allies for votes in the same areas served "as a check on each other's [electoral] shenanigans in the west and center."[38] As a result, electoral manipulation declined dramatically. In short, the coalitional structure of Yushchenko's regime—in stark contrast to that of Kuchma—meant that the president's power was hemmed in from the start.

Political competition was also enabled by the persistence of old regime institutions. Among the most important of these were media organizations with ties to Yanukovych and his party. Even after his defeat and resignation in 2004, pro-Yanukovych media ensured that he received positive or at least neutral coverage (ODIHR 2006, 17–19). In general, although the Ukrainian press during this period was wracked by endemic corruption, it was also quite pluralistic, making it very hard for Yushchenko to impose a single official line. And with key oligarchs supporting the opposition, a relatively equal playing field among the major parties emerged.[39]

A key player in the opposition to Yushchenko was Yanukovych's powerful Party of Regions. Drawing on the support of extraordinarily wealthy energy oligarchs and the country's strongest regional political machine in Donetsk province, the Party of Regions had "more money at its disposal" and was "more organized" than other parties in Ukraine.[40] It was also less personalized than other Ukrainian parties, had the largest network of primary organizations in the country, and retained strong voting discipline in the legislature.[41] Yanukovych was also backed by powerful oligarchs—including Viktor Medvedchuk and Rinat Akhmetov, who controlled the major television stations *1 + 1* and *TV Ukraina*, respectively.

After Yanukovych was defeated in 2004, he did not disappear but remained a powerful force. The Party of Regions possessed a large and loyal base of electoral support in the east, and thus quickly became a key player in the new Ukrainian political system. Yushchenko and Tymoshenko each used Yanukovych to try to neutralize the other's influence. In the summer of 2005, Yushchenko obtained Yanukovych's support to oust Tymoshenko as prime minister in exchange for a promise to cease attacks on the latter and provide amnesty for his 2004 electoral fraud.[42] Yanukovych's enormous financial base therefore remained intact, providing his party with the resources to capture a plurality of seats in the 2006 parliamentary elections and ultimately seize the prime minister's office (after Yushchenko and Tymoshenko failed to forge a coalition).[43] In the 2010 presidential elections, both Tymoshenko and Yushchenko ran against Yanukovych. Yushchenko— whose campaign was wracked by defections, severe underfunding, and disorganization—obtained just 5 percent of the vote.[44] Tymoshenko made it to the second round against Yanukovych, who beat Tymoshenko 49 percent to 45 percent in free and fair elections.

As in Moldova, the emergence of a better organized party put an end to Ukraine's democratic moment. Drawing on a disciplined party and a compliant prime minister, Yanukovych packed the courts and increased the formal powers of the president. Under the guise of combating corruption, the government jailed Tymoshenko and other opposition activists.

However, a third democratic moment emerged after Yanukovych fell in 2014 to large-scale protests that both forced the president to flee the country and led to civil war. Large sections of the Ukrainian state collapsed. Police and special forces "disappeared from the streets" (Puglisi 2014). The new authorities in Kyiv lacked any effective means of imposing order—outsourcing security functions to local oligarchs and opposition paramilitaries (Puglisi 2014). Ukrainian president Petro Poroshenko came to power in 2014 with a party that was "no more than a myth," with no website or known address or telephone number.[45]

War with Russia created challenging circumstances for democratic development. In significant parts of eastern Ukraine, weakened security made it impossible to carry out the election. Furthermore, the conflict threatened democracy by encouraging government efforts to restrict opposition Russophile media. For example, in 2018, the opposition *Radio Vesti*, operating in Kyiv and Kharkiv, was shut down due to its "rude and derogatory remarks addressed to the heroes [of the EuroMaidan Revolution]" (quoted in Way 2019, 55). Therefore, Ukraine cannot be considered a full democracy between 2014 and 2019.

Nevertheless, the opposition was given substantially greater freedom to operate than under Yanukovych, and politics were extraordinarily open and competitive in those parts of the country under Ukrainian control. In parliamentary and presidential elections in 2014 and 2019, there was little fraud and the media, while biased, represented diverse and opposing political forces.[46] Each election witnessed dramatic shifts in political power. Most notably, in 2019, Poroshenko was defeated 25 percent to 73 percent in presidential elections while his party lost 80 percent of its seats in parliament.

Democratic success may partly be traced to Ukraine's vulnerable international position. Under attack from a power three times its size, the government was heavily dependent on Western military and economic support. As a result, Poroshenko faced constraints in undertaking overtly undemocratic behavior that might undermine the country's international reputation. Such constraints may have prevented democratic backsliding early in Poroshenko's term. Thus, it was rumored that President Obama successfully discouraged Poroshenko from imposing martial law when the two leaders met in June 2014. Perhaps more importantly, Poroshenko was unable to convince his own allies to support limitations on democracy. In late 2018, following a Russian naval attack, Poroshenko *did* declare martial law, which would have postponed upcoming presidential elections. However, this move sparked widespread opposition from within his own supporters and the Ukrainian elite in general. As a result, Poroshenko amended the law and held the elections as scheduled. He was then soundly defeated by a total outsider, the comedian Volodymyr Zelensky. Under Zelensky, Ukraine has maintained similar levels of democracy: restrictions on Russophile media (supported by the Biden administration)[47] have continued at the same time that the system has remained extremely open and competitive. In 2021, Ukraine was very nearly democratic.

Georgia

Suffering a complete breakdown of social order and descent into warlord rule in the early 1990s, Georgia arguably faced more serious obstacles to democracy than Moldova and Ukraine.[48] Perhaps as a result, Georgia since independence has not been as democratic as Moldova or Ukraine.[49] Georgia nevertheless experienced a surprising democratic moment in the 2010s. In 2012, the country witnessed the first peaceful democratic turnover of power in its history. In subsequent years, elections improved in quality and the opposition faced relatively few constraints in mobilizing support before early 2021, when the government arrested the main opposition leader. While short-lived, Georgia's democratic moment is unexpected given the country's unpromising conditions. This outcome, I argue, can best be explained by Georgia's vulnerability to external pressure, the weakness of the ruling party, and the strength of old regime forces that remained intact after the fall of President Mikheil Saakashvili in 2013.

After becoming independent in 1991, Georgia experienced a short-lived dictatorship under Zviad Gamsakhurdia that led to total state breakdown and civil war in 1991–92, and ethnic conflict involving the country's ethnic enclaves of Ossetia and Abkhazia, as well as Russian military interventions in the early 1990s and in 2008. While no dictator lasted for long, Georgia *also* lacked a strong opposition. Opposition challenges have been weakened by the fact that old regime forces tended to disappear completely following their ouster—leaving the new government with fewer checks on its power. In 1991, 1992, and 2004, new leaders came to power with more than 80 percent support before completely collapsing as political forces. Each time, the near total collapse of the prior regime (the Communists in 1991, Gamsakhurdia in 1992, and Shevardnadze in 2003) meant that new leaders ruled without an effective political opposition that could check their power.

Georgia's democratic moment emerged out of the Rose Revolution of 2003. In the late 1990s and early 2000s, Georgia was ruled by President Eduard Shevardnadze, who had been brought in by a warlord in the early 1990s in the wake of the collapse of the Gamsakhurdia regime. While Shevardnadze brought a measure of stability, corruption was rampant, the central government faced regional challenges in Ajaria, Ossetia, and Abkhazia, and the police often went unpaid for months at a time (see Devdariani 2003). As the popularity of Shevardnadze declined in the early 2000s, Shevardnadze's government fell apart.

Top officials—including most notably Justice Minister Mikheil Saakashvili—split from the president and went into opposition.

Marked by significant fraud, parliamentary elections in 2003 sparked mass protests after official results showed Shevardnadze's coalition winning a narrow plurality. Confronting an underfunded police force, Saakashvili easily stormed parliament and forced Shevardnadze to flee.[50] At the same time, Shevardnadze was isolated internationally. He lacked support from Russia and was highly dependent on US aid.[51] In mid-2003, President Bush sent Shevardnadze a letter expressing hope that he would cede power to a "new generation of leaders" (Devdariani 2004). Unable to rely on the weakened coercive apparatus and isolated from both Russia and the West, Shevardnadze had little choice but to resign.

Like previous Georgian governments, Shevardnadze disappeared as a political force. Power shifted dramatically to Mikheil Saakashvili and his United National Movement (UNM). Saakashvili won the presidency with 96 percent of the vote and his UNM captured nearly two-thirds of parliament. Saakashvili quickly built a relatively well-disciplined party and strengthened the state. Reforms by Saakashvili increased the coercive capacity of the police, and key regions—such as Ajaria, a province on the Black Sea coast that had enjoyed de facto autonomy from the weak central government—were brought under central control (Fairbanks and Gugushvili 2013, 117).

Saakashvili's government was not democratic.[52] Media harassment persisted, including tax raids of independent television stations, prosecution of journalists, and government pressure to cancel programs critical of Saakashvili (see Dolidze 2007; Fuller 2005; Peuch 2004). In 2008, Saakashvili was reelected in a presidential election that was marred by harassment of opposition supporters and numerous irregularities in voting (ODIHR 2008).

Contrary to widespread expectations, however, Saakashvili's tenure ended in an important democratic moment made possible by Western pressure, incumbent weakness, and the survival of old regime forces. First, Western involvement in Georgian politics created future opportunities for international actors to discourage autocratic measures. There existed strong public and elite support for the European Union in Georgia (Muller 2011). Furthermore, in the wake of the Russian invasion of 2008, the country was heavily dependent on Western military assistance—relying on the United States for thirty percent of its military expenditures.[53] Georgia's increasing dependence on the West as a bulwark against Russian aggression made it potentially vulnerable to democratizing pressure.

Opposition to Saakashvili began to coalesce around a powerful Georgian billionaire, Bidzina Ivanishvili, after the 2008 election. Educated in Moscow in the 1980s, Ivanishvili had amassed significant wealth in the privatization gold rush in Russia in the early 1990s. In 2013, Forbes estimated that his wealth was

$ 5.3 billion—almost half of Georgia's annual GDP (Gente 2013, 4). A Georgian citizen, Ivanishvili invested heavily in Georgia—paying to repair Tbilisi State University and building hospitals and parks (van Peski 2013, 72). He initially backed Saakashvili (Gente 2013, 6), but his support shifted after the 2008 presidential election (Gente 2013, 7). Criticizing government abuse, Ivanishvili began funding opposition parties (Gente 2013, 7). Then, less than a year before the 2012 parliamentary elections, he created the "Georgian Dream" coalition consisting of six opposition parties that included a mix of NGO activists, a chess champion, and a football player (Aprasidze 2013, 223; Fairbanks and Gugushvili 2013, 119; van Peski 2013). The coalition lacked any ideological coherence—combining European-minded liberals and hardcore Georgian nationalists (Gilbreath 2015, 107; van Peski 2013, 72). At the same time, Ivanishvili's vast riches meant that the coalition was much more centralized than coalitions described above in Ukraine under Yushchenko and Moldova under the AEI.

Saakashvili responded aggressively to Ivanishvili's decision to go into opposition. Accused of being a "Kremlin stooge," Ivanishvili was deprived of his Georgian citizenship shortly after he announced his intention to create the Georgian Dream coalition.[54] The government began harassing Ivanishvili's supporters, and imposed enormous fines on Ivanishvili and his allies (Cecire 2013, 237; Fairbanks and Gugushvili 2013, 120, 121; Freedom House 2014, 228). However, two factors hampered Saakashvili's efforts to quash opposition. First, the opposition was powerful and united. In contrast to earlier oligarchs who opposed Saakashvili, Ivanishvili did a much better job coopting and unifying opposition parties—allowing Ivanishvili to present a united front that was backed by an extraordinary amount of money. Second, in part due to the strength of the opposition, it was harder for Saakashvili to garner Western support. In the absence of any serious challenges to Saakashvili in the early 2000s, unconditional support had been costless to the West. However, in the runup to the 2012 parliamentary election, President Barack Obama faced the prospect of backing Saakashvili amid protests provoked in reaction to a stolen election.[55] Thus, when Obama met with Saakashvili in early February 2012, Obama stressed that the conduct of the upcoming elections would be a "litmus test" for US–Georgian relations.[56] Simultaneously, various international agencies funded by the US government gave extensive coverage of Saakashvili's abuses (Cecire 2013, 247; Mueller 2014, 344). Finally, Ivanishvili engaged significantly with the United States. He met regularly with the US ambassador to Georgia and hired a number of Western lobbyists to bolster his image in the West.[57] In early 2012, Ivanishvili paid to take out a full-page ad in both the *New York Times* and the *Washington Post* making the case for free and fair elections in his country.[58] Saakashvili, sensitive to international criticism, passed a "must carry" law that required all cable services to carry a diversity of news channels in order to ensure the population access to all types of information (Freedom House 2013).

In the end, the Georgian government backed off from attempts to steal the election from Ivanishvili. Saakashvili did not yield on the citizenship question but instead made a change in the constitution to allow Ivanishvili as a European Union citizen to run in Georgian elections.[59] Though in August the government declared that Ivanishvili's coalition would be barred from taking part in the elections due to violations of spending laws, it "flinched" in the end, fearing foreign disapproval (Fairbanks and Gugushvili 2013, 121). As a result, the campaign was relatively free and fair. The media gave Georgian Dream significant coverage (ODIHR 2012, 2). While Saakashvili's government had tried to pad the electoral rolls in the hopes of manipulating the vote, the margin of victory for Georgian Dream was simply too large and efforts at manipulation were seemingly abandoned (Fairbanks and Gugushvili 2013, 123; Mitchell 2013, 79–80). The Georgian Dream coalition obtained 85 seats and the National Movement 65. Faced with such a clear outcome and internationally isolated, Saakashvili took to the airwaves to concede his party's defeat and announce that it would go into opposition (Cecire 2013, 239; Fairbanks and Gugushvili 2013, 123). Despite retaining control of the presidency, he gave up entire control of the government to Georgian Dream (Kvashilava 2019, 230). (Georgia was a semi-presidential regime from 2004 to 2018.)

As the first peaceful, democratic turnover in Georgia's history, the 2012 election marked a major milestone in Georgia's democratic development. The country became "unquestionably the most open polity of the South Caucasus" (Cornell 2014, 185; see also Fumagalli 2014, 396) and more democratic than any other post-Soviet state (van Peski 2013, 50). In the words of one commentator, politics in Georgia became "boring" (Gilbreath 2015).

The dramatic transformation of Georgian politics during this period can be seen in the improvement of the quality of elections in 2012, 2013, 2016, and 2018 (Mitchell 2016; see also Freedom House 2013, 2015, 2019b). Each election was highly competitive.[60] In contrast to Saakashvili, the Georgian Dream government during this period relied less on coercion and much more on cooptation to remain in power (Freedom House 2019b). The political system no longer saw the widespread use of government-sponsored threats and violence that had plagued Georgian politics in its first two decades of independence. In contrast to elections in the past, the opposition was given the freedom to campaign in all parts of the territory under government control. Incidents of violence became "isolated" (ODIHR 2017, 2). In elections in 2013 and 2016, international monitors carrying out parallel vote counts confirmed the accuracy of the official results (NDI 2013; NDI 2016, 4). Many issues raised by international actors—including the use of government web pages for campaigning—were ones that exist in countries that most consider to be democratic (ODIHR 2019, 11–12).

As electoral quality improved under Georgian Dream, so too did media pluralism. While some popular talk shows were unexpectedly canceled and government leaders expressed frustration that media were "circulating lies and creating tension in the society" (Freedom House 2015, 2016), media were generally vibrant and frequently aired critical voices (Freedom House 2017; Mitchell 2016). Georgian television frequently featured lively debates and a diverse range of views (Freedom House 2015). Candidates during election time had nearly unfettered access to media. Due in part to laws passed under Saakashvili in 2012, media coverage during election was relatively balanced (ODIHR 2016, 19). Finally, civil society operated without harassment and nongovernmental organizations were given ample opportunity to express critical opinions (Freedom House 2015).

The surprising emergence of genuine, if flawed, pluralism can be at least partly explained by the persistence of old regime forces and party weakness. First, the new regime was heavily shaped by the persistence of Saakashvili-era media and Saakashvili's party. As noted above, previous transitions had witnessed the complete disintegration of the old government—leaving the new administration without serious competitors. Things were different in 2012. Prominent pro-Saakashvili forces—the UNM and the pro-Saakashvili Rustavi 2 television station—remained in place after he left power, creating important checks on the new government. In particular, the United National Movement remained a potent political force—even after Saakashvili left the country in 2015. The UNM had an ideology focusing on reform and a core group of convinced loyalists in a position to challenge the new administration (Fairbanks and Gugushvili 2013, 124; Orovec and Holland 2019, 39). In 2012, the party won 40 percent of the vote, and in 2018, it won a plurality and forced the Presidential election into two rounds—before being defeated by the Georgian Dream candidate.

Most importantly, Rustavi 2, the most popular television station in Georgia, watched by 80 percent of the public, provided an important democratic check on Georgian Dream. A critical source of pro-opposition coverage under Shevardnadze, the station had been transformed from a government critic into a pro-Saakashvili "propaganda machine" after 2003.[61] But, under the directorship of Nika Gvarmia, a former UNM deputy and minister of justice, it survived Saakashvili's fall. The station aired hundreds of stories exposing government corruption and Ivanishvili's business activities.[62] In the 2013, 2016, and 2018 national elections, it provided a prominent source of criticism of the incumbent.

Rustavi 2's persistence was not a foregone conclusion. Indeed, immediately after taking power, the government began an effort to silence the station by transferring ownership to Kibar Khalvashi, a government ally—an avenue made possible by questionable changes of ownership under Saakashvili (Welt 2015). In mid-2015, a Tbilisi court supported the transfer of ownership to Khalvashi, who claimed that his shares had been illegally liquidated by Saakashvili's government in 2005. However, international outcry convinced the government to allow the station to remain in the hands of pro-UNM forces until the case was ruled on by the European Court of Human Rights. As a result, the station continued to air criticism of the government (Freedom House 2017).

Second, Georgian pluralism was bolstered by divisions within Georgian Dream itself. Founded as a loose coalition of ideologically diverse forces just a few months before it came to power, the party suffered significant defections— especially in its first years in government (see Aivazian 2019, 112–13). These divisions undermined government efforts to curb the opposition. In 2013, Giorgi Margvelashvili, a former minister of education in the Georgian Dream government and a member of the opposition under Shevardnadze (Fumagalli 2014, 396), won presidential elections with 62 percent of the vote. After assuming office, Margvelashvili became a check on the prime minister's power and "a clear voice for democracy, reform and human rights in Georgia" despite being a member of the same party (Freedom House 2016, 2017; Mitchell 2016). Together with the Georgian Dream parliamentary chairman, Margvelashvili opposed government attacks on Rustavi 2 (Bukia 2015; Welt 2015). Margvelashvili successfully thwarted efforts by the government to weaken bureaucratic independence and preserve government surveillance capacities inherited from Saakashvili (Freedom House 2016). Similarly, the Georgian Dream speaker of Parliament, Davit Usupashvili, condemned police attacks on protesters (Freedom House 2014).

At the same time, problems existed. After taking power, the government regularly used state agencies to target potential sources of opposition. Fulfilling a campaign promise, Ivanishvili immediately began to target UNM officials for prosecution (Cecire 2013, 237; Fumagalli 2014, 397; Human Rights Watch 2015). By the end of 2012, more than twenty former government officials had been detained on criminal charges (Freedom House 2013, 2014). In 2014, the government began efforts to prosecute Saakashvili himself for abuse of office. The government seized his property and tried but failed to convince Interpol to put Saakashvili on its international wanted list.[63] In response, Saakashvili was forced to flee the country. Media independence, too, suffered. In July 2019, the European Court for Human Rights found no evidence of government interference in Georgian court decisions transferring ownership of the opposition television station Rustavi 2 to a Georgian Dream ally.[64]

Increased problems might be linked to the fact that the Georgian Dream coalition became less fractured over time as members of the coalition defected from the core group controlled by Ivanishvili. In 2016, Georgian Dream won a majority 115 of 150 seats in the legislature. In the runup to the 2020 parliamentary elections, the government began carrying out more serious attacks on the opposition. Shortly after the banker Mamuka Khazaradze announced his intention to form an opposition bloc to challenge Georgian Dream, prosecutors brought fraud charges for a violation that had allegedly occurred eleven years prior[65]—a move that was widely interpreted as an open attack on the opposition.[66] After parliamentary elections in late 2020, opposition parties alleged fraud and boycotted legislative sessions.[67] Then, in early 2021, police raided the headquarters of the UNM and arrested the party's leader, Nika Melia.

At the same time, electoral life remains more pluralistic than in Georgia's past or most of the rest of the former Soviet Union. Indeed, the 2020 parliamentary elections were characterized by open campaigning of the opposition and wide coverage of the major parties. Opposition leader Khazaredze's party was allowed to campaign for the parliamentary election and gained seats in the legislature.[68] The kind of pervasive violence that characterized Georgia's first decades of independence was almost entirely absent. Finally, in 2021 there was still some hope that internal divisions might prevent a more complete descent into authoritarianism. Even though the party was much more unified than it had been in 2013, it remained divided over the regime's authoritarian trajectory. Thus, the arrest of Melia caused a major rupture within Georgian Dream. The Prime Minister Giorgi Gakharia resigned in protest over Melia's arrest.

Conclusion

In contrast to other chapters in this volume, Georgia, Moldova, and Ukraine did *not* witness the emergence of stable democracy. At the same time, an exclusive focus on the global failure of democracy in the post-Soviet region blinds us to very real instances of democratic success that emerged even in hostile conditions. During the "democratic moments" described in this chapter, elections were (very nearly) free and fair, the opposition was given free reign, and media gave extensive and often positive coverage to those who were critical of the government. In such cases, incumbents confronted intense political competition and often lost power in peaceful and democratic elections. At the same time, democracy was not consolidated in the sense that leaders regularly tried to abuse their power and change the fundamental rules of the game. Such moments were particularly evident in Georgia, Moldova, and Ukraine—that had on average the greatest democratic success in the former Soviet Union since 1991. The chapter focuses on three such moments in Ukraine, two in Moldova, and one in Georgia.

I argue that three factors helped facilitate democratic moments in the cases above. First, authoritarian weakness—in particular the weakness of authoritarian states and ruling parties—undermined efforts to consolidate authoritarian control. Such weakness hardly guaranteed democracy, but it created the possibility of pluralism in the absence of a robust civil society or well-organized opposition. In each of these cases, weak parties and weak states undermined efforts to suppress opposition challenges and contributed to relatively free and highly competitive elections. Second, the persistence of parties and media from the previous authoritarian government created key checks on leaders and enhanced the likelihood of a democratic moment. In both Ukraine in the late 2000s and Georgia in the 2010s, old regime media and parties provided an important source of democratic contestation that hemmed in the autocratic ambitions of incumbents (Loxton and Mainwaring 2018). Third, and finally, Russian intervention in the region had a contradictory impact. On one hand, it likely strengthened pro-Russian authoritarian forces such as Kuchma and the Party of Regions in Ukraine and the Communist Party in Moldova. It has also periodically motivated anti-Russian governments to suppress opposition Russophile media. At the same, it has left anti-Russian governments vulnerable to Western democratizing pressure. Such pressure clearly played a role in convincing Saakashvili to step down in Georgia in 2012–13 and may have undermined efforts to consolidate authoritarian rule in Ukraine in 2014.

What does this analysis add to the discussion of democracy in hard places? First, it suggests that important cases of democratic success can emerge short of long-term consolidation. (Indeed, the breakdown of democracy in Benin in 2019 and the democratic crisis in India show that cases that might seem consolidated are often not so.) The democratic moments analyzed in this chapter were relatively short-lived but quite real and thus require explanation. Second, in line with the analyses of Reidl and Slater (Chapters 4 and 3, respectively, this volume) and *contra* Varshney and Mainwaring (Chapters 2 and 7, respectively, this volume), this chapter suggests that democracy emerges less from normative commitment and more from constraints on behavior. While we can never know for sure if leaders might somehow have monopolized power if they had been more autocratically inclined, we do know that each leader willingly engaged in antidemocratic behavior and faced identifiable constraints on authoritarian behavior.

Finally, the argument presented here may account for democracy in other hard places. In particular, pluralism by default appears to explain the emergence of democratic competition in some parts of sub-Saharan Africa, which, like the former Soviet Union, includes numerous countries with relatively weak states and ruling parties. For example, incumbent weakness at least partly explains Benin's long and very surprising period of democratic success that is analyzed in Chapter 4, by Rachel Reidl. (For other examples of pluralism by default in the African context, see Levitsky and Way 2010, chap. 6.)[69] Comparing Benin and South Africa, Reidl argues that democracy in Benin emerged out of a balance of forces between the incumbent and the opposition. Yet, given the weakness of both the opposition and civil society in Benin, it is not obvious how such a balance emerged after the country's transition to democracy in 1991. (In economically developed South Africa, which had a robust civil society, such a balance seems less surprising.) Indeed, opponents of Mathieu Kérékou's military dictatorship in Benin were quite weak in the late 1980s and early 1990s (Allen 1992, 74; Nwajiaku 1994, 431; Riedl 2014, 161).[70]

A closer look at Benin suggests that pluralism by default may explain the balance of forces described by Reidl. Here, we see interesting parallels to the post-Soviet examples of pluralism by default described above. As in many post-Soviet cases, opposition to the old regime in Benin emerged less from a robust civil society and much more from the fragmentation of the old regime.[71] Furthermore, the ruling Peoples' Revolutionary Party of Benin (PRPB), like the Soviet Communist Party, completely disappeared during the transition. In April 1991, following a National Conference in which PRPB officials called for an end to dictatorship, the party effectively dissolved itself (Allen 1992, 72; Riedl 2014, 166). Like post-communist *apparatchiks* who rapidly abandoned the Communist Party in 1991 to save their own skins, former supporters of the PRPB felt that dissolving the party was their best root to survival (Riedl 2014, 166). In turn, the rapid demise of the PRPB resulted in a political vacuum and the proliferation of an extremely large number of very weak parties with particularistic and narrow geographic bases of power (Kuenzi and Lambright 2001, 450; Riedl 2014, 197–98). Finally, as in many parts of the former Soviet Union, Benin emerged from the transition with a weak state (Heilbrunn 1993, 285).[72]

The combination of party and state weakness created prime conditions for pluralism by default. Between 1991 and 2016, democratic competition in Benin can be directly traced to party and state weakness. First, in the March 1991 elections that pitted Kérékou against Soglo, President Kérékou was deprived of virtually any incumbent advantages. Kérékou ran without a party. The opposition leader, Nicéphore Soglo, who had been appointed as prime minister by the National Conference, was given control over the military. All of Kérékou's allies in the government were removed (Englebert 1996, 164–65). Soglo trounced Kérékou in the second round 68 percent to 32 percent.

Soglo, in turn, came to power with "neither a political base nor a political following" (Amuwo 2003, 163).[73] He was forced to "cobble together" a three-party coalition that collapsed within a year (Decalo 1997, 57; Englebert 1996, 166). Because of Soglo's inability to create a stable majority, the legislature gained significant de facto power and voted to establish an autonomous electoral commission that was opposed by Soglo (Englebert 1996, 166; Magnusson 1999, 225). Soglo also lacked firm control over the means of coercion.[74] Both opposition and incumbent had paramilitaries with the capacity for intimidation (Amuwo 2003, 166). As a result, Soglo enjoyed relatively few incumbent advantages in the runup to the 1996 election, when Soglo again faced Kérékou in the second round. After losing to Kérékou by five points, Soglo—*the incumbent*—"alleged massive rigging" and threatened to contest the results in the courts. However, facing little chance of success, he backed down and accepted defeat (Amuwo 2003, 166–67; Levitsky and Way 2010, 295).

While Kérékou lacked a strong party,[75]he was a relatively skilled backroom politician and pulled together a coalition of elite supporters—buying the support of Houngbédji by naming him prime minister (Levitsky and Way 2010, 295). In 2001, Kérékou won reelection. However, Kérékou failed to keep the support of Houngbédji, whose *Parti du Renouveau Démocratique* (PRD) became one of the main opposition parties in the country (Africa Confidential 2002). Without a party, Kérékou was unable in 2006 to decide on a successor—creating an election that was wide open (Levitsky and Way 2010, 296). While Kérékou made a concerted effort to cancel elections and hold onto power, domestic and international backlash convinced him to let the elections go forward (Africa Confidential 2006; Seely 2007, 198). As a result, Boni Yayi, a political outsider, won without the backing of a party in an election that was widely considered free and fair (Africa Confidential 2006; Seely 2007, 197–99). After winning reelection in 2011, Yayi sought to change the constitution and seek a third term.[76] He was only dissuaded after a series of defections from his party, Cowry Forces for an Emerging Benin, and this party's failure to secure a majority in the 2015 legislative elections.[77] In 2016, Patrice Talon, a former financial backer of Yayi who had fallen out with the president, beat out Yayi's chosen successor in relatively free elections.[78]

The dynamics described above suggest that, to an important extent, the balance of forces in Benin were rooted in incumbent weakness. Such weakness both thwarted efforts by leaders to engage in backsliding and allowed relatively unorganized opposition (all of whom ran as independents) to successfully challenge incumbent power.

However, pluralism by default is not a durable basis for democracy and thus we would not expect pluralism to survive indefinitely. Indeed, after 2016, Benin slipped unambiguously back into competitive authoritarian rule. Sébastien Ajavon, a successful businessman who came in third in the 2016 election, was forced into exile after being sentenced in absentia for a drug trafficking charge that many considered to be politically motivated.[79] The legislature also voted in July 2018 to lift the immunity of three opposition deputies so that they could face corruption charges.[80] Then, the government passed a new electoral law in September that effectively made it impossible for opposition parties to compete in the 2019 parliamentary elections.[81] As a result, the National Assembly only included government supporters.

In sum, there is at least some evidence of pluralism by default outside the former Soviet Union. As in Georgia, Moldova, and Ukraine, state and party weakness undermined efforts by successive incumbents to consolidate political power in Benin. And, as in the post-Soviet cases, democracy never consolidated in Benin. Leaders repeatedly sought to undermine the rules of the game, and democracy collapsed by the late 2010s. At the same time, the comparison between post-Soviet cases, on one hand, and both Benin and the other cases covered in this book, on the other, raises an important question. Why did democracy in the former Soviet Union fare worse than in the cases covered in the book? Indeed, democracy survived for at least twenty-five years in Benin—and longer in the other cases covered in the book. What might have prevented post-Soviet cases from establishing more stable democratic rule?

One possible answer lies in the differing regional environments. In contrast to the other cases covered in this book, post-Soviet cases have been shaped by the existence of a dominant regional autocracy intent on interfering with the politics of smaller countries. As discussed above, Russia has influenced regime politics in contradictory ways. On one hand, Russian threats have periodically enhanced these countries' vulnerability to Western democratizing pressures and strengthened challenges to their rule. At the same time, such interference has undermined democracy in two ways. First, as we saw in Ukraine, Russian security threats encouraged the government to suppress opposition Russophile media. Furthermore, the Russian government has given support to pro-Russian autocrats in Moldova and Ukraine. Thus, in both countries, democratic moments were cut short by the election of pro-Russian politicians and parties (President Kuchma and the Party of Regions in Ukraine; the Communist Party in Moldova). While the case studies presented evidence that organizational factors helped undermine democracy, it is also possible that Russian influence pushed these governments toward greater autocracy as well. Russian influence is too contradictory and/or weak to stamp out pluralism, but, given the already weak conditions for democracy in the region, it may make true democracy in hard places harder to maintain for significant periods of time.

Notes

1. In line with other scholars of the region, I use "post-Soviet" to describe the twelve republics of the Soviet Union excluding the Baltic states, which entered the Soviet Union much later than the other republics and had traditions of independent statehood the others lacked.
2. "Consolidated" democracies are democratic regimes in which major rules regulating the structure and acquisition of power change very infrequently and are taken for granted by virtually all major regime actors.
3. See, for example, Anderson 1999; Fish 1995; Hough 1997; and McFaul 1999; for more pessimistic early assessments, see Jowitt 1992 and Roeder 1994.

4. For example, Levon Ter-Petrosian in Armenia, Yeltsin in Russia, and Kuchma in Ukraine all continued to receive significant aid following serious democratic abuses in the mid- and late 1990s. See Bureau of European and Eurasian Affairs 2009.

5. Such peaceful democratic turnovers took place in Belarus in 1994; Moldova in 1996, 2001, and 2019; Ukraine in 1994, 2010, and 2019; and Georgia in 2013.

6. Compared to my own assessment, V-Dem is rather easy on Georgia after 2003 and puzzlingly stringent on Ukraine after 2014, showing a *decline* in democracy after the Euromaidan revolution of 2014. Unfortunately, V-Dem's reliance on expert surveys does not allow us to identify which specific incidents or government behavior (or whether such incidents/government behavior took place in parts of the country controlled by the national government) motivated V-Dem's divergent assessments.

7. For example, Russia's President Boris Yeltsin was clearly more tolerant of media criticism than his successor, Vladimir Putin.

8. The coding of post-Soviet cases is based on World Bank data on natural resource wealth as share of exports (World Development Indicators, n.d.).

9. The other nonresource cases varied between those that were highly authoritarian (Belarus and Tajikistan) and competitive authoritarian (Armenia and Kyrgyzstan).

10. Incumbents backed by weak ruling parties are those who are supported by no party, who are part of a ruling coalition of multiple parties, or who are running backed by a new (and therefore not well established) party that has not run in two elections. See Way (2015) for a full discussion of causal variables and codings.

11. "Nationalists Send Party to Scrapyard as They Take Control," *The Times* (London), August 31, 1991.

12. This concept is similar to Michael Mann's (1984) "despotic power" and Brian Taylor's (2011) "exceptional state power."

13. As Sidney Tarrow notes, "[r]ational people do not often attack well-fortified opponents" (Tarrow 1996, 54). See also Beissinger 2002, 152–53.

14. Helsinki Watch 1993, 18–19; Waters 1996, 398; author interviews with Viorel Cibatoru (former military advisor), Chișinău, Moldova, February 7, 2002; and Nicolai Chirtoaca (former National Security advisor), February 5, 2002.

15. It is coded as weak according to my criteria because when it first backed Snegur, it had not run in any elections.

16. Author interview with Alexandru Muravschi (parliamentary deputy from 1994 to 2001), Chișinău, January 31, 2002.

17. Ibid.

18. "Presidential Campaign in Moldova Is Likely to Have Its Own 'Lebed,'" *Infotag*, July 13, 1996.

19. Author interview with Adrian Usatii, Chișinău, July 30, 2004.

20. "Moldova: Parliament Speaker Calls for Radio, TV Chief's Ouster," *Infotag*, July 28, 1997.

21. In the elections, the Communists gained forty seats; the BDPM, twenty-four; the Democratic Convention of Moldova, twenty-six; and the Party of Democratic Forces, eleven.

22. Author interview with Dumitru Diacov (head of parliament, 1998–2000), Chișinău, February 1, 2002.

23. Ibid.; author interview with Alexandru Mosanu (leader of the Front), Chişinău, February 4, 2002; author interview with Anatol Golea (journalist), Chişinău, February 1, 2002.

24. Diacov interview, 2002.

25. Quoted in "Political Commentary Examines Ousted TV Chief's Case," *Basapress*, July 30, 1997. See also Diacov interview, 2002; Golea interview, 2002; Muravschi interview, 2002.

26. "Moldova: Parliament Approves New Teleradio Management," *Infotag*, November 30, 1997.

27. Author interview with Angela Sarbu, Independent Journalism Center. Chişinău, February 6, 2002.

28. For details of these proposed amendments, see Roper 2001, 12.

29. *RFE/RL Newsline*, December 16, 1999.

30. Diacov interview, 2002.

31. For a detailed description, see Way 2015, chap. 3.

32. Because of this closure, Moldova cannot be considered a full democracy during this period.

33. See OSCE election reports for these elections in "Elections in Moldova," at https://www.osce.org/odihr/elections/moldova/.

34. See Robert Petraru, "Is Moldova Heading into Uncertainty as the Democratic Party of Moldova Grows Stronger?," *Vocaleurope*, March 4, 2019, https://www.vocaleurope.eu/is-moldova-heading-into-uncertainty-as-the-democratic-party-of-moldova-grows-stronger/.

35. Ukraine is a semi-presidential system. While the formal powers of the president have fluctuated since 1991, the president has consistently been considered the most powerful figure in the country.

36. See Trochev (2010) and "Президент и правящая Партия регионов не только постарались укрепить вертикаль. . ." [The President and the ruling Party of Regions not only tried to strengthen the vertical of executive power . . .], *Зеркало Недели*, September 25, 2010.

37. Trochev (2010, 136); "Голубая контрреволюция: Виктор Янукович ликвидирует последствия 'оранжевой революцииь'" [Blue counterrevolution: Viktor Yanukovych liquidates the consequences of the 'Orange Revolution'], *Gazeta.Ru*, September 30, 2010.

38. US Embassy Cable, September 7, 2007.

39. James Marson and Dariya Orlova, "Nation's News Media: Free or Still Captive to Their Owners?," *Kyiv Post*, October 15, 2008.

40. US Embassy Cable September 7, 2007. See also Kushnarev 2007.

41. US Embassy Cable, September 28, 2007; "'Партия регионов и "Единый центр' имеют самые большие сети первичных организаций в стране – Минюст" [The Party of Regions and the 'United Center' have the largest networks of primary organizations in the country—Ministry of Justice], *Униан*, March 24, 2010; US Embassy Cable, April 15, 2008.

42. "Меморандум порозуміння між владою та опозицією" [Agreement memorandum between the government and opposition], *Ukrainska Pravda*, September 22, 2005. Quoted in Kudelia and Kuzio 2014.

43. The Orange coalition (including Moroz's Socialist Party) garnered just over 40 percent of the vote and slightly more than half of the legislature. However, Moroz defected to Yanukovych.

44. Andriy Konovalenko, "Баба Поразка Віктора Ющенка" [Baba defeat of Victor Yushchenko], *Ukrainska Pravda*, January 26, 2010.

45. Serhii Leshchenko, "Порошенко і порожнеча" [Poroshenko and the vacuum], *Ukrainska Pravda*, May 16, 2014, www.pravda.com.ua/articles/2014/05/16/7025568.

46. See the OSCE election reports available at https://www.osce.org/odihr/elections/Ukraine (accessed July 2021).

47. In early February 2021, the government shut down three television stations owned by an oligarch, Viktor Medvedchuk, with personal ties to Putin. This move was supported by the US government as a "defense of [Ukraine's] sovereignty and territorial integrity" against "Russia's malign influence" (Kalashnyk 2021).

48. Conflicts in Moldova in 1991–92 and Ukraine after 2014 were much more geographically confined than in Georgia, where civil war encompassed the whole country in the early 1990s. In addition, Georgia, in contrast to Moldova and Ukraine, was surrounded on all sides by nondemocratic states—Turkey, Russia, Azerbaijan, and Armenia. Finally, Way (2015) argues that identity divisions between relatively equal groups sustained political competition in Moldova and Ukraine, whereas the absence of this kind of division in Georgia made the monopolization of power easier.

49. Between 1991 and 2021, Moldova witnessed four peaceful, institutionally regular democratic turnovers (1996, 2001, 2016, and 2020) and Ukraine experienced three (1994, 2010, and 2019), while Georgia experienced only one.

50. On these events, see Fairbanks 2004, 117; Karumidze and Wertsch 2005, 15, 39, 54; and Mitchell 2004, 348.

51. The US government provided more than $1 billion in aid between 1992 and 2002, making Georgia one of the highest per capita recipients of aid in Eurasia (Nichols 2003, 5).

52. See Dolidze 2007; "Viewing Georgia, without the Rose-Colored Glasses," *New York Times*, September 25, 2008. As Nodia (2005, 1) stated, "strengthening the state was accompanied by certain setbacks in democratic freedoms."

53. Joshua Kucera, "Georgia, Tajikistan, among Countries Most Dependent on U.S. Military Aid," *Eurasianet*, March 11, 2016, https://eurasianet.org/georgia-tajikistan-among-countries-most-dependent-on-us-military-aid.

54. Margarita Antidze, "Georgian Tycoon Takes on Saakashvili," *Reuters*, October 17, 2011, https://www.reuters.com/article/us-georgia-tycoon/georgian-tycoon-takes-on-saakashvili-idUSTRE79G1CT20111017.

55. Lincoln Mitchell, "Could Georgia Be 2012's October Surprise?," *RealClearWorld*, September 22, 2012, https://www.realclearworld.com/articles/2012/09/22/could_georgia_be_2012s_october_surprise.amp.html.

56. See Liz Sherwood-Randall, "President Obama Meets with Georgian President Mikheil Saakashvili," *The White House, President Barack Obama* (blog), February 3, 2012, https://obamawhitehouse.archives.gov/blog/2012/02/03/president-obama-meets-georgian-president-mikheil-saakashvili; Vladimir Socor, "Georgia and the United States: De-Alignment through Regime Change? (Part Two)," *Eurasia Daily Monitor*,

March 18, 2013, https://jamestown.org/program/georgia-and-the-united-states-de-alignment-through-regime-change-part-two/; Lebanidze 2014, 211.

57. Socor, "Georgia and the United States: De-Alignment through Regime Change? (Part Two)"; Giorgi Lomsadze,. "Saakashvili and Ivanishvili: Bonkers for Obama," *Eurasianet*, January 31, 2012, https://eurasianet.org/saakashvili-and-ivanishvili-bonkers-for-obama; Cecire 2013, 247.

58. Josh Rogin, "Inside the Other Georgian Lobbying Effort in Washington," *Foreign Policy*, January 30, 2012, https://foreignpolicy.com/2012/01/30/inside-the-other-georgian-lobbying-effort-in-washington/.

59. Cecire 2013, 237; "Saakashvili Comments on Ivanishvili," *Civil.ge*, May 21, 2012, https://civil.ge/archives/121944.

60. "Georgian Dream Shown the Exit Door," *Nezavisimaya gazeta*, October 30, 2018, p. 5.

61. "The Fall and Rise of Georgia's Most Watched TV Channel—Rustavi 2," *Jam News*, August 21, 2019, https://jam-news.net/the-fall-and-rise-of-georgias-most-watched-tv-channel-rustavi-2/.

62. Ibid.

63. "Georgia Seeks Interpol 'Red Notice' for Saakashvili," *Civil.ge*, August 31, 2014, https://old.civil.ge/eng/article.php?id=27628.

64. Margarita Antidze, "Europe's Human Rights Court Rules against Owners of Georgian Pro-Opposition TV Channel in Ownership Row," *Reuters*, July 18, 2019, https://www.reuters.com/article/us-georgia-politics-tv-court/europes-human-rights-court-rules-against-owners-of-georgian-pro-opposition-tv-channel-in-ownership-row-idUSKCN1UD1YY.

65. Giorgi Lomsadze, "In Georgian Politics, It's Millionaire vs Billionaire," *Eurasianet*, August 7, 2019, https://eurasianet.org/in-georgian-politics-its-millionaire-vs-billionaire.

66. See Freedom House (2020b) and the detailed report on this by Transparency International (David 2020). Furthermore, in early 2020, the government canceled a major port project that Khazaredze's company benefited from—a move that was seen by some as punishment for Khazaredze's political activity. See Giorgi Lomsadze, "Georgia Cancels Contract for Black Sea Megaport," *Eurasianet*, January 9, 2020, https://eurasianet.org/georgia-cancels-contract-for-black-sea-megaport.

67. Georgian Dream won 90 of 150 seats.

68. "Lelo's Khazaradze Speaks of Church, Queer Rights, Foreign Policy," *Civil.ge*, June 8, 2020, https://civil.ge/archives/355161.

69. See, in particular, discussions of Kenya, Zambia, Mali, and Madagascar.

70. All successful opposition candidates from 1991 to 2016 ran as independents and lacked any party organization backing them.

71. Kathryn Nwajiaku (1994, 435) argues that groups pushing the democratic transition emerged out of the "splintering" of Kerekou's patrimonial networks.

72. Benin's armed forces were "the least coherent in Francophone Africa" and existed as a "patchwork of conflicting political allegiances" (Decalo 1976, 53).

73. Soglo's allies were not bound together by any political organization or "any grand ideals beyond the immediate wrenching of power and sharing in the spoils of office" (Amuwo 2003, 163).

74. The military attempted coups in 1992 and 1994—the latter of which was only halted because of US intervention (Magnusson 2005, 223, 224).

75. In 1994, Kérékou created Action Front for Renewal and Development (FARD) which won just ten seats in 1995 and relied on an extremely localized base of support (Bierschenk, Thiolèron, and Bako-Arifari 2003, 163). As a result, he was forced to cobble together a relatively loose and unstable coalition that suffered numerous defections.

76. David Lewis, "Third Term Doubts Overshadow Benin Legislative Vote," *Reuters,* April 22, 2015, https://jp.reuters.com/article/benin-politics-idAFL5N0XJ4TO20150422.

77. While Yayi ran as an independent, the Cowry Forces supported him in the legislature. See "Benin Votes in Key Test for President Boni Yayi," *Agence France Presse*, April 26, 2015; and Albert Trithart, "Mixed Results as Term Limits Put to the Vote on Africa's 'Super Sunday,'" *IPI Global Observatory*, March 28, 2016.

78. Tyson Roberts, "Here's Why Benin's Election Was a Step Forward for African Democratic Consolidation. And Why It Wasn't," *The Washington Post*, March 22, 2016.

79. Freedom House, "Freedom in the World 2019: Benin," https://freedomhouse.org/country/benin/freedom-world/2019; Virgile Ahissou, "African Court Slams Benin's Treatment of 'Chicken King' Ajavon," *Bloomberg.com*, March 30, 2019, https://www.bloomberg.com/news/articles/2019-03-30/african-court-slams-benin-s-treatment-of-chicken-king-ajavon.

80. Freedom House, "Freedom in the World 2019: Benin"; Ahissou, "African Court," 2019.

81. "Benin MPs Adopt New Electoral Law," *BBC Monitoring Africa*, September 4, 2018.

6

The Puzzle of Timor-Leste

Nancy Bermeo

When Timor-Leste voted for independence in 1999, the deck seemed stacked against successful democracy.* The nation had a miniscule middle class, over 40 percent of the population lived on less than 55 cents per day (UNDP 2002), fewer than 50 percent were literate (Millo and Barnett 2004), and life expectancy was only forty-eight years (Karatnycky 2002). Only seventeen countries on the planet had worse human development indicators (Harris and Goldsmith 2011). When it held its first national elections in 2002, Timor-Leste's GDP per capita was distressingly distant from the average for other nominally consolidated democracies. Figure 6.1 illustrates this using a seventeen-year threshold for consolidation (Svolik 2015, 717). Seen in the light of the vast literature linking democracy's longevity to economic development, Timor-Leste was the quintessential outlier.

Social homogeneity is thought to advantage new democracies, but Timor-Leste seemed disadvantaged on this dimension as well. Area specialists pointed to at least thirty ethnic or tribal groups (Anderson 2001), sixteen different languages, multiple dialects, and an East–West regional divide (Palmer and McWilliams 2018). Observers saw it as "not one place but many" (Shiosaki 2017, 55).

These socio-structural obstacles combined with historical factors that might work against success. First, the continued presence of strong and legitimate traditional authorities at the village level could pose a challenging counterforce to democratically elected leaders (McWilliams 2008; Swenson 2018). Second, the nation lacked any previous experience with a working democracy. Quite the contrary, when the fall of the Portuguese dictatorship made independence possible in 1974, many local elites believed that "society was ill-prepared . . . to engage in political activity" and that the few political organizations that existed were merely "small cells" operating "in ignorance of one another" (CAVR 2005, 14, 23). The movements for national liberation that had emerged in Portugal's African colonies had never emerged. To make matters worse, the country's tentative steps toward a democratic transition in 1975 had ended in a bloody internal war between inchoate political parties. This armed struggle was quickly followed by an invasion from Indonesia and then a brutal, twenty-four-year separatist war.

Nancy Bermeo, *The Puzzle of Timor-Leste* In: *Democracy in Hard Places*. Edited by: Scott Mainwaring and Tarek Masoud, Oxford University Press. © Oxford University Press 2022. DOI: 10.1093/oso/9780197598757.003.0006

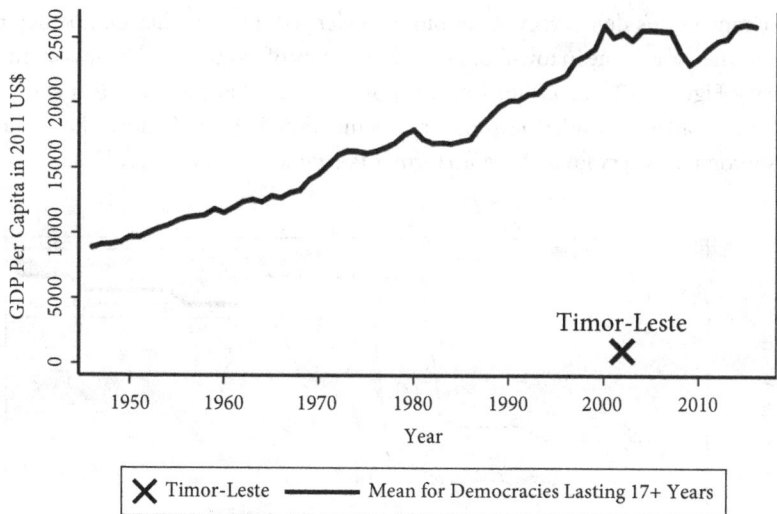

Figure 6.1. Transition year GDP vs. mean for existing democracies, 1945–2015
Sources: Bolt et al. (2018) and Marshall and Jaggers (2018)

Timor-Leste's watershed wars produced a third raft of factors that might undercut democratic success. Demobilized troops have often been harmful in new democracies (Lyons 2004), and Timor-Leste's democracy would have to be built as thousands of "demobilized" troops re-entered a ruined economy with arms in hand. Relatedly, the devastation wrought by decades of violence meant that Timor-Leste would be creating a new democracy not simply in a new state but in a weak and "mendicant state" (Shoesmith 2003, 234). Finally, FRETILIN, the largest and most visible party associated with the new nation's wars, had strong historical ties with FRELIMO, the party that led what many deemed a hybrid regime in Mozambique. This led observers to predict that if a lasting electoral democracy emerged in Timor-Leste at all, it would very likely be a one-party-dominant system.

Surprising Success

Despite the long litany of liabilities listed above, Timor-Leste has maintained a democracy of surprising durability. The democratic regime that emerged amid so much uncertainty in 2001–02, is still in place some twenty years later. Profound challenges remain but, if Milan Svolik (2015) is correct in predicting that democracies that survive this long have a breakdown risk of only one in two hundred, Timor-Leste has already crossed a meaningful threshold.

Timor-Leste's democracy is seriously challenged, but whether democracy remains the "only game in town" or not, the longevity of its current regime is extraordinary. Figures 6.2 and 6.3 illustrate the point, using a Polity Score of 6 or above as the threshold for considering a country a democracy. Figure 6.2 shows that Timor-Leste compares very favorably with former Portuguese colonies in Africa.

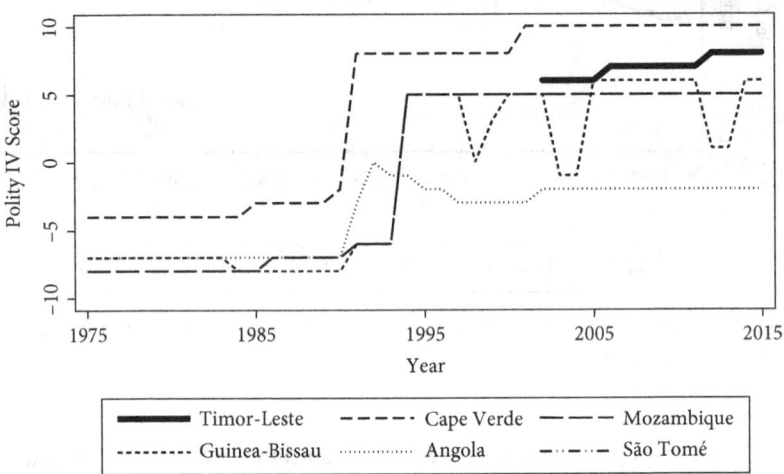

Figure 6.2. Polity scores for former Portuguese colonies, 1975–2015

Source: Marshall, Gurr, and Jaggers 2016

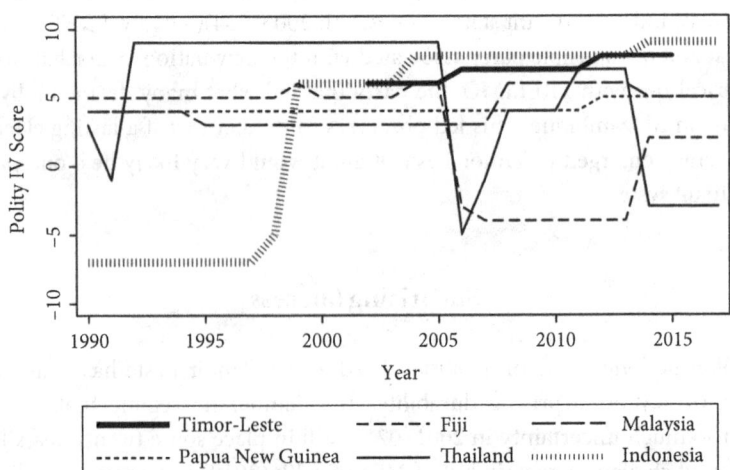

Figure 6.3. Polity scores for post-1989 Asian democracies, 1990–2017

Source: Marshall and Jaggers 2018

Figure 6.3 shows that the durability of Timor-Leste's democracy compares very favorably to many of its Asian neighbors. Even in richer countries, such as Fiji, Malaysia, Papua New Guinea, Sri Lanka, and Thailand, democratic spells have been shorter lived.

Timor-Leste's democracy confounds the common wisdom in terms of quality as well as durability. Figure 6.4 shows how Timor-Leste compares to some of its Asian neighbors on a widely used Civil Liberties Index. Figure 6.5 provides the same case comparison with a widely used Liberal Democracy Index.

Closer case analysis justifies the positive assessments in these large data sets. Knowledgeable observers report that the "country's population is deeply engaged politically" (Aspinall et al. 2018, 155). In fact, voter turnout for national polls has averaged 78 percent since the founding of the nation with only a modest decline over time. This figure matches that of South Korea and compares favorably with those of much richer and more established democracies such as Germany and Norway (IFES 2018). Most important, voters are participating in elections of consistently good quality. Sérgio Vieira de Mello, of the United Nations, deemed Timor-Leste's first elections of a standard which could make "many democratic countries . . . jealous" (King 2003, 751). The 2007 elections actually brought a turnover in power, marking "the emergence of a genuinely competitive multi-party system" (Leach and Kingsbury 2013, 22). The 2012 elections were deemed "a resounding success" (Shiosaki 2017, 61–62), and the 2017 elections brought a remarkable, second turnover in power. Timor-Leste is noted for a "lively public

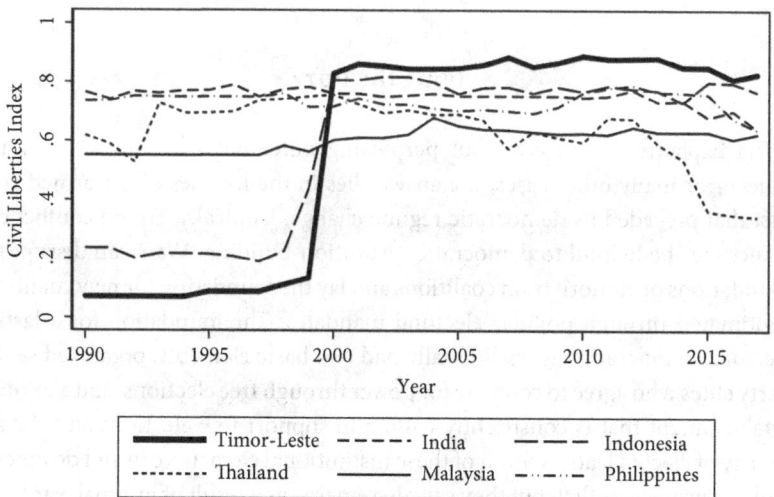

Figure 6.4. Civil liberties for Southeast Asia and India, 1990–2017
Source: Coppedge et al. 2018

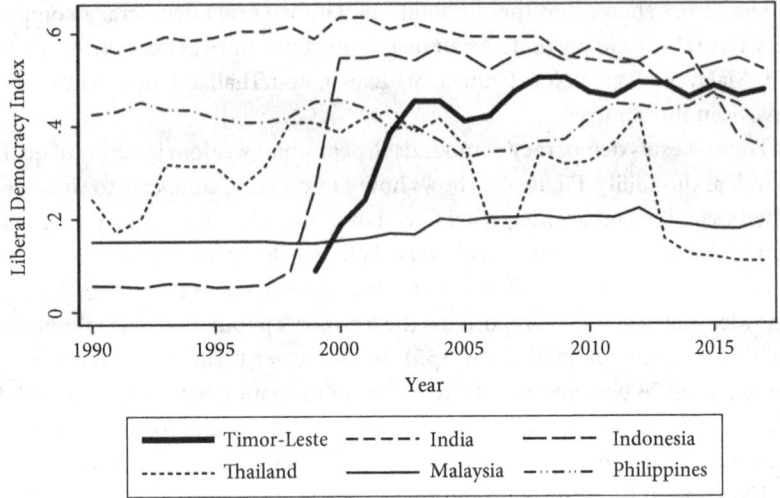

Figure 6.5. Liberal democracy for Southeast Asia and India, 1990–2017
Source: Coppedge et al. 2018

sphere," "vigorous competition among parties," the absence of retail vote buying (Aspinall et al. 2018, 153–54), and the fact that "parties do offer real choices" with "some response to public interest" (Shoesmith 2013, 126). Borrowing Varshney's distinction we can conclude that Timor-Leste's democracy appears both vibrant *and* liberal (2015).

Solving the Puzzle

What explains this positive but perplexing outcome? For Timor-Leste, and indeed for many other cases, the answer lies in the legacies of the armed conflict that preceded its democratic regime change. Ironically, armed conflict can sometimes be helpful to democratic institution-building. Wars can disrupt the foundations of authoritarian coalitions and lay the foundation for new coalitions legitimated through popular electoral mandates. The foundation for a lasting electoral democracy has traditionally had two basic elements: organized sets of party elites who agree to compete for power through free elections, and a military establishment that is consistently willing to support free elections and the authority of elected leaders. Both of these institutional elements can and do emerge without armed conflict, but they can also emerge as a result of internal war.[1]

Of course, internal wars do not always produce changes that are helpful to democracy. The legacies of internal war vary with the nature and outcome of the war itself. Which sorts of war are helpful and which are not? Quantitative analysis of all new democracies emerging between 1946 and 2011 reveals that revolutionary wars have a significant, positive effect on democratic durability; that identity wars, in the aggregate, have no statistically significant effect on durability in either direction; but that a small subset of identity wars appear to produce democracies of notable resilience. Successful separatist wars which simultaneously generate both a new state *and* a new democracy produce highly durable regimes. I call these *breakaway democracies*.[2] They are few in number but relatively resilient, and Timor-Leste is one of these.[3]

The Kaplan-Meir Plot in Figure 6.6 shows the survival probabilities of new democracies with various conflict histories.

These patterns derive, in large part, from the divergent effects that different sorts of conflict have on political parties and military institutions. Revolutionary wars are fought for "*the* people," a group without fixed boundaries. Identity wars are fought for "*a* people" instead. Though identities are certainly malleable, the relatively fixed social boundaries so often reinforced by identity wars can complicate the creation of inclusive, and therefore viable, political party systems. They can also complicate the creation of inclusive and non-interventionist armed forces. Breakaway democracies have three advantages which make them better able to cope with these complications. First, the act of warring with the "rump" state can build new solidarities across divisions that were problematic before the separatist victory. Second, the act of separation itself typically produces more

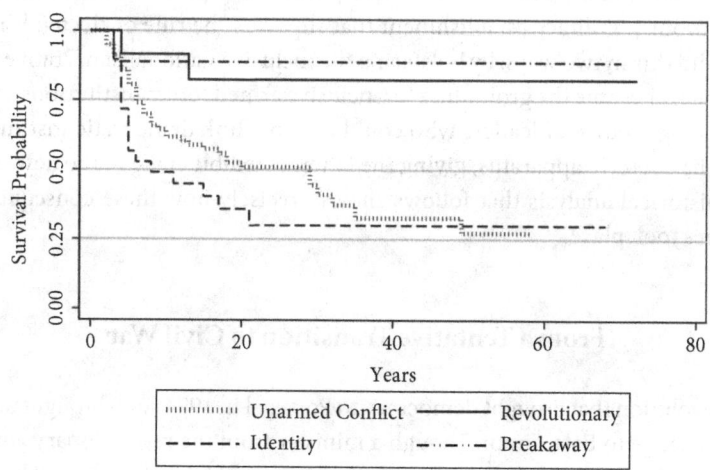

Figure 6.6. Conflict history and democratic durability, Kaplan–Meier Plot

Sources: Boix-Miller-Rosato (BMR) dichotomous coding of democracy, 1800–2015; Cederman, Wimmer, and Min 2010; Geddes, Wright, and Frantz 2014; Kalyvas and Balcells 2010; Marshall and Jaggers 2018; Toft 2012; UCDP/PRIO Armed Conflict Dataset.

homogeneous polities. Finally, separation offers the opportunity to custom-craft new institutions to lower the risks of democratic competition.[4]

This is simply a brief summary of a much broader project, but the argument's core and the quantitative evidence that sustains it suggest that the surprising endurance and quality of Timor-Leste's democracy derives, in large part, from the institutional and ideational legacies of the wars that preceded its founding. Historical analysis of the armed struggles that raged between the end of Portuguese colonialism in 1975 and the beginning of Timor-Leste's new democracy in 2002 illustrates these points. A conflict history that included both a brief war with revolutionary elements and a successful separatist war resulting in a new state created the institutional and ideational landscape for a relatively robust democracy.

Together Timor-Leste's wars provoked four major changes that bolstered successful democracy. First, they weakened the forces that undergirded dictatorship by diminishing the ranks of the local actors who had formed the anti-democratic coalition of the past. Second and relatedly, they strengthened an inclusive national identity that not only replaced the diffuse dependency-based identities of the past but also gave rise to a series of inclusive institutions (and mindsets.) Third, the wars reinforced the infrastructure for a competitive party system. They did this by producing a host of heroic leaders who were willing and able to compete successfully in free elections, by creating the infrastructure for several viable party organizations, and by attracting the external resources to make the rewards of democratic competition greater than its risks. Fourth and finally, Timor-Leste's wars produced a professionalized, noninterventionist, military establishment that supports the rule of elected leaders. They did this in two ways: by bolstering the inclusive nationalist narratives that eventually became the grounding for inclusive armed forces institutions and by producing a range of leaders who could credibly link democratic institutions with the coercive apparatus, giving the latter a credible stake in the new order. The historical analysis that follows shows precisely how these consequential changes took place.

From a Tentative Transition to Civil War

The revolution that brought democracy to Portugal in 1974 soon brought unwelcome change to East Timor. Though a minister from the revolutionary government in Lisbon quickly arrived to tell a hopeful crowd that "Timor will be what the majority of people want it to be" (quoted in Dunn 2003, 64–65), the "people" would not get to rule for nearly a quarter of a century. Two bloody wars and a brutal dictatorship intervened.

The trouble to come was not immediately apparent. As soon as the Portuguese eased restrictions on associational life, local elites established three proto-parties representing a credible spectrum of ideologies. The Timorese Democratic Union (UDT) was founded by Catholic professionals and *assimilados*, many of whom were plantation owners and senior officials in the Portuguese colonial administration (Hicks 2016). The party was divided between a centrist, liberal wing represented by Mário Viegas Carrascalão and an ultraconservative, fiercely anticommunist wing led by Francisco Lopes da Cruz.

The Timorese Social Democratic Association (ASDT) situated itself on the UDT's left. Its founders were similar to the UDT's founders in terms of social background, and they too worked in government service, but they tended to be less senior and, often, teachers. Like the UDT, the party embraced a range of ideologies. A center-left group was led by Xavier do Amaral, a progressive Catholic who had studied theology in Macau. A more radical leftist group was led by Mari Alkatiri, who had studied topography in Angola, made contact with the MPLA, and become a Marxist (Magalhães et al. 2007). Though the election of Xavier do Amaral as president suggested that moderate forces in the party were probably numerically dominant, by September 1974 the more radical wing of the party changed the organization's name to the Revolutionary Front for an Independent East Timor (FRETILIN) and revised its official program to focus much more explicitly on a social revolutionary agenda.

The third party to be founded was the Popular Democratic Association of Timor (APODETI). Its founding President, Arnaldo dos Reis Araújo, was a cattle baron, but its organizers included landowners in other sectors, leaders of the sizable Arab community in Dili, and a number of *liurai* (local chiefs), who feared that free party competition and an independent state would erode their considerable power. Despite the social diversity of its founders, APODETI was more ideologically homogeneous than its competition: the group was fiercely anticommunist and single-minded about the goal of integration with Indonesia. In fact, the party's original name was the Association for the Integration of Timor in Indonesia (AITI) (Hicks 2016).

APODETI's focus on making Timor-Leste part of Indonesia was emblematic of a major obstacle to a successful democratic transition. At both the elite and the mass level, the people of Timor-Leste lacked a consistent and encompassing vision of national identity. They thus lacked the sense of national unity that Rustow (1970) and others have found essential for viable democracy. Ambivalence about nationhood was not confined to one party. A traditionalist, monarchist party called KOTA sought fusion with Indonesia too, and another, smaller party sought integration with Australia. Along with the small Labour Party, the UDT initially sought federation with Portugal. Even FRETILIN, which had sought independence from its inception, initially envisioned a gradual separation process. Benedict Anderson noted an "unsureness of identity" among "East Timorese leaders" and concluded that in 1974–75 "true East Timor nationalism was still quite thin on the ground" (2001, 237).

Unsettled national identity soon mixed with rabid anti-communism to turn an incipient party system into a theater for civil war. Haunted by the possibility of independence under a FRETILIN government, Indonesian security forces and APODETI leaders convinced right-wing anti-communists in the UDT that FRETILIN would soon use Chinese arms and Vietnamese support troops to turn Timor-Leste into a communist regime (Jardine 1999). After meeting with a group of Indonesian generals, the ultraconservative president of the UDT, Lopes da Cruz, joined forces with APODETI and launched a coordinated, armed action throughout the country on August 11, 1975 (CAVR 2005). The pro-Indonesian forces lacked discipline and often executed FRETILIN supporters on the spot (Dunn 2003), but FRETILIN's ranks grew quickly. It offered fierce resistance and swiftly drove the Indonesian-backed coalition into West Timor. Though this first war lasted less than two months, it killed between 1,500 and 3,000 people and displaced more than 20,000 others (Hicks 2016; Taylor 1999).

The brief but brutal war left lessons in several quarters. Ordinary people were "profoundly traumatized by the partisan conflict of 1975" and were left "deeply apprehensive" about the reemergence of cross-party violence (Ingram 2018, 369). Party leaders in both the UDT and FRETILIN recognized the chaos unleashed by armed men on both sides and openly admitted that they had "lost control of the situation" (CAVR 2005, 31–40). Recognizing that the UDT had politicized the upper ranks of the (still) colonial military and that FRETILIN had politicized enlisted men, many East Timorese civilians and soldiers came to recognize the danger of partisan division of the armed forces (CAVR 2005). Finally, pivotal party leaders used the lessons of war to highlight the need for inclusive nationalism: when he was inaugurated president of the FRETILIN government in the war's aftermath, Francisco Xavier do Amaral affirmed, "After more than 400 years of . . . ignorance and massacres, what are we waiting for? . . . *we* have to be the first and the last to resolve our problems. So, from this day on, *we all,* yes, *we all,* will build *our nation, Timor-Leste*" (quoted in CAVR 2005, 56; emphasis added).

Tragically, the Indonesian government was already launching a military invasion as these words were being spoken. Amaral's presidency would last only ten days while the occupation, and the war against it, would last over twenty-four years. This second, very long, separatist war would reinforce the lessons emerging from the civil war and leave additional legacies that eventually advantaged the new nation's new democracy.

The Democratizing Effects of the Separatist War

Being notoriously well armed, decidedly wealthier and much larger, Indonesia expected a quick victory. It never came. The armed and unarmed supporters of the resistance proved surprisingly resilient. FALINTIL, FRETILIN's armed wing, was nearly obliterated by the end of 1978, and defeat looked imminent as five central committee members surrendered and FRETILIN president, Nicolau Lobato, was shot dead. Yet the resistance fought on. In June 1980, FALINTIL even managed an attack on the capital, Dili, "to show the world" that FRETILIN still existed (CAVR 2005, 90). Though a notoriously brutal Indonesian officer boasted in 1983 that his forces had reduced the resistance to "five hundred members" with "one hundred weapons" (quoted in Kammen 2009, 73), the Indonesians initiated a cease-fire in the same year. The costs of containing the resistance through armed force were beginning to strain Indonesia's dictatorship.

The resistance raised costs further by changing tactics. FALINTIL reorganized into small, mobile guerrilla units. Meanwhile, resistance leaders began to invest more in both clandestine work at home and diplomacy abroad (Robinson 2010). Violence continued until 2001, but the course of the war eventually brought changes that would be helpful to Timor-Leste's new democracy.

Weakening the Anti-Democratic Coalition

The first change involved diminishing the power and ranks of the actors who had poisoned party politics in 1974–75. Property owners helped derail democracy in the mid-1970s, but the occupation benefited very few of them. Quite the contrary, landowning families were often targets of individual greed as local stooges of the Indonesian military seized plantations (Kammen 2015). Coffee planters, sandalwood producers, and other agriculturalists were forced to sell their products at low prices when Indonesian military officers established commercial monopolies in the vacuum created by their slaughter of ethnic Chinese (Dunn 2003; Jardine 1999). Ironically, the anti-democratic coalition built around the fear of communist expropriation found many of its members subject to expropriation from ardent *anti*-communists. As Figure 6.7 illustrates, property rights were abysmally weak until after democracy was established.

The Special Forces Command sent to "preserve order" in Timor-Leste treated the province as "their special property" (Dunn 2003, 299–300), making the province "a virtual fiefdom" (Aspinall and Berger 2001, 1011). As a consequence, an increasing number of aristocratic and mestizo planter families came to play "a leading role in the resistance" (Kammen 2015, 135). The harm done to local property owners explains why even Indonesia's local *development* programs

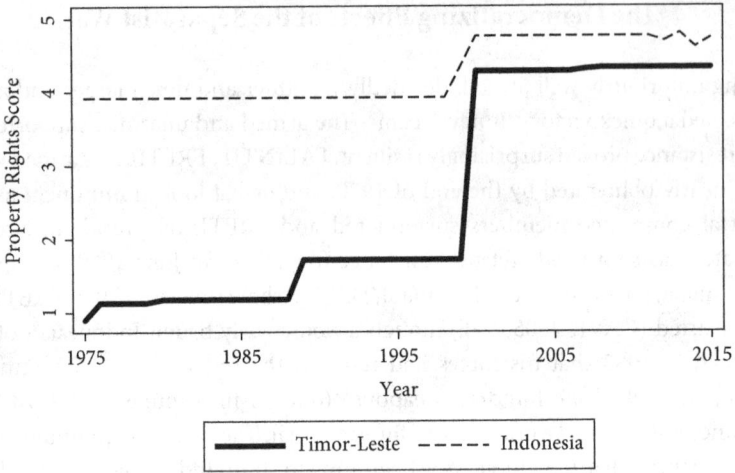

Figure 6.7. Property rights in Timor-Leste vs. Indonesia, 1975–2015
Source: Coppedge et al. 2018

backfired and eventually "encouraged the emergence of a 'nationalist conscious-ness'" (Mendes 2005, 205; my translation).

The nature of wartime violence weakened the foundations of the authoritarian party coalition as well. The Indonesian Army used indiscriminate violence—often killing APODETI and UDT supporters in their homes and in the streets—especially in the early weeks of the invasion. This and the military's engagement in extensive robbery and rape produced a sharp decline in popular support for in-tegration as early as 1976 (Dunn 2003). After the slaughter of university students in the Santa Cruz Cemetery in 1991, insiders report that "Apodeti people started to side with the resistance" *en masse* and that the organization began "to drown" as a party (Anderson, Djati, and Kammen 2003, 21).

The UDT was shaken too as members scrambled to distance themselves from the dictatorship. A number of party members were so revolted by the af-termath of invasion and annexation that they attempted a coup in April 1976. João Carrascalão, who had led the armed Anti-Communist Movement against FRETILIN in 1975, soon became a prominent organizer for the resistance in Australia, even aligning with FRETILIN activists (Durand 2016). Another UDT founder, Mário Carrascalão, served as the Indonesian-appointed governor of Timor-Leste but met with FRETILIN leaders several times, framed himself as part of the resistance in 1983, and openly joined the broad resistance front in 1988 (Fernandes 2011).

The Catholic Church was never part of the dictatorial coalition but any officials who might have sympathized were soon silenced by the overwhelming support the local church gave to the resistance and to FRETILIN's sympathizers specifically. The local church was no longer "a bastion of the Portuguese colonial system" (CAVR 2005, 93). From the war's beginning it served as a "sanctuary" for ordinary people, a "vital link to the outside world" (ibid.) and a bridge between legality and clandestinity for the opposition (ibid., 99–104).

The enlisted men who were conscripted into what became the Indonesian-led army constituted a final coalition group that changed during the war. As the conflict wore on, hundreds of Timorese deserted Indonesian battalions with their weapons in hand and joined the resistance instead. As the occupation army's brutality grew, thousands went into hiding to avoid conscription altogether (Dunn 2003).

Strengthening National Identity

Changes in group behavior were intimately tied to the fact that war strengthened a sense of national identity. Years of lonely struggle against Indonesian annexation gave the people of Timor-Leste a strong sense of who they were and who they were not. The "different visions of East Timorese nationalism" that were problematic in 1975 were largely "subsumed" by the resistance struggle itself and gave rise to a national identity that was independent but also inclusive (Aspinall and Berger 2001, 1012). Annexation and the war against it made the "colonized" more aware of their commonalities and their ability to "emancipate themselves" by working in concert (Anderson et al. 2003). The "'occupied-occupier' binary . . . [still] frames national identity today" (Arthur 2019, 10), trumping alternative identities based on ethnicity, religion, language and, to lesser extent, region. As FRETILIN leader Mari Alkatiri himself put it, "national cohesion was built upon opposition to the occupant" (quoted in Shoesmith 2003, 242–43).

Invasion opponents within the local clergy provided key mechanisms for brokering cohesion and for bolstering inclusivity. They were uniquely suited to do so because (regardless of party) "almost all" of the political leaders who spanned the period from 1974 through the occupation had studied in the same Jesuit schools (Cristalis 2009, 23), and even Alkatiri, a Muslim, had published political criticism in the local Jesuit magazine. Local clerics drew on these long-standing networks to initiate dialogue and cooperation across party boundaries. In 1982, for example, the highest Catholic official in the province met secretly with FALINTIL's leader, Xanana Gusmão, to highlight both "the need for national unity" and "his understanding of the Resistance" as a purely "nationalist" rather than a leftist struggle (CAVR 2005, 97–98). The following year, a priest who had invited Gusmão to speak in his church accompanied him to a meeting with Mário Carrascalão, the Indonesian-appointed governor.

The role of the local church as a mechanism for creating a national identity extended beyond elites. Benedict Anderson argues that "a popular Catholicism . . . emerged as an expression of a common suffering, just as it did in nineteenth-century Ireland" and that the emphasis on "commonality" became a substitute "for the kind of nationalism . . . which comes from print-capitalism" (Anderson 2001, 238).

The fact that the local church chose Tetum as the language of the liturgy (deliberately eschewing both Indonesian and Portuguese) had "profoundly nationalizing effects" (Anderson 2001, 238). These connections between war, language, and identity construction were obvious to FRETILIN leader José Ramos-Horta years before he and Bishop Carlos Belo would win a Nobel Prize for their role in the resistance:

> Independence is now the desire of everyone, including those who had illusions . . . years ago. . . . Indonesia's efforts to "pacify" us have failed, as have the attempts to destroy Timorese cultural identity. Throughout the country . . . there is a tremendous cultural movement. . . . The Tetum language, which was once spoken by slightly over 50% of the population, is now used by everyone and has gained tremendous strength and vitality. (Ramos-Horta 1987, 205)

Despite the role that Catholic clerics played in the strengthening of Timor-Leste's national identity, the identity itself was not religiously exclusive. To the contrary, the war of liberation gave rise to what Tudor and Slater call "inclusive nationalism," a form of nationalism that explicitly challenges "colonial practices of divide and rule" and instead serves to mobilize "active, direct support across class . . . ethnic and religious divisions" (Tudor and Slater 2016, 28–29). This is one of the second war's most important legacies. As Tudor and Slater have shown convincingly, inclusive nationalism has been a powerful "source of democratic strength" in countries such as India (and later, Indonesia) where democracy developed against the odds (Tudor and Slater 2016, 28; Tudor 2013).

National identity in Timor-Leste draws on the highly inclusive concept of *Mauberism*, an identity frame that began to develop in the last years of Portuguese colonialism. *Mauberism* glorifies an indigenous "brotherhood" united in suffering from external oppression but elevated by ancient traditions of "self-rule" (Myrttinen 2013, 214), fearlessness, "cooperation[,] and consensus" (Cristalis 2009, 24). The celebration of *Maubere* identity enabled FRETILIN, and later, the resistance as a whole, to "Timorize the idea of 'the people' (in a nationalist sense)" (Shoesmith 2003, 239).

In keeping with the prototype of "inclusive nationalism," diversity is intrinsic to the definition of who "the people" of Timor-Leste are. In 1986 Gusmão himself wrote that independence was "the only path" for the "preservation of the *identities* that distinguish our people" (Niner 2000, 124). Specialists observe "a national identity that preserves and promotes cultural diversity" (Sousa 2001,194); "a strong sense of aggregated nativeness that infuses [various]Timorese identities with a sense of unity" (Palmer and McWilliams 2018); and a "general and diffuse nationalism" in which "diversity" is not only a key component "of identity" but of "national dignity" as well (Sousa 2001, 193–94).

The new inclusive nationalism emerging from war explains why—despite deadly intimidation—nearly 80 percent of the people of Timor-Leste chose independence over autonomy when they were finally allowed to vote on the issue in 1999. Timor-Leste's second war had eroded and subsumed the divisions that facilitated its first war, and had given rise to an inclusive nationalism instead.

Bolstering a Competitive Party System

In addition to bolstering inclusive nationalism, separatist war produced the leaders and organizations essential to a competitive party system. By the time of independence, Timor-Leste had a broad array of leaders who were willing and able to win free elections. Some emerged on the battlefield, others in the exile community. Still others emerged in the arenas the occupiers established as means of control: including the sham local government institutions and the expanded student community. Each leader became visible as a result of the challenges and tactical conflicts inherent in waging a decades-long resistance war—and each became associated with a party organization as Timor-Leste's new democracy developed. Thus, by the time of its founding elections in 2002, the cores of several competitive parties had developed in Timor-Leste, producing a party system that was balanced enough to avoid single-party domination.

FRETILIN was Timor-Leste's most visible party as its founding elections approached, and the nature of the war explains why. FRETILIN managed to confine the invasion force to only 30 percent of the province for over two years, and used liberated zones to expand its base, not just by keeping people alive but by promoting literacy, agricultural cooperatives, healthcare, and participatory democracy (Capizzi et al. 1976; CAVR 2005; Taylor 1999). Its "great strength . . . was to never use violence against civilians" (Durand 2016, 119).

The resistance was harboring some 450,000 civilians when Indonesia closed in on the liberated zones (Durand 2016). But the experience of governance had already ensured FRETILIN "support in most regions" (Taylor 1999, 96) and forced party cadres to bureaucratize and gain administrative skills.

Later watershed moments of the war worked to FRETILIN's advantage as well. When the Indonesians interned over 300,000 civilians to cut resistance support (CAVR 2005), FRETILIN exploited the camps to recruit even more (Budiarjo and Liong 1984). When the occupiers called a cease-fire after recruiting locals into the Indonesian Army, FRETILIN successfully lobbied recruits to defect in droves (Kammen 2009). When the death toll for men skyrocketed, FRETILIN recruited women (Loney 2018; Niner 2015).

These wartime successes help explain why FRETILIN leaders were willing to compete in fair elections. As a militant told an interviewer in 1992, "politically, we [have] won" already (Jardine 1999, 75). Positive prognostications were appropriate. FRETILIN won the new nation's founding elections with 59 percent of the vote, but it did not become a hegemonic party because war had helped produce powerful electoral alternatives.

A first set of alternatives emerged from within FRETILIN itself. This is because a long and intense struggle with a better-armed power inevitably raises tactical dilemmas. Different leaders responded differently to a range of dilemmas and in so doing laid the foundation for different organizations.

The first fissure with organizational consequences involved Xavier do Amaral, FRETILIN's founding president. Recognizing that Indonesia's 1977–79 encirclement campaign would inevitably kill thousands of innocent civilians under FRETILIN "protection," Amaral led a group back to his home region and began to negotiate a local truce. Other FRETILIN leaders declared this treasonous and had him arrested (Taylor 1999). When the war ended, he organized the ASDT, an alternative party attracting strong support in his home region, and among "older . . . revolutionaries who had grown disillusioned with FRETILIN" (King 2003, 754).

A second, more powerful party grouping emerged from tactical changes initiated by Xanana Gusmão, the charismatic head of FALINTIL. His eyewitness experience of the war gave him a vision that many exiled FRETILIN leaders did not share. It was a more pluralist, more inclusive vision of both the resistance and the regime that should emerge after victory.

Beginning in 1983, he insisted that FRETILIN "must mobilize people who [seek] an Independent Country," regardless of their ideology, and that the UDT and FRETILIN should consider "a course of National Unity" to secure independence and peace (quoted in Kammen 2009, 87).

In December 1987, he rejected Marxist revolution altogether and made his commitment to democracy explicit in a seminal speech that was taped and shared worldwide (Weldemichael 2013). He stated clearly, "We have come to recognize through these long years that what inspires the people of East Timor to struggle is not the making of the revolution . . . [but the desire] to liberate the Homeland . . .and . . . to live freely and independently. . . . I publicly declare my total and wholehearted rejection of those doctrines that promote suppression of democratic freedoms in East Timor" (Niner 2000, 134–35). In a further effort to signal his inclusive approach, Gusmão resigned from the party and declared FALINTIL "a national army" officially separate from FRETILIN (Niner 2000, 131–35).

Gusmão's turnabout met with fierce condemnation from party leaders, but his charismatic authority could not be challenged. His success in founding an inclusive resistance coalition in 1988 meant that FRETILIN was no longer "*the* party of the resistance" (Weldemichael 2013, 203) and that the war would leave multiple heroes and multiple organizations in its wake. By 2007, a party founded by Gusmão, the CNRT, would win control of government through the nation's second parliamentary elections.[5]

The war of resistance had effects on actors outside of FRETILIN as well, and thus left still other party organizations in its wake. These represented a broad range of ideologies. The Social Democrat Party (PSD) was founded by Mário Carrascalão, who drew on his visibility as provincial governor and then resistance-front activist to create what became FRETILIN's major opponent on the right and represent the type of reformed conservative party that Dan Ziblatt has convincingly associated with stable democratic trajectories in Europe (Ziblatt 2017). A resurrected and reformed UDT, led by João Carrascalão, served the same purpose in representing a moderate but unambiguously democratic center-right (Shoesmith 2013). Both parties emerged from a strengthened sense of national identity and the deep disillusionment brought on by war with an authoritarian occupier (Anderson et al. 2003).

Another competitive party that emerged as a direct result of Timor-Leste's conflict history is the center-left Democratic Party (PD). The PD was founded by Fernando de Araújo, the heroic and (once imprisoned) leader of RENETIL—a student resistance movement that began among East Timorese students in Indonesia. Although the PD came into being less than three months before the founding elections, it polled remarkably well, garnering 8.7 percent of the vote nationwide. It drew (and draws) its support from the younger cohort of the resistance who worked in common cause with FALINTIL "to make the territory ungovernable" (Leach 2016). Many had shown themselves "ready to risk the wrath of a ruthless military" in demonstrations and clandestine activities of great consequence (Dunn 2003, 297). All were alienated by FRETILIN's exiles whom they "perceived as arrogant, privileged, and authoritarian" and likely to claim a disproportionate share of power and employment (King 2003, 755). Suspicious of the Marxist exile group that had come to be known as "the Maputo clique" (Croissant 2008, 656), the PD, like other new parties, was born of the strengthened national identity and commitment to democracy that emerged as a legacy of war with an authoritarian occupier (Myrttinen 2013). The breadth and strength of the parties emerging in the wake of the separatist war led to a party system that was not simply viable but diverse and competitive.

Producing a Noninterventionist Military

The nature of Timor-Leste's wars had profound effects on its armed forces as well as its political parties, producing a professionalized, noninterventionist military that has also been essential to democratic durability. The positive outcome was not inevitable. The civil war, the Indonesian invasion, and the war that followed left a regional division within the coercive apparatus that caused a serious security crisis in 2006 and might have reversed democratization altogether. However, the inclusive nationalist ideology strengthened by the war plus a series of inclusive institutions associated with the resistance helped resolve the crisis and even dampen regional divisions (Bexley and Tchailoro 2013; Braithwaite et al. 2012).

The professional and noninterventionist nature of Timor-Leste's military has long been recognized. The military was seen as "unthreatening" when democracy first began (Smith 2004, 157) and is still generally viewed as "an instrument rather than an actor in politics" (Mietzner 2012, 13; see also Croissant and Kuehn 2009). The fact that a military coup has never even been *attempted* in Timor-Leste bears this out and sets the case apart from several of its Asian neighbors.

There can be little doubt that the professionalization and the political neutrality of Timor-Leste's military emerged as a result of conflict history and that both qualities were widely recognized before the nation's founding elections. FALINTIL's prestige as a professional fighting force began with its role as the triumphant underdog in the 1975 civil war (CAVR 2005), but its warriors were elevated to truly heroic status during the war of resistance as participants in a "David-and-Goliath battle" (Cristalis 2009, 4).

The elevated image of the armed forces was easily joined to the image of being "above politics" among locals, but the professionalism of the armed forces was obvious to outsiders as well (Robinson 2010, 146–47). Military officers from abroad assessed FALINTIL as decidedly "more professional" than its (better funded and US-trained) Indonesian counterpart even before the democratic transition formally began (ibid.). FALINTIL's "extraordinary discipline" (Dunn 2003, 297) and exemplary behavior in the face of horrid provocations from anti-independence militias in the aftermath of the referendum confirmed its professional image further (Ballard 2008; Robinson 2010).

The armed forces' nonpartisan stance, like the array of political parties described above, was very much a product of changes occurring during the course of the resistance war. Though FALINTIL was founded as the armed wing of FRETILIN, it eventually operated with extraordinary "organizational autonomy" from the party (Sindre 2016, 504). Autonomy was a necessity at first. Many FRETILIN leaders were killed as the war began, and the distance of the exiled party leadership from the war itself diminished their influence considerably (Weldemichael 2013), leading, as one exile recalls, to nearly "total silence" until after 1982 (Gama 1995, 102). But FALINTIL's autonomy from FRETILIN was due to ideas too. Gusmão's decision to broaden the resistance coalition made it essential that FALINTIL was "rebadged as a non-partisan nationalist army" (Ingram 2018, 368), and the move worked. FALINTIL was effectively and permanently separated from FRETILIN control (Shoesmith 2013).

There was certainly a strategic rationale for the separation: since FALINTIL was fighting a guerrilla war without "any significant external funding" (Morjé Howard 2008, 263) the broadening of its domestic resource base was essential to its survival, but Gusmão laid out detailed ideological reasons for the separation as well. In a public letter he insisted that FALINTIL would be "outside the party-political game" altogether and dedicated instead "*to the defense of the homeland of everyone*" and to the defense of a constitution that guarantees "individual and collective freedoms and the respect for the interests of *all citizens and social classes in East Timor*" (Niner 2000, 132–33; emphasis added).

As the neutral defender of the freedoms of "all citizens," FALINTIL became an institutional agent of the inclusive nationalism that developed during the war. Unfortunately, its success in this role would be severely tested in 2006, because of wartime legacies that worked against democratization. Prime among these were: the masses of veterans seeking employment in a ruined economy; a police force drawn primarily from the Western region where FRETILIN was least popular; the veterans of an armed group led by Cornelio Gama which had broken away from FALINTIL in 1985 and had aligned with FRETILIN's Interior Minister, Rogério Lobato (Shoesmith 2003); and, finally, the longstanding personal divisions between the new nation's two elected executives, FRETILIN's Prime Minister Mari Alkatiri and President Xanana Gusmão.

These potential fault lines opened wide in the spring of 2006. Though FALINTIL had been transformed into the national armed forces and renamed the F-FDTL in 2001, it had been cut dramatically in size. Veterans with seniority were allocated most of the positions in the first battalion formed and, because of the war's geography, they came disproportionally from the east of the country (Boyle 2014). The police force (PNTL) was also restructured, but there mostly westerners were rehired. Eventually, wartime regional and political differences became explosive.

The security crisis erupted after westerners within the F-FDTL signed a public petition charging the military with discrimination and then abandoned their posts after deeming the government response inadequate (United Nations 2006). Though protests were peaceful at first, after several hundred men were dismissed, deadly riots led by Gama, a police major named Alfredo Reinado, and others mobilizing regional animosities spread throughout the country. As the death toll rose, the government invited troops from Australia, New Zealand, Malaysia, and Portugal to help restore order. The prime minister was forced to resign but was replaced lawfully by Nobel laureate José Ramos-Horta. The nation held free and fair elections for a new government as scheduled and produced a peaceful transfer of power.

Timor-Leste's democracy survived its security crisis through the skillful use of inclusivity. Four mechanisms stand out as important. The first is the semi-presidential system adopted from Portugal (which served as a key geographic base for the exiled resistance and a center for institutional diffusion). Semi-presidentialism allowed one major leader to check the inadequacy of another while giving two sets of citizens representation in the new nation's executive (Feijó 2016).

Gusmão used an inclusive executive institution to democracy's advantage, but the skillful use of inclusivity extended to the party system too. Several of the potentially "anti-system" movements that were problematic during the first elected government were successfully integrated into the party system during the second. Some movement leaders joined the Social Democratic Party, others joined the Democratic Party, and still others formed new parties such as UNDERTIM (which, despite its leaders' previous hostility to Gusmão, was invited to join the ruling coalition). Timor-Leste's party system has thus far managed to absorb potentially disruptive movement activity and thus meet one of the major challenges for new democracies (Bermeo and Yashar 2016b).

A third inclusive means of coping with the divisions provoking the crisis involved the creation of institutions in which the police and the military work together. In a peacetime version of the coalition formation developed during the resistance war, a joint military-police command has been established in the hope that "collaboration" will enable the "reconciliation of previous enmities" (Wilson 2012, 193). Though the fusion of functions under control of the military contradicted the advice of foreign actors, it has become a point of "nationalistic pride" (ibid.). It accompanies a whole series of public gestures in which governing elites use the wartime experience as a means of strengthening common bonds—such as having conflict protagonists sign a highly publicized "peace agreement" and involving previously warring groups in "peace demonstrations" to commemorate the Santa Cruz massacre (Scambary 2011).

Finally, the national budget was used inclusively as well. Gusmão might have used solely punitive measures against those who mobilized against "Xanana's Boys" in 2006, but he organized a series of highly inclusive grants and pension programs instead—and these too have been widely credited for dampening disorder (Kingsbury 2014; Roll 2014).

Ironically, the emergence and resolution of the crisis may enable the armed forces to be even more supportive of democracy in the future. Security scholars note that "the crisis led to an improvement in East Timor's security outlook" (Tansey 2009, 107), that "institutional rivalries between the police and the army . . . [have] receded," that "regionalist . . . divisions" have "virtu-ally disappeared," and that coups are "unlikely" because civilian leadership enjoys "charismatic authority" throughout the senior ranks of the defense forces (MacQueen 2015a, 763; see also Harris and O'Neil 2011).

It is noteworthy that even at the height of the crisis, no viable coup coalition emerged within the military. This provides a convincing illustration of the lasting "acceptance for civilian supremacy" among the nation's armed forces (Kammen 2011, 127). Specialists argue that this acceptance stems from the early Marxist-Leninist orientation of the resistance movement (Scambary 2011). But the ac-ceptance of *elected* civilian authority is likely to have come from a later period when the armed resistance embraced democracy instead. Over time, the accept-ance of elected civilian authority was reinforced by other factors too. First, the example of military rule furnished by the Indonesians provided no grounds for emulation—quite the opposite.[6] Second, the heroic status that the armed forces enjoyed among citizens and politicians alike made it unlikely that democratic institutions would ignore the organization's needs. Finally, the fact that military heroes have often been elected to high office means that the armed forces cur-rently have easy access to power and thus, no need to seize it unlawfully.

Alternative Hypotheses

Clearly, the legacies of Timor-Leste's wars have contributed to democratic dura-bility in important ways. But before concluding, it is useful to weigh two alterna-tive explanations for success.

A first involves oil and gas revenue from the seabed between the island of Timor and Australia.[7] Timor-Leste has indeed benefited from natural resource income in a variety of ways. Its use in the funding of the veterans' pension system is a case in point (Roll 2018).[8] Yet it would be wrong to accord this revenue de-cisive weight in determining democratic success. After all, a great deal of careful scholarship finds that the connection between oil revenue and lasting democracy is strongly negative (Ahmadov 2014; Aslaksen 2010; Ross 2001). In the specific case of Timor-Leste, oil revenue has sometimes outpaced state spending capacity (Lundahl and Sjöholm 2007), always fallen far short of expectations for job cre-ation, sometimes focused on the needs of imagined tourists rather than those of the overwhelmingly rural population (Nygaard-Christensen 2016), and often fostered communal conflicts (Bovensiepen and Nygaard-Christensen 2018).

Thanks to natural resource revenue, Timor-Leste is now, technically, in the lower band of middle-income countries, but this categorization belies the fact that half the people in Timor-Leste still live below the two-dollar-a-day pov-erty line and that the nation remains among the poorest countries in the world by several measures (Kingsbury 2018). Thus, country experts are right to view Timor-Leste's resource revenue as "both destructive and . . . productive" for political institutions (Bovensiepen and Nygaard-Christensen 2018, 414). It may have sometimes contributed to democracy's durability but was certainly not its sufficient or its principal cause.[9]

A second and seemingly more powerful explanatory hypothesis involves assistance from abroad. International assistance was not just massive but long lasting: the UN spent over $52 million on the 1999 independence referendum and twenty nations deployed 11,000 troops to combat the terror unleashed by Indonesian-led militias in its aftermath. After order was restored, the UN established the United Nations Transitional Administration in East Timor (UNTAET), a costly authority with "the broadest mandate of any peacekeeping mission before or since" (Ingram 2018, 366). It involved 9,150 military personnel, 1,640 police, 1,670 international civilian staff, and nearly 2,000 local staff—all in an area the size of Connecticut (Morjé Howard 2008, 260). Support from abroad continued years after democratic elections began. In fact, the UN did not secure its "metaphorical 'exit visa'" until 2012, after Timor-Leste held its third successful set of legislative elections (MacQueen 2015a, 762).

It is tempting to conclude that the success of Timor-Leste's democratization is due to foreign assistance rather than to the legacies of war, but a closer look at the evidence suggests that this is incorrect. First, we have to recognize that most of the foreign assistance received by Timor-Leste was itself a legacy of war. The massive aid for reconstruction was allocated because war had turned the territory into what a British diplomat aptly described as "hell on earth" (Durand 2016, 173). The massive peacekeeping missions were deployed precisely because the peace had not been kept. In this respect, foreign assistance is not an alternative to my argument but an intrinsic element of it. To the extent that aid had a positive effect, it illustrates the positive consequences of armed conflict.

Yet there are other reasons to reject foreign assistance as the primary explanation for Timor-Leste's success. To start with, quantitative analysis suggests that there is no clear association between foreign assistance and the durability of post-conflict democracies in general. Table 6.1 presents hazard models based on data for all new, post-conflict democracies emerging between 1946 and 2011. Controlling for the major structural, institutional, and regional variables associated with democratic longevity, plus conflict type, we find that the likelihood of breakdown diminishes with GDP, with GDP growth, and (as predicted earlier in this chapter) with a revolutionary conflict history. But we also find that neither aid per capita (models 1–3) nor UN Peacekeeping (models 4–6) has a significant effect in either direction.

Table 6.1. Aid, Peacekeeping, and Democratic Durability

	Model 1	Model 2	Model 3	Model 4	Model 5	Model 6
Aid per capita (SL)	0.145 (0.292)	0.500 (0.326)	0.075 (0.399)			
UN peacekeeping				-0.989 (0.618)	-0.518 (0.695)	-0.448 (0.531)
Revolutionary conflict		-1.655* (0.694)	-1.886** (0.665)		-1.533* (0.657)	-1.894** (0.638)
Identity conflict		0.339 (0.395)	0.389 (0.367)		0.214 (0.402)	0.435 (0.377)
GDP per capita (SL)		-1.973*** (0.353)	-1.829*** (0.550)		-1.863*** (0.368)	-1.750** (0.551)
GDP growth (SL)		-0.308** (0.112)	-0.341** (0.115)		-0.274* (0.107)	-0.322* (0.113)
Trade openness (SL)		1.094* (0.449)	1.097* (0.547)		0.963* (0.459)	1.016 (0.542)
Ethnic fractionalization			0.482** (0.162)			0.459** (0.152)
PR			-0.546 (0.356)			-0.411 (0.414)
Presidentialism			-0.525 (0.315)			-0.539 (0.301)
Region fixed effects	No	No	Yes	No	No	Yes
Country clusters	97	94	94	99	95	95
Number of observations	2,363	2,266	2,266	2,394	2,279	2,279

Note: A country-year was coded as democratic if it scored 6 or above on the Polity IV index. Standard errors were clustered on country. Coefficients estimated from Cox proportional hazards models using the Efron model for ties. Proportional hazard tests at the 0.05 threshold were used to check for Time Varying Covariates. SL indicates a variable is standardized (S) and lagged (L) by 1 year.

$* p < .1; ** p < .05; *** p < .01$

In Timor-Leste specifically, the effects of foreign resources on successful democratization were decidedly mixed. Foreign troops were critical to the restoration of order after the independence referendum and again in 2006–7. This is why Timor-Leste is so frequently cited as an example of successful international intervention (Morjé Howard 2007). But the role of UNTAET and other international assistance bodies in promoting democracy in Timor-Leste is hotly contested. They were deemed by some to be the *cause* of dangerous intra-elite conflict (King 2003) and were sometimes viewed as "profoundly undemocratic" (Caplan 2005, 171) or even "absolutist" themselves (Chopra 2002, 979).

Criticism was not ubiquitous, but the failure of international assistance was sometimes more obvious than its success. The United Nations Mission to East Timor's (UNAMET's) attempt to run the independence referendum in an orderly and secure environment exemplifies the point. Though UNAMET agents were determined to quell regional violence by establishing a watchful presence throughout the territory, running extensive voter education programs, and arranging that only aggregate rather than district referendum results would be reported (Shiosaki 2017), anti-independence paramilitaries killed over 2,000 people anyway. UNAMET's staff and offices became targets themselves, whole villages were razed to the ground, thousands had to flee their homes, and 70 percent of public buildings were destroyed (CAVR 2005). The international community's failure to provide sufficient security, despite "unassailable" evidence that it was desperately needed, left Timor-Leste in even worse condition after the balloting than before (Martin and Mayer-Rieckh 2005).

After independence, the UN's failed attempts at police reform contributed decisively to the 2006–7 security crisis. Though the development of "a credible, professional and impartial police service" was a centerpiece of the UN intervention, its officials made several highly consequential errors along the way (Hood 2006), including relying excessively on the advice of Indonesian police officials, hiring hundreds of inevitably distrusted Indonesian police veterans for the "new" national police force (Arnold 2009), excluding "key stakeholders" (Powles 2015, 212), and failing to consult with the local population in general (Chopra 2002; Hood 2006).

In addition to suffering from "all but non-existent" civilian oversight (Hood 2006), the PNTL had deeply conflictual relations with the national armed forces. These conflicts reflected the widespread perception that the PNTL was controlled by and biased toward people from the western districts and a related perception that the donor community was overfunding the police and underfunding the military (Hood 2006). Though an expert outside evaluation team concluded in 2003 that the UN police program had produced an institution that was both "weak" and "unsustainable" (International Policy Institute 2003, 102), peacekeeping forces were withdrawn in May 2005 anyway. The withdrawal proved "catastrophically premature" (MacQueen 2015b, 692), leading to "crippling chaos" and the greatest political crisis in the new democracy's history thus far (MacQueen 2015a, 765).

Beyond evidence that assistance policies sometimes threatened democratic longevity, there are other reasons to question the relative strength of assistance effects. One of the most powerful relates to sequencing. The extraordinary external resources described above were forthcoming in large part because Timor-Leste's political elites had made a credible commitment to democracy before the transition even got underway. This is one of the reasons why a senior UNTAET official concluded that the new nation offered "conditions for success rarely available" to peace missions elsewhere (Chopra 2000, 28). As Rebecca Strating puts it, democratic values were not "simply imposed on East Timor." A new, "state-based identity . . . formulated around principles of pluralism [and] democracy . . . developed *during* the independence movement" and then "justified and sustained it" (Strating 2016, 3; emphasis mine). Kammen argues, similarly, that the amalgam of new organizations, political discourse, and popular activism that emerged as part of the resistance to the Indonesian occupation constituted "a perverse form of democratization" in itself (Kammen 2015, 159). After independence, foreign advisors "guided institutional design," but institutions "evolved in response to local political drivers" (Ingram 2018, 365).

International efforts to build and protect democracy in Timor-Leste did contribute, in part, to the durability of Timor-Leste's democratic institutions but as a secondary influence. As both Thomas Carothers (1999) and Richard Caplan (2005) have argued, even the most successful democracy-promotion initiatives do not determine political traditions, citizen values, the nature of major political organizations, or the strength of anti-democratic groups. Since these are the political forces that shape the trajectory of new democracies most, the role of foreign assistance is rarely, if ever, determinant.

In sum, democracy in Timor-Leste was locally grown. It was nurtured by foreign actors, but foreign resources did not guarantee either its founding or its durability. A whole host of national heroes had come to embrace democracy during the war of resistance and had started building inclusive pluralist institutions on their own—before international aid was forthcoming. This is why outsiders surveyed the scene in 2002 and concluded that "no" local institutions posed a "serious threat" to democracy (Smith 2004, 157). Oisín Tansey is right to remind us that "all the significant parties . . . were unequivocally pro-democratic" before foreign funded democracy-building began and that Timor-Leste's transition was largely a process driven by local actors in which even the UN eventually "became a minor partner" (Tansey 2009, 68–69).

Conclusion

My explanation for the resilience of Timor-Leste's democracy resonates with many of the conclusions drawn from the other cases in this volume. We see parallels with South Africa, and Benin regarding the decisive role of leaders' perceptions: in Timor-Leste, as in both of these very different cases, democracy emerged and endured, in part, because all of the major political actors had "faith" in their ability to survive under democratic rule. This faith derived from an extreme version of the "authoritarian weakness" that helps explain democracy's resilience in Benin, Ukraine, and elsewhere: resistance leaders in Timor-Leste rightly recognized the profound weakness of the institutions created by the occupation forces and thus had faith that democracy would work to their advantage.

The decisive role played by resistance leaders offers striking parallels with the case of India. In India, as in Timor-Leste, it was emerging and not incumbent elites who mattered most because those who eschewed participation in the independence movement simply could not "be counted as powerful political actors." The "democratic temper" that these emerging elites developed during decades of struggle proved decisive in both cases, as well.

The subject of "democratic temper" brings us to a parallel between Timor-Leste and cases as diverse as Argentina and Indonesia. We see parallels with Argentina in the discrediting of extremism and in the pivotal role of changes in elite "normative preferences." And we see parallels with Indonesia not simply in the inclusive/egalitarian nationalism adopted by key elites but in the very mechanism through which adoption occurred. In Indonesia, as in Timor-Leste, the inclusive form of nationalism that eventually worked to "secure" and "sustain" its 1999 democracy was in part "a product of its revolutionary path to independence" (Chapter 3, this volume). In Timor-Leste, Indonesia, India, and much of Southern Africa, durable democracy emerged not from slow, structural changes but from "extreme political, economic, and ideological crisis" instead (Chapter 4, this volume).

Despite our longing for parsimonious theory, no outcome as important as democratic durability can be attributed to a single explanatory variable, even in a single case. The puzzling longevity of democracy in Timor-Leste is no exception. But durability can be explained through generalizable causal stories, and I have offered one here. In this case (and in many others), the roots of democratic durability lie in conflict-history, that is, in how ideas and institutions changed (or failed to change) during the conflicts that preceded democratization. My argument, like many of the others in this volume, is about the impact of what Slater calls "historical inheritance" (Chapter 3, this volume). As I stated at the outset, armed conflict *per se* does not boost democratic longevity: only certain sorts of conflict-histories have positive effects. New democracies emerging from revolutionary conflicts and new democracies emerging from successful separatist wars are associated with increased durability. It is essential to underscore the fact that separatist conflict is only helpful if it produces a new democracy in a new state. Most separatist conflicts do not produce separate states, and even fewer become democracies when they do.

Timor-Leste's new democracy was disadvantaged by a whole host of structural factors, but because it emerged on the heels of a successful separatist war (with revolutionary beginnings), it was advantaged as well. As the historical analysis presented here illustrates, Timor-Leste's conflict-history left four legacies that undergirded democratic survival. First, it weakened the ranks of the elites and parties that had formed the local anti-democratic coalition. Second, it strengthened a potent and inclusive nationalism that not only replaced the diffuse identities of the past but gave rise to a series of inclusive institutions. Third, it bolstered a competitive party system with genuinely popular leaders who could win free elections. Finally, it produced a professionalized, pro-democratic military.

Most of these changes were wrought during twenty-four years of separatist war. Yet the country's first internal war left prodemocratic legacies as well. Like many revolutionary struggles, it projected a framing of "the people" and "a nation" that was ethnically and religiously inclusive, produced a number of electable heroic figures, strengthened an electable party, and laid the early foundations for a military apparatus that obeyed civilian authority.

***

I am not alone in relating regime durability to particular types of nationalism (Tudor 2013; Tudor and Slater 2016; Varshney 2015), to pro-democratic leaders (Mainwaring and Pérez-Liñán 2013), to strong parties (Riedl 2014), or to supportive militaries (Brownlee et al. 2013; Levitsky and Way 2013; Slater 2020). Each of the collaborators in this project has related regime durability to at least one of these factors, and most have done so in studies of democratic regimes. My findings here contribute to the literature by showing how variables used by others in very different cases help explain both a failed and a successful attempt at democratization in Timor-Leste. But the chapter makes other contributions as well.

One contribution lies in advancing our thinking about how the factors that bolster regime longevity actually emerge. Here, too, my collaborators have made great strides. They have urged us to recognize the lasting importance of "inherited political structures" (Brownlee et al. 2013, 43), to see that "strong coercive and party organizations" are the fruit of long-term processes and not "short-term crafting" (Levitsky and Way 2010, 83), to recognize that "divergent pathways to democracy" have considerable "long run" consequences (Riedl 2016, 124), and to see the strong connection between revolutionary histories and the parties and militaries that sustain dictatorships (Lachapelle et al. 2020; Levitsky and Way 2013). I extend this literature by linking *democratic* durability to the ideational and political structures inherited from conflicts of all sorts, including revolutionary *and* non-revolutionary struggles alike. In so doing, I explore and highlight a cause of the causes we know to be important.

The study's third contribution emanates from expanding our thinking about democracy to *literally* new (as opposed to merely different) states. Our most influential arguments about the evolution of durable democracies have emerged from cases where a new democracy replaces a dictatorship in an already existing state (Haggard and Kaufman 2016; Linz and Stepan 1996). These arguments focus on incumbent parties, on incumbent authoritarian elites, and on the coercive apparatus of existing states. What happens if the regime *and* the state are new? Studying democracies emerging from successful separatist wars gives us a more refined understanding of the varieties of identity conflict and better purchase on the critical policy questions they generate.

The final contribution of this chapter lies in offering an explanation for democracy in hard places. The institutions and ideas that are helpful to democratic longevity have often emerged from the cluster of slow-moving changes wrought by economic development. I have shown that these same factors can also be brought about by the disequilibria and dilemmas caused by certain types of war. This argument is certainly counterintuitive, and by associating something evil with something good it is normatively problematic. Yet it is also perversely hopeful—for it shows us that even poor countries can enjoy democracy if they are mobilized to fight for it.

Notes

* The author thanks Mário Rebelo for excellent research assistance.
1. External war can have positive effects on democratic durability, too (Bermeo 2010).
2. I thank Steve Fish, Rachel Riedl, and the participants in this project for this and other helpful suggestions.
3. By new democracies I mean regimes that are given a Polity score of 6 or above in Marshall, Gurr, and Jaggers (2018). My results are robust to using the democracy coding of Boix, Miller, and Rosato (Boix-Miller-Rosato [BMR] dichotomous coding of democracy, 1800–2015). I emphasize my exclusive focus on "*new democracies*." I make no generalizations about the effects of war on the likelihood of democratic *transitions*. (Indeed, the vast majority of wars are *not* followed by new democracies.) I also make no generalization about war and the durability of new (or existing) *dictatorships*. For insights on war and dictatorship, see Lachapelle et al. (2020). For more discussion of the effects of conflict history on democratic durability, see Bermeo (forthcoming).
4. Secessionist rebels are often advantaged in several ways by their wartime conduct. When they try to build strong local support *and* get recognition and resources from the international community, they are less likely to kill civilians and more likely to provide civilians with services. See Jo 2015; Mampilly 2011; and Staniland 2012.
5. Gusmão enjoyed a landslide win in the 2002 presidential elections as an independent.
6. Timor-Leste's post-independence state institutions were affected by what scholars have aptly termed an "anti-past" vision—that is, "an inversion of everything wrong" about

the Indonesian regime (Bovensiepen and Nygaard-Christensen 2018, 423), including military rule.

7. This was discovered before independence and is a major reason Australia turned a blind eye to the Indonesian invasion. Australia and Timor-Leste were involved in a costly maritime boundary dispute until 2018 which hampered optimal use of the resource revenue too. For a brief overview with a discussion of democracy, see Feijó (2018).

8. Roll shows how the pensions funded by oil money were key to both state-building and stabilization. Like the oil wealth in Middle East dictatorships, oil revenue was sometimes used to "contain challenges" (Brownlee et al. 2013, 30).

9. Quite the contrary, it may, in the future, harm the legitimacy of elites who are already being accused of oil- and gas-related corruption (Kingsbury 2018).

7

Economic Crises, Military Rebellions, and Democratic Survival

Argentina, 1983–2021

Scott Mainwaring and Emilia Simison

What enables democracies to survive under difficult circumstances?* Why do actors support democratic regimes when they experience deep material losses? This chapter addresses these questions, focusing on the survival of democracy in Argentina since 1983.

Argentina was a difficult case for building enduring democracy in different ways from the other countries studied in this volume. At the time of the transition to democracy, Argentina was wealthier than the other countries. Nor did it face the challenges of religious, linguistic, and ethnic diversity that Benin, India, and Indonesia did; these cleavages are not very salient politically in Argentina. The challenges in Argentina were rather a past history of repeated failures of democracy and of authoritarian actors that had repeatedly subverted democracy, plus three severe economic crises and military rebellions.

Our argument unfolds in two stages. The first is that the military dictatorship of 1976–83 was a dreadful failure. Its economic results were terrible; it waged a disastrous war against the United Kingdom by invading the Falkland/Malvinas islands in 1982; and it committed more human rights abuses than any previous Argentine dictatorship in the twentieth century. These outcomes generated a widespread repudiation of the past that led actors across the political spectrum to a new valuing of democracy and to a rejection of extremism.

Since 1983, Argentina has been a world leader in memorializing the repudiation of the dictatorship's crimes and in creating a collective memory about the importance of human rights. This effort has made it difficult for authoritarian actors to gain a political toehold and has helped sustain commitment to democracy.

The second stage of the argument focuses on two proximate explanatory variables: the demise of extremist anti-system actors and actors' changing normative preferences about authoritarianism and democracy. Extremist anti-system actors on the left and right bear great responsibility for the destruction of Argentina's previous democratic experiment from 1973 to 1976.

Scott Mainwaring and Emilia Simison, *Economic Crises, Military Rebellions, and Democratic Survival* In: *Democracy in Hard Places*. Edited by: Scott Mainwaring and Tarek Masoud, Oxford University Press. © Oxford University Press 2022.
DOI: 10.1093/oso/9780197598757.003.0007

The revolutionary left, right-wing death squads, and by 1975 the military engaged in widespread violence that left much of Argentine society clamoring for a coup that finally arrived on March 24, 1976. After the coup, through ruthless repression, the dictatorship crushed the revolutionary left. What remained of it rejected the totalitarian temptation and largely accepted democracy (Ollier 2009). The revolutionary left ceased to exist as a meaningful actor after 1983. The extremist authoritarian right was also much weaker after 1983. The fiasco of the dictatorship from 1976 to 1983 discredited the authoritarian right and the military. Although the military remained a threat to the new regime at the time of the democratic transition, it was a chastened actor. An important part of the story of democratic survival after 1983 has to do with the demise of the revolutionary left and the paramilitary death squads, the acceptance of democracy within the armed forces, and the gradual establishment of civilian control over the military. Without these extremist anti-system actors, democracy stood a much better chance.

The second proximate factor that helped democracy survive after 1983 was that the actors that remained important after 1983 shifted their attitudes about democracy. If political parties, other organized actors, and citizens value democratic rights and procedures, a regime can survive severe crises. Conversely, as Argentina's breakdowns of 1951,[1] 1962, 1966, and 1976 showed, if most powerful actors are indifferent toward democracy or prefer an authoritarian regime, democracy can crumble under economic conditions that were much better than those from 1983 to 1990, 1998 to 2002, and 2012 to 2020.

Graphically, the argument has the form presented in Figure 7.1.

In Argentina, democracy broke down in 1930, 1951, 1962, 1966, and 1976 despite the country's relatively high income and moderate inequalities. It survived

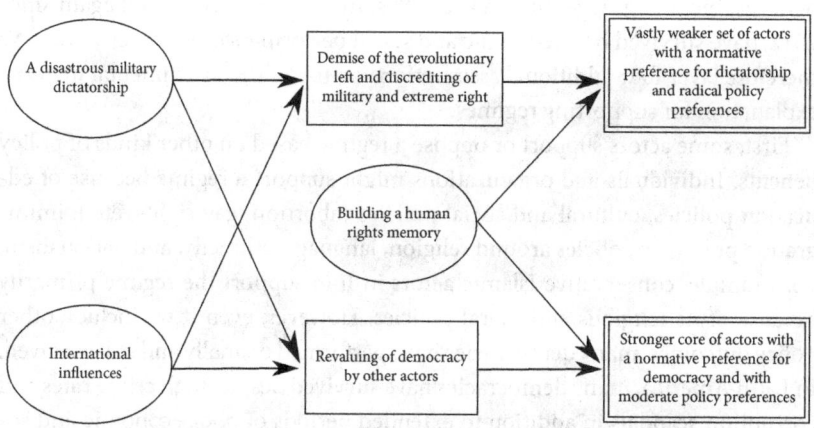

Figure 7.1. Graphic summary of the argument

after 1983 despite hyperinflation, three severe recessions, a dramatic worsening of poverty and income inequality, and several military rebellions. But the actors and their attitudes about democracy changed radically in Argentina's democratic experiment that began in 1983, and this is the key to understanding why democracy survived.

Why Do Actors Support Democratic Regimes?

The survival of democracy hinges on the balance of power between forces that support or accept the regime and those that would like to undermine it. Democratic regimes survive when powerful actors support them. They collapse when the actors that want to undermine them are more powerful than those that support democracy.[2] Why, then, do actors support democracies?

An instrumental material logic to this question focuses on economic benefits: actors support a democratic regime if it generates good material outcomes for them. Some class approaches that focus on whether different classes gain materially exemplify this instrumental material logic. Acemoglu and Robinson (2006) and Boix (2003) claim that the poor support democracy when revolution is not feasible because democracy redistributes income to the poor. The wealthy support authoritarianism under conditions of high inequality because democracy redistributes income to the poor, and they want to avoid this outcome. These class and some other political economy approaches (Ansell and Samuels 2014) focus exclusively on material gains and losses.

Support for regimes is undoubtedly sometimes conditional on material outcomes. If a new democracy produces poor material outcomes over an extended time, some actors are likely to withdraw their support. Yet countless democracies, including Argentina in the 1980s, from 1998 to 2002, and again since 2012, have survived bad economic and social performance (Remmer 1996). We therefore layer four additional assumptions on top of the instrumental material explanation for supporting regimes.

First, some actors support or oppose a regime based on other kinds of policy benefits. Individuals and organizations might support a regime because of education policies, cultural and social policies (abortion, gay rights, etc.), immigration policy, or policies around religion, language, ethnicity, and nationalism. For example, conservative Islamic actors in Iran support the regime primarily because of its religious and moral policies. However, even if we include other policy outcomes, many democracies have performed dismally and still survived. In Latin America, many democracies have survived despite high crime rates and corruption scandals in addition to extended periods of poor economic and social results.

Second, actors and individuals implicitly compare their expected utility under democracy with their expectations about utility under dictatorship. They might believe that a democratic regime has produced poor substantive outcomes, but they lack confidence that a dictatorship would do better. In that case, they would have no incentive to support a move to dictatorship. They might not actively support the democracy, but neither they would actively support a coup. This perspective that actors implicitly compare utility under democracy and dictatorship helps illuminate the logic of some Argentine actors after 1983. Real wages fell dramatically in Argentina from 1983 to 1990 (by 30 percent) and from 1998 to 2002 (by 27 percent) (ECLAC 1993, 2004). However, the recent memory of wage contraction under the military dictatorship reduced workers' willingness to support another coup.

Nevertheless, an approach that posits that actors focus exclusively on material outcomes and compare utility under different regime types often has difficulty explaining actors' positions. Under Argentina's semi-democratic regime of 1963 to 1966, the economy grew at a rate that had few matches in the twentieth century (Gerchunoff and Llach 2010, 300). Per capita GDP grew by 8.5 percent in 1964 and 8.9 percent in 1965 (but then fell 2.1 percent in 1966) (World Development Indicators, n.d.).[3] Growth was much better than it had been during the two previous authoritarian regimes (1955–58 and 1962–63). Unemployment dropped from 8.8 percent in 1963 to 5.2 percent in 1966 (García Vázquez 1994, 294), and real wages grew more than 10 percent (Gerchunoff and Llach 2010, 296). Yet organized labor and most business groups supported the 1966 coup that overthrew the government. In light of the weak economic performance of the previous dictatorships (1955–58 and 1962–63), it is unlikely that most actors concluded that a new dictatorship would have better economic performance.

Third, actors might incur some costs for opposing democracy, or they might be constrained by strong institutions. Most individuals and organizations would consider the probability of a successful attempt to overthrow a democracy and the likely costs of attempting but failing to do so. Even if opposition actors despise the incumbent democracy, if the probability of overthrowing it is very low and the potential costs of supporting a failed attempt to achieve a regime change are high, most actors will remain on the sidelines.

However, if a democracy produces bad substantive outcomes for most powerful actors, the costs of signaling subtle support to change the regime should not be terribly high. Under democracy, actors can signal opposition to the regime at a much lower cost than they can under repressive dictatorships. Because liberal democracies are reluctant to repress anti-system actors that do not engage in violence or otherwise go beyond the law, these actors have considerable latitude to signal their support for a regime change. If actors choose regimes based on what they deliver substantively, under circumstances of extended poor performance, a broad coalition of actors should oppose it. Powerful opposition to a democracy does not ensure that it will erode or break down, but it makes this outcome much more likely. If a regime produced bad outcomes for vast swaths of society, as has been the case in Argentina for extended times since 1983, and if actors supported or opposed regimes based only on material outcomes, it would be difficult for democracy to survive.

Fourth, some individuals and organizations have preferences about the regime in addition to caring about substantive outcomes. By definition, democracy affords free and fair elections, nearly universal adult voting and citizenship rights, respect for a panoply of political and civil rights, and civilian control over the military. Many citizens, political leaders, and organized actors might value these procedural aspects of democracy. They might not benefit materially from democracy, and they might endure policy losses. However, following Winston Churchill's famous maxim that "democracy is the worst form of government except all those other forms that have been tried," they still might conclude that democracy is the best possible regime. Voters emerging from the tyranny of communist rule valued democracy even when most post-communist economies were struggling in the 1990s (Hofferbert and Klingemann 1999; Rose and Mishler 1996). Following Mainwaring and Pérez-Liñán (2013), we refer to actors that value the procedural aspects of democracy as having a normative preference for democracy. We argue that in Argentina, a change in actors' normative preferences and the demise of extremist anti-system actors are key to explaining the survival of democracy after 1983.

We divide actors' utility into two broad baskets. The first basket includes all outcomes and policies that are not related to the political regime. Second are the outcomes and procedures that are an intrinsic part of democracy as a political regime.[4] Liberal democracy has four characteristics:

1. Free and fair elections for the national assembly and the head of government.
2. Almost universal adult suffrage among citizens and no exclusions from citizenship that were not common at a given historical moment.
3. A broad set of rights (freedom of expression, freedom of speech, freedom of assembly, freedom of religion, freedom from prosecution based on political beliefs), and state institutions that function to ensure these rights.
4. Civilian control over the military and ability to choose policies without having them dictated by armed actors.

Many individuals and organizations value these defining features of democracy—as Ashutosh Varshney argues in his chapter on India. Human rights organizations value rights that are an intrinsic part of democracy. In democracies, most journalists, media companies, artists, and academics value freedom of expression. Many churches, religious leaders, and followers value freedom of religion. Many people believe in basic principles of human dignity and sanctity; such beliefs could prompt favoring democracy and could lead to moral repudiation of repressive authoritarian regimes. Some citizens want the right to choose their leaders in free and fair elections. Political parties and politicians might want to maintain free and fair elections as a hedge against authoritarian regimes that cut them out entirely—or worse, that ban and persecute them. Many individuals value procedural fairness and not only substantive outcomes (Frey, Benz, and Stutzer 2004). Democracy is more likely than most authoritarian regimes to offer procedural fairness in who gets to run for office, how they get elected, who governs, and how they govern. Democracy is also more likely to offer fair legal procedures. Some business leaders might value the checks and balances and procedural guarantees of democracies. Some individuals have a moral compass that leads them to repudiate the rights violations that authoritarian regimes commit and to value democracy's guarantees of rights. When individuals or organizations give some weight to these considerations that are defining features of democracy, they have a normative preference for democracy. This preference is based on the guarantees, procedures, and rights that democracy enshrines.

Skeptics believe that actors favor democracy only out of self-interest. Indeed, some powerful Argentine actors (the Peronist Party and the labor movement, for example) whose attitudes about democracy underwent profound transformations acknowledged after 1983 that democracy was in their interests. But these actors did nothing to support democracy from 1973 to 1976, and they passively accepted a coup in 1976. If democracy was not in their (perception of their) interests between 1945 and 1976 but was in their (perception of their) interests after 1983, it is because they came to a new valuing of democracy after the harsh realities of the military dictatorship. Actors' perceptions of their interests are deeply infused with their normative beliefs.

Organizations and individuals weight instrumental policy interests and normative preferences about the regime differently. Many might weight substantive outcomes other than those that are defining features of a democracy for almost 100 percent of their implicit calculus. But others value the procedures and rights that democracy guarantees. This orientation might be especially prevalent after individuals and organizations have experienced or witnessed deprivations because of dictatorships, or because they have been socialized in well-functioning democratic regimes.

If political actors value the rights and procedures that are defining features of democracy, democracy is more likely to survive. A normative preference for democracy refers to actors' willingness to incur other policy costs in order to defend or achieve democracy; an actor values democracy because of these rights and procedures. It does *not* mean that they always prefer democracy at any cost. Normative preferences about democracy include some substantive outcomes (protection of rights), and they can also be based on "procedural utility"—the well-being derived from procedures above and beyond the outcomes they generate (Frey et al. 2004).[5]

When actors value the rights and procedures of democracy, it can survive bad governing performance (Linz 1988; Linz and Stepan 1989; O'Donnell 1986; Remmer 1996). They are less willing to subvert democracy. Conversely, in contexts of weak accountability institutions, democracy that rests exclusively on regime performance is almost inevitably precarious. With weak accountability institutions such as courts and the national legislature, if no actors were committed to democracy, powerful narrowly instrumental actors would not feel constrained by the rules of the game. If actors preferred democracy exclusively because of the instrumental advantages it confers to them, any equilibrium would be vulnerable to easy disruption unless institutions such as courts and the congress were strong, or unless a tight balance of power remained in place over time.

Preferences are not static; individuals and organizations change how much they value democracy on its intrinsic merits. The legacies of different types of authoritarian regimes, for example, affect future support for democracy; people who have experienced exclusionary authoritarian regimes are less likely to hold anti-democratic beliefs (Neundorf et al. 2019). In fact, survey data show that Argentines valued democracy more after 1983, almost certainly in response to the gross human rights violations, ineptitude of the last military dictatorship, and the powerful memorialization of human rights abuses.

The values that individuals and organizations implicitly assign to these two categories of outcomes and procedures are not observable. The point is that some individuals and organizations attach a positive value to the rights and procedures that characterize democracy. This positive value is part of the glue that sometimes enables democracies to survive in difficult conditions.

No observational evidence can definitively show that actors support a democracy solely because of its other substantive outcomes or also in part because they value the rights, guarantees, and procedures of a democracy. However, in Argentina, large swaths of society experienced major economic losses from 1983 to 1990, 1998 to 2002, and 2012 to 2020. Despite these losses, powerful organized actors did not merely accept democracy because they had no choice; they actively defended the regime in the face of military rebellions. Therefore, we can definitively rule out simple material explanations.

Moreover, the discourse and behavior of powerful actors changed profoundly relative to the past, and these actors actively supported democracy. A look at the discourse and behavior of some actors suggests that they had a normative preference for democracy and that this preference helped democracy survive. The demise of radical anti-system actors also made it easier for democracy to survive; it is an equally important part of our account.

A Failed Dictatorship

The dictatorship of 1976–83 was a spectacular failure. Initially, it enjoyed broad support despite massive human rights violations. However, this support dwindled as the economy sputtered, and then it collapsed when the generals initiated a war against the United Kingdom by invading the Falkland/Malvinas Islands. The damage wrought by the dictatorship pushed important actors and countless citizens toward a commitment to democracy.

Economic Results

The dictatorship's economic policies failed dismally. As the Economic Commission for Latin America and the Caribbean reported, when the new democratic government took office in December 1983, "The economic problems were very grave. . . . The per capita product was similar to what it had been fifteen years earlier. . . . Domestic savings and the availability of external financing had declined sharply; the government was operating at a great deficit; workers . . . were trying to recoup levels of consumption that had been put off for a long time . . . and external debtors were reluctant to refinance their credits much less offer new loans. . . . The very high inflation rate revealed a large disequilibrium in public finances . . . and stimulated speculative behavior in financial and exchange rate markets" (ECLAC 1985, 1–2). Real wages fell by 41.3 percent between 1975 and 1982 (Graña and Kennedy 2008, table 7). Per capita GDP was lower in 1983 than it had been in 1975, the last full year of democracy (World Development Indicators, n.d.). The external debt ballooned, leaving an enormous burden for the new government. Inflation surged, reaching 380 percent in 1983 (World Development Indicators, n.d.). The economic legacy for the incoming democratic regime was ruinous.

A Reckless and Disastrous War

By 1981, the dictatorship was in disarray, with support faltering because of the economy mismanagement. Military cohesion had cracked, and public opinion had turned sharply against the dictatorship. In response to the crumbling support, the dictatorship gambled that it could galvanize public support by invading the Falkland/Malvinas islands. Both the British and the Argentines had claimed the islands since the nineteenth century, but the British had long exercised control.

Waging war against the United Kingdom was a reckless and disastrous gamble. The dictators launched the war by invading the Falklands on April 2. Their expectation that the invasion would generate renewed public support was absolutely right in the short term. Because the British had almost no military presence on the islands, the Argentine troops quickly took over without bloodshed, generating a jingoistic response that the dictatorship had expected. In the UK, the Thatcher government responded with equal nationalistic fervor and determination, quickly dispatching a fleet of warships across the Atlantic.

To garner support for the war, until the day the Argentine military surrendered, with a gigantic propaganda output, the generals proclaimed that they were winning the war. The press coverage was massive and jingoistic; the tightly controlled media proclaimed that the Argentine military was winning. Most Argentines swallowed the lies and applauded the invasion; even much of the left, which had been the object of savage repression by the dictatorship, rallied to the cause. Millions of Argentines mobilized on the streets to express their support for the war.

It took several weeks for British warships to reach the islands and engage the Argentine military, initially in naval battles. The British military landed on East Falkland Island on May 21 and subsequently routed the Argentines, leading to the surrender on June 14, 1982. The cost in lives (about 649 Argentine soldiers died and another 1,177 were wounded) and economic ruin was high. The logistical preparation was dismal, leading to appalling conditions for the mostly young Argentine conscripts who invaded. Without adequate food, boots, and coats, they starved and froze on the cold, wind-swept islands until the generals capitulated. Argentine military documents that came to light in the 2010s indicate that some officers tortured and abused the conscripts to keep them in line.[6] The dictatorship's brazen lies about winning the war reinforced the effects of the bellicose disaster, discrediting the military as a bunch of incompetents *and* liars.

The fallout was immediate and profound; it brought down the dictatorship, although the actual transfer of power did not take place for almost eighteen months, on December 10, 1983. President Leopoldo Galtieri was forced to resign only four days after the Argentine surrender, June 18, 1982, and he was placed under (comfortable) house arrest in a military compound. His entire cabinet resigned the same day, although they remained in place until new appointments could take over.

Human Rights Abuses and Their Memorialization

The dictatorship of 1976–83 was Argentina's most repressive of the twentieth century. The country's governments, courts, human rights NGOs, and countless artists, scholars, and journalists have helped to build an enduring commitment to never allowing something similar to occur. The memorialization of human rights abuses under the dictatorship has helped build and preserve an anti-authoritarian sentiment.

Few countries in the world have ever done as much as Argentina to memorialize the atrocities of the terrible past and to prosecute those responsible for human rights crimes under a dictatorship (González Ocantos 2016, 2020; Sikkink 2008). The report commissioned by the Alfonsín government in its first days in office, *Nunca Más: Informe de la Comisión Nacional sobre la Desaparición de Personas* (Never Again: Report of the Argentine National Commission on the Disappearance of Persons), has sold more than 700,000 copies, and it had a huge impact (Crenzel 2015). Argentina became a world pioneer in prosecuting military dictators who presided over gross human rights abuses. In 1985, the world's most publicized human rights trials since the Nuremburg trails in Germany in 1945–46, galvanized public opinion against the atrocities committed by the military. The top leaders of the dictatorship ended up in jail. President Carlos Menem (1989–99) later pardoned them, but subsequent court cases put them back in jail. As of November 2018, 3,007 individuals had faced charges for human rights abuses during the dictatorship (Human Rights Watch 2019), and by July 2019 courts had convicted 915 individuals of human rights abuses (González-Ocantos 2020, 14). Many trials and convictions were highly publicized, creating an ongoing sense of a repudiation of the terrible past.

In 2002, the Argentine Congress created the National Day of Memory for Truth and Justice, commemorated as a national holiday every year on March 24, the day of the 1976 coup. Around that day, all schools focus on human rights. The country continues to have one of the most vibrant human rights movements in the world.

Prize-winning films such as *The Official Story* (1985) and *The Secret in Their Eyes* (2009),[7] both of which dramatized the human rights abuses committed under the dictatorship, drew huge audiences in Argentina and internationally. Countless other films, works of theater, works by journalists,[8] memoirs, novels, and academic works also memorialized the gross human rights violations. As of 2019, Argentina had thirty-four official public museums, parks, and other institutions that "have permanent activities related to the transmission and promotion of human rights."[9] Among the best known is the *Museo Sitio de Memoria ESMA* (Museum and Site of Memory ESMA) in Buenos Aires, which opened in

2015. It functions at the site of what had been the largest torture and extermination center during the dictatorship.[10]

The reinforcement of the importance of human rights and democracy coming both from state institutions and civil society organizations has reduced the space for authoritarian candidates, parties, social movements, and civil society organizations. Conversely, these efforts have kept alive a message about the importance of human rights and democracy.

The trials against the former dictators in 1985 and the guilty verdicts in December 1985 riveted the attention of the world's human rights and democracy advocates on Argentina. The courts effectively prosecuted many abusers, communicating a message about the importance of human rights (González Ocantos 2016). The governments of Néstor Kirchner (2003–7) and Cristina Fernández de Kirchner (2007–15) reopened trials against the former abusers, invoked the importance of human rights, and criticized the dictatorship's abuses, activating the memory of how depraved that dictatorship was and affirming the value of democracy.

Advantages and Three Potential Threats to Democracy

Argentina had five democratic advantages in 1983—three domestic and two international. First, it was an upper-middle-income country with one of the highest standards of living and highest educational levels in Latin America. Second, although income inequality had worsened during the previous decade, it remained one of the least unequal countries in Latin America. Third, the dictatorship of 1976–83 was thoroughly defeated and discredited after its disastrous invasion of the Falkland/Malvinas Islands in 1982, and after its mishandling of economic policy. The discrediting of the military gave operating space to the new democratic government. Fourth, the neighborhood and region were starting to transform in a democratic direction. After several false starts and coups between 1978 and 1982, Bolivia completed a precarious transition to democracy in 1982. Brazil's and Uruguay's transitions to democracy were well under way. These changes were incomplete when Argentina transitioned back to democracy in December 1983, but the tide was shifting away from dictatorship. A democratic neighborhood makes it easier for a country to sustain democracy. Fifth, notwithstanding considerable wavering by the Reagan administration in Central America, US policy had shifted toward putting more emphasis on supporting democracy in South America. In the Argentine case, the US veered toward supporting a democratic transition after the dictatorship initiated war with the United Kingdom in 1982.

Given these advantages, Argentina was not among the most difficult cases of democracy, but it was not an easy case from 1983 through the early 1990s. Democrats in Argentina faced three formidable threats to democracy: a long antecedent history of coups and authoritarian actors, severe economic crises, and military rebellions.

Argentina had a long history of democratic failures despite a high level of modernization and moderate inequalities, so its structural advantages did not guarantee democratic survival. The country had experienced democratic breakdowns in 1930, 1951, 1962, 1966, and 1976. It was one of the world champions of breakdowns in the twentieth century. Powerful authoritarian actors had repeatedly subverted democracy. Previous studies have shown that a past history of breakdowns is a good predictor of a future breakdown (Przeworski et al. 2000, 124, table 2.17). Given this fact and the reality that no previous experience with democracy in Argentina had begun under economic conditions nearly as bad as those that the Alfonsín government faced, and that the country was more unequal and marginally poorer than it had been at the beginning of the previous failed democratic experiment (1973–76), democratic survival was not a foregone conclusion.

Argentina has confronted three punishing economic crises, with three of the largest declines in per capita income under democracy in Latin America since 1978. Only the Peruvian per capita GDP decline from 1980 to 1992 was greater than the declines Argentina experienced from 1983–90, 1998–2002, and 2012–20 (World Development Indicators, n.d.),[11] and democracy in Peru broke down at the end of that period, in April 1992. By 1990, Argentina's per capita GDP was 17.5 percent lower than it had been in 1984 (World Development Indicators, n.d.),[12] and inflation reached 4,923 percent in 1989 (CEPALSTAT, n.d.).[13] Per capita GDP dropped 22.0 percent from 1998 to 2002, accompanied by a massive increase in unemployment and poverty. Another long and cumulatively terrible slump began in 2012 and culminated in an estimated 10.8 percent decline in per capita GDP in Covid-plagued 2020 (World Development Indicators, n.d.).[14] By 2020, per capita GDP was 20.1 percent lower than it had been in 2011. No third-wave democracy has survived three equally devastating economic crises.

These economic crises could have derailed democracy—especially the first one, when the military leadership from the previous dictatorship was still partly intact. Indeed, simple materialist understandings of what makes democracy viable probably would have predicted breakdown. The second crisis provoked massive social mobilizations. But at no time did these crises break democracy. Whereas Argentina's economic problems of 1929–30, 1966, and 1975–76 solidified support for coups, the severe crises of 1989–90, 2001–2, and 2018–20 did not. Focusing on a democracy that survived severe and prolonged economic crises that led to losses for most sectors of society rules out simple materialistic explanations for regime support. During the crises, most sectors of society experienced economic losses.

For the first part of this democratic period, roughly 1983 to 1990, Argentina has one other advantage for case selection. Several military rebellions in the 1980s could have led to a breakdown, especially in tandem with the economic crises. The investigations of human rights abuses committed by the dictatorship proved to be destabilizing. At that time, the military was still divided between factions that accepted civilian control and democracy and sectors that remained wedded to the authoritarian tradition. Members of the authoritarian factions engaged in uprisings in 1987 and 1988 that could have threatened the stability of the democratic regime. However, the revolts failed to garner political support. Large numbers of people, as well as the main political and societal actors, actively mobilized in defense of democracy.

The frequent military rebellions distinguish Argentina from other transition cases at that time. In McGuire's (1995a, 194–95) analysis of seven transitions from authoritarian rule in Latin America and Southern Europe, Argentina, with four rebellions, had the most military uprisings. Therefore, it would be wrong to argue that actors tolerated democracy only because they had no chance of forming a winning coalition to install an authoritarian regime. Indeed, the rebellions failed in part because they generated a massive outpouring of public support for democracy and because powerful actors such as labor unions and business associations came to the regime's defense.

The notion that Argentina's democratization was easy also ignores the perspectives of actors at that time. Around 1982–84, many Argentine analysts underscored the difficult challenges to democratic survival. The obstacles included profound economic problems such as a massive foreign debt incurred by the dictatorship, a history of an authoritarian political culture, a military that although defeated was still profoundly authoritarian and powerful, a history of many failed regimes, and weak democratic institutions. Acuña (1984, 261–62) wrote that if business interests felt attacked by the economic policies of the new democratic government, they might try to provoke a new military intervention. Amadeo (1984, 94) doubted that a return to democracy would take place in the medium term unless some deep structural problems were resolved. Bruno (1984, 128) warned that "actors that represented the oligarchy and imperialism" would attempt to undermine democracy if the constitutional government did not protect their interests.

Cavarozzi (1983, 69–70) wrote that "from the perspective of the stabilization of a democracy, the situation is not too promising."[15] De Riz argued, "The democratic reconstitution of the relationships between the state and society in Argentina does not seem to be attainable in the short term" (De Riz 1982, 1215–16). Oszlak (1984, 12) wrote that the establishment of democratic practices and institutions "will be a difficult and slow process." O'Donnell (1983) warned that "once again, the political opening could be perceived as a transitory refugee of an authoritarianism in crisis, without a path to democracy." Nearly a quarter-century after the 1983 transition, well-known historian Luis Alberto Romero (2006, 29) wrote, "It is unquestionably possible that without the military dictatorship, democracy would have quickly sunk . . . because in 1983, there was nothing great with which to build democracy, except for hope."

Moreover, Argentine citizens were also skeptical that democracy would last. In a national survey carried out in late 1985, 95 percent of respondents said that "the authoritarian regimes will return if the government does not organize things well," against only 5 percent who believed that "democracy will become stronger in our country, and authoritarian governments are something of the past" (CID 1985).[16]

Democracy in Argentina, 1983–2020

The new democratic regime began on December 10, 1983, when Raúl Alfonsín assumed the presidency. Democracy in Argentina has now survived for thirty-eight years, and it has had a solid quality. According to V-Dem and Freedom House, since 1984, Argentina has consistently had one of the highest levels of democracy in Latin America. Figure 7.2 shows Argentina's V-Dem Liberal Democracy Index scores and Freedom House scores from 1983 to 2020. Freedom House scores are inverted so that a high score represents a high level of democracy, and then standardized from 0 to 1 so that they are on the same 0-to-1 scale as V-Dem's Liberal Democracy score.[17]

Three Severe Economic Crises

Many scholars have shown that economic crises can imperil new democracies (Gasiorowski 1995; Przeworski et al. 2000; Sing 2010; Svolik 2015). Economic slumps that were much milder than what Argentina experienced in the 1980s and 1998–2002 contributed to breakdowns in 1930, 1951/55, and 1976.

The dictatorship (1976–83) left the economy in a ruinous state, and the Alfonsín administration never got a solid grip on the economy. From 1983 to 1991, the country lurched from one crisis to the next, culminating in the hyperinflation of 1989–90, when inflation reached 4,923 percent and 1,343 percent, respectively (CEPALSTAT, n.d.). Few democracies have survived worse economic conditions. Inflation remained high during Alfonsín's whole term, ranging from 82 percent in 1986 to 4,923 percent in 1989 (CEPALSTAT, n.d.). GDP per capita

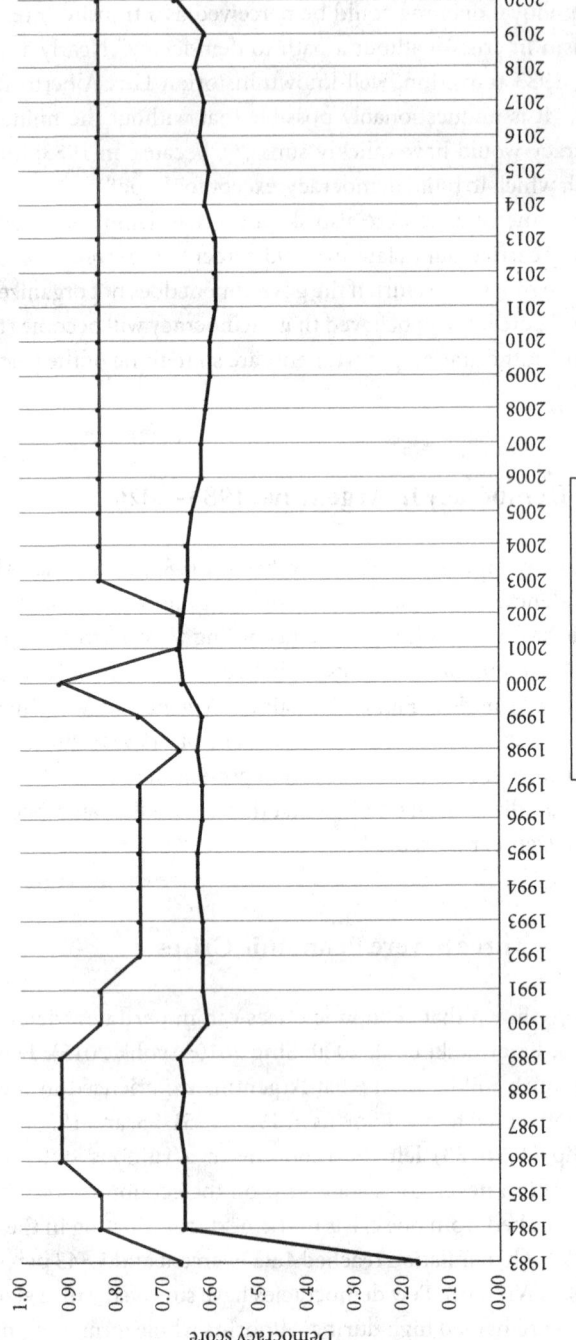

Figure 7.2. Argentina, V-Dem liberal democracy and Freedom House scores, 1983–2020
Sources: Coppedge et al. 2021; Freedom House 2021a.

diminished on average 2.1 percent yearly between 1981 and 1990, and the foreign debt reached 70 percent of the GDP (Novaro 2010, 226). According to the IMF database on systemic banking crises (Valencia and Laeven 2012), the output lost during the 1989–91 crisis reached 12.6 percent of GDP and the fiscal costs of the crisis, defined as the component of gross fiscal outlays related to the restructuring of the financial sector, were equivalent to 6 percent of GDP.

This crisis impoverished millions of Argentines and generated widespread suffering and uncertainty. It precipitated the early resignation of President Alfonsín on July 8, 1989, five months before his term was due to end, and the early assumption of the presidency by his elected successor, Carlos Menem. Despite the severity of the economic crisis, democracy survived. Argentina became an early exemplar of how to displace a failed government but preserve a democratic regime.

Another potential challenge to democracy occurred during the severe financial and economic crisis of 2001–2. The urban poverty rate hit 45.4 percent in 2002, shocking for a country where it had been only 16.1 percent eight years earlier (ECLAC 2006, 317). Since ECLAC started regularly publishing data on poverty at the beginning of the 1990s, no other country in Latin America registered such an extraordinary increase in poverty until Venezuela in the 2010s. We wonder if there is another case of a democracy that experienced such an extraordinary increase in poverty without a breakdown. During the crisis of 1999–2002, per capita GDP declined sharply, from $8,729 to $6,817 (World Development Indicators, n.d.).[18] Unemployment surged from 7.4 percent in 1990 to 11.5 percent in 1994, 14.9 percent in 1997, and 15.1 percent in 2000 (ECLAC, 2001).

By 1998, the economy had slid into a recession. With support from other parties in addition to the Radical Civic Union (*Unión Cívica Radical*, UCR), Fernando de la Rúa won the 1999 presidential election, in part because the high economic and social toll had tarnished the Justicialist Party (*Partido Justicialista*, PJ). The situation worsened in November 2001 with the collapse of the capital market. In the face of massive demonstrations, De la Rúa resigned on December 20, 2001, beginning a period of great political instability and unpredictability. Argentina had five different presidents in thirteen days, from December 20, 2001, to January 2, 2002. In Argentina's past democratic periods, when actors readily conspired against the regime, this instability could easily have led to a breakdown. After resignations by four presidents, Congress elected Eduardo Duhalde to serve from January 2, 2002, to May 25, 2003. By the time Duhalde left office, the economic situation had improved greatly.

The economic and social costs of the 1994–2002 period were extremely high. According to the IMF database on systemic banking crises, the output lost in the 2001–3 crisis was 70.97 percent of GDP, and its fiscal costs amounted to 9.6 percent of GDP (Valencia and Laeven 2012). In terms of GDP drop, this crisis was the worst by a Latin American democracy that was established in the third wave and survived. According to the data of the Economic Commission on Latin America and the Caribbean, no democracy in Latin America has experienced as great an increase in poverty. Average incomes fell 22 percent between 1998 and 2002 (Steinberg 2015, 2). The national unemployment rate reached 19.7 percent in 2002 according to the World Development Indicators, while the urban unemployment rate was also 19.7 percent according to ECLAC (2004). The crisis implied forty-two months of decline in the level of economic activity (Novaro, Bonvecchi, and Cherny 2014, 25).

The third economic slump began in 2012 (−2.1 percent per capita growth), followed by six years of cycling between low growth and recessions that consistently more than wiped out the previous year's tepid growth: 1.3 percent per capita growth in 2013, a 3.5 percent drop in 2014, 1.7 percent growth in 2015, a 3.1 percent drop in 2016, and 1.8 percent growth in 2017. In 2018, the economy began a steady decline with a drop in per capita GDP of 3.5 percent that year, another decline of 3.0 percent in 2019, and a sharp drop of 11.5 percent in 2020 (ECLAC 2021, 117, table A1.3).

The Military Rebellions of the 1980s

Another challenge that Argentine democracy confronted was subordinating the military. This was not an easy task. Although the dictatorship suffered a humiliating defeat in the 1982 war with the United Kingdom, the unreconstructed military was still intact at the time of the democratic transition. Most of the military had a profoundly authoritarian worldview (Franco 2009). Massive human rights violations committed by the dictatorship created a delicate balancing act for the government. On one hand, Alfonsín won the 1983 election in part because of his firm stance on behalf of human rights. Human rights movements that had been important actors in the struggle against the dictatorship demanded legal action against the killers and torturers in the military and security forces. On the other hand, the military and security forces had a high level of self-justification of their activities during the "dirty war." They believed that they were fighting to preserve Western Christian civilization against a subversive threat. Acting against a powerful entrenched military with this profile could have fostered a coup.

Of the new democracies in Latin America in the third wave, the Alfonsín government clashed with the military more than any other, and it made more efforts than any other foundational democratic government to punish human rights abusers.[19] As mentioned earlier in this chapter, just five days after his inauguration, Alfonsín formed a commission to investigate human rights abuses during the dictatorship. The National Commission on the Disappearance of

People's report, *Nunca Más*, documented the "disappearance" of 8,961 people and the widespread use of torture and clandestine detention centers. It quickly became a bestseller in Argentina and internationally, and it provoked international outrage about the widespread human rights abuses. The Alfonsín government prosecuted the leaders of the military dictatorship, and courts convicted and sentenced them to lengthy prison terms in 1986.

In the context of a partly unreformed military, the ongoing investigations into human rights abuses threatened to be destabilizing. The military was divided between sectors that accepted civilian control and democracy and others that remained wedded to the authoritarian tradition and engaged in uprisings in April 1987 and January and December 1988 (Jaunarena 2011; Norden 1996). During these military rebellions, citizens risked their lives by mobilizing on the streets on behalf of democracy, and the main parties, labor unions, social movements, and business groups came to the defense of democracy. This support helped enable democracy to survive the rebellions, and it was telling of the shift in Argentine public opinion regarding military rule.

A new army revolt took place in late 1990, but loyal army units repressed the insurgents. By the early 1990s, the military was under civilian control and began to acknowledge excesses during the "dirty war." Military extremism was buried. The military declined in relevance after 1990 and ceased being an important player in regime politics (Diamint 2006; Norden 1996; Palermo and Novaro 1996, 252). Since the early 1990s, there has been no chance of a successful military coup.

Explaining Democratic Survival in Difficult Economic Conditions

Why did powerful actors not mobilize against democracy during the severe economic crises since 1983? Most powerful actors have been committed to preserving democracy, and since the subordination of the military in the early 1990s, there have been no important authoritarian actors. Normative commitments to democracy helped the regime to survive economic crises that were more severe than the economic problems faced during earlier breakdowns. Because all important actors have agreed that preserving democracy is important, the pro-democracy coalition has remained intact even in moments of enormous turmoil and economic crisis. All actors, even those that do not have a strong normative preference, have accepted democracy.

The rest of this section shows how the preferences of the main political actors changed after the last military dictatorship. To trace these changes, we used primary and secondary sources. Among the primary sources consulted are the interviews available at the Oral History Archive of the Gino Germani Institute,[20] the Archive on Argentine Unionism at Torcuato Di Tella University,[21] the General Confederation of Labor (Confederación General del Trabajo, CGT) archives,[22] and the digital archives of the newspapers *Clarín* and *La Nación* (available since 1995).

The Justicialist (Peronist) Party

For democracy to endure, the preferences and behavior of governing parties and presidents are especially important because they are the main actors that can lead executive suffocations of democracy. Radical leftist governments can also jeopardize democracy by promoting a backlash among conservative actors, potentially leading to a military coup.

From 1983 to 2015, the Radicals and Peronists were consistently the core of the democratic coalition (although the Radicals became a much weaker electoral contender after 2001). The Peronist party, *Partido Justicialista* (PJ), experienced a deep change in its attitudes toward democracy. Although Juan Perón was democratically elected in 1945, he governed as an authoritarian populist until he was ousted by a coup in 1955. From 1973 to 1976, Perón and his hand-picked predecessor and successor after his death in 1974 displayed indifference toward the preservation of democracy. Most Peronist labor unions and other Peronist actors also did. The Peronist right, which included the country's most powerful right-wing death squads, and the Peronist left actively conspired against democracy. An unreconstructed Peronism would have been disastrous for democracy after 1983.

The Peronists won the presidency in 1989, 1995, 2003, 2007, 2011, and 2019, and they were the main opposition party in 1983–89, 1999–2001, and 2015–19. They left behind their more authoritarian tendencies. The highly authoritarian revolutionary Peronist left and the right-wing Peronist death squads ceased to exist. The disastrous experience of the dictatorship of 1976–83 led most PJ leaders to value democracy. By 1984 the *Renovación* ("Renewal") movement had become the dominant force inside the PJ, pushing for further democratization within the party. This movement included among its principles the true acceptance of party competition, faith in the Constitution, and the distinction between the partisan and corporatist spheres (Novaro 1994, 60–61). In the words of one of Peronism's most important leaders from the 1950s until 2005, Antonio Cafiero, "It is necessary to learn to live together in a pluralist and fragile democracy" (quoted in Novaro 1994, 61). This idea is clear also in declarations made by Juan Gabriel Labaké, a member of the Supreme Peronist Command (*Comando Superior Justicialista*), in 1985 on the steely determination of party members to fight for the stability of the institutions and the constitutional order.[23] A leading Peronist politician and well-known political scientist and public intellectual, Juan Abal Medina, wrote that "[t]he extremely difficult experience of the dictatorship led actors to recognize the value of . . . tolerance and diversity, which had been absent in all of the previous democratic episodes" (Abal Medina and Suárez Cao 2003, 78).[24]

Sectors within Peronism have been willing to sacrifice *some* democratic practices (de Ipola 1987), but the movement distanced itself from the authoritarian proclivities of its past. The PJ accepted its role as a loyal opposition (in Linz's terms [1978b]) under democracy from 1983–89, 1999–2001 and 2015–19.

Once labor and the PJ became committed to democracy as a value, the withering economic crises under democracy did not cause them to favor an authoritarian outcome. In the midst of the 2001–2 financial meltdown, the Peronist members of the Chamber of Deputies voted to approve March 24 (the anniversary of the 1976 coup) a day of memory of truth and justice: "The Peronist deputies support this measure not only as Peronists but also as democrats. . . . We have a commitment to democracy. Having suffered through the infamous dictatorship, we must always celebrate the memory of those who were disappeared, persecuted, and jailed, of our colleagues who needed to leave the country, and of all those who fought to restore democracy and to ensure that we would never again have a dictatorship in our beloved country" (in García Lerena 2007, 613).[25]

The military revolt of April 1987 showed the profound transformation among PJ leaders, who offered unwavering support to the Radical administration. Notwithstanding the failures of Alfonsín's economic policies, the PJ did not attempt to destabilize the regime. During the military revolts, the transformation among partisan actors was clear. As Menem expressed in January 1989, the democratic regime was not going to be jeopardized (quoted in Masi 2014, 319).

The five Peronist presidents who lasted more than a few weeks (Carlos Menem, 1989–99; Eduardo Duhalde, 2002–3; Néstor Kirchner, 2003–7; Cristina Fernández, 2007–15; Alberto Fernández, 2019–) were much more respectful of democratic norms than Juan Perón had been from 1946 to 1955 and from 1973 to 1974, and than Isabel Perón had been from 1974 to 1976. They occasionally ran roughshod over mechanisms of intrastate accountability, but they trespassed within bounds that did not undermine democracy even when congressional majorities would probably have allowed them to go further than they did. Courts and the national Congress sometimes impeded presidential encroachments; the story after 1983 is not exclusively about normative preferences and policy moderation. While the Peronist presidents were not ideal democrats, they displayed none of the four *ex ante* markers of authoritarian characteristics that Levitsky and Ziblatt (2018) enumerate.[26] They recognized the opposition as legitimate, and they were less aggressive in pushing to expand presidential power than leaders who have engineered executive takeovers.

The Illiberalism Index of the Varieties of Party Identity and Organization (V-Party) project is useful for indicating the degree to which political parties support democratic norms (Lührmann et al. 2020). The index is based on four expert survey questions about party leaders' use of severe personal attacks on or demonization of political opponents; their acceptance of free and fair elections and freedom of speech, media, assembly, and association; their acceptance of minority rights; and their rejection of political violence. All four questions tap essential democratic norms. The scale ranges from 0 (parties that fully embrace liberal democratic values) to 1 (extremely illiberal parties).

Figure 7.3 shows V-Party's Illiberalism scores for the PJ and the UCR from 1983 to 2019 and for Republican Proposal (*Propuesta Republicana*, PRO), former President Mauricio Macri's party, from 2015, when it was created, until 2019. As the conclusion to this volume (Chapter 8) shows, Argentine parties have embraced the liberal values embodied in V-Party's Illiberalism index to a greater degree than the governing parties of other countries in this volume. The PJ has adhered to liberal principles less than the UCR and PRO but more than most governing parties represented in this volume. V-Party's Illiberalism index supports the narrative that follows.

The Menem administration was reasonably open toward the opposition, generally tolerant of public criticism, and somewhat accepting of congressional checks (Cheresky 2008, 122–24; Llanos 1998; Palermo and Novaro 1996, 202–3, 256–66). Menem took some actions that, if unchecked, would have expanded his powers, including packing the Supreme Court in 1990, successfully pushing for a constitutional amendment that allowed him to run for reelection in 1995, and flirting with running for a third term in 1999. However, other actors committed to preserving democracy, including parts of the PJ, blocked him from going down the path of eroding democracy. Moreover, Menem's closest associates concur that he never remotely had any intention of grabbing power; rather, he packed the court and pushed to expand executive power as ways of dealing with the severe economic crisis he inherited.

The PJ encouraged the sometimes violent popular mobilizations that led to de la Rúa's fall in December 2001 (Auyero 2007; Novaro 2006, 297). However, it did not become an anti-democratic actor (Novaro 2002, 83). Its commitment to preserving democracy helped the regime to survive in the face of a bruising social and economic crisis. During the crisis of December 2001, the PJ accepted its role as a loyal opposition. In December 2001, when new authorities for both chambers of the national Congress were elected, Eduardo Camaño, the newly elected president of the lower chamber, said that his task and that of Ramón Puerta, who

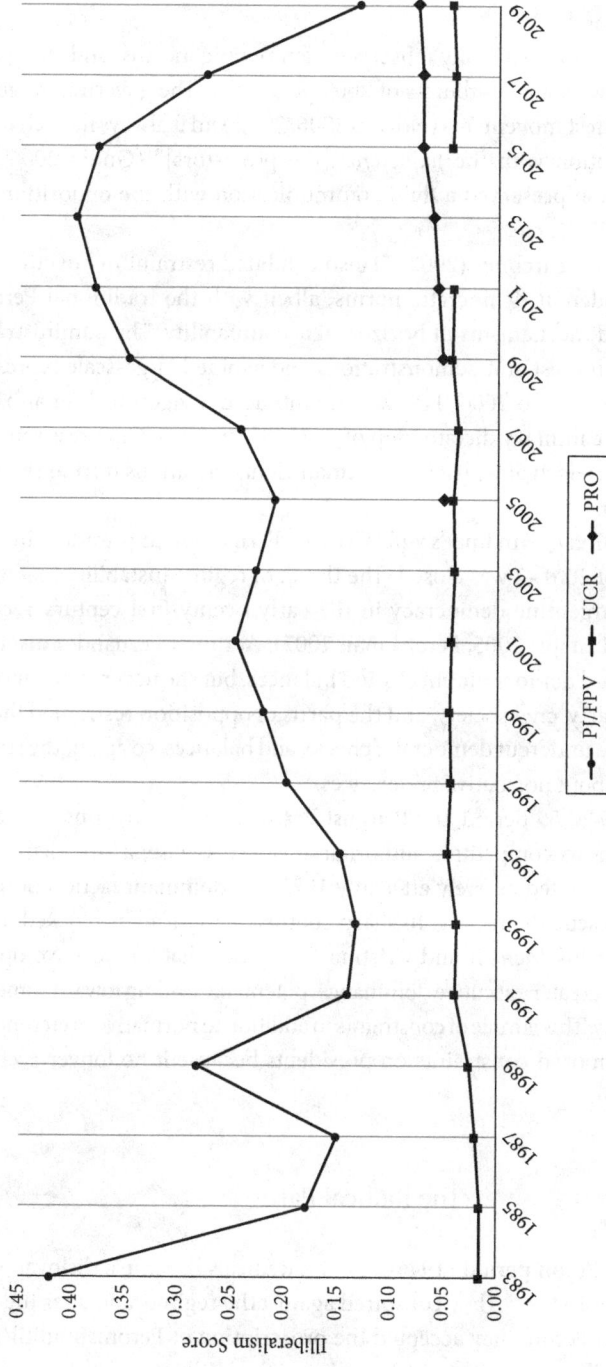

Figure 7.3. V-Dem illiberalism scores—FPV-PJ, UCR, and PRO, 1983–2019

Note: For 2017, we use the data for *Unidad Ciudadana*, as all Kirchnerista candidates ran under this ticket following a split in the PJ.

Source: Lührmann et al. 2020 (variable: v2xpa_illiberal).

had been elected as provisional president of the Senate, was to guarantee the stability of the regime.[27]

President Duhalde generally observed democratic norms and sought to handle the massive social outbursts of 2002 peacefully. The government generally tolerated protest movements (Novaro 2006, 295), and it always had "channels open for negotiation with the *piqueteros* [the protestors]" (Godio 2006, 47). The administration preserved a fluid communication with the opposition and avoided radical discourse.

President Néstor Kirchner (2003–7) also exhibited restraint in how much he attempted to undercut democratic norms, albeit with the traditional Peronist antipathy toward mechanisms of horizontal accountability. The administration tolerated public protest and demonstrations and avoided large-scale repression of the *piqueteros* (Godio 2006, 119–23). It embraced a vigorous human rights policy against the military dictatorship of 1976–83. In 2003, Congress removed the last legal barriers against trials for human rights violations during the military dictatorship.

With the election of Kirchner's wife, Cristina Fernández, as president in 2007, the great crisis of 2001–2 was closed. The threat of regime instability that might have besieged Argentine democracy in the early twenty-first century receded (Bosoer 2006; Mustapic 2005; Pérez Liñán 2007). At times, Fernández displayed intolerance toward democratic checks and balances, but she never went far down that path. Her party, civil society, and the partisan opposition restrained the degree to which she undercut democratic checks and balances, so again, the story is not exclusively about normative preferences.

During the 1946–55 period, the Peronist Party never did anything to prevent the rapid descent to competitive authoritarianism. Likewise, as the democracy of 1973–76 deteriorated severely after July 1975, the dominant faction of the PJ did nothing to rescue the regime. In sharp contrast, party leaders blocked moves by Presidents Carlos Menem and Cristina Fernández that would have opened pathways toward greater executive dominance, potentially leading toward some erosion of democracy. This is a tale of constraints in addition to normative preferences—but the party imposed constraints on presidents because it no longer accepted authoritarianism.

The Radical Party

During the first Perón period (1946–55), the Radicals became a disloyal opposition, by the late 1940s.[28] They conspired against the regime, and after the 1955 coup that ousted Perón, they accepted the proscription of Peronism until 1970. The UCR's unwillingness to accept Peronism as a legitimate actor between the late 1940s and 1970 helped sink the semi-democratic regimes of 1958–62 and 1963–66 (O'Donnell 1973). The UCR's transformation to a normative preference for democracy occurred in 1970. The signing of an agreement, "*La Hora del Pueblo*" (The Hour of the People), in 1970 to work together with the Peronists to reestablish democracy signaled a commitment to support the regime, no matter who would win the elections. The UCR was a staunch advocate of democracy between 1973 and 1976.

From 1983 to 2001, the UCR was one of the two main parties, and it won the 1983 and 1999 presidential elections. In the post-1983 period, both parties recognized each other as legitimate and long-term actors in politics, refraining from the use of non-democratic strategies (McGuire 1995b, 178–80). The Radical Party has had an unwavering commitment to tolerance and democratic pluralism, and consistently moderate policy preferences. President Alfonsín (1983–89) was a committed democrat (Norden 1996, 80–82). He accepted congressional decisions that blocked his government from undertaking reforms that he deemed important. He inherited from the Radical tradition the idea of a democratic pact, which played a central role in his electoral campaign in 1983 (Novaro and Palermo 2006, 530–31). This pact implied a commitment to protect civil and political rights, strengthen democratic institutions, and limit authoritarian powers including the influence of the armed forces (Novaro 1994, 58). In interviews for the Oral History Archive, Alfonsín's economic team, including former Ministry of Economy Juan Vital Sourrouille and former secretaries and collaborators José Luis Machinea, Carlos Bonvecchi, and Pablo Gerchunoff, stated that consolidating democracy was their paramount goal, and that policy decisions were affected by it.[29]

The other UCR president, Fernando de la Rúa (1999–2001), also was committed to observing democratic norms and constraints. He supported freedom of speech, freedom of the press, political tolerance, and public sector transparency (Bonvecchi 2002, 125; Charosky 2002, 210–13; Novaro 2002, 85–91; see also Freedom House 2002 and US Department of State 2002).

The UCR behaved as a loyal opposition during Peronist governments. It showed an unyielding support for democracy when it institutionally backed President Duhalde (2002–3) in order to guarantee the stability of the regime (Jaunarena 2011). Moved by "a fundamental commitment to democracy," Radical deputies and senators supported Duhalde's policies (Godio 2006, 190).

This change in normative preferences also reached smaller political parties. An example was the Record of Agreements (*Acta de Coincidencias*), signed on June 7, 1984, by sixteen political parties including the UCR and the PJ (Aboy Carlés 2004). It included a commitment to reject terrorism and any attempt to forcibly remove the legitimately elected authorities.[30]

The Military

The military is the main actor outside government that can directly topple democracy. After 1983, the Argentine military went from being an anti-democratic actor to accepting democracy and rejecting authoritarianism. The armed forces have moved far from the anti-democratic ideologies that guided many officers during most of the twentieth century. Since 1990, its leadership has adhered to the idea of civilian democratic control of the armed forces.[31] It is not clear whether the military has a normative preference for democracy (this is possible, but we do not have enough evidence to make the assertion), but it has moved very far from its past, when it usually had a normative preference for dictatorship. Its acceptance of democracy has closed the doors to coups.

Like other sectors of Argentine society, the armed forces experienced major substantive losses during the first two decades of democracy. Many military officials who committed human rights abuses during the dictatorship went to jail. As of 2005, 1,070 individuals were imprisoned for human rights crimes, the overwhelmingly majority of which were committed during the dictatorship.[32] In addition, as president, Alfonsín drastically reduced the military budget, from 3.47 percent of the GDP in 1983 to 1.88 percent in 1989. In the same period, military personnel declined by 60 percent (Battaglino 2010). The reduction in the military budget continued in the following presidencies; it was slightly above 1 percent of the GDP by 2002 (World Development Indicators, n.d.).

During the early years of the democratic regime, the military was divided between factions that accepted civilian control and democracy, including groups vocally in favor of democracy, such as the Center of Military Members for Argentine Democracy (*Centro de Militares para la Democracia Argentina*, CEMIDA),[33] and minority sectors that remained wedded to the authoritarian tradition and engaged in uprisings in 1987 and 1988 (Jaunarena 2011; Norden 1996). Another army revolt took place in late 1990, but loyal army units repressed the insurgents. After Menem quelled the last major military rebellion in 1990, the armed forces became a less relevant political actor (Norden 1996). By the early 1990s, the military was under civilian control and began to acknowledge excesses during the "dirty war." Military extremism was buried. During the protests of December 2001, the military refused to suppress the protests without an explicit law from the National Congress. Godio (2002, 126) states that by then the armed forces were unified in the preservation of democracy. The military is more constrained now by other democratic actors than it was between 1930 and 1983, but these constraints imposed by other actors are themselves a product of changing attitudes about democracy and authoritarianism.

Organized Labor

In Argentina, organized labor was frequently an important actor in the fate of political regimes. Before 1983, most of the organized labor movement was at best indifferent toward democracy. Labor mobilized against the semi-democratic regimes of 1958–62 and 1963–66 and supported coups against them. Most of the movement was wedded to Perón (1946–55, 1973–4) despite his turn toward a repressive competitive authoritarian regime in the 1940s and his ambiguous practices toward democracy in 1973–4. Incessant demands for higher wages, coupled with minority radical left-wing mobilizations that included countless factory occupations, helped galvanize the opposition to the democratic regime of 1973–6 (Torre 1983). The Peronist right wing of the labor movement supported the death squads, enabling a severe degradation of democracy as human rights abuses escalated.

Workers suffered substantial economic losses during the Alfonsín period. The average income of the employed active population in Greater Buenos Aires declined 24 percent between 1986 and 1990 (ECLAC 1993). Workers' economic losses were deeper than those they experienced during the military dictatorship. Contrary to the argument that democracy favors income redistribution to the poor (Acemoglu and Robinson 2006; Boix 2003), exactly the opposite happened in Argentina during the first two decades of democracy: income inequality increased sharply and the median income declined.

Despite these losses, organized labor was deeply committed to preserving democracy. One month after Alfonsín's inauguration, in January 1984 the unified CGT issued a document that captured labor's new position on representative democracy. "The rule of law, liberty guaranteed by the legal system, responsible pluralism, and institutionalized participation constitute the only path by which economic development is viable, social justice is possible, and the realization of the human person is guaranteed. For this reason, the labor movement must be a zealous guardian of democratic stability for all Argentines" (quoted in García Lerena 2007, 240–41). In March 1984, the CGT called upon business associations, parties, and youth and religious organizations to integrate a broad national front to help protect democracy (Senén González and Bosoer 2009, 235). McGuire (1997, 21) writes that by the end of the Alfonsín period, the main contending factions within the labor movement "acquired an instrumental stake in the survival of elections and legislative activity" and that the leader of the CGT, Saúl Ubaldini, was committed to democracy "was beyond any serious dispute." In the words of Ramón Baldassini, one of the four Secretary Generals of the CGT, Argentines needed to become conscious of the fact that an institutional break would hurt everyone in the long run and workers in particular.[34]

Labor vigorously mobilized against the Alfonsín government. Even during strikes and demonstrations against the government, however, organized labor stressed its commitment to democracy. In a gathering in the Plaza de Mayo in May 1985, Ubaldini stated that there would not be a coup because workers would stop anyone who might try (quoted in García Lerena 2007, 250). In November 1984, José Luis Castillo, the secretary general of the Union of Ship Technicians of the Argentine Republic (*Sindicato de Conductores Navales de la República Argentina*, SICONARA) expressed concern with rumors about a coup and stated that it was necessary to defend democracy, no matter who the president was.[35]

Some of labor's criticisms of the Alfonsín government were based on the idea that democracy was not deep enough. These criticisms called for deepening democracy rather than rejecting it to prioritize social or economic outcomes or corporatist interests. A constant in these declarations was the claim that workers were crucial in the fight for getting democracy back and that they were now crucial in defending it.[36]

Labor commitment to democracy was also evident in cross-sectional actions such as the "Democratic Compromise in the Face of the Situation of Rebellion and Threat against the Constitutional Order" (*Compromiso democrático ante la situación de rebeldía y amenaza del orden constitucional*) signed in 1987 by the CGT, political parties, the Argentine Industrial Union, a powerful business association (*Unión Industrial Argentina*, UIA), and the government in response to the military uprisings (more on this below). The signatories endorsed democracy as the only option for Argentines (García Lerena 2007, 264).

Labor's defense of democracy was especially important during the military uprisings. During the Easter 1987 uprising, the CGT declared a strike for an unlimited time starting the following Monday if the rebels did not surrender (Pucciarelli 2006, 136). An official CGT resolution stated that the Argentine people had to be united against any threat to democracy and defend it without hesitation.[37] As labor leader José Pedraza stated in an interview, CGT leaders "monolithically defended democracy . . . regardless of our differences with Alfonsín, with the Radical Party, because we stood by democracy."[38] As Luis Sartori highlighted in a newspaper article published right after the events, that was the first time that a non-Peronist government received unanimous support from the unions against a military rebellion.[39] This unanimous support was repeated during the next military uprising in January 1988.[40]

In June 1988, a group of union leaders led by Ubaldini, who opposed the Due Obedience law that gave amnesty to human rights violators who had not yet been prosecuted, issued a joint statement saying, "The armed forces . . . [should] subordinate themselves to the democratic system and guarantee the people that nothing will stand in the way of the prosecution of those who . . . violated human rights" (quoted in McGuire 1992, 54–55). Writing at a time of severe economic problems that had terrible consequences for many workers, Ranis (1992, 6) stated that "Argentine workers' commitment to and support for democracy seemed to reach a new plane in the light of the contrast between the military *Proceso* and the new democracy."

During the economic and financial meltdown of 2001–2, although labor organizations protested and criticized the government, they did not oppose the democratic regime. In a massive demonstration in downtown Buenos Aires, co-organized by unions and labor organizations in August 2001, Hugo Moyano, the leader of the most combative faction of the CGT, urged Argentines to use the "lethal weapon" of elections to express their dissatisfaction with the government.[41]

Popular Mobilizations

During the military rebellions, massive demonstrations in support of democracy showed citizens' commitment to the regime (Jaunarena 2011). The first big pro-democracy, anti-coup demonstration took place in Córdoba province on Holy Thursday, April 16, 1987, one day after the first signs of military revolt became evident in Córdoba. Local parties, together with social and professional organizations including the student movement and the local branch of the CGT, organized a popular demonstration in defense of democracy and a multiparty condemnation of the revolts. Famous singers, actors, and actresses took part in many of the popular demonstrations, called by their professional associations (Pucciarelli 2006, 123–24). Alfonsín later said, reflecting on the Easter uprising, that his only force for deterrence in this dramatic situation was the gigantic and patient crowd covering Plaza de Mayo and other public squares (quoted in Masi 2014, 162). As Gabetta (quoted in Pucciarelli 2006, 134) stated in 1987, the crowd was willing to risk their lives for the democratic regime, showing that Argentines' attitude toward democracy had changed.

The economic crisis of 2001–2 generated widespread social protest. However, these protests were different in kind and political impact from the radicalized labor and student mobilizations of the 1973–76 period. In the 1973–76 period, radicalized labor groups and student organizations occupied countless factories and universities, adding to the tumult and the sense of chaos that weakened the democratic regime. These movements were at best indifferent to the fate of democracy; some favored the installation of a revolutionary socialist regime, and others engaged in behavior that destabilized democracy.

After 1983, even most radical movements protected democracy. An example of this was the emergence of organizations of unemployed that became known as "*organizaciones piqueteras*" (picketer organizations), due to their utilization of roadblocks (Svampa and Pereyra 2003, 25). These movements of unemployed and informal poor workers emerged in the late 1990s in the face of very high unemployment and a weak public safety net. These mobilizations initiated a dynamic of protest for social benefits and provisions, including the use of roadblocks as their main tool. The protests intensified as social conditions deteriorated and the government failed to provide adequate responses to the demands (Garay 2016, 169–71).

Although the *piqueteros* adopted a repertoire of contentious action, their policy demands seldom acquired overtones against democracy. The *piqueteros* employed confrontational tactics by blocking roads and highways, vandalizing toll booths, blocking the pay booths for subways, and encouraging people to ride the subways without paying (Cheresky 2008, 189). In 2004 some groups committed violent acts, including an attack on a police station (Botana 2006, 140). However, most factions were not anti-system (Godio 2006, 307, 319).

The protest movements in 2001–2 never questioned democracy as a political regime. Their main demands were oriented to the state (Schuster et al. 2006). The movements expressed discontent with the political establishment but not against democracy. On the contrary, they demanded more democracy in the form of better representation or the possibility of intervening more directly in public affairs. Some neighborhood assemblies referred to elections as an opportunity for people to use their vote to kick everyone out (Dinerstein 2004, 262).

Many social movements involved in the protests aimed at recovering the participatory component of democracy, faced with a democracy that they considered insufficiently democratic (Natalucci 2011, 198). The protests were thus aimed at defending and not attacking democracy. In the words of one participant, after De la Rúa's call for the "state of siege," "I lived through the *junta* (military government); I know what it means. . . . [P]eople saw this as the first step in the return to political repressions . . . A reversal of rights that we were not willing to lose" (in Onuch 2014, 105).

Business Associations

Business associations openly supported the 1930, 1955, 1966, and 1976 coups (Sidicaro 2002). Their behavior changed to pro-democratic after 1983, partially in response to the failed economic policies of the dictatorship.

Many business sectors experienced heavy setbacks during the periods from 1983 to 1991 and from 1998 to 2003. According to Central Bank data, the main index for the Argentine stock market, Merval, fell more than 60 percent between February 2000 and October 2001.[42] If we consider the devaluation of the peso, the drop in real terms during that period was 90 percent (to one-tenth of its value).[43] This collapse of the Argentine stock market negatively affected many business and elite interests.

Despite these economic losses for business, the experience of the last military dictatorship brought about a change in business's preferences for democracy. Acuña (1995, 232) identifies the democratic transition as a turning point with respect to previous patterns of political struggle for business interests. He observed a change in the meaning that authoritarianism and democracy have for their economic interests. Business interests ceased seeing dictatorships as friendly and predictable. Dictatorships might pursue ill-conceived policies with negative impacts for the main economic actors or perilous "adventures" such as the Falkland/Malvinas War (Acuña 1995, 268–69). Because of the failures of the economic policies of the dictatorship of 1976–83, business stopped perceiving the military as an agent of modernization. This led to support for democracy in the months leading to the elections of 1983 (Pucciarelli 2006, 216). The business sector's bet on the democratic regime seemed to be a long-term one (Acuña 1995, 272). In 1985, the "Group of 11," made up of the CGT and the main business associations, stated in a public communication that democracy is a patrimony of the whole nation and an unquestionable value.[44] Business associations defended the Alfonsín government during all of the military uprisings (Acuña 1995, 269; Beltrán 2006, 217). Business leaders viewed the leaders of the military rebellions with suspicion and skepticism. Their modes of action, populist slogans, and references against "imperialism" made them a risky and uncertain alternative for business. Associations such as the Argentine Rural Society (SRA), the Argentine Industrial Union (UIA), and the Argentine Chamber of Commerce (*Cámara Argentina de Comercio*, CAC) spoke out in favor of democracy during the military crises (Acuña 2004, 180–81). Acuña (1995) argues that business changed its normative preferences regarding the political regime, and not only its instrumental policy preferences after 1983 in response to the failures, closed nature, and erratic character of the 1976–83 regime.

An act that illustrated the support for democracy by opposition parties, unions, and business organizations was the signing of the "Democratic Compromise in the Face of the Situation of Rebellion and Threat against the Constitutional Order" in response to the military uprising of April 1987. The document expressed the determined resolution of the signatories to defend the Constitution and democracy as the "single life destiny of the Argentine people."[45] The document was signed by representatives of most political parties including the Radical Party, the Peronist Party, the Intransigent Party, the Union of the Democratic Center (Unión del Centro Democrático, UCEDE), the Christian Democratic Party, and many provincial parties. Representatives of the CGT and many business organizations, including the SRA, the UIA, the Construction Union, the CAC, and the Argentine Rural Confederations, also signed.[46]

By 2001, thus, all the main actors had accepted democracy. No actors have an explicit preference for dictatorship, and none has attempted to form an authoritarian coalition since the failed coups toward the end of the Alfonsín government.

The Decline of Extremist Actors and the Rise of the Human Rights Movement

The changes in attitudes toward democracy and authoritarianism were accompanied by a concomitant demise of radicalism in Argentine politics. Powerful actors with extremist agendas no longer exist. The revolutionary left was annihilated during the "dirty war". Most individuals who came from the revolutionary left and survived the dictatorship underwent political and personal conversions. Many became staunch supporters of democracy (Ollier 2009). The demise of the revolutionary left and of radical sympathizers such as the Peronist Youth (*Juventud Peronista*) and far left-wing unionism lowered the stakes of democratic politics. Conservative and centrist actors no longer feared politically motivated assassinations and kidnappings, factory takeovers, and the sense of chaos and disorder that permeated the 1973–76 period.

The extremist right wing, which included death squads that killed hundreds of people before the March 1976 coup, also weakened greatly, discredited by its association with a disgraced regime. The radical right-wing temptation— the idea that Argentina could recover its golden era through right-wing authoritarianism—died. The defeat in the 1982 Falkland/Malvinas War, the military regime's mishandling of economic policy, the international notoriety and condemnation that surrounded the state terror of the military regime, and the domestic repudiation of the human rights violations committed by the armed forces during the "dirty war" discredited the far right. After 1983, other political actors rejected extremist policy positions and intransigent behavior.

The end of extremism, which was closely associated with changing attitudes toward democracy, had profound consequences for democratic survival. In periods of economic downturn, some of which have been severe in the post-1983 period, most people, companies, and sectors have suffered losses, but democracy has given them an institutionalized, peaceful way of fighting for their interests without resorting to coups or violence.

During the dictatorship, some courageous individuals created new human rights organizations. They established one of the most innovative, vociferous, and effective human rights movements in the world. They were a key part of the opposition to the dictatorship, and a consistent advocate thereafter clamoring for transitional justice. Although thirty-eight years have now lapsed since the end of the last dictatorship, these organizations have continued their work, thereby continuously activating a message on behalf of human rights and, by extension, on behalf of democracy (Sikkink 2008).

Understanding Changes in Actors' Preferences

The deep failures of the military dictatorship of 1976–83 were a major cause of the reorientation of actors' preferences about the political regime. Repressive failed dictatorships do not always generate change in actors' preferences toward democracy (Roberts 1998), but they sometimes do (Bermeo 1992). In this respect, the reorientation of many Argentine actors toward democracy after the 1976 coup followed a path similar to what Bermeo describes in her chapter on Timor-Leste. A process of political learning occurred. The building of collective memory through human rights trials resulting in the imprisonment of hundreds of abusers, human rights museums and other public spaces, a vigorous human rights movement, and a vast outpouring of arts, journalism, and academic work on the abuses of the dictatorship has constantly renewed a message about human rights and democracy.

An extensive literature has documented that international influences, especially regional influences, affect political regimes. Two international influences supported the demise of extremist actors and a stronger commitment to democracy and greater political moderation among most of the rest. First, US policy toward Latin America changed after 1977. For the most part, from 1977 until 2017, the US supported democracy in Latin America, although the periods from 1981 to 1985 and from 2017 to 2021 were exceptions. Except for these two periods, the US generally withdrew support for right-wing authoritarians. Because actors knew that the US would oppose coups against democracy, the cost of attempting coups increased. A decisive turning point in the US's relationship with Argentina's right-wing authoritarians came when President Carter signaled clear opposition to the military dictatorship of 1976–83. Another came when President Reagan sided with the United Kingdom when the Argentine dictators went to war against the US's close ally in 1982. US opposition to the generals' bellicose miscalculation reduced the space for Argentina's right-wing authoritarians. US support for Argentine democrats bolstered the pro-democracy camp.

Second, the transformation of the Argentine left was influenced by a similar development on the left in Brazil, Chile, and Uruguay, as well as in much of Europe. The left began to reject revolutionary socialism and to embrace liberal democracy as a necessary part of a desirable political order (Ollier 2009). In Uruguay, Chile, and Brazil, the devastating experiences of military dictatorships pushed the left toward democracy. The left in these countries and the democratic left in Europe influenced leftist Argentine intellectuals, politicians, artists, and political activists. The crushing of dissent in Poland in 1981 laid bare the bankruptcy of Soviet-style communism. The motto of the Argentine human rights movement, "*nunca más*," meaning, "never again [will we allow such depraved human rights abuses]," could also apply to most of the left's attitude about revolutionary socialism: never again would these individuals and organizations embrace revolutionary socialism.

A Few Alternative Explanations

Some scholars argue that institutional constraints, rather than actors' normative preferences and their location on the moderate–radical policy scale, help explain the survival of democracy. Institutional constraints might be sufficient to protect democracy in countries with long-established democracies and strong institutions. However, Argentina has relatively weak democratic institutions (Levitsky and Murillo 2005; Spiller and Tommasi 2007). The courts (Helmke 2005; Larkins 1998) and Congress have sometimes imposed limits on presidents, and in so doing, they have helped defend democracy against presidential encroachments. But by themselves, they do not provide a convincing explanation for the stabilization of Argentine democracy. They were not significant actors in defeating the military rebellions of the 1980s. Congress sometimes limited initiatives by the UCR and Macri administrations, but for the most part it was highly deferential to the PJ presidents. As Jones and Hwang (2005, 127–28) summarized, "The majority party leadership in the Chamber and Senate is in most instances a faithful servant of the president." Moreover, as Jones et al. (2002) and Jones and Micozzi (2013, 72) noted, the combination of very short legislative careers (usually, one term only for federal deputies), governors' control over deputies, and ample party switching after elections (usually in the direction of the president's coalition) weakens legislative controls over the executive. Notwithstanding occasional exceptions, the courts have been generally deferential to presidents (Berbecel, 2022; Helmke 2005; Spiller and Tommasi 2007). The hypertrophy of presidential power during the Menem period led O'Donnell (1994) to coin his famous concept, "delegative democracy," one of whose central features was the weakness of mechanisms of horizontal accountability.

In the post-1983 period, some institutional constraints have been stronger than they were in the democratic experiences of 1946–51 and 1973–76. The fact that the governing party has not always had a majority in Congress has enhanced congressional checks and balances. The fact that no party consistently wins the presidency has been salutary for democracy. Nevertheless, the ability of many provincial governors to construct competitive authoritarian provincial enclaves

(Gervasoni 2018) and the weakness of Argentina's court system in checking presidents indicate that institutions alone are unlikely to suffice to preserve democracy. The ability of presidents and prime ministers in seemingly once solid democracies such as Venezuela until the 1990s, Hungary until 2010, and Poland until 2015 to overrun democracy points in the same direction.

Some excellent scholars included in this volume (and others) posit that a balance of power constrains powerful actors to abide by democratic rules of the game and that this balance of power explains democratic survival. We agree that a balance of power is generally good for democracy. Dominance by one party or individual makes executive takeovers easier, and it could make military coups more likely if powerful actors strongly oppose the government. However, after the fall of the De la Rúa government in 2001, except for the 2015–19 interlude, the Peronists have dominated the electoral and political landscape against a highly fragmented opposition. In the context of generally deferential courts and a national congress that is not strong, it is difficult to argue that the opposition was powerful enough to have kept a president who really wanted to undermine democracy from doing so. The fact that courts and Congress have occasionally limited presidential encroachments does not show that they have consistently been decisive constraints in safeguarding democracy. In contexts of fairly weak institutional constraints and clear electoral dominance, power-hungry presidents who are bent on eroding democracy are difficult to stop.

Could public opinion favorable to democracy explain its survival? In the Latin American Public Opinion surveys, Argentines have consistently expressed more favorable attitudes about democracy than respondents in most Latin American countries. For example, in 2018–19, 71.1 percent of Argentine respondents agreed that "Democracy may have problems, but it is better than any other form of government." In Latin America, this was the third highest percentage, behind only Uruguay (76.2 percent) and Costa Rica (72.4 percent) (Zechmeister and Lupu 2019, 12). Moreover, at critical times such as the military rebellions discussed above, citizen mobilization on behalf of democracy helped a great deal. Certainly, favorable public opinion has been a substantial asset for democracy. But it is hard to know how much weight to give it. Venezuelans expressed a high attachment to democracy as their country became more and more authoritarian, so citizen support in the usual survey questions certainly does not guarantee the survival of democracy. More generally, it is not easy for voters to force governments to remain faithful to democracy (Graham and Svolik 2020).

Gibson (1996) and Ziblatt (2017) argued that strong conservative parties help stabilize democracy by protecting the interests of conservative elites such as business groups. This argument is generally right, but it does not help explain the survival of democracy in Argentina. From 1983 to 2015, Argentina had nothing that resembled a strong conservative party.[47] The most successful conservative parties in presidential elections were the UCEDE in 1983 with 0.4 percent of the vote and again in 1989 with 6.5 percent, MODIN in 1995 with 1.8 percent, *Acción por la República* in 1999 with 10.2 percent, and *Recrear* in 2003 with 16.4 percent and in 2007 with 1.4 percent. No conservative party had a presidential candidate in 2011. Democracy can endure despite the lack of a powerful conservative party. Unless the major parties are committed to democracy, it is doubtful that it can survive powerful extremist actors committed to the destruction of democracy, as Argentina experienced from 1973 to 1976.

The absence of a solid conservative party was not a hindrance to democracy despite the fact that the main conservative actors suffered large losses. The military, business, and the Church hierarchy (which was mostly a conservative actor in Argentina from 1976 to 1983)[48] accepted large losses under democracy. As noted previously, many military leaders ended up in jail, military budgets were slashed, and the military was downsized. Most business interests faced losses during the economic crises of 1983–90, 1998–2002, and 2018–20. Agricultural exporters were subjected to large export taxes under the government of Cristina Fernández de Kirchner (2007–15). Most of the leadership of the Argentine Catholic Church supported the military coup of 1976 and the ensuring dictatorship. Under democracy, the Church lost important political battles in 2006, when the Law of Integral Sexual Education passed; in 2010, when Argentina became the first Latin American country to pass a bill legalizing gay marriage at the national level; in 2012, when it passed one of the most progressive laws in the world in support of the rights of transgender individuals; and in 2015, when a new civil code affirmed the equal rights of all individuals regardless of gender and sexual orientation. Yet the Church has accepted democracy and generally embraced it since 1983.

A modernization explanation can explain the survival of democracy after 1983, but it cannot explain why democracy has fared better since 1983 than it did between 1973 and 1976, and it offers at best a weak explanation for why democracy has fared better since 1983 than in the breakdowns of 1930, 1951, 1962, and 1966. Although Argentina's level of development has long been favorable to democracy, the initial level per capita GDP in 1983 was slightly lower than it was in 1973. Per capita GDP was $6,717 in 1983, 3 percent lower than the per capita GDP of $6,947 at the beginning of the previous democratic regime in 1973 (World Development Indicators, n.d.).

Class theories of democratization based on the power of the working class do not explain Argentina's democratic stability since 1983. The organized working class is smaller and less powerful now than it was during Argentina's competitive regimes of 1946–51, 1958–62, 1963–66, and 1973–76. The share of the economically active population engaged in manufacturing, mining, transportation, and construction declined from 28 percent in 1970 to 22 percent by 2005 (ILO

1975; LABORSTA, n.d.). Union density declined steeply from 42.5 percent in 1954 (Doyon 1988, table 5) to 24.4 percent for 1990–95 (ILO 2002). Therefore, Argentina's post-1983 democratic stabilization is not a result of a larger, more powerful working class.

Theories of democratization based on income inequalities also fail to explain Argentina's transformation from repeated breakdowns to stable democracy after 1983. Argentina's income distribution was relatively equal between 1960 (and almost certainly well before then) and 1976. From 1960 until 1976—the first decades for which hard data are available—Argentina's Gini coefficient for income distribution was almost always below 0.40 and was as low as 0.33 (1972), one of the lowest figures ever recorded in Latin America. Income inequalities became much worse in Argentina in the decades after the 1976 coup. From 1976 until 2003, Argentina experienced the greatest increase in inequality of any country in Latin America. The Gini index increased from 34.7 in 1973 (the inaugural year of the last democratic regime before the current one) to 52.8 in 2003. Few countries in the world outside the former communist countries experienced such a staggering increase in inequality in this time. When the main actors were committed to democracy and there were no extremist actors, the regime could withstand a profound increase in inequality (SEDLAC 2018).

Conclusion

In Latin America, democracy has infrequently broken down since the beginning of the third wave in 1978. Democracy has survived in most countries despite formidable obstacles and deep economic crises. The specific story behind the survival of democracy varies from country to country, but a common story is that more actors are committed to democracy than before, fewer authoritarian actors abound, extremist actors have been less powerful, and US policy has been largely favorable to supporting democracy since Jimmy Carter's presidency (1977–81) (Schenoni and Mainwaring 2019).

In Argentina, democracy survived despite a past history of coups and strong authoritarian actors, and despite three severe economic crises and several military uprisings. Because substantive outcomes were terrible for many actors during the first two decades of democracy when it was more likely to be vulnerable, it is impossible to explain the survival of democracy by claiming that actors benefited in substantive terms. And because factions of the military were probably willing to launch a coup, it is clear that actors did not merely accept democracy because they had no choice. Some of the actors and millions of people who experienced the deepest losses in the 1983–91 period mobilized in defense of democracy when the military rebellions occurred.

Democracy survived in part because of the demise of extremist actors. With less at stake, there was less reason to destroy democracy. In addition, a fundamental transformation occurred in several key actors' beliefs regarding democracy after the last military dictatorship. Some actors came to believe that democracy was worth defending even if its substantive results were dismal. Other actors were less committed to democracy, but they were more committed than they had been in the past to not flagrantly violate democratic norms even when they had the power to do so. This normative preference and the demise of radical extremist actors has helped preserve democracy.

Notes

* A few paragraphs of this chapter come from Mainwaring and Pérez-Liñán 2013. We are grateful to Fernando Bizzarro, Michael Coppedge, Candelaria Garay, Steve Levitsky, Raúl Madrid, Tarek Masoud, Aníbal Pérez-Liñán, Luis Schiumerini, Maggie Shum, Jazmín Sierra, Guillermo Trejo, Deborah Yashar, and colleagues at the conference on Democracy in Hard Places that took place in May 2019 at the Ash Center for Democratic Governance and Innovation of the Harvard Kennedy School for helpful comments. Thanks to Vicky De Negri and Luis Elizondo for research assistance.

1. A military coup ended the presidency of Juan Perón in 1955. In our view, democracy had broken down by 1951 because of severe infringements of opposition rights and a grossly uneven playing field. Thus, we situate the breakdown as occurring four years before the coup that deposed Perón.

2. The exposition that follows focuses on coups, but the logic applies equally to executive takeovers.

3. Measured in annual percentage (indicator: NY.GDP.MKTP.KD.ZG).

4. For a similar logic with voters, see Graham and Svolik (2020).

5. Frey et al. (2004, 381) define procedural utility as "the well-being people gain from living and acting under institutionalized processes as they contribute to a positive sense of self."

6. "Argentine Falklands War Troops 'Tortured by Their Own Side,'" BBC News, September 14, 2015, https://www.bbc.com/news/world-latin-america-34252025.

7. Both movies won Oscar awards for Best Foreign Language Film as well as many other international film awards.

8. For example, a best-selling book by renowned journalist Horacio Verbitsky (1995) reported confessions of naval officer Adolfo Scilingo that the Argentine military had dumped the live bodies of countless political prisoners into the Atlantic Ocean on "death flights."

9. "7 sitios para recordar y volver a decir: 'Nunca más' [7 sites to remember and say once more: 'Never again']." Ministerio de Cultura, March 23, 2019, https://www.cultura. gob.ar/espacios-para-no-olvidar-7-sitios-de-horror-y-resistencia_7297/.

10. For evidence that human rights museums make individuals, in the short term, more supportive of democracy and transitional justice, and less supportive of authoritarianism, see Balcells et al., 2022.

11. Measured in annual percentage (indicator: NY.GDP.MKTP.KD.ZG).

12. Measured in constant 2010 US dollars (indicator: NY.GDP.PCAP.KD).

13. Annual growth in consumer prices.

14. GDP per capita growth (annual %) (NY.GDP.PCAP.KD.ZG).

15. Authors' translation. All translations in this chapter are ours.

16. Thanks to Luis Schiumerini for pointing out this survey result.

17. The formula is (14-FH score)/12, where FH score is the combined score for civil liberties and political rights. Although the scale is the same, the scores are not exactly commensurable; Freedom House has far more scores equal to or approaching 1 than V-Dem. V-Dem counts the first year of democracy as 1984, thus accounting for the sharp discrepancy in the 1983 scores.

18. Measured in constant 2010 US dollars (indicator: NY.GDP.PCAP.KD).

19. The government of Patricio Aylwin in Chile (1990–94) and the Chilean courts vigorously punished a large number of human rights abusers. However, their efforts were not as publicized as those in Argentina, and they never induced a military rebellion that could have resulted in a coup. In most other Latin American countries, early efforts at transitional justice were timid (González Ocantos 2016).

20. Archivo de Historia Oral de la Argentina Contemporánea, Instituto de Investigaciones Gino Germani, http://iigg.sociales.uba.ar/cdi-2/archivos/.

21. Archivo del Sindicalismo Argentino "Santiago Senén González" (ASASG), Universidad Torcuato Di Tella, https://www.utdt.edu/ver_contenido.php?id_conten ido=2280&id_item_menu=4559.

22. This includes all the public declarations and speeches available at the library of the CGT for the period 1981–90 (although there are only a couple of documents for the last three years).

23. "Iniciativa de Labaké para recrear la estructura del movimiento peronista [Labaké's initiative to recreate the structure of the Peronist movement]," *Tiempo Argentino*, March 3, 1985.

24. Abal Medina served as chief of cabinet for President Cristina Fernández de Kirchner (2011–13) and national senator (2011–17). His father was one of the founding leaders of the Montoneros.

25. Along similar lines, Tcach and Quiroga (2006, 13) wrote that "[t]he dictatorship taught the society . . . to value the preservation of democracy. . . . Argentine society learned the lesson well: the rejection of political violence that undermines and annuls institutional legitimacy and the rule of law."

26. Levitsky and Ziblatt (2018, 23–24) propose four key indicators of authoritarian orientations: (1) "Rejection of . . . democratic rules of the game," (2) "Denial of the legitimacy of political opponents," (3) "Toleration or encouragement of violence," and (4) "Readiness to curtail civil liberties of opponents, including media."

27. Quoted in "El nuevo Parlamento: los límites del justicialismo. La fortaleza institucional no disimula debilidades internas [The new Parliament: the limits of Justicialism. Institutional strength does not conceal internal weaknesses]," *Clarín*, December 6, 2001, https://www.clarin.com/politica/fortaleza-institucional-disim ula-debilidades-internas_0_rkVxzPUgRFl.html.

28. Linz's (1978b) concept of "disloyal opposition" referred to actors that wanted to undermine a democratic regime. Because Perón installed a repressive competitive authoritarian regime, we use the term "disloyal opposition" here to refer to the UCR's attitude toward this regime, not toward democracy *per se.*

29. Oral History Archive interview recorded during July 2005 (first part, first cassette).

30. Martín Prieto, "Peronistas y radicales firman en Argentina un remedo de los 'pactos de la Moncloa [Peronists and Radicals sign in Argentina an imitation of the Moncloa pacts]." *El País,* August 6, 1984, https://elpais.com/diario/1984/06/08/internacional/455493620_850215.html.

31. A few prominent military leaders published memoirs or gave interviews that endorsed the intrinsic value of democracy. See Ballester (1996, 14) and the interview with former president Alejandro Lanusse (1971–73; Lanusse 1988, 59–63).

32. Procuraduría de Crímenes contra la Humanidad, n.d. [Attorney's Office for Crimes against Humanity] "Estadísticas" (Statistics), https://www.fiscales.gob.ar/lesa-humanidad/?tipo-entrada=estad%C3%ADsticas (accessed April 2021).

33. See "Nucleamiento de militares retirados [Grouping of retired military officials]." *Clarín,* November 18, 1984.

34. "Ramón Baldassini se define como un socialdemócrata [Ramón Baldassini defines himself as a social-democrat]. *La Razón,* December 26, 1984.

35. "Preocupa a la C.G.T. la desestabilización [CGT worried by destabilization]." *Clarín,* November 6, 1984. Castillo later served as a federal deputy from the Peronist (Justicialist) Party for the province of Buenos Aires from 1987 to 1999.

36. " 'Tenemos una democracia sólo formal [We have only a formal democracy]." *Tiempo Argentino,* April 27, 1984; "Casella dialogó con el titular de la CGT [Castella conversed with the head of the CGT]." *Clarín,* April 27, 1984; "Los trabajadores aspiramos a una democracia real, con justicia social e independencia económica ["We workers aspire to a real democracy, with social justice and economic independence"]. *Tiempo Argentino,* April 30, 1984; "CGT: Multitudinaria Concentración [CGT: Mass Concentration]." May 2, 1984; "CGT: Rechaza la advertencia oficial [CGT: Rejects the governmental warning]." *Clarín,* November 22, 1984.

37. "Resolución del Comité Central Confederal [Central Confederate Committee's resolution]." CGT, March 25, 1987.

38. Third session, minutes 56:50–58:00. Interviewed by members of the Oral History Group at IIGG *Archivo de Historia Oral de la Argentina Contemporánea.*

39. Luis Sartori, "Un respaldo sin fisuras [Unfailing support]." *Clarín,* April 20, 1987.

40. Ricardo Roa, "Acordes y disonancias frente a la crisis [Harmonies and dissonances in the face of the crisis]." *Clarín,* December 12, 1988.

41. Quotes published in "Las CGT pidieron derrotar en las urnas el modelo económico [The CGTs call for the defeat of the economic models in the ballot box]." *La Nación,* August 30, 2001, https://www.lanacion.com.ar/331412-las-cgt-pidieron-derrotar-en-las-urnas-el-modelo-economico.

42. Banco Central de la República Argentina [Central Bank of the Argentine Republic], Informe Monetario Mensual [Monthly monetary report] (March 2000 and November

2001; accessed August 2, 2021), http://www.bcra.gob.ar/PublicacionesEstadisticas/Informe_monetario_mensual.asp.

43. Marc Garrigasait, "Qué hizo la Bolsa en Argentina durante el corralito y qué nos enseña [What the Argentine Stock Market did during the 'corralito' and what that teaches us]." *El blog de Marc Garrigasait* (blog), August 6, 2012, https://investorsco nundrum.com/2012/08/06/que-hizo-la-bolsa-en-argentina-durante-el-corralito-y-que-nos-ensena/.

44. "Apoyo a la democracia de gremios y empresarios [Support for democracy from unions and businessmen]." *Clarín*, April 20, 1985.

45. Quoted in Martín Prieto, "Alfonsín logra personalmente la rendición de los sublevados en Campo de Mayo [Alfonsín personally achieves the surrender of the rebels of Campo de Mayo]." *El País*, April 20, 1987, https://elpais.com/diario/1987/04/20/internacional/545868006_850215.html.

46. National broadcast of the signature ceremony by *Radio Nacional*. Audio available at the La Plata University archive, April 24, 1987, http://sedici.unlp.edu.ar/handle/10915/44452.

47. President Carlos Menem (1989–99), a Peronist, governed on the center-right. However, the PJ was not a conservative party, and it returned to its left-of-center roots from 2002 on.

48. See Mignone (1986).

8

Why Democracies Survive
in Hard Places

Scott Mainwaring

This volume addresses a puzzle that has important theoretical consequences for how social scientists and historians understand democracy: why does democracy sometimes survive in very inauspicious conditions?[*] Because many structural and cultural conditions are unfavorable in these contexts, in this chapter I focus on a debate about institutions and actors.[1] Do democracies survive because narrowly self-interested actors are constrained by a balance of power and institutions, or do they also survive in part because some actors are committed normatively to democracy? We believe that this is the first volume to take this puzzle up directly and in great detail.

The volume does not offer definitive answers, but it brings the debate about these questions to the fore in new ways. No analysis of why democracy survives can ignore actors' instrumental interests and behavior, formal institutions, or the balance of power, but I argue that actors' normative preferences about democracy and dictatorship also help explain the longevity of democracy in hard places.[2] Actors have very different attitudes and preferences about democracy and authoritarianism, and these preferences about the regime are important for sustaining democracy or leading to its demise. Actors that are normatively committed to democracy can help sustain it even in difficult circumstances. Conversely, illiberal rulers and other actors can often tear it down in less institutionalized regimes.

In Argentina, India, South Africa, and Timor-Leste, a repudiation of the terrible past generated a new appreciation of democracy that has helped these regimes survive despite many adverse conditions. The Argentine military dictatorship of 1976–83 was a resounding failure, and in response to the very high price that they paid, actors that had previously been indifferent to democracy strongly embraced it (Chapter 7, this volume). These democratic commitments have stuck over time, perhaps because the previous dictatorship was such a failure, and also because of the memorialization of human rights abuses under that regime. In India, a broad, inclusive, democratic nationalism formed in response to British colonialism (see Chapter 2, this volume). Although there have been important challenges to that inclusive, democratic nationalism in the

Scott Mainwaring, *Why Democracies Survive in Hard Places* In: *Democracy in Hard Places*. Edited by: Scott Mainwaring and Tarek Masoud, Oxford University Press. © Oxford University Press 2022. DOI: 10.1093/oso/9780197598757.003.0008 fifty-seven years since Nehru died in 1964, the primary original organizational carrier of that inclusive democratic nationalism, the Congress Party, has usually remained a solidly democratic actor. In South Africa, the primary opponent to the apartheid regime, the African National Congress, became a strongly pro-democratic actor in the 1990s. For the most part, it has remained one since then. Finally, as Nancy Bermeo describes, in Timor-Leste, a broad democratic, inclusive, national consensus also emerged in response to the widespread repudiation of Indonesia's brutal occupation of 1975–99.

In Benin since 2019, Georgia since 2008, India under the BJP, and Moldova and Ukraine during many periods, ruling parties have been measurably (based on expert surveys) less committed to liberal norms than in Argentina, India during most of the time under the Congress Party, South Africa, and Timor-Leste. In these contexts, democracy has broken down (Benin in 2019), never really taken hold (Georgia, Moldova, Ukraine), and eroded sharply (India under the BJP). Indonesia is an intermediate case according to expert surveys; the ruling parties at times (2009–14 and 2019–present) have been less committed to liberal norms than in Argentina, India under Congress, South Africa, and Timor-Leste, but without being as illiberal as some governing parties in Georgia, Moldova, and Ukraine, or the BJP in India in recent years.

My argument does not pit actors' normative preferences against institutions. To understand why democracies survive in hard places, we also need to analyze external constraints that bind actors. Institutional constraints are essential because, as James Madison (1788) famously noted in the Federalist #51, "Men are not angels."[3] For this reason, Madison argued, strong checks and balances are needed to protect a republic. Without institutional constraints, democracy's survival would rest solely on actors' willingness to accept costs to protect democracy. Although some rulers and parties are law- and norm-respecting democrats, such people and parties do not always hold power. Hence, the need for institutional constraints that make it more difficult and costly to attempt to erode or overthrow democracy. Even fairly weak institutions sometimes constrain would-be authoritarian rulers.

Perspectives that emphasize institutional constraints have put forth two potentially complementary arguments. First, a strong opposition can constrain the government and prevent executive takeovers of democracy. Enough actors find democracy an acceptable compromise that it becomes a stable equilibrium. Arguments that posit that democracy rests on a balance of power are intuitively sensible, and some empirical evidence supports the idea that democracy is on more solid ground when there is a strong partisan opposition (Pérez-Liñán et al. 2019). However, these arguments do not go very far in explaining the surprising democratic endurance in our six cases of long-lasting democracy.[4] In five of the six cases, for extended times, government dominance could have enabled rulers with authoritarian predilections to engage in a power grab.

Second, *institutions* constrain actors that would of their own accord seek to expand their power at the expense of democracy. This was James Madison's focus. At first blush, it might seem that institutional arguments should not hold much sway in democracies in hard places. Institutional checks and balances are not strong in such contexts. Nevertheless, several of the authors in this volume (Mainwaring and Simison on Argentina, Riedl on Benin and South Africa, Slater on Indonesia, and Varshney on India) indicate—perhaps surprisingly—that even in these contexts of usually weak checks and balances, institutions such as courts, federalism, and legislatures sometimes protect democracies. Institutional constraints are not sufficient to generate regime stability in most democracies in hard places, but they sometimes induce players to stay in the game.

I briefly discuss two other constraints that could in principle push actors to stick to democracy: external actors, of which the European Union and the United States are by far the most important, and voters. The EU and the US sometimes have encouraged transitions to democracy and prevented outright coups, but they have little capacity to thwart incremental executive takeovers. An older literature on voters argues that democratic voters induce regimes to be democratic. But this literature did not make convincing arguments about the mechanisms by which such an outcome would occur. Much of the recent literature is skeptical that voters care deeply about democracy above and beyond the outputs that it produces, and hence that voters will keep democracy intact (Graham and Svolik 2020; Svolik 2019). Even if voters care deeply about democracy, voting is such a blunt way of conveying citizen preferences that it is not certain that they could push politicians to abide by democratic rules of the game.

Normative Preferences about the Political Regime

Democracies survive either because of actors' own preferences—they embrace democracy as the best possible political regime—or because they are constrained to abide by democratic rules of the game. In this section, I discuss internal constraints that stem from actors' normative commitments. I begin with three claims: first, that actors have very different preferences about the political regime; second, that these differences in preferences are measurable; and third, that these preferences have highly important consequences for regime outcomes. Actors committed to democracy make it more viable; actors committed to its destruction or indifferent to its survival make a breakdown more likely.

Actors' preferences regarding the political regime form a continuum ranging from a strong normative commitment to democracy to intense hostility to it and a preference for some kind of authoritarian regime. Imagine five points on an underlying continuum regarding actors' preferences about the political regime:

1. An actor has a strong normative preference for democracy. A normative preference for democracy means that an actor is willing to forego some instrumental benefits in order to preserve democracy. As an example, in August 2020, Republican Senator Mitt Romney criticized President Trump's attacks on mail-in voting. "We should make every effort to assure that people who want to vote get the chance to vote, and *that's even more important than the outcome of the vote. We have got to preserve the principle of democracy*" (emphasis added).[5] For Romney, democracy is more important than winning. For actors and individuals who have a strong normative preference for democracy, building and retaining democracy and protecting human rights are central objectives. Human rights activists and organizations, religious leaders and churches that value human rights and democracy, and some exceptional political leaders such as Nelson Mandela and Jawaharlal Nehru are examples.

2. An actor has a modest normative preference for democracy. The actor believes that democracy is the best possible political regime and is willing to forego some instrumental advantages in order to protect democracy. Most of the mainstream political parties in the advanced industrial democracies normatively favored democracy throughout most of their histories as mass, representative polyarchies. For the most part, these parties practiced what Levitsky and Ziblatt (2018) call mutual tolerance and forbearance.[6] They accepted the legitimacy of the other mainstream parties, and they refrained from constitutional hardball. In contrast, narrowly self-interested instrumental actors that have no normative interest in preserving democracy would frequently question the legitimacy of other mainstream parties and engage in constitutional hardball on a regular basis.

3. The actor is indifferent to regime type.

4. On normative grounds, the actor rejects some aspects of liberal democracy and would prefer to dismantle it. Advocates of "illiberal democracy" such as Viktor Orbán and critics of representative democracy such as Hugo Chávez are examples. Many populists fit into this category. Their claim to be the true representative of the people or the nation leads them to hostility toward democratic checks and balances and toward political opposition, which they see as illegitimate (Galston 2018; Madrid and Weyland 2019; Müller 2016a; Norris and Inglehart 2019; Weyland 2013, 2020).

5. The actor despises liberal democracy and would like to overthrow it and install an authoritarian or totalitarian regime. The revolutionary left,

theocrats such as the leaders and supporters of the Iranian regime, Islamic terrorist groups, and right-wing extremists such as the Nazis are examples. So are personalistic autocrats who are convinced of their special, almost innate qualities for ruling. Examples include traditional advocates of the divine right of kings and more modern autocrats such as Rafael Trujillo (1930–61) in the Dominican Republic. These actors are deeply (sometimes fanatically) ideologically committed to a personalistic authoritarian or totalitarian regime.

Commitments to democracy are important because in weakly institutionalized democracies, international actors and domestic formal checks and balances are unlikely to deter rulers who have authoritarian proclivities and significant institutional and popular support. Just as positive normative commitments help protect democracy, illiberal actors can help to sink it. A durable democratic equilibrium with no democrats is extremely unlikely.

The normative preferences of presidents and prime ministers and of their parties are particularly important; they are the prime movers of democratic politics (Pérez-Liñán et al. 2019). Executive-led suffocations of democracy hinge on presidents, prime ministers, and governing parties who want to cripple checks and balances and diminish opposition rights. Presidents and prime ministers who are committed to democracy avoid such transgressions.[7]

Actors' preferences about the political regime and their other programmatic preferences are not voluntaristic individual agency. These preferences are embedded in organizational histories, identities, donor bases, activists, and voters. Organizational preferences are not as static as Berman (1998) suggests in her excellent book on Social Democratic parties in Germany and Sweden, but nor are they part of a voluntaristic world. Parties (and other actors) do not change their programmatic profiles—including on issues related to the political regime—overnight. There is some element of choice in these organizational preferences, and they do change over time, but choice is bounded by the organizational histories, identities, ideological commitments, donors, activists, and bases. These are not (in my understanding) *structural* constraints, but they are constraints.

Illiberalism and Democracy in Hard Places

Data from the Varieties of Party Identity and Organization (V-Party, Lührmann et al. 2020) project are useful for indicating the degree to which the main parties in our nine countries have embraced democratic norms. This project created an illiberalism index based on expert surveys in 169 countries. The index is based on four questions about party leaders' severe personal attacks on or demonization of political opponents; their acceptance of free and fair elections and freedom of speech, media, assembly, and association; their acceptance of minority rights; and their rejection of political violence. All four questions tap essential democratic norms. The scale ranges from 0 (parties that fully embrace liberal democratic values) to 1 (extremely illiberal parties). I expect that low illiberal scores make it easier for democracy to endure, and that high illiberal scores, especially for governing parties, make it difficult for democracy to survive in hard places.

Figure 8.1 provides information about the governing parties' scores on V-Party's illiberalism scale in our nine countries at each national election. In Argentina, South Africa, and Timor-Leste, the main parties have embraced liberal democratic norms, as has the party that has governed India during most of the period since independence—the Congress Party. The authors of the chapters on Argentina, Timor-Leste, and India point to these normative preferences as central to the survival of democracy in difficult circumstances.

In Argentina, consistent with Chapter 7 (this volume), two of the three governing parties since 1983, the UCR (1983–89 and 1999–2001) and PRO (2015–19), had extremely low illiberalism scores: 0.02 to 0.03, 0.04 to 0.05, and 0.07 to 0.08, respectively. The Peronist (PJ) presidents did not always fully embrace liberal democratic norms, but they never came close to the full-throated illiberalism that endangers democracy. For example, President Carlos Menem (1989–99) packed the Supreme Court in 1990 and made extensive use of presidential decrees to implement his neoliberal economic reforms, but he did not attempt to muzzle the press, demonize the opposition, or ensconce himself in power. As a governing party, the PJ's illiberalism score ranged between 0.13 and 0.28 from 1989 to 1999 and between 0.21 and 0.40 from 2001 to 2015, and it was 0.13 in 2019. Except for the PJ in the first two years of democracy (1983–85), with an illiberalism score of 0.42, the main opposition parties have consistently had low illiberalism scores. These scores are consistent with Mainwaring and Simison's argument that the most important actors have been democracy-preserving.

Regarding South Africa, according to V-Party, the ANC initially strongly embraced liberal democratic values, with illiberal scores of 0.15 in 1994, 0.12 in 1999, and 0.13 in 2004. Among the forces that opposed the apartheid regime, those with a genuine commitment to democracy prevailed—the ANC faction led by Nelson Mandela. Mandela and inner allies promoted the idea that the first democratic government of South Africa (1994–99) would be a national unity government that included the ruling white National Party.[8] At Mandela's instigation and notwithstanding some internal critics who opposed this move,[9] the ANC prioritized democratic stability over radical change. It made many concessions to ensure that white South Africans would not feel threatened (see

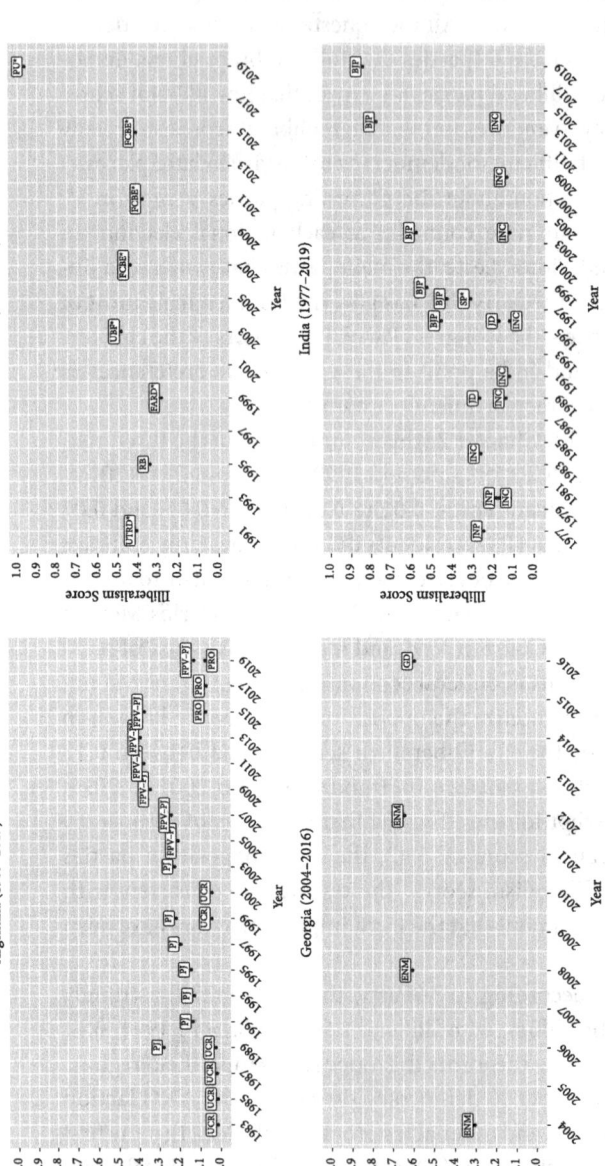

Figure 8.1. Governing party illiberalism scores

Notes: The figures include all national elections (presidential and legislative) beginning with the first democratic election, and show the illiberalism score (V-Party variable v2xpa_illiberal) for the governing party. We define the "governing party" as the party of the head of government, that is, the prime minister or the president. For each election, we show the illiberalism score for the party of the incumbent head of government at the time of the election and for the winner in that election (i.e., if the government changes hands, then the election year will show two Illiberalism scores). For the first election of the democratic regime, Figure 8.1 shows only the incoming governing party. If the head of government is an independent, Figure 8.1 shows the score for the largest party of their supporting coalition, measured in share of seats in the legislature (Moldova 1998; Ukraine 1994, 1998, 2002; Benin 1991, 1999, 2007, 2011, 2015, 2019). These parties are marked with an asterisk (*). We exclude elections for which there are no illiberalism data for the party of the head of state (Ukraine 1999, 2004, 2010; Moldova 1996, 2001, 2006, 2016; Georgia 2013, 2018; Timor-Leste 2018), unless this party took part in an electoral coalition for which there are data. In this case, Figure 8.1 includes the coalition's data and marks them with an * (Benin 2003, India 1998, and Timor-Leste 2018). Georgia: We classify the system as presidential until and including the 2012 election, and parliamentary since the 2013 election, as a constitutional amendment significantly reduced the powers of the president in favor of the prime minister. India: For 1991, there are no illiberalism data for the outgoing party, SJP(R), which had no allies (so I cannot use another party's illiberalism data as proxy). For 1996: The incoming PM following the April/May elections belonged to BJP, but he lasted only fifteen days; he resigned when it became clear that he did not have enough support to form a government. The new PM belonged to JD. Figure 8.1 includes both BJP and PD as incoming governing parties. Timor-Leste: For 2018, there are no illiberalism data for PLP, the incoming party. Ukraine: Ukraine is a semi presidential system. Following Lucan Way's suggestions (private communication), I classify the more powerful executive as the president until the 2004 election, and as the prime minister between the 2006 and the 2012 elections, and as the president since the 2012 election. For further details, see online Appendix 8.2.

Sources: Lührmann et al. 2020 for illiberalism scores. For sources for the head of governments and their parties, see online Appendix 8.1. For coding decisions about independent heads of government and about elections for which V-Party did not code the party of the head of the head of government, see online Appendix 8.2.

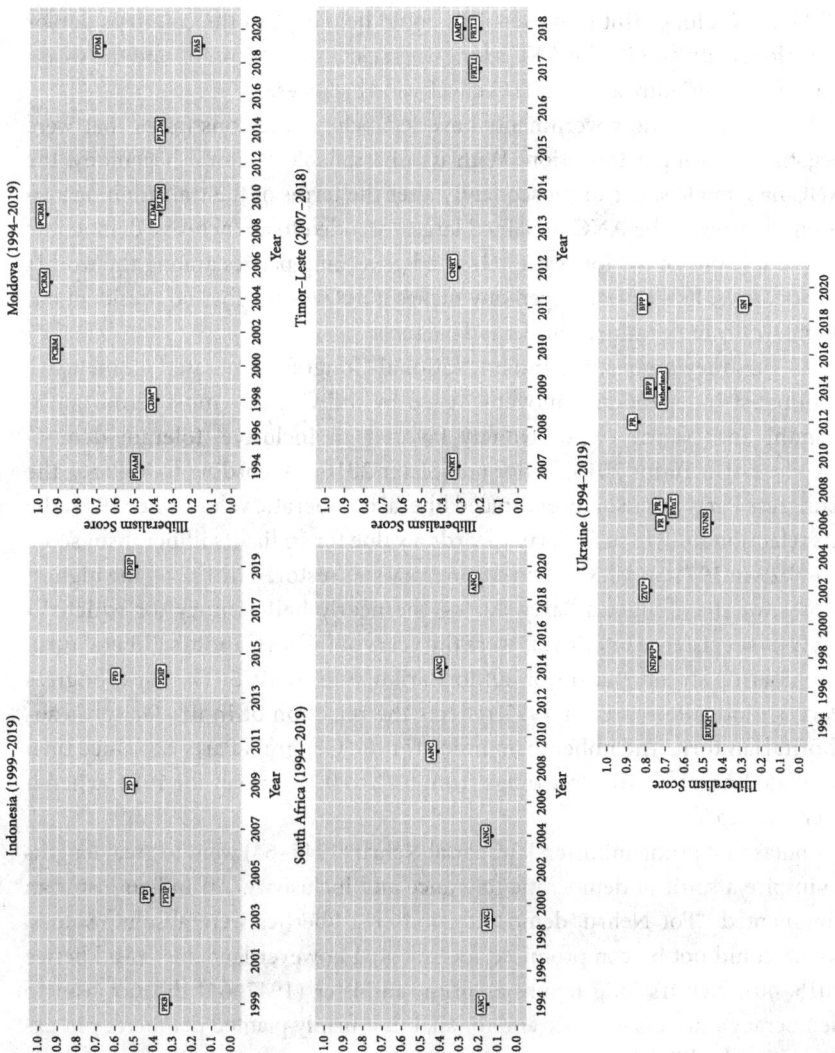

Figure 8.1. Continued

Chapter 4). As president (1994–99), Mandela emphasized national reconciliation and forgiveness, launching the democratic period in a promising way.

According to V-Party, the ANC took an illiberal turn in 2009 (0.41) and 2014 (0.37), but then shifted back to greater liberalism in 2019 (0.19). By V-Party's measure, solid support for liberal democratic principles has characterized most of the ANC's long stint in power. This could help explain the country's democratic longevity despite the ANC's long-term electoral hegemony and the weakness of the legislature and courts as checks and balances.

Many democratic governments have left behind the constraints that were negotiated during a transition. With its unassailable electoral hegemony, the ANC had ample space to subsequently alter the terms of the transition negotiations. However, the ANC remained largely wedded to an inclusive democratic vision. It is one of the longest-established governing parties among the world's democracies. Its electoral hegemony makes it noteworthy that no president has dramatically undermined checks and balances.

As Varshney argues, the Indian National Congress generated an inclusive nationalist independence movement led by individuals—most importantly, Gandhi and Nehru—who strongly favored an inclusive, tolerant democracy (see also Tudor 2013; Tudor and Slater 2016). According to V-Party, the Congress Party has usually embraced liberal democratic values since 1971, the first election for which V-Party records a value for India. Its illiberalism score was 0.29 in 1971 and 0.31 when democracy was restored in 1977—the highest scores for the Congress Party during the nearly half-century for which V-Party has registered one. These were the years of Indira Gandhi's illiberal turn, culminating in her period of authoritarian rule in 1975–77. The Congress Party's moderate score for 1977 reflects the rejection of Indira Gandhi's authoritarian turn. The illiberalism index for the Congress Party has since then oscillated narrowly in a low range from 0.12 to 0.18, except for 1984, when it increased to 0.26.

India's first prime minister, Jawaharlal Nehru (1947–64) went to great lengths to inspire a spirit of democratic tolerance and inclusivity. An Indian historian commented, "For Nehru, democracy and civil liberties were absolute values, which could not be compromised for any goal however laudable" (Mukherjee 2015, 40). Nehru's long tenure as prime minister (1947–64) did not lead to democracy's success for once and for all, but it firmly planted democracy in extraordinarily difficult conditions. During this period, a strong court system, a robust federal system, a vibrant free press, a norm of vigorous electoral competition, acceptance of many official languages, a majority position within the Congress Party that India should have an inclusive and secular democracy, and civilian control of the military emerged. Democracy is on surer footing with these institutions and norms in place.

Except for the period from 1971 to 1977, even during periods of overwhelming electoral dominance (1952–77, 1980–89) when it could have run roughshod over democracy, the Congress Party has generally hewed to democratic norms. Indira Gandhi temporarily shattered the marriage between the Congress Party and democracy with her declaration of Emergency Rule in 1975, but in the 1977 elections voters punished her for abrogating democracy. The Congress Party emerged from the 1975–77 period and its 1977 electoral defeat with a revitalized commitment to democracy.

The BJP, the Hindu nationalist party, has much higher illiberal scores, consistent with Varshney's chapter. Also consistent with his argument, the BJP's illiberalism represents a grave threat to democracy. During its first brief period in government in 1996, the BJP's illiberalism score was 0.46. During its subsequent periods in government, its score increased from 0.43 from 1998 to 1999, to 0.53 from 1999 to 2004, to 0.58 from 2004 to 2009, and to an alarming 0.77 from 2014 to 2019, and 0.84 from 2019 to the present. Even with India's long democratic tradition, illiberal rulers put democracy in hard places at risk.

V-Party's illiberal index supports Nancy Bermeo's contention that the main parties have been committed to democracy in Timor-Leste. Both the governing parties and the main opposition parties have consistently scored low or moderately on the illiberalism index. The National Congress for Timorese Liberation, which headed the government from 2007 to 2017, scored 0.31 on the illiberal index in both of its terms in office. The three largest other parties from 2007 to 2012 scored 0.32, 0.12, and 0.14, and the three largest parties after the 2012 elections scored 0.20 and 0.12, respectively. The Revolutionary Front for an Independent Timor, which headed the minority government that took office in 2017, scored 0.20 on the illiberal index. V-Party records illiberal scores for four other parties for the 2017 election in the very low to moderate range, ranging from 0.11 to 0.32. A coalition, the Coalition for Change and Progress, won the 2018 election; its illiberalism score was 0.28. The other three parties for which V-Party registered an illiberalism score ranged from 0.11 to 0.26—again, from very low to moderate. Solid support for liberal democratic principles has helped preserve democracy in Timor-Leste.

The argument that normative commitments can help explain the durability of democracy under difficult circumstances works partially for Benin but with a caveat: independent candidates won five of the country's first seven presidential elections between 1991 and 2015. Because independents are not tethered to a party, how parties score on the illiberalism scale is less relevant for understanding dynamics in the political regime.

From 1991 until 2019, the forty-two parties in Benin for which V-Party has illiberalism scores had low to moderate scores, ranging from 0.21 to 0.48, compared to a mean of 0.50 for the entire V-Party database. Illiberalism scores of the governing party or the largest supporting party when the presidents were independents ranged from 0.28 to 0.44 between 1991 and 2019. Until 2019, these scores are moderate, again consistent with the argument that parties committed to democracy can help it survive.

Two new large parties formed to support President Patrice Talon in the 2019 national assembly elections; they won 100 percent of the seats. In 2019, both received extraordinarily high illiberal scores in V-Party (0.96 and 0.95, respectively). These scores are completely consistent with the argument that if the governing parties are hostile to democracy, its prospects in difficult structural and cultural environments are dim.

In sum, for five of our six long-standing democracies, V-Party evidence supports the assertion that executives' and parties' attitudes about the political regime correlate strongly with the fate of democracy. This argument also works reasonably for our final case of long-standing democracy—Indonesia. V-Party's experts score Indonesia's presidential parties in the early years of democracy (1999–2004) as fairly liberal—the National Awakening Party (1999–2001) at 0.31 and the Indonesian Democratic Party of Struggle (2001–4) at 0.30. The ruling Democratic Party (2004–14) represented a mild illiberal turn, with scores of 0.41 (2004–9) and 0.49 (2009–14). The Indonesian Democratic Party of Struggle won the 2014 and 2019 presidential elections; V-Party's illiberalism scores for it were 0.33 in 2014 and 0.49 in 2019. V-Party scores some of Indonesia's other parties as profoundly illiberal. These powerful illiberal actors would seem to make it difficult to deepen democracy and make democracy vulnerable to erosion.

V-Party's illiberalism scores are also highly consistent with the difficulty of establishing stable democracy in Georgia, Ukraine, and Moldova. In all three countries, some of the governing parties and some of the other main parties have displayed highly illiberal attitudes. Consistent with Lucan Way's account in Chapter 5, V-Party's illiberalism scores of the governing parties and main support parties (when independents were head of government) oscillate from moderate to extreme illiberalism in Moldova and Ukraine, and from moderate to high illiberalism in Georgia.

Table 8.1 summarizes information about V-Party's coding of the governing party, expectations about regime outcomes based on V-Party's coding, and actual outcomes in our nine countries. To present the data in a synthetic way, I focus exclusively on the governing parties; they are the prime movers in executive suffocations of democracy. I considered illiberalism scores of less than 0.15 extremely low, less than 0.30 low, 0.30 to 0.50 moderate, 0.50 to 0.80 high, and above 0.80 extremely high.[10] Using categorical variables for this table rather than the actual V-Party illiberalism score makes it more efficient to summarize periods during which scores fluctuated some but remained within these categories.

Table 8.1. Illiberalism Scores of Governing Parties and Regime Outcomes

Country	Elections coded by V-Party	Number of elections coded during this time	V-Dem Party illiberalism (governing party)	Probability of democratic survival based on governing party illiberalism	Actual outcome
Argentina	1983–2007	13	Extremely low or low	Very high	Survival
	2009–13	3	Moderate	High	Survival
	2015–19	3	Extremely low	Very high	Survival
Benin	1991–95	2	Moderate	High	Survival
	1999*	1	Low	Very high	Survival
	2003*–15*	4	Moderate	High	Survival
	2019*	1	Extremely high	Breakdown	Electoral authoritarianism (2020)
Georgia	2004	1	Moderate	High	Survival
	2008–16	3	High	Low	Survival
India	1977–96	6[a]	Low or extremely low	Very high	Survival
	1998	1	Moderate	High	Survival
	1999	1	High	Low	Survival
	2004, 2009	2	Extremely low	Very high	Survival
	2014–20	2	High to extremely high	Breakdown	Electoral authoritarianism
Indonesia	1999–2019	5	Moderate	High	Survival
Moldova	1994–98	2	Moderate	High	Survival
	2001–9	3	Extremely high	Breakdown	Electoral authoritarianism
	2009–14	3	Moderate	High	Survival
	2019	1	Extremely low	High	Survival

Continued

Table 8.1. *Continued*

Country	Elections coded by V-Party	Number of elections coded during this time	V-Dem Party illiberalism (governing party)	Probability of democratic survival based on governing party illiberalism	Actual outcome
South Africa	1994–2004	3	Low or extremely low	Very high	Survival
	2009–14	2	Moderate	High	Survival
	2019	1	Low	Very high	Survival
Timor-Leste	2007–12	2	Moderate	High	Survival
	2017–18*	2	Low	Very high	Survival
Ukraine[b]	1994*	1	Moderate	High	Survival
	1998*–2002*	2	High	Low	Competitive authoritarian in 1998
	2006–7	2	High	Low	Competitive authoritarian in 2011
	2012–14	2	Extremely high or high	Very low	Competitive authoritarian
	2019	1	Low	Low	Survival

Note: Illiberalism scores correspond to the party of the head of government elected in each election. An asterisk (*) indicates that the head of government is an independent and that the illiberalism data correspond to the largest party of their supporting coalition, measured in share of seats in the legislature, or that illiberalism data reflect the head of government's electoral coalition for cases for which V-Party does not code their party but does code the coalition. Coding of regime outcomes is based on V-Dem version 11.1 (Coppedge et al. 2021) and follows Lührmann et al.'s (2018) coding rules.

Sources: For governing parties, see online Appendix 8.1. For illiberalism scores, Lührmann et al. 2020.

[a] Following the 1996 general elections, the new BJP Prime Minister stepped down after two weeks when he could not form a government. Table 8.1 does not include this very short-lived BJP government. The United Front coalition then assumed office without new elections.

[b] Ukraine is a semi-presidential system. Following Lucan Way's suggestions, I classify the more powerful executive as the president until the 2004 election, as the prime minister between the 2006 and the 2012 elections, and as the president since the 2012 election. For further details, see online Appendix 8.2.

All fifty-nine elections in which the ruling incumbent party scored low or moderate on V-Party's illiberalism scale were associated with the subsequent survival of democracy during that administration according to V-Dem.[11]

Benin and India were democracies for a long time but then suffered severe erosions under an independent who created highly illiberal ruling parties (Benin after 2015) and the BJP, also a highly illiberal party (India since 2014). Moldova and Ukraine have frequently had illiberal ruling parties, and they have not been able to build durable democracies. Only India in 1999 and 2004 had governing parties with illiberalism scores above 0.50 without an erosion or breakdown of democracy—and both illiberal scores were not much above 0.50 (0.53, and 0.58, respectively). In short, all fifty-nine illiberalism scores under 0.50 were associated with the survival of democracy according to Lührmann et al.'s (2018) coding rules, and most scores above 0.50 were associated with sharp erosion or breakdown. These bivariate relationships do not show cause, and there is a reasonable possibility of some coding of illiberalism based on what actually transpires in the regime (i.e., a contamination effect). But the association between governing party adherence to liberal principles and the survival of democracy is still striking.

What Generates and Sustains a Commitment to Democracy? The Repudiation of the Terrible Past

In my view, actors' normative preferences about the political regime are critically important for understanding outcomes. For example, the biggest difference between Hungary before and after 2010 was the ascension to power of an authoritarian populist who was determined to weaken democratic checks and balances and tilt the playing field toward his governing party. Thinking about actors' attitudes about democratic norms directs us to some essential questions such as the one I turn to in this section: what generates and sustains commitments to democracy?

The extant literature has given little attention and few answers to this question.[12] Our volume suggests one answer for Argentina, South Africa, Timor-Leste, and India: a widespread repudiation of the terrible past and/or a common enemy generated broad support among organized actors and citizens for democracy (see also Bermeo 1992). In Argentina, India, South Africa, and Timor-Leste, the alternative to democracy was too unpalatable. *Sustained* democracy was not an inevitable outcome, but most powerful actors and the transition leaders perceived democracy as the best way to overcome the terrible past. A strong and broad commitment to democracy did not immunize the regime from subsequent challenges, but the memory of the terrible past weighed heavily on political leaders and in favor of democracy.

In Argentina, the failures of the dictatorship of 1976–83 were many and profound, as Mainwaring and Simison argue in Chapter 7. Economic performance was dismal. When the regime's support faltered because of economic mismanagement, the government waged a reckless and disastrous war against the United Kingdom by invading the Falkland/Malvinas Islands in 1982. The cost in lives (about 650 Argentine soldiers died) and economic ruin was enormous. The logistical preparation was dismal, leading to appalling conditions for the mostly young Argentine soldiers who invaded; without adequate food, boots, and coats, they starved and froze until the generals capitulated. To garner support for the war, even as the Argentine military was being routed, right up until the day they surrendered, with a massive propaganda effort, the generals proclaimed that they were winning the war. Their brazen lies reinforced the effects of the bellicose disaster, discrediting the military as a bunch of incompetents *and* liars. After the transition, in 1985–86, the world's most publicized human rights trials since Nuremburg in 1945–46 galvanized public opinion against the human rights atrocities committed by the military.

Mainwaring and Simison argue that the broad repudiation of the dictatorship of 1976–83 generated new commitments to democracy and a rejection of extremist positions (see also Ollier 2009). The Peronist Party and the labor unions, which had never been committed to democracy, became ardent supporters; some leaders risked their lives to protect democracy during the military rebellions of the 1980s and 1990. The revolutionary left was vanquished, and a few of its participants became intellectual leaders celebrating the virtues of democracy. Business associations, which had embraced the coups of 1955, 1962, 1966, and 1973, now recognized that untethered dictatorships could be very destructive; they, too, rejected the authoritarian past. Since 1983, a strong human rights movements, successful prosecutions of the human rights abuses committed during the military dictatorship, and a powerful memorialization of the past abuses have helped maintain aversion to authoritarian leaders.

Nancy Bermeo argues that armed conflict in Timor-Leste paved the way to a durable democracy. The primary armed conflict pitted different groups in Timor-Leste against the Indonesian invaders and intruders, thereby creating cohesion among previously fractious groups against the hated enemy. The independence war "strengthened an inclusive national identity" and "gave rise to a series of inclusive institutions (and mindsets)" (Chapter 6, this volume). First, a sanguinary civil war broke out in 1975 between warring factions within Timor-Leste. Then the Indonesian military invaded, leading to a twenty-four-year-long brutal occupation (1975–99) that generated widespread resentment toward the occupying force and a newfound sense of inclusive nationalism. If before the occupation the East Timorese had conflictual understandings of national identity, the Indonesian occupation created a sense of a common enemy that in turn created a cohesive inclusive nationalism. Bermeo notes that in response to the need for a cohesive national project forged in opposition to Indonesia, the charismatic party leader Xanana Gusmão renounced his and his party's Marxist revolutionary path and instead embraced democracy as a project that would bring Timor-Leste together. The war of independence also had a professionalizing effect on the military.

In South Africa, as Riedl argues, the leadership of the African National Congress, the vast majority of the Black population, and most of the international community widely abhorred apartheid. The South African regime's extreme racial discrimination made it a worldwide pariah.

Just as the Argentine military dictatorship, the South African apartheid regime, and the Indonesian invaders of Timor-Leste formed hated enemies that helped forge a widespread democracy movement, so did the British colonialists in India. To help defeat the British and achieve independence, by the 1930s, the Indian National Congress mobilized scores of millions of Indians in opposition to colonial rule and on behalf of independence. The broad, inclusive, tolerant nature of the movement also entailed a deep commitment to inclusive democracy on the part of Gandhi and Nehru, as well as many other Congress Party leaders.

Gandhi and Nehru's vision for this inclusive democracy shaped India's constitution and the Congress Party, generating momentum for democracy that lasted for the first two decades (Tudor 2013; Tudor and Slater 2016). Congress's commitments helped lead to a constitution that enshrined the principle that democracy had to be for all Indians, including the poorest, all religious groups, and the lower castes (see Chapter 2, this volume). They set the tone for the Congress Party and for India's political system during the first decades after independence in 1947.

In Argentina, India, South Africa, and Timor-Leste, because of the widespread repudiation of the terrible past, no electorally successful party reclaimed the legacy of the previous regime. The only very partial and ephemeral exception to this rule was the National Party in South Africa, which won 20.4 percent of the vote in the founding election of 1994, but it was still dwarfed by the ANC, which won 62.7 percent. The party rebranded itself the New National Party in 1997 to create some distance from its apartheid past, but its vote share collapsed to 6.9 percent in 1999 and 1.7 percent in 2004 before the party disbanded in 2005. The absence of parties to reclaim the legacy of the authoritarian or colonial past in these four cases underscores the thorough rejection of the previous dictatorships. No authoritarian successor party can mobilize authoritarian sentiments. This absence is a dramatic contrast to the many democracies in the world that have thriving authoritarian successor parties (Loxton and Mainwaring 2018).

In India, Timor-Leste, South Africa, and Argentina, the commitment to democracy evinced by the governing party or parties and the main opposition parties was enormously helpful. Commitment to democracy enabled these regimes to survive in contexts of great adversity. A critical question for future research is how to keep alive normative commitments to democracy.

These four cases were not unique in generating commitments to democracy that endured for some time based on a repudiation of the terrible past. In Chile, after the left experienced severe repression during the Pinochet dictatorship (1973–90), it became firmly committed to democracy (Roberts 1998; Walker 1990). In similar fashion, most of the Brazilian, Uruguayan, and Spanish left became converts to democracy after the dictatorships of 1964–85, 1973–85, and 1939–75, respectively. A traumatic experience such as a repressive dictatorship (Argentina, Timor-Leste, and South Africa), a foreign invasion and civil war (Timor-Leste), or an extremely racist regime that oppressed the great majority of the population (South Africa) does not inexorably lead individuals and actors to value democracy—but it did so in these cases for an extended time.

Democracy as an Equilibrium of Narrowly Self-Interested Actors

Some explanations posit that democracy endures because self-interested actors reluctantly conclude that democracy is their best option because of a power equilibrium, or because institutions constrain the military and the executive from overthrowing the regime. These approaches focus exclusively on constraints external to actors and regard actors as narrowly self-interested. They do not consider actors' normative commitments part of what makes democracy viable. These approaches often help explain democratic stabilization, but I am skeptical that they are sufficient.

By nakedly or narrowly self-interested, I mean something along the lines that Przeworski (2019, 19–20) wrote: "The dream of all politicians is to conquer power and to hold on to it forever. It is unreasonable to expect that competing parties would abstain from doing whatever they can do to enhance their electoral advantage."[13] I discuss two approaches that view democracy as an equilibrium among narrowly self-interested actors. One posits that democracy is an equilibrium among actors, none of which can overpower the others. These actors accept democracy because they can't overpower the others, and because democracy is a tenable compromise that gives them enough of what they want. The other sees democracy as an equilibrium in which formal institutions—the legislature, the courts, and other mechanisms of accountability—prevent rulers from overthrowing democracy. My own view is that scholars must seriously consider both possibilities, but that they do not go far toward explaining democratic stability in hard places—at least for the cases studied in detail in this book.

A Large Partisan Opposition

One plausible answer to what sustains democracies is a large partisan opposition; the opposition controls enough levers of power (such as seats in the national assembly, governorships, etc.) to prevent the government from encroaching deeply on democracy or from enacting radical measures that would deeply threaten established interests, potentially leading to the formation of a coup coalition. Government majorities present two potential threats to democracy. On one hand, they facilitate executive takeovers. A minority opposition usually cannot block political reforms that enhance executive power, bolster the position of the governing party, allow the executive to capture supposedly independent institutions, and marginalize the opposition. On the other, because governments with majorities might not face meaningful checks and balances, it might be easier for them to pursue potentially destabilizing radical agendas.

The focus on partisan checks on the government has a long pedigree. Przeworski (1991,10–50; 2019) advanced a partisan balancing argument. He wrote (2019, 177) that "checks and balances do not operate effectively when different powers of the government are controlled by the same party." Rustow (1970) and other scholars have advocated a balance-of-power argument to explain pacted democratic transitions—although Rustow explicitly did not extend his argument to explaining democratic endurance.[14] Lijphart (1977) advocated power-sharing arrangements including multipartism, especially in contexts of democracy in plural societies, as a way of balancing power. In this volume, Riedl's chapter on Benin and South Africa advocates a balance-of-power argument as a way of understanding democratic stability.

Little empirical work has systematically tested arguments about the impact of a balance of power on the survival of democracy. One exception is Pérez-Liñán et al. (2019), who provide compelling evidence that a sizable opposition was helpful for democratic longevity in Latin America from 1925 to 2016. When presidents controlled the legislature and courts, democratic breakdowns were more likely.

Our volume offers surprisingly thin evidence to support the idea that opposition majorities help protect democracy in hard places. Figure 8.2 shows the percentage of assembly seats controlled by the governing party and by the governing coalition for our nine countries. To operationalize whether a party is part of the government, I used the parties that hold cabinet portfolios. The dataset on cabinet composition is based on data in July of every year, and it extends until at least 2016 and for some countries later. Figure 8.2 includes data for the upper chamber only for Argentina, the only case in this volume that has symmetrical bicameralism. In Georgia, cabinets have included only the governing party, so Figure 8.2 has no second line for this country for the seat share of the governing coalition.

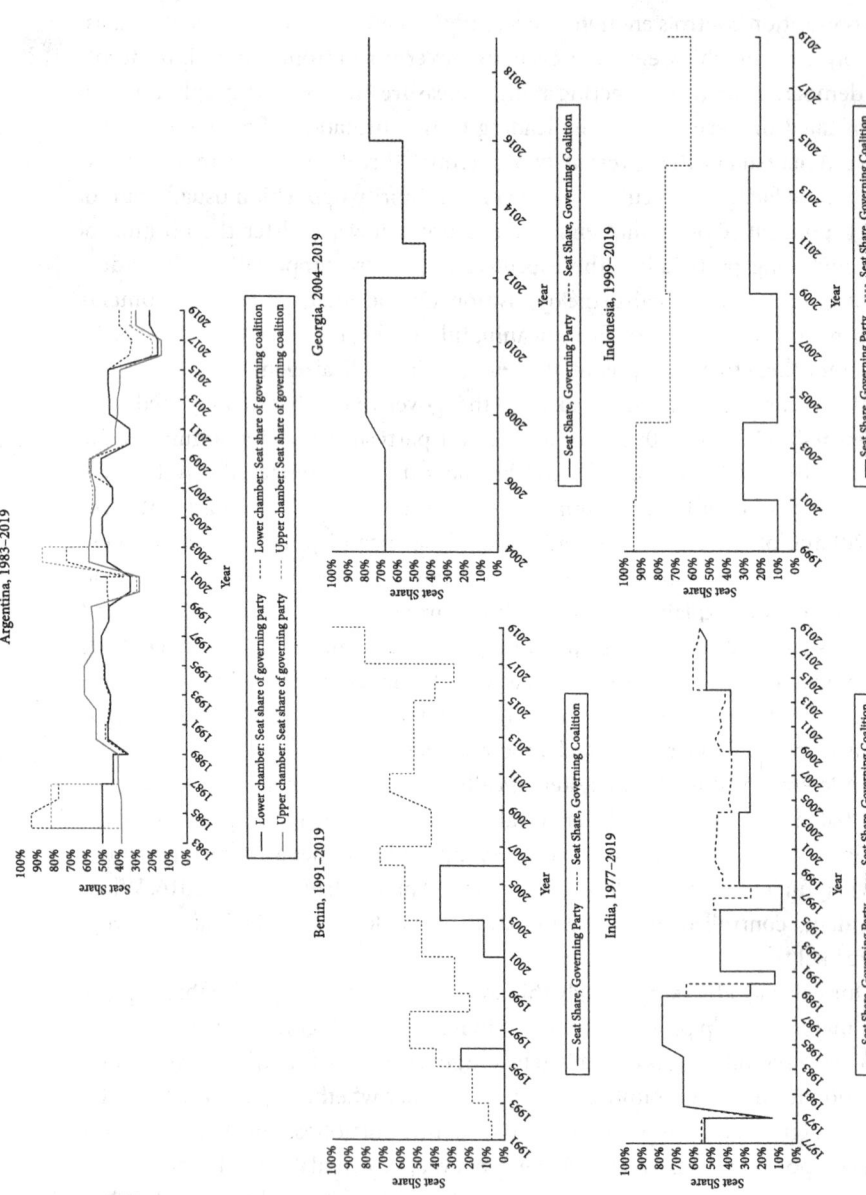

Figure 8.2. Percentage of national assembly seats controlled by the governing party and coalition

Note: When the head of government is an independent, the seat share of the governing party is 0%. When cabinet periods do not begin on the first day of a month, we assigned them to the next month (e.g., the period beginning on 10/29/84 is set as beginning in 11/1984).

Sources: For a complete list of references, see online Appendix 8.1.

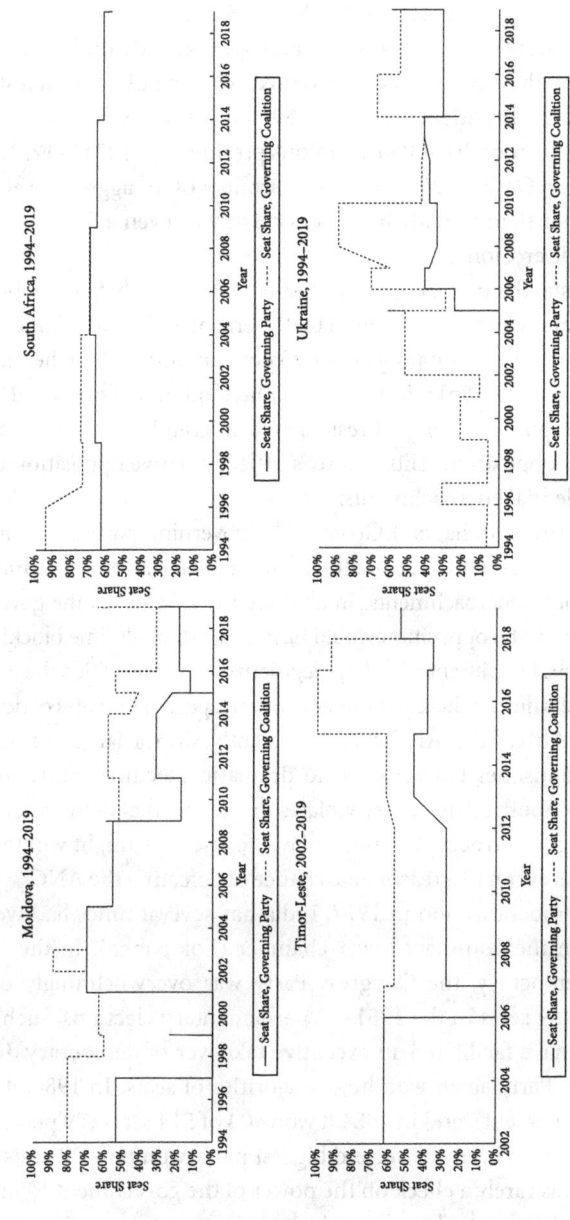

Figure 8.2. Continued

Among our nine cases, none has consistently exhibited a strong partisan opposition. In Benin, the governing coalition enjoyed a modest majority (55 percent) in 1996–98, 2003–6 (58 percent), and 2011–15 (52 percent) and a commanding majority in 2006–7 (72 percent), 2010–11 (66 percent), and 2017–19, at which point the president's attacks on democracy were already under way (81 percent from 2017–19, then 100 percent). Paradoxically, one of the smallest seat shares controlled by the president's coalition, 29 percent of the seats, occurred during the first eighteen months of Patrice Talon's presidency, in 2016–17. Talon's supermajorities from October 2017 on were a product of his aggressive attacks on democracy rather than initially being a necessary or even a facilitating condition for democratic erosion.

In Indonesia, the president's coalition has consistently had sizable majorities in the national assembly, reaching 93 to 95 percent in the early democratic period (1999–2004) and never dipping below 73 percent until 2014, when it dropped to 60 percent. Slater (2018b) referred to this phenomenon of oversized coalitions as "promiscuous power-sharing." Presidents form grand coalitions, and few parties end up in the opposition. Thus, there is little legislative opposition to block potential presidential encroachments.

In South Africa, India, and Georgia, the governing party has sometimes had large majorities that would make it easier for a president or prime minister to engage in executive encroachments. In all three cases, at times, the government was so dominant that the opposition would have had a difficult time blocking executive encroachments. Despite enjoying large legislative supermajorities, the presidents and prime ministers during these periods generally respected the rules of democracy.

In South Africa, the ANC has consistently won a large majority of seats. Consistent landslides have not led to dramatic executive efforts to erode democracy. The South African case violates the notion that democracy rests on the losers' willingness to accept results today because they might win tomorrow; no contender has ever had a reasonable chance of defeating the ANC.

Since redemocratization in 1977, India has several times had weak partisan opposition in the dominant lower chamber (Lok Sabha). In the first decades of India's democracy, the Congress Party was overwhelmingly dominant. It won 364 of 489 seats in the 1951–52 parliamentary elections; such dominance could easily have facilitated an executive takeover of democracy. In the 1980s, the Congress Party again won huge majorities of seats. In 1980, it won 353 of 529 seats (67 percent), and in 1984 it won 404 of 514 seats (79 percent), its most dominant election ever; the second biggest party won only 30 seats. The Indian parliament was rarely a check on the power of the government.[15] Since the 2019 elections, the BJP has had a solid majority (56 percent) in parliament, facilitating the attacks on liberal rights that Varshney details in Chapter 2.

In Argentina, the data in Figure 8.2 about the seat share of the governing party and the governing coalition understate the degree to which Peronism has dominated elections and the political system since 2001. Peronists have won four of five presidential elections, three times in landslides (2003, 2007, 2011). In 2003, a fractured Peronist field won 61 percent of the valid vote distributed among three different PJ candidates. The leading non-Peronist won only 16.4 percent of the vote. In 2007, Cristina Fernández de Kirchner won 45 percent of the vote, a 22 percent margin over her closest competitor, and in 2011 she won 54 percent of the vote, a 37 percent margin over the runner-up. In 2019, Alberto Fernández won by an 8 percent margin. Peronism has also usually dominated the national congress. Moreover, some of the nominally non-Peronist parties in an increasingly fragmented party system fairly consistently align with the president. Although the national congress has occasionally blocked presidential initiatives, it would be far-fetched to attribute the survival of democracy in Argentina to a strong partisan opposition.

In Timor-Leste, oversized majority governing coalitions have been the rule rather than the exception. At the extreme, in 2015–17, the president's cabinet included parties that occupied all of the seats in the national assembly. In 2017–18, the presidential coalition controlled 92 percent of the seats.

In Moldova, the governing coalitions under both democracy and authoritarianism between 1994 and 2005 and again since 2019 controlled large majorities (more than 60 percent) in the national legislature. The same was true in Ukraine from 2006 to 2010 and from 2014 to 2016.

In sum, although a partisan balance of power is an asset for democratic stability, in all of our cases, governing coalitions have had large majorities during extended periods. The stability of democracy in our nine cases has not rested on the opposition's capacity to block the executive.

Moreover, in some cases (although not among our nine until perhaps Benin since 2016), rulers with authoritarian ambitions have undermined democracy in part *because* they faced partisan shackles in the national legislature. Well-known cases include Alberto Fujimori in Peru (1990–2000), who closed the congress and courts in April 1992 to eliminate legislative constraints that blocked him from taking actions (Kenney 2004); Hugo Chávez in Venezuela (1999–2013), who almost immediately and with dubious legality convened a constitutional congress to circumvent the recently elected congress, whose partisan composition was not favorable to him; and Rafael Correa in Ecuador (2007–17), who did the same for the same reason. Correa created a new party when he ran for president, but his party did not have any congressional candidates, so the legislature had no Correa copartisans when he assumed office in January 2007.

Democracy as an Intertemporal Bargain

A variant of the partisan balance argument posits that democracies are stable because of an intertemporal bargain. Müller (2016a, 254) expressed this idea clearly: "Democracies rely on the idea that losers in elections have every reason to continue playing the political game, because they might form a majority the next time" (see also Przeworski 1991, 10–50). Rulers who were initially freely and fairly elected but then presided over executive takeovers manifest a flaw in this logic. These rulers rigged the system in their own favor, thus simultaneously reaping more of the system's benefits today (e.g., through patronage and cronyism) *and* diminishing, perhaps radically so, the likelihood of losing tomorrow. If the winners of elections today did "whatever they can to enhance their electoral advantage" (Przeworski 2019), they should seize their temporary electoral advantage and cripple the opposition. This does occur, but when it is a regular part of politics, it signals that a democracy is already ill.

In sum, in contexts of weak institutions, illiberal rulers can sometimes maneuver around partisan constraints. Rules and procedures that should in principle bind these heads of government do not. If I were designing electoral rules to reduce the likelihood of a breakdown of a generic democracy in a hard place, other things equal, I would recommend rules that promote multipartism, aim to create a partisan balance of power, and make it difficult for one party to command majorities. But in the cases in this volume, democratic survival has not rested on a consistently strong partisan opposition.

Many accounts of pacted democratic transitions have convincingly argued that they involved a power balance among self-interested actors. Outgoing regime elites won some protections for their interests, and incoming democrats won democracy (Riedl's chapter, this volume; Rustow 1970; Ziblatt 2017). Both sides won some advantages by agreeing to the democratic transition. But the fact that pacted transitions constitute an equilibrium of narrowly self-interested actors does not explain why it *remains* in the interests of the government to not defect at subsequent moments. The initial balance of power at the time of the democratic transition does not get frozen in time. An account of democracy as a balance of power among self-interested actors must explain not only the initial transition but also why the actors continue to find democracy an acceptable compromise.[16]

Implicitly, the argument that democracy is a stable equilibrium because narrowly self-interested actors find it in their interests to preserve the regime rests on the assumption that actors pay a fairly high price for defecting from democracy, or that democracy consistently yields substantial payoffs to all powerful players. If narrowly self-interested rulers do not pay a price for encroachments, they should regularly seize opportunities to grab advantages and reduce the likelihood of having to relinquish power. This kind of behavior does occur, but when it is the norm, democracy rests on precarious bases.

Legislatures and Courts as Protectors of Democracy

Several chapters in this volume suggest that while formal institutions are far from sufficient, they do help protect democracies. Riedl on South Africa and Benin, Slater on Indonesia, and Varshney on India convincingly argue that formal institutions have helped protect these democracies. This is perhaps somewhat surprising because as Brinks et al. (2019), Levitsky and Murillo (2005, 2014), and O'Donnell (1993, 1994) have suggested, formal institutions are almost always much weaker in democracies in hard places. They do not consistently provide robust protection for democracy.

In several of our nine countries, institutional arrangements have protected democracy in at least two ways. First, some institutions have promoted power sharing and inclusion; they are contra-majoritarian. They have given a broader range of actors and interests a stake in the game, and therefore, they dampen incentives to overthrow democracy. In Benin, proportional representation for the national assembly helped ensure the representation of different ethnicities and averted "ethno-regional political dominance" (Riedl, Chapter 4, this volume). Varshney on India and Riedl on Benin and South Africa argue that constitutional and institutional design helped bring about democratic stability. Quasi-federalism in India has allowed groups that are minorities at the country level to govern at the state level, thus helping to integrate a hugely diverse country (Stepan et al. 2011; Varshney 2013, chapter 6).[17] Federalism thereby facilitated the peaceful articulation of some ethnic, religious, and linguistic demands in a context of extraordinary diversity. Varshney points to another way in which federalism has contributed to the survival of democracy in India: the parties that rule at the state level but in the opposition at the country level push back against executive encroachments.

In South Africa, the transitional compromise resulted in a constitution that protected whites' economic interests and fostered moderation; both decisions were favorable to the establishment and preservation of democracy. Riedl argues that federalism in South Africa gave the Zulu and white minorities control over at least one of the nine provinces and protected elite economic interests. This arrangement helped create buy-in among these groups and thereby helped pave the way for democracy. Likewise, an asymmetrical quasi-federal arrangement in Indonesia has helped balance what Slater (Chapter 3) calls inclusive nationalism with some regional ethnonationalist demands (Bertrand 2007).[18] Federalism in South Africa and quasi-federalism in Indonesia and India have helped democracy. In large countries with as much "riotous diversity," to use Dan Slater's felicitous expression, as India and Indonesia have, federalism has been an asset for democratic stability.

Contra-majoritarian, consensus-building, inclusive institutions are generally favorable to preserving democracy (Ginsberg and Huq 2018, 164–204; Lijphart 1977; Pérez-Liñán et al. 2019; Reynolds 2002) in contexts of politically salient ethnic, national, or religious cleavages—a huge challenge in India and Indonesia, among many other democracies in hard places. They divide and limit power. They encourage accommodation and efforts to build a consensus across different groups, and they give a broader range of actors access to parts of state power.

A second way in which institutions have helped democracy is that legislatures and courts have sometimes limited executive power. The Argentine case provides some examples. When Carlos Menem attempted to run for a third consecutive term for president in 1999, the Supreme Court's public lack of support made it impossible for him to go ahead (Helmke 2005, 135–41).

However, institutions don't offer a general explanation for the longevity of democracy in hard places because the institutions that are designed to check executive power are rarely strong. Legal systems are vulnerable to executive influence and control. In contexts of weak institutions, popular rulers who want to run roughshod over democratic checks and balances often can find ways to do so. This is the peril now facing democracy in Benin and India—and a common peril of democracies with relatively weak institutions.

As an example of institutional fragility in the face of a determined executive assault, Patrice Talon, Benin's wealthiest businessman, won the 2016 presidential election, running as an independent. When he assumed office, little indicated that he would quickly set about undermining Benin's democracy. Unlike many populists, he did not rail against democracy during his campaign. The national assembly, which had been elected in 2015, was fragmented along party lines. Talon initially had a minority in the National Assembly, and the largest party was in the opposition. As a result, he was seemingly poorly positioned to capture institutions. He initially pledged that he would not seek reelection after his five-year term.

This innocuous beginning soon gave rise, however, to presidential incursions against democracy. Talon attacked the independence of the courts and the media and began to target political opponents. In February 2018, he appointed his personal attorney as head of the Constitutional Court. Before this move, Benin's Constitutional Court had a history of judicial independence. With his personal attorney as head of the Constitutional Court, this independence quickly eroded.

Before Talon's presidency, Benin had a strong history of free and fair elections. The Electoral Integrity Project scored Benin as having the second freest and fairest elections in Africa from 2012 to 2018, marginally behind Cape Verde (70 points for Benin and 71 for Cape Verde on a scale of 0 to 100), and ahead of the United States (61 points on the 100-point scale) (Norris and Grömping 2019). This changed dramatically after Talon captured the courts and the national assembly. In 2018, at Talon's behest, the national assembly passed a new, highly restrictive electoral law that regulated the 2019 elections for the new assembly. The Constitutional Court also required that parties obtain a "certificate of conformity" to be eligible to run for the elections. Only two parties, both of which backed Talon, qualified to run. The new rules "essentially made it impossible for anyone other than Mr. Talon's supporters to run for office" (Maslin Nir 2019).

Intimidated opposition observers canceled plans to monitor the elections. When the opposition boycotted the elections because of the highly skewed playing field, turnout plummeted to about one-fourth of eligible voters, down from 68 percent in 2015. One hundred percent of the national assembly seated in 2019 supports Talon; there is no opposition. The government also greatly stepped up harassment of the opposition. Former president Thomas Boni Yayi (2006–16) was under house arrest for fifty-two days after the April elections, and then he fled Benin. Talon's main rival in the 2016 presidential election, Lionel Zinsou, was banned from running for office for five years. In 2018, the third-place finisher in the 2016 presidential election, Sebastian Ajavon, was condemned to twenty years in prison. The High Authority for Audiovisual Media and Communication shut down some opposition media. In 2017, a new digital media law facilitated subsequent harassment and legal cases against opposition and independent media. The police and military have violently suppressed opposition protests.

It seems stunning how quickly and easily Talon was able to undo the previous twenty-five years of democracy. The institutions that had been in place during Benin's democracy from 1991 to 2016 were intact when Talon took office, but a president determined to subvert democracy was able to do so in short order. As Ashutosh Varshney writes in Chapter 2 of this volume, India under Prime Minister Narendra Modi is another example of a leader with an authoritarian orientation who has been able to carry out a project of eroding democracy despite the country's long democratic tradition. Democratic institutions that once appeared to be solid have crumbled under pressure.

Institutional Weakness: Legislatures

Legislatures and courts in our nine cases are not strong. Presidents and prime ministers have an arsenal of weapons that often enable them to circumvent constraints that legislatures and courts should constitutionally be able to impose. Legislatures are supposed to provide a counterbalance to presidents and prime ministers, and they sometimes do—although less so if the governing party has a majority in the national legislature. While legislatures sometimes constrain executive power,[19] in the cases in this volume, there is limited evidence that they have fostered the longevity of democracy by successfully pushing back against executive power grabs.

Legislatures often fail to constrain rulers. As noted in the previous section, in our nine countries, heads of government have often enjoyed supermajorities in the national assemblies. In such situations, legislative checks generally do not work in weakly institutionalized democracies. Moreover, even when heads of government do not enjoy solid majorities in the national assembly, in most third-wave democracies, they have powerful tools at their disposal that could enable them to push beyond the limits of democracy. Many presidential systems grant strong constitutional powers to the executive, giving presidents more leeway than they have in the US (Cox and Morgenstern 2001). Most democratically elected presidents have more extensive lawmaking and decree capacity than the US president (Carey and Shugart 1998; Figueiredo and Limongi 1999). These features make it easier for the executive to capture institutions and run over democracy. Other things equal, prime ministers who have majorities in the national assembly might be even more likely to be dominant politically because parliamentary systems have a fused election and survival of the head of government. Therefore, they usually do not contend with a legislature whose purpose is, in part, to serve as a counterbalance to the executive.

Chernykh et al. (2017) constructed an index of legislative powers (the Weighted Legislative Powers Score) for 158 countries based on expert surveys for the years around 2005–7. Scores are based on legislatures' legal and constitutional authority, and they range from 0 (an extremely weak legislature) to 5.93 (Germany). Only one of our nine legislatures, Moldova, has strong constitutional powers. The other eight countries featured in our volume scored in the second and third quartiles (see Table 8.2), although the sample included many authoritarian regimes with weak legislatures. In many third-wave democracies, presidents can circumvent legislatures that they view as obstructionist.

In principle, if the upper chamber of the national assembly is powerful, bicameralism might serve as a protection against power-hungry executives eager to undermine democracy. However, of our nine cases, only Argentina has a powerful upper chamber, and its greatly malapportioned Senate has hampered rather than bolstered democracy. Argentina's federal system has rarely been a roadblock for presidents who wanted to expand their power. On the contrary, it has benefited authoritarian provincial political bosses, with negative consequences for democracy at the country level (Gervasoni 2018).

In sum, legislatures sometimes limit executive encroachments. But as the above discussion of Benin suggests, and as cases such as Venezuela in 1999 and Ecuador in 2007 also show, even majority opposition legislatures do not always block executive takeovers. Legislative constraints are not sufficient to protect

Table 8.2. Weighted Legislative Powers Scores for Nine Countries

	Weighted legislative powers score	Weighted legislative powers rank (out of 158)
Argentina	3.60	76
Benin	4.13	58
Georgia	4.35	50
India	4.51	47
Indonesia	4.25	47
Moldova	5.29	21
South Africa	4.57	43
Timor-Leste	3.43	82
Ukraine	4.08	62

Source: Chernykh et al. 2017.

democracy, and in some contexts, especially when the executive's party also controls the legislature, they do not protect it at all. In weakly institutionalized democracies, presidents and prime ministers typically have an arsenal of tools that enable them to be dominant players.

Institutional Weakness: Courts

A similar story is true for courts. In an era of increasing judicialization of democratic politics, courts have become meaningful actors in many third-wave democracies. They sometimes issue rulings that limit or prevent executive encroachments (see Varshney, Chapter 2 in this volume), and in a small number of third-wave democracies they are powerful actors that can limit executive encroachments. However, in most third-wave democracies, courts are not strong, independent actors. Presidents and prime ministers with hegemonic ambitions are often able to violate or quietly ignore court rulings and constitutional norms. They may be able to intimidate or offer rewards to judges to step down and replace them with more pliant individuals. They might be able to pack the courts. In most poor democracies, courts are underfunded, understaffed, and ill prepared to take on presidents and prime ministers with authoritarian instincts.[20] The judiciary struggles to achieve independence in relation to the executive and other powerful actors.

Expert surveys show a perception of relatively weak courts in most of our nine cases. Four V-Dem questions focus on judicial capacity to check the government. Question 3.7.0.11 of V-Dem Version 10 (February 2020) asks, "When the high court . . . is ruling in cases that are salient to the government, how often would you say that it makes decisions that merely reflect government wishes regardless of its sincere view of the legal record?" (Item v2juhcind). Question 3.7.0.12 asks, "When judges *not* on the high court are ruling in cases that are salient to the government, how often would you say that it makes decisions that merely reflect government wishes regardless of their sincere view of the legal record?" (Item v2juncind). Scores range from 0 ("always") to 4 ("never").[21] Columns 2 and 3 of Table 8.3 show V-Dem's linearized original scale posterior estimate, which treats the ordinal values on the original scale as if they were linear (Coppedge et al. 2020b, 25–26).

According to V-Dem's experts, the high courts in South Africa do not often issue rulings simply to accommodate the government. But the coders judge that the other eight countries have pliant courts that with some frequency make "decisions that merely reflect government wishes regardless of their sincere view of the legal record." In Argentina, Benin, Georgia, Moldova, Timor-Leste, and Ukraine, the point estimate in Table 8.3 is closer to a judgment that courts'

Table 8.3. Expert Perception of Judicial Capacity to Constrain Governments, V-Dem (2019)

	High court independence (3.7.0.11)	Lower court independence (3.7.0.12)	Government compliance with high court (3.7.0.13)	Compliance with other courts (3.7.0.14)
Argentina	2.35	2.36	3.04	2.99
Benin	2.22	2.33	2.84	2.37
Georgia	2.11	1.30	3.05	2.66
India	2.72	2.13	2.84	2.82
Indonesia	2.73	2.10	3.22	2.96
Moldova	2.60	2.74	2.66	2.63
South Africa	3.40	3.05	3.09	3.03
Timor-Leste	2.07	2.45	1.77	2.48
Ukraine	1.64	1.72	1.58	1.27
Denmark	*3.67*	*3.68*	*3.63*	*3.43*

Note: The V-Dem question number is in parentheses in the top row.

Source: Coppedge et al. 2020b.

decisions bow to government preferences about half the time "regardless of their sincere view of the legal record." The surveys judged the lower courts in Ukraine and Georgia to be particularly pliant. The final row, in italics, shows perceptions for Denmark, a country with strong legal institutions, to provide one benchmark.

Question 3.7.0.13 is "How often would you say the government complies with important decisions by the high court with which it disagrees?" (Item v2juhccomp). Question 3.7.0.14 is "How often would you say the government complies with important decisions by other courts with which it disagrees?" Scores range from 0 ("never") to 4 ("always") (Item v2jucomp).[22]

As the final two columns of Table 8.3 show, no country's score is much above 3.00 for either question. A score of 3.00 indicates a perception that the government "usually" "complies with important (judicial) decisions . . . with which it disagrees." Obviously, it is very problematic for a democracy if a government often does not comply with important judicial decisions.

The World Bank Governance Indicators include two measures that are relevant to understanding perceptions of institutional capacity to check rulers with authoritarian proclivities: control of corruption and rule of law. Where corruption is pervasive and where the rule of law is weak, it is presumably easier for would-be authoritarians to run over institutions and degrade democracy. Hence, democracy should be on firmer footing with solid scores for perceptions of control of corruption and rule of law.

Table 8.4 shows how our nine countries scores on these two measures. Scores are the number of standard deviations above and below the world mean in a

Table 8.4. World Bank Governance Indicators: Perceptions of Control of Corruption and Rule of Law in Nine Hard Cases, 2019

	Control of corruption	Rule of law
Argentina	−0.07	−0.43
Benin	−0.32	−0.66
Georgia	0.67	0.31
India	−0.23	−0.03
Indonesia	−0.42	−0.34
Moldova	−0.62	−0.37
South Africa	0.08	−0.08
Timor-Leste	−0.38	−1.11
Ukraine	−0.71	−0.70

Source: Worldwide Governance Indicators, n.d.

given year, and they are based on expert and public opinion surveys. With the surprising exception of Georgia, none of the eight countries scores well on these indicators. Benin and Timor-Leste (and Moldova and Ukraine, which are not cases of long-lasting democracy) have poor perceptions for control of corruption and rule of law, making the longevity of their democracies all the more notable.

The ease with which executives with authoritarian predilections have steamrolled courts in weakly institutionalized democracies makes us skeptical that the reason for democratic resilience in our cases has much to do with a vigorous and independent legal system. None of the authors of the cases suggests that the court system has been a major asset for democratic longevity.

In sum, in almost all democracies in hard places, institutional weakness is an ongoing problem. Counting on institutions alone, or even in combination with a partisan balance, to protect democracy is a poor bet.

Effective Governance and Durable Democracy

An obvious hypothesis for why democracy might endure in hard places is that governments function well despite the difficult environmental circumstances. Some of the extensive literature on economic performance and democratic endurance supports this argument, but the findings in this literature are mixed. In Table 1.1 in the introduction to this volume, Models 1 and 4 show a weakly statistically significant correlation (p < .10) between poor growth performance and democratic breakdown; in the other four models, economic growth is not significant.[23]

The authors in this volume do not invoke solid government performance as a reason for why democracy endured for a considerable time in difficult circumstances. In fact, it is difficult or impossible to attribute democratic endurance in most of our cases of long-standing democracy to good government performance. Table 8.5 shows one common measure of government performance, per capita GDP growth under democracy. Among our six long-standing democracies, India and Indonesia registered strong average growth rates. The average growth record in Argentina and South Africa has been poor, and in Benin, it has been mediocre. Table 8.5 also provides the data for the three post-Soviet cases.

Table 8.5 also shows the World Governance Indicator for Government Effectiveness for 2019. Scores are the number of standard deviations above or below the world mean of 0 in a given year. Except for Georgia and South Africa, the World Governance Indicator registers average (Argentina, India, Indonesia) or fairly poor (Benin, Moldova, Timor-Leste, and Ukraine) perceptions of government effectiveness. Effective governance certainly helps protect democracy,

Table 8.5. Perception of Government Effectiveness and Per Capita GDP Growth in Nine Hard Cases

Country	Period	Average GDP per capita growth	Perception of government effectiveness (2019)
Argentina	1983–2019	0.97%	−0.09
Benin	1991–2019	1.45%	−0.44
Georgia	2012–2019	4.51%	0.83
India	1977–2019	4.00%	0.17
Indonesia	1999–2019	3.69%	0.18
Moldova	1994–2019	3.61%[a]	−0.38
South Africa	1994–2019	1.12%	0.37
Timor-Leste	2002–2019	1.82%	−0.88
Ukraine	1994–2019	0.90%	−0.30

Sources: GDP per capita growth, World Development Indicators, n.d.; government effectiveness, Worldwide Governance Indicators, n.d.
[a] There are no data for 1994 and 1995.

but it does not explain why democracy has survived for a considerable time in most of our cases.

International Constraints: The EU, the US, and the OAS

Another possible reason why democracies might survive is international support for democracy and pressures against individuals and groups that attempt to erode or overthrow it. Two generations of research have shown that international actors and influences affect prospects for democracy (Brinks and Coppedge 2006; Gleditsch 2002; Gleditsch and Ward 2006; Levitsky and Way 2010; Mainwaring and Pérez-Liñán 2013; Pevehouse 2005; Vachudova 2005, 2010; Whitehead 1986).

In the 1970s and 1980s, EU support for democratization in Greece, Portugal, and Spain helped nurture democratic consolidation (Pridham 1991; Whitehead 1986). The 1990s generated optimism that international actors and influences could help sustain democracies. The European Union embarked on the most ambitious democracy promotion ever. With EU support, the Baltics, the Czech Republic, Hungary, and Poland quickly and robustly democratized after the fall of communism. In Bulgaria, Romania, and Slovakia, in the second half of the 1990s, EU leverage induced a turn toward liberalism and democracy (Vachudova 2005, 2010). In the Western Hemisphere, pressures from the US and the Organization of American States sometimes thwarted executive takeovers and coups in the 1990s.

However, as Levitsky and Way (2010) have argued, international influences are likely to have significant protective effect for democracy only in cases of high vulnerability to external influence *and* strong linkages to the West—mainly, countries in the Western Hemisphere and Eastern Europe. This includes only one case in our volume—Argentina—although, as Riedl argues, international pressures were crucial in the transition to democracy in South Africa.

What do the case studies in this volume tell us about the capacity of international actors to sustain democracy in hard places? The only author who points to international pressures and support as an important factor in sustaining what he calls democratic moments is Lucan Way, writing on Georgia (2013–present), Moldova (1991–2001), and Ukraine (1991–98, 2005–10). He asserts that a factor in the emergence of democratic moments in the post-Soviet countries is that anti-Russian leaders are susceptible to democratizing pressures. But, Way argues, these international pressures have not been sufficient to nudge any of these three countries into becoming even low-level electoral democracies. International pressures were central to the decision of the apartheid regime elite to democratize in South Africa, but they are not a part of Riedl's account of democratic maintenance after the transition.

Mainwaring and Simison on Argentina and Bermeo on Timor-Leste explicitly note that international pressures and support are not a central part of their explanations for democratic stability. Mainwaring and Simison argue that a largely democratic neighborhood has supported democracy in Argentina, but it is not the main part of their explanation for democratic survival. Bermeo argues that democracy assistance was not a major contributing factor to democratic endurance in Timor-Leste, although she writes that peacekeeping forces were important. As many scholars have demonstrated, being part of a friendly neighborhood increases a democracy's chances of survival. However, except for Argentina, the countries in our volume are not in neighborhoods that are friendly to democracies. International constraints are not a major part of the story of democratic longevity in these cases.

Beyond the case studies in this volume, in the new millennium, international actors have been less successful in supporting democracy than they were in the 1990s. The US and the EU have been the main pro-democracy actors in the post–Cold War period, but they have been hard-pressed to block incremental executive takeovers. The US and OAS were unable to prevent incremental democratic erosions in Venezuela (1999–present), Bolivia (2006–19, followed by a coup in late 2019), Ecuador (2007–17), and Nicaragua (2007–present), and they were not able to thwart a coup in Honduras in 2009. The European Union has not been able to prevent severe backsliding in Hungary since 2010 and Poland since 2015—countries that, based on their wealth, education levels, membership in the EU, and proximity to Western Europe, should have been immune to erosion. Chinese ascendance and Russia's muscular support for authoritarian regimes has further tipped the balance away from democracy. The ability of international actors to sustain democracies is more questionable now than it was in the 1990s.

Voters and Democratic Stability

A long lineage in some ways dating back to Tocqueville's classic *Democracy in America* has seen the broader political culture as responsible for maintaining democracy. In recent decades, the work by Inglehart and Welzel (2005) exemplified the view that democratic voters make for democratic regimes (Almond and Verba 1963; Inglehart 1997, 160–215). Nevertheless, as Claassen (2020) noted, until his work, the empirical evidence to support these claims was thin. Moreover, work that claimed that mass values accounted for democracy prior to Claassen's was subject to trenchant criticisms (Seligson 2002).

None of the authors in this volume argues that voters constrain politicians to maintain democracy and thereby are responsible for sustaining democratic regimes in hard places. This issue is the subject of an ongoing debate in the social sciences, and it would be folly to attempt to resolve it here. Nevertheless, I would be remiss if I did not say something about the subject because voters' preferences on some issues can hold politicians somewhat accountable.

In an excellent recent analysis, Claassen (2020) argued that public support helps democracies survive. I have no doubt that strong democratic commitments in the mass public help protect democracy and that, conversely, the absence of such commitments makes democracy more vulnerable. Nevertheless, I am skeptical that voters' attitudes are responsible for maintaining democratic regimes in our cases or more generally. Several streams of literature underpin this assumption. First, electoral accountability is blunt. Politicians in democracies do not faithfully reflect mass preferences. Even when politicians claim to represent mass publics, there are serious monitoring problems (Achen and Bartels 2016; Przeworski et al. 1999). Politicians have significant autonomy and preferences of their own, and elections do not suffice to induce them to mirror mass preferences. As was displayed when President Trump claimed that widespread fraud had cheated him out of the 2020 US presidential election and 70 percent of Republican voters believed this assertion, politicians' preferences and discourse shape voter preferences and beliefs (Achen and Bartels 2016; Lenz 2012).

Even if voters were able to constrain politicians within tighter boundaries than is feasible, it is not evident how much they would be willing to sacrifice in other outcomes in order to achieve or preserve democracy. Recent work by Graham and Svolik (2020) and Svolik (2019) based on survey experiments raises serious doubts that US voters impose much of a penalty on politicians for being flagrantly undemocratic. Their evidence suggests that the great majority of voters care more about other things, especially in the context of high polarization. At best, the evidence that voters care deeply about democracy and push politicians and parties to sustain democracy is mixed. The many executive takeovers led by authoritarian populists who repeatedly won elections further suggests that large numbers of voters do not greatly value democracy.

Along related lines, Bermeo (2003) argued that voters' attitudes were not responsible for democratic breakdowns in Latin America and Europe; voters did not defect from democracy, but key politicians and elite groups did. If this argument is correct, it suggests that even fairly widespread democratic commitments among voters might not do much to protect democracy. Elites matter most for democratic stability.

Because most voters in most democracies in hard places have less political information and more pressing material needs than most voters in the advanced industrial democracies, it seems even less likely that voters will highly prioritize democracy over substantive outcomes, and less likely that they will have the means to push politicians into observing democratic norms.

Conclusion: External Constraints and Actors' Motivations

This volume advances knowledge about what enables democracy to survive in inhospitable terrain. I close with a few summary thoughts about how partisan oppositions, institutional constraints, and actors' own preferences sustain democracy.

1. It is extremely helpful for democratic stability that the ruling party and the other main parties be committed to democracy. Such parties exhibit what Levitsky and Ziblatt (2018) call tolerance and mutual respect, and they reject naked power grabs. If the governing parties are committed to democracy, the regime can survive for an extended time even in inhospitable terrain.

2. Scholars don't know a great deal about what generates and sustains normative preferences for democracy. This volume suggests that a widespread repudiation of the terrible past and the memorialization of that terrible

past can help generate commitments to democracy that endure for an extended time. The chapters in this volume by Bermeo on Timor-Leste and Mainwaring and Simison on Argentina each point to extremely costly antecedent authoritarian regimes as generators of normative preferences for democracy. The South African apartheid regime and British colonialism in India generated similar widespread repudiation. The Argentine case suggests that large-scale and ongoing efforts at memorializing human rights abuses under dictatorship through human rights trials, public education, human rights museums, and human rights movements can help nurture commitments to democracy even if government performance is mediocre or worse.

3. Unfortunately, scholars and democracy advocates cannot always count on the long-term sustainability of normative commitments to democracy. In this volume, this is especially clear in Varshney's chapter on India. The solid commitment of the Congress Party to democracy during most of its history—excepting the 1975–80 interlude—did not insulate democracy from subsequent erosion when the BJP came to power.

4. Despite the large and illuminating outpouring of works on democratic erosion and/or populism, we do not know a great deal about how to limit support for illiberal politicians and parties.

5. If the governing parties are naked power maximizers, democracy is not likely to endure in countries with the challenges we describe in this volume. Institutional constraints are not likely to be sufficient to hold democracy together. Indeed, as scholars and democrats have discovered to great alarm, even in developed countries with solid institutions, democracy is not always able to withstand attacks from illiberal power maximizers. If all politicians always pushed to constantly gain a political advantage (as some do) at the expense of democracy, democracy in hard places would be an extremely unlikely equilibrium.

6. The volume opens, rather than resolves, the question of how best to sustain normative commitments to democracy. Effective democratic governance is sometimes part of the answer, but in the new media environment in which bizarre and far-fetched conspiracy theories can gain widespread traction, it might not be enough.

7. A partisan balance of power is useful for sustaining democracy, but in contexts of weak institutions, it is far from sufficient. Moreover, and perhaps surprisingly, our volume suggests that a partisan balance of power is far from necessary to sustain democracy even in difficult contexts. In six countries analyzed in detail in this volume, democracy lasted for an extended time even though the governing party or coalition sometimes enjoyed indisputable electoral hegemony.

8.   Strong legislatures and solid courts are helpful for sustaining democracy, but they do not exist in most third-wave democracies—and certainly not in most democracies in "hard places." Strong legislatures are often not effective as checks and balances if the executive's party or coalition holds a majority in the assembly.[24] Moreover, in the medium term, they are not likely to emerge in the third-wave democracies that do not already have them.

9.   The combination of a majority partisan opposition and strong legislatures and courts probably makes democracy impregnable from executive takeovers. However, because of the institutional weakness of most legislatures and most judicial systems, this combination does not exist in any of the countries studied in depth in this volume. Surprisingly, democracy has survived for an extended time in six of these countries despite often having the combination that seems least propitious: weak institutions and frequent government majorities. In my view, this highlights the importance of actors' normative commitments.

10. Institutional constraints must complement actors' normative dispositions, and vice versa. In all but well-established democracies, institutional constraints can be vulnerable to rulers with authoritarian predilections. On the flip side, democracy would be vulnerable if its existence always hinged on the normative preferences of rulers and other actors.

Notes

*   Many stimulating conversations and exchanges with Tarek Masoud and Aníbal Pérez-Liñán shaped my thinking about this chapter. I am grateful to María Victoria De Negri, Hannah Early Bagdanov, and Luis Elizondo Gracia for research assistance; to Hannah Early Bagdanov, Nancy Bermeo, Benjamín García Holgado, Frances Hagopian, Tarek Masoud, Ashutosh Varshney, and Kurt Weyland for comments; to Jacob Nyrup and Stuart Bramwell for data on cabinet composition; and to Lucan Way for information on governing parties in Georgia, Moldova, and Ukraine.

1.   My understanding of actors includes organizations such as political parties, militaries, labor and business associations, interest groups, and social movement organizations, as well as heads of government and the ruling parties.

2.   Some of the very distinguished authors who write in this volume offer divergent views.

3.   The exact quote is "If men were angels, no government would be necessary. If angels were to govern men, neither external nor internal controls on government would be necessary" (Madison 1788).

4.   Georgia, Moldova, and Ukraine are not cases of long-lasting democracy, as Lucan Way's chapter makes clear.

5. "Mitt Romney Blasted Trump's Handling of the Pandemic and His Repeated Attacks on Mail-In Voting," *New York Times*, August 15, 2020, https://www.nytimes.com/2020/08/15/world/coronavirus-covid-19.html#link-32696171.

6. Some exceptions deviate from this rule. In the US, the dominant faction of the Southern Democrats rejected liberal democracy from before the Civil War until around the 1960s. With the effort to overturn the results of the 2020 election, Donald Trump and most of the contemporary Republican Party are also exceptions.

7. Harvard political theorist Danielle Allen (2020, 60–61) wrote that "[p]eople can have the chance of self-government through the institutions of constitutional democracy if and only if they prioritize the preservation of these institutions over wins in substantive domains of policy." My argument is not as demanding, but I agree that democracy is likely to be imperiled if the main political parties consistently prioritize "wins in substantive domains of policy" above "the preservation of the institutions of constitutional democracy."

8. The National Party left the coalition government in 1995 because of its limited influence on policy-making.

9. The African National Congress was ideologically very heterogeneous. It included some Leninists and some African nationalists who were indifferent to democracy.

10. In the dataset as a whole, 0.50 represents the median score. However, for democracy to survive for an extended time in difficult circumstances, it is problematic if the governing party is only moderately committed to democratic norms. This is why I code the median point on the scale as high illiberalism.

11. In contrast to Lührmann et al.'s (2020) coding for Georgia for the period after 2004, Lucan Way (Chapter 5 of this volume) views the subsequent Saakashvili government as competitive authoritarian. V-Party codes the victorious ENM party (United National Movement) as 0.31 on the illiberalism scale in the 2004 elections.

12. An important body of literature has argued that high polarization erodes democratic commitments. See Graham and Svolik 2020; Levitsky and Ziblatt 2018; McCoy et al. 2018; and Svolik 2019. Although the evidence for this argument is solid based on the cases these authors analyze, among our nine country cases the relationship between party system polarization and illiberalism as measured by V-Party data is weak. For example, Indonesia combines mostly high illiberalism scores with consistently low party system polarization. I measured party system polarization based on the V-Party question about parties' left-right position on a 0-to-6 scale (V2pariglef); each party's distance from the country's mean weighted ideological score is weighted by its vote share. At the *country-election* level for our nine countries, the bivariate correlation between party system polarization and a weighted (again by vote share) illiberalism score is only 0.01 ($N = 57$ country elections). Moreover, contrary to Mainwaring and Pérez-Liñán (2013), who showed a strong relationship between actors' moderation and commitment to democracy, the correlation between actors' distance from the ideological center and their illiberalism score is also very weak. At the party-election year for our nine countries ($n = 265$), the bivariate correlation between a party's ideological distance as an absolute value from the median distance of 3.00 and its

illiberalism score is only 0.15. In other words, party illiberalism is weakly related to party distance from the center, and party system illiberalism is extremely weakly correlated with party system polarization.

13. Many politicians have willingly stepped down from office even when they enjoyed high approval ratings. For example, every two-term US president until Franklin D. Roosevelt willingly decided against running for a third term. Chilean President Patricio Aylwin (1990–94) shortened his term, ruled out running for reelection, and left office with extraordinarily high approval ratings. Many ruling parties have engaged in what Levitsky and Ziblatt (2018) call forbearance; they do not consider using every possible tool to expand their advantage. In the same book, Przeworski (2019, 20) talks about democratic and anti-democratic forces. If all politicians were willing to do "whatever they can . . . to enhance their electoral advantage," there is no difference between democratic and anti-democratic forces; there are no democrats.

14. Rustow (1970) claimed that democratic transitions often result from stalemates among clashing actors under authoritarian rule. As a way of breaking the impasse, the actors agree to transition to democracy even though none of them really wants democracy. Although his article focused on transitions, and although Rustow himself argued that democratic survival is a different issue, his logic could in principle apply to survival as well.

15. On one of the few occasions in which the government proposed a measure that could have weakened democracy, namely, a September 1988 draft bill to restrict freedom of the press, the Congress Party rebelled; it was not willing to curb democratic rights. The parliament walked out (Guha 2017, 593). It was not a partisan balance of power but rather the Congress Party's unwillingness to support a bill that would have weakened freedom of the press that sank the measure.

16. Rustow was aware of this fact. He argued that democratic transitions could come about without any actor being committed to democracy, but that democratic stabilization rested on other processes.

17. The northern, Muslim-majority state of Jammu and Kashmir has been a notable failure in this effort to combine a strong central government with substantial autonomy at the state level. Kashmir has experienced frequent violent conflict and frequent violations of citizen rights (Guha 2017, 237–57, 344–58, 609–12, 642–45; Stepan et al. 2011, 109–15). In August 2019, the Modi government abrogated Jammu and Kashmir's autonomous status, which had been enshrined in Article 370 of the Indian Constitution. De facto, this state now has a subnational authoritarian regime.

18. This is not to assert that federalism is *consistently* good for democracy. In the US, for generations, southern states used claims of state rights to preserve authoritarian enclaves and oppress African Americans (Mickey 2015). In Argentina, provincial political bosses have used a fiscal federal system with perverse incentives to build and preserve provincial authoritarianism, which in turn has dragged down the country's level of democracy (Gervasoni 2018). One province of Indonesia, Aceh, has used its special federal status as a way of defending sharia rule and downplaying the rights of religious minorities.

19. Legislatures sometimes help impede executive takeovers; Gamboa (2017) analyzes the example of Colombia under Álvaro Uribe (2002–10). In Argentina, the congress

blocked attempts to expand executive power by populist presidents Néstor Kirchner (2003–7) and Cristina Fernández de Kircher (2007–15).

20. Reenock et al. (2013) found that independent courts favor democratic survival only in contexts of moderately high economic development. Because most of our countries are poor, by implication, independent courts would not be expected to have an impact on democratic survival. In some other studies, independent courts have had a more consistently positive impact on democratic survival. See Gibler and Randazzo (2011) and Pérez-Liñán and Mainwaring (2013).

21. 1 = Usually; 2 = About half the time; 3 = Seldom.

22. 1 = Seldom; 2 = About half the time; 3 = Usually.

23. Some scholars have reported that democracies are more likely to break down during times of economic crisis (Gasiorowski 1995; Kapstein and Converse 2008, 58–68; Przeworski et al. 2000; Slater et al. 2014, 362). Others have reported no effect (Alemán and Yang 2011, 1140; Haggard and Kaufman 2016, 238–43; Mainwaring and Pérez-Liñán 2013) or even that low growth was associated with a lower probability of breakdown (Remmer 1996). Still others have reported results that vary across different sets of cases (Bernhard et al. 2001; Houle 2009, 612; Svolik 2015, 726).

24. As Wu (2020) wrote, "Structural checks can be overrated. The survival of our Republic depends as much, if not more, on the virtue of those in government. . . . We have grown too jaded about things like professionalism and institutions, and the idea of men and women who take their duties seriously. . . . No external constraint can fully substitute for the personal compulsion to do what is right."

References

Abal Medina, Juan, and Julieta Súarez Cao. 2003. "Más allá del bipartidismo: El sistema argentino de partidos." *Iberoamericana* 3, no. 9 (March): 65–87.

Aboy Carlés, Gerardo. 2004. "Parque Norte o la doble ruptura alfonsinista." In *Historia reciente: Argentina en democracia*, edited by Marcos Novaro and Vicente Palermo, 11–33. Buenos Aires: Edhasa.

Acemoglu, Daron, Simon Johnson, James A. Robinson, and Pierre Yared. 2008. "Income and Democracy." *American Economic Review* 98, no. 3: 808–842.

Acemoglu, Daron, and James A. Robinson. 2006. *Economic Origins of Dictatorship and Democracy*. New York: Cambridge University Press.

Achen, Christopher H., and Larry M. Bartels. 2016. *Democracy for Realists: Why Elections Do Not Produce Responsive Government*. Princeton, NJ: Princeton University Press.

Acuña, Carlos Hugo. 1995. "Intereses empresarios, dictadura y democracia en la Argentina actual (o sobre por qué la burguesía abandona estrategias autoritarias y opta por la estabilidad democrática)." In *La nueva matriz política argentina*, edited by Carlos Hugo Acuña, 231–84. Buenos Aires: Ediciones Nueva Visión.

Acuña, Carlos Hugo. 2004. "The Industrial Bourgeoisie as a Political Actor: The Logic of Its Organization and Strategies in Argentina (from Its XIX Century Origins to the Present)." PhD diss., University of Chicago, Department of Political Science.

Acuña, Marcelo Luis. 1984. *De Frondizi a Alfonsín: la tradición política del radicalismo*. 2 vols. Buenos Aires: Centro Editor de América Latina.

Adejumobi, Said. 2000. "Elections in Africa: A Fading Shadow of Democracy?" *International Political Science Review* 21, no. 1: 59–73.

Adjaho, Richard. 1992. *La faillite du contrôle des finances publiques au Bénin (1960–1990)*. Cotonou: Editions du Flamboyant.

Africa Confidential. 2002. "The Old Order Please." *Africa Confidential* 43, no. 24 (December 6): 7.

Africa Confidential. 2006. "Twilight of the Chameleon." *Africa Confidential* 47, no. 7 (March 31): 7.

Afrobarometer Data (South Africa and Benin, round 7, 2016–2018; accessed July 2021). http://www.afrobarometer.org.

Agnes, Flavia. 2016. "Personal Laws." In *The Oxford Handbook of the Indian Constitution*, edited by Sujit Choudhry, Madhav Khosla, and Pratap Bhanu Mehta, 903–20. Oxford: Oxford University Press.

Ahmadov, Anar. 2014. "Oil, Democracy, and Context: A Meta-Analysis." *Comparative Political Studies* 47, no. 9: 1238–67.

Ahmed, Sadiq, and Ashutosh Varshney. 2012. "Battles Half Won: The Political Economy of India's Growth and Economic Policy." In *Oxford Handbook of the Indian Economy*, edited by Chetan Ghate, 56–102. Oxford: Oxford University Press.

Aivazaian, Anna. 2019. "ПЕРСПЕКТИВЫ ПАРЛАМЕНТСКИХ ВЫБОРОВ В ГРУЗИИ В 2020 Г." *Научно-аналитический вестник ИЕ РАН* 6, no. 12: 111–15.

Alemán, José, and David D. Yang. 2011. "A Duration Analysis of Democratic Transitions and Authoritarian Backslides." *Comparative Political Studies* 44, no. 9 (September): 1123–51.

Allen, Chris. 1992. "Restructuring an Authoritarian State: Democratic Renewal in Benin." *Review of African Political Economy* 19, no. 54: 42–58.

Allen, Danielle. 2020. "The Constitution Counted My Great-Great-Grandfather as Three-Fifths of a Free Person: Here's Why I Love It Anyway." *The Atlantic* 326, no. 3 (October): 58–63.

Almond, Gabriel A., and Sydney Verba. 1963. *The Civic Culture: Political Attitudes and Democracy in Five Nations*. Princeton, NJ: Princeton University Press.

Amadeo, Eduardo. 1984. "Empresarios y democracia." In *Democracia, orden político y parlamento*, edited by Hilda Sabato and Marcelo Cavarozzi, 94–103. Buenos Aires: Centro Editor de América Latina.

Amuwo, 'Kunle. 2003. "The State and the Politics of Democratic Consolidation in Benin, 1990–1999." In *Political Liberalization and Democratization in Africa*, edited by Julius Omozuanvbo Ihonvbere and John Mukum Mbaku, 141–78. Westport, CT: Praeger.

Anderson, Benedict. 1983. "Old State, New Society: Indonesia's New Order in Comparative Historical Perspective." *Journal of Asian Studies* 42, no. 3 (May): 477–96.

Anderson, Benedict. 2001. "Imagining East Timor." *Lusotopie* 8: 233–39.

Anderson, Benedict, Alief Djati, and Douglas Kammen. 2003. "Interview with Mário Carrascalão." *Indonesia* 76: 1–22.

Anderson, John. 1999. *Kyrgyzstan: Central Asia's Island of Democracy?* Amsterdam, ND: Harwood Academic Publishers.

Ansell, Ben, and David Samuels. 2010. "Inequality and Democratization: A Contractarian Approach." *Comparative Political Studies* 43, no. 12 (December): 1543–74.

Ansell, Ben, and David J. Samuels. 2014. *Inequality and Democratization: An Elite-Competition Approach*. New York: Cambridge University Press.

Aprasidze, David. 2013. *Nations in Transit 2012: Georgia*. New York: Freedom House.

Arnold, Matthew B. 2009. "Challenges Too Strong for the Nascent State of Timor-Leste: Petitioners and Mutineers." *Asian Survey* 49, no. 3: 429–49.

Arthur, Catherine. 2019. *Political Symbols and National Identity in Timor-Leste*. Cham, Switzerland: Palgrave Macmillan.

Aslaksen, Silje. 2010. "Oil and Democracy: More than a Cross-Country Correlation?" *Journal of Peace Research* 47, no. 4: 421–31.

Aspinall, Edward, and Mark Berger. 2001. "The Break-Up of Indonesia? Nationalisms after Decolonisation and the Limits of the Nation-State in Post-Cold War Southeast Asia." *Third World Quarterly* 22, no. 6 (December): 1003–24.

Aspinall, Edward, Allen Hicken, James Scambary, and Meredith Weiss. 2018. "Exchange: Timor-Leste Votes—Parties and Patronage." *Journal of Democracy* 29, no. 1 (January): 153–67.

Austin, Granville. 1966. *The Indian Constitution: Cornerstone of a Nation*. Delhi: Oxford University Press.

Auyero, Javier. 2007. *Routine Politics and Violence in Argentina: The Gray Zone of State Power*. New York: Cambridge University Press.

Balcells, Laia, Valeria Palanza, and Elsa Voytas. 2022. "Do Transitional Justice Museums Persuade Visitors? Evidence from a Field Experiment." *Journal of Politics* 84, no. 1 (January): 496–510. https://doi.org/10.1086/714765.

Ballard, John. 2008. *Triumph of Self-Determination: Operation Stabilise and United Nations Peace-Making in East Timor*. Westport, CT: Greenwood Publishing Group.

Ballester, Horacio. 1996. *Memorias de un coronel democrático: medio siglo de historia política argentina en la óptica de un militar*. Buenos Aires: Ediciones de la Flor.

Banégas, Richard. 2003. *La démocratie à pas de caméléon. Transition et imaginaires politiques au Bénin*. Paris: Karthala.

Banégas, Richard. 2014. "Briefing Benin: Challenges for Democracy." *African Affairs* 113, no. 452: 449–59.

Barkan, Joel D. 1995. "Debate: PR and Southern Africa: Elections in Agrarian Societies." *Journal of Democracy* 6, no. 4: 106–16.

Basu, Deepankar. 2021. "Majoritarian Politics and Hate Crimes against Religious Minorities: Evidence from India, 2009–2018." *World Development* 146: 105540. https://doi.org/10.1016/j.worlddev.2021.105540.

Bates, Robert H. 1984. *Markets and States in Tropical Africa: The Political Basis of Agricultural Policies*. Berkeley: University of California Press.

Battaglino, Jorge. 2010. "La política militar de Alfonsín: la implementación del control civil en un contexto desfavorable." In *Discutir Alfonsín*, edited by Roberto Gargarella, María Victoria Murillo, and Mario Pecheny, 161–84. Buenos Aires: Siglo XXI.

Bayart, Jean-François. 1989. *L'état en Afrique. La politique du ventre*. Paris: Fayard.

Beissinger, Mark R. 2002. *Nationalist Mobilization and the Collapse of the Soviet State*. New York: Cambridge University Press.

Bellin, Eva. 2004. "The Robustness of Authoritarianism in the Middle East: Exceptionalism in Comparative Perspective." *Comparative Politics* 36, no. 2: 139–57.

Bellin, Eva. 2012. "Reconsidering the Robustness of Authoritarianism in the Middle East: Lessons from the Arab Spring." *Comparative Politics* 44, no. 2: 127–49.

Beltrán, Gastón J. 2006. "Acción empresaria e ideología. La génesis de las reformas estructurales." In *Los años de Alfonsín, ¿el poder de la democracia o la democracia del poder?*, edited by Alfredo Raúl Pucciarelli, 199–243. Buenos Aires: Siglo XXI.

Berbecel, Dan. 2022. *Presidential Power in Latin America: Examining the Cases of Argentina and Chile*. New York: Routledge.

Berman, Sheri. 1998. *The Social Democratic Movement: Ideas and Politics in the Making of Interwar Europe*. Cambridge, MA: Harvard University Press.

Bermeo, Nancy. 1992. "Democracy and the Lessons of Dictatorship." *Comparative Politics* 24, no. 3 (April): 273–91.

Bermeo, Nancy. 2003. *Ordinary People in Extraordinary Times*. Princeton, NJ: Princeton University Press.

Bermeo, Nancy. 2010. "Armed Conflict and the Durability of Electoral Democracy." In *In War's Wake: International Conflict and the Fate of Liberal Democracy*, edited by Elizabeth Kier and Ronald Krebs, 67–94. New York: Cambridge University Press.

Bermeo, Nancy. Forthcoming. *Democracy after War*. Princeton, NJ: Princeton University Press.

Bermeo, Nancy, and Deborah J. Yashar, eds. 2016a. *Parties, Movements, and Democracy in the Developing World*. New York: Cambridge University Press.

Bermeo, Nancy, and Deborah Yashar. 2016b. "Parties, Movements, and the Making of Democracy." In *Parties, Movements, and Democracy in the Developing World*, edited by Nancy Bermeo and Deborah Yashar, 1–27. New York: Cambridge University Press.

Bernhard, Michael, Timothy Nordstrom, and Christopher Reenock. 2001. "Economic Performance, Institutional Intermediation and Democratic Breakdown." *Journal of Politics* 63 (3): 775–803.

Bertrand, Jacques. 2007. "Indonesia's Quasi-Federalist Approach: Accommodation among Strong Integrationist Tendencies." *International Journal of Constitutional Law* 5, no. 4 (October): 576–605.

Bexley, Angie, and Nuno Rodrigues Tchailoro. 2013. "Consuming Youth: Timorese in the Resistance against Indonesian Occupation." *Asia Pacific Journal of Anthropology* 14, no. 5: 405–22.

Bierschenk, Thomas. 2009. "Democratization without Development: Benin 1989–2009." *International Journal of Politics, Culture, and Society IJPS* 22, no. 3: 337–57.

Bierschenk, Thomas, Elizabeth Thioléron, and Nassirou Bako-Arifari. 2003. "Benin." *Development Policy Review* 21, no. 2: 161–78.

Bockelie, Josette. 2013. "Democratic Consolidation in Benin: A Study of Socio-Economic and Political Development." Undergraduate thesis, Paris Institute of Political Studies.

Boix, Carles. 2003. *Democracy and Redistribution*. Cambridge: Cambridge University Press.

Boix, Carles. 2011. "Democracy, Development, and the International System." *American Political Science Review* 105, no. 4 (November): 809–28.

Boix, Carles, and Susan C. Stokes. 2003. "Endogenous Democratization." *World Politics* 55, no. 4 (July): 517–49.

Boix-Miller-Rosato (BMR). dichotomous coding of democracy, 1800–2015 (Version 3.0). Accessed August 2019. https://sites.google.com/site/mkmtwo/data.

Bolt, Jutta, Robert Inklaar, Herman de Jong, and Jan Luiten van Zanden. 2018. "Maddison Project Database, version 2018." Accessed July 2018. www.ggdc.net/maddison.

Bonvecchi, Alejandro. 2002. "Estrategia de supervivencia y tácticas de disuasión. Los procesos políticos de la política económica después de las reformas estructurales." In *El derrumbe político en el ocaso de la convertibilidad*, edited by Marcos Novaro, 107–93. Buenos Aires: Norma.

Booysen, Susan. 2014. *Twenty Years of South African Democracy: Citizen Views of Human Rights, Governance and the Political System*. Washington, DC: Freedom House. https://freedomhouse.org/sites/default/files/Twenty%20Years%20of%20South%20African%20Democracy.pdf.

Booysen, Susan, and Grant Masterson. 2009. "South Africa." In *Compendium of Elections in Southern Africa 1989–2009: 20 Years of Multiparty Democracy*, edited by Denis Kadima and Susan Booysen, 399–402. Johannesburg: EISA.

Bosoer, Fabián. 2006. "¿Crisis con salvataje? Una hipótesis sobre el componente parlamentario en el auto-rescate de las democracias sudamericanas: 1999–2004." In *Instituciones, democracia e integración regional en el Mercosur*, edited by Giorgio Alberti, Elsa Llenderrozas, and Julio Pinto, 245–66. Buenos Aires: Bononiae Libris-Prometeo.

Botana, Natalio. 2006. *Poder y hegemonía. el régimen político después de la crisis*. Buenos Aires: Emecé.

Bovensiepen, Judith, and Maj Nygaard-Christensen. 2018. "Petroleum Planning as State Building in Timor-Leste." *Asia Pacific Journal of Anthropology* 19, no. 5: 412–31.

Boyle, Michael. 2014. *Violence after War: Explaining Instability in Post-Conflict States*. Baltimore, MD: JHU Press.

Braithwaite, John, Hilary Charlesworth, and Adérito Soares. 2012. *Networked Governance of Freedom and Tyranny: Peace in Timor-Leste*. Canberra, Australia: ANU Press.

Bratton, Michael, and Chris Landsberg. 1998. "Aiding Reconstruction and Development in South Africa: Promise and Delivery." In *Good Intentions: Pledges of Aid for Postconflict Recovery*, edited by Shepard Forman and Stewart Patrick, 259–314. Boulder, CO: Lynne Rienner Publishers.

Bratton, Michael, and Nicholas van de Walle. 1997. *Democratic Experiments in Africa: Regime Transitions in Comparative Perspective*. Cambridge: Cambridge University Press.

Brinks, Daniel, and Michael Coppedge. 2006. "Diffusion Is No Illusion: Neighbor Emulation in the Third Wave of Democracy." *Comparative Political Studies* 39, no. 4 (May): 463–89.

Brinks, Daniel M., Steven Levitsky, and María Victoria Murillo. 2019. *Understanding Institutional Weakness: Power and Design in Latin American Institutions*. New York: Cambridge University Press.

Brownlee, Jason. 2007. *Durable Authoritarianism in an Age of Democratization*. New York: Cambridge University Press.

Brownlee, Jason, Tarek Masoud, and Andrew Reynolds. 2013. "Tracking the 'Arab Spring': Why the Modest Harvest?" *Journal of Democracy* 24, no. 4: 29–44.

Bruno, Ángel. 1984. "Derechos humanos y el parlamento." In *Democracia, orden político y parlamento*, edited by Hilda Sabato and Marcelo Cavarozzi, 127–35. Buenos Aires: Centro Editor de América Latina.

Budiardjo, Carmel, and Soei Liong Liem. 1984. *The War against East Timor*. London: Zed Books.

Bukia, Sopho. 2015. "Georgian TV Dispute Gets Nasty." Institute for War and Peace Reporting, Congressional Research Service, Issue 794 (October 27). https://www.refworld.org/docid/564c41a64.html.

Bureau of European and Eurasian Affairs. 2009. "Foreign Operations Appropriated Assistance: Belarus." Washington, DC: US Department of State.

Burnell, Peter J. 2010. *Is There a New Autocracy Promotion?* Madrid: Fride.

Capizzi, Elaine, Helen Hill, and Dave Macey. 1976. "FRETILIN and the Struggle for Independence in East Timor." *Race & Class* 17, no. 4: 381–95.

Caplan, Richard. 2005. *International Governance of War-Torn Territories*. New York: Oxford University Press.

Carey, John M., and Matthew Soberg Shugart, eds. 1998. *Executive Decree Authority*. New York: Cambridge University Press.

Carothers, Thomas. 1999. *Aiding Democracy Abroad: The Learning Curve*. Washington DC: Carnegie Endowment.

Cavarozzi, Marcelo. 1983. *Autoritarismo y democracia (1955–1983)*. Buenos Aires: Centro Editor de América Latina.

CAVR (Timor-Leste Commission for Reception, Truth, and Reconciliation). 2005. *Chega! The Report of the Commission for Reception, Truth, and Reconciliation in Timor-Leste*. Part 3. http://www.etan.org/etanpdf/2006/CAVR/03-History-of-the-Conflict.pdf.

CBM (Consultative Business Movement). 1997. *Submission to the Truth and Reconciliation Commission of South Africa*. Johannesburg, South Africa: CBM.

Cecire, Michael. 2013. "Georgia's 2012 Elections and Lessons for Democracy Promotion." *Orbis* 57, no. 2 (Spring): 232–50.

Cederman, Lars-Erik, Andreas Wimmer, and Brian Min. 2010. "Why Do Ethnic Groups Rebel? New Data and Analysis." *World Politics* 62, no. 1 (January): 87–119.

CEPALSTAT. Databases and Statistical Publications. Accessed January 2019. http://estad isticas.cepal.org/cepalstat.

Chabi, Maurice. 1993. *Banqueroute: Mode d'emploi (Un marabout dans les griffes de la mafia béninoise).* Cotonou: Editions Gazette Livres.

Chakrabarti, Poulomi. 2019. "One Nation, Many Worlds: Education, Health and Dignity in India." PhD diss., Brown University.

Challenor, Herschelle. 1970. "French-Speaking West Africa's Dahomeyan Strangers in Colonization and Decolonization." PhD diss., Columbia University.

Charosky, Hernán. 2002. "Honestos y audaces: realizaciones y límites de la política anticorrupción." In *El derrumbe político en el ocaso de la convertibilidad*, edited by Marcos Novaro, 195–252. Buenos Aires: Norma.

Chauchard, Simon. 2017. *Why Representation Matters: Ethnic Quotas in Rural India.* New York: Cambridge University Press.

Cheeseman, Nic. 2015. *Democracy in Africa: Successes, Failures, and the Struggle for Political Reform.* New York: Cambridge University Press.

Cheresky, Isidoro. 2008. *Poder presidencial, opinión pública y exclusión social.* Buenos Aires: Ediciones Manantial.

Chernykh, Svitlana, David Doyle, and Timothy J. Power. 2017. "Measuring Legislative Power: An Expert Reweighting of the Fish-Kroenig Parliamentary Powers Index." *Legislative Studies Quarterly* 42, no. 2 (May): 295–320.

Chhibber, Pradeep. 2014. *Religious Practice and Democracy in India.* New York: Cambridge University Press.

Chopra, Jarat. 2000. "The UN's Kingdom in East Timor." *Survival* 42, no. 3 (Autumn): 27–29.

Chopra, Jarat. 2002. "Building State Failure in East Timor." *Development and Change* 33, no. 5: 979–1000.

CIA (Central Intelligence Agency). 2021. "Georgia." Last updated September 22, 2021. Accessed October 10, 2021. https://www.cia.gov/the-world-factbook/countries/georgia/.

CID (Consultoría Interdisciplinaria en Desarrollo S. A.). 1985. *USIA Poll # 1985-I85110: Youth Attitudes Survey.* Buenos Aires: Consultoría Interdisciplinaria en Desarrollo S. A.

Claassen, Christopher. 2020. "Does Public Support Help Democracy Survive?" *American Journal of Political Science* 64, no. 1 (January): 118–34. https://doi.org/10.1111/ajps.12452.

CONADEP (Comisión Nacional sobre la Desaparición de Personas). 1984. *Nunca más: informe final de la Comisión Nacional sobre la Desaparición de Personas.* Buenos Aires: EUDEBA.

Coppedge, Michael. 2002. "Theory Building and Hypothesis Testing: Large- vs. Small-N Research on Democratization." Paper prepared for presentation at the Annual Meeting of the Midwest Political Science Association, Chicago, IL, April 25–27.

Coppedge, Michael, Benjamin Denison, Paul Friesen, Lucia Tiscornia, and Yang Xu. 2022. "International Influences: The Hidden Dimension." In *Why Democracies Develop and Decline*, edited by Michael Coppedge, Amanda Edgell, Carl Henrik Knutsen, and Staffan I. Lindberg. New York: Cambridge University Press.

Coppedge, Michael, John Gerring, Carl Henrik Knutsen, Staffan I. Lindberg, Svend-Erik Skaaning, Jan Teorell, David Altman, Michael Bernhard, M. Steven Fish, Agnes Cornell, Sirianne Dahlum, Haakon Gjerløw, Adam Glynn, Allen Hicken, Joshua Krusell, Anna Lührmann, Kyle L. Marquardt, Kelly McMann, Valeriya Mechkova, Juraj

Medzihorsky, Moa Olin, Pamela Paxton, Daniel Pemstein, Josefine Pernes, Johannes von Römer, Brigitte Seim, Rachel Sigman, Jeffrey Staton, Natalia Stepanova, Aksel Sundström, Eitan Tzelgov, Yi-ting Wang, Tore Wig, Steven Wilson, and Daniel Ziblatt. 2018. "V-Dem Country-Year Dataset v8." *Varieties of Democracy (V-Dem) Project.* https://doi.org/10.23696/vdemcy18.

Coppedge, Michael, John Gerring, Carl Henrik Knutsen, Staffan I. Lindberg, Jan Teorell, David Altman, Michael Bernhard, M. Steven Fish, Adam Glynn, Allen Hicken, Anna Luhrmann, Kyle L. Marquardt, Kelly McMann, Pamela Paxton, Daniel Pemstein, Brigitte Seim, Rachel Sigman, Svend-Erik Skaaning, Jeffrey Staton, Agnes Cornell, Lisa Gastaldi, Haakon Gjerløw, Valeriya Mechkova, Johannes von Römer, Aksel Sundström, Eitan Tzelgov, Luca Uberti, Yi-ting Wang, Tore Wig, and Daniel Ziblatt. 2020a. "V-Dem Codebook v10." Varieties of Democracy (V-Dem) Project. https://www.v-dem. net/media/filer_public/28/14/28140582-43d6-4940-948f-a2df84a31893/v-dem_c odebook_v10.pdf.

Coppedge, Michael, John Gerring, Carl Henrik Knutsen, Staffan I. Lindberg, Jan Teorell, David Altman, Michael Bernhard, M. Steven Fish, Adam Glynn, Allen Hicken, Anna Luhrmann, Kyle L. Marquardt, Kelly McMann, Pamela Paxton, Daniel Pemstein, Brigitte Seim, Rachel Sigman, Svend-Erik Skaaning, Jeffrey Staton, Steven Wilson, Agnes Cornell, Nazifa Alizada, Lisa Gastaldi, Haakon Gjerløw, Garry Hindle, Nina Ilchenko, Laura Maxwell, Valeriya Mechkova, Juraj Medzihorsky, Johannes von Römer, Aksel Sundström, Eitan Tzelgov, Yi-ting Wang, Tore Wig, and Daniel Ziblatt. 2020b. "V-Dem Country–Year Dataset v10." Varieties of Democracy (V-Dem) Project. https://doi.org/10.23696/vdemds20.

Coppedge, Michael, John Gerring, Carl Henrik Knutsen, Staffan I. Lindberg, Jan Teorell, Nazifa Alizada, David Altman, Michael Bernhard, Agnes Cornell, M. Steven Fish, Lisa Gastaldi, Haakon Gjerløw, Adam Glynn, Allen Hicken, Garry Hindle, Nina Ilchenko, Joshua Krusell, Anna Luhrmann, Seraphine F. Maerz, Kyle L. Marquardt, Kelly McMann, Valeriya Mechkova, Juraj Medzihorsky, Pamela Paxton, Daniel Pemstein, Josefine Pernes, Johannes von Römer, Brigitte Seim, Rachel Sigman, Svend-Erik Skaaning, Jeffrey Staton, Aksel Sundström, Ei-tan Tzelgov, Yi-ting Wang, Tore Wig, Steven Wilson and Daniel Ziblatt. 2021. "V-Dem Country–Year Dataset v11.1." Varieties of Democracy (V-Dem) Project. https://doi.org/10.23696/vdemds21.

Cornell, Svante E. 2014. "Getting Georgia Right." *European View* 13: 185.

Corrales, Javier. 2018. *Fixing Democracy: Why Constitutional Change Often Fails to Enhance Democracy in Latin America.* New York: Oxford University Press.

Coveney, Joseph. 2021. "FIRTHLOGIT: Stata Module to Calculate Bias Reduction in Logistic Regression." https://econpapers.repec.org/software/bocbocode/s456948.htm.

Cox, Gary, and Scott Morgenstern. 2001. "Latin America's Reactive Assemblies and Proactive Presidents." *Comparative Politics* 33, no. 2 (January): 171–89.

Crenzel, Emilio. 2015. "Genesis, Uses, and Significations of the *Nunca Más* Report in Argentina." *Latin American Perspectives* 42, no. 3: 20–38. https://doi.org/10.1177/0094582X15570875.

Cristalis, Irena. 2009. *East Timor: A Nation's Bitter Dawn.* London: Zed Books.

Croissant, Aurel. 2008. "The Perils and Promises of Democratization through United Nations Transitional Authority—Lessons from Cambodia and East Timor." *Democratisation* 15, no. 3: 649–68.

Croissant, Aurel, and David Kuehn. 2009. "Patterns of Civilian Control of the Military in East Asia's New Democracies." *Journal of East Asian Studies* 9, no. 2: 187–217.

Crowther, William. 1991. "The Politics of Ethno-National Mobilization: Nationalism and Reform in Soviet Moldavia." *Russian Review* 50, no. 2: 183–202.

Crowther, William. 2007. "Moldova, Transnistria, and the PCRM's Turn to the West." *East European Quarterly* 61, no. 3: 273–304.

Dahl, Robert A. 1971. *Polyarchy: Participation and Opposition*. New Haven: Yale University Press.

Dahl, Robert A. 1973. *Polyarchy: Participation and Opposition*. New Haven: Yale University Press.

Dahl, Robert A. 1989. *Democracy and Its Critics*. New Haven: Yale University Press.

Darwich, May. 2017. "Creating the Enemy, Constructing the Threat: The Diffusion of Repression against the Muslim Brotherhood in the Middle East." *Democratization* 24 (7): 1289–1306.

David, Pauline. 2020. "TBC Bank Case: Money Laundering Prosecution." Transparency International. https://transparency.ge/en/post/assessment-money-laundering-prosecution-mamuka-khazaradze-badri-japaridze-and-avtandil.

de Ipola, Emilio. 1987. "La difícil apuesta del peronismo democrático." In *Ensayos sobre la transición democrática en la Argentina*, edited by José Nun and Juan Carlos Portantiero, 333–74. Buenos Aires: Puntosur Editores.

de Jager, Nicola, and Cindy Steenekamp. 2019. "Political Radicalism: Responding to the Legitimacy Gap in South Africa." In *Democracy under Threat: A Crisis of Legitimacy?*, edited by Ursula van Beek, 147–69. Cham, Switzerland: Palgrave Macmillan.

De Riz, Liliana. 1982. "Argentina: ni democracia estable ni régimen militar sólido." *Revista Mexicana de Sociología* 44, no. 4: 1203–23. https://doi.org/10.2307/3540128.

de Souza, Peter, Suhas Palshikar, and Yogendra Yadav, eds. 2008. *The State of Democracy in South Asia: A Report*. Delhi: Oxford University Press.

Decalo, Samuel. 1976. *Coups and Army Rule in Africa Motivations and Constraints*. New Haven: Yale University Press.

Decalo, Samuel. 1997. "Benin: The First of the New Democracies." In *Political Reform in Francophone Africa*, edited by John F. Clark and David E. Gardinier, 43–61. Boulder, CO: Westview Press.

Decalo, Samuel. 2018. "Benin: First of the New Democracies." In *Political Reform in Francophone Africa*, edited by John Clark and David Gardinier, 43–61. New York: Routledge.

Devdariani, Jaba. 2003. "Georgia: Security at Stake." *Transitions Online*, April 9.

Devdariani, Jaba. 2004. "Georgia: The Year of Revolution." *Transitions Online*, April 15.

Diamint, Rut. 2006. "Crisis, Democracy, and the Military in Argentina." In *Broken Promises? The Argentine Crisis and Argentine Democracy*, edited by Edward Epstein and David Pion-Berlin, 163–79. Lanham, MD: Lexington Books.

Diamond, Larry, Seymour Martin Lipset, and Juan Linz. 1987. "Building and Sustaining Democratic Government in Developing Countries: Some Tentative Findings." *World Affairs* 150, no. 1 (Summer): 5–19.

Dinerstein, Ana Cecilia. 2004. "Más allá de la crisis. Acerca de la naturaleza del cambio político en Argentina." *Revista Venezolana de Economía y Ciencias Sociales* 10, no. 1 (January–April): 241–69.

Ding, Iza, and Dan Slater. 2021. "Democratic Decoupling." *Democratization* 28, no. 1 (January): 63–80.

Diop, Omar. 2006. *Partis politiques et processus de transition démocratique en Afrique noire: Recherches sur les enjeux juridiques et sociologiques du multipartisme dans quelques pays de l'espace francophone*. Paris: Editions Publibook des Ecrivans.

Divan, Shyam. 2016. "Public Interest Litigation." In *The Oxford Handbook of the Indian Constitution*, edited by Sujit Choudhry, Madhav Khosla, and Pratap Bhanu Mehta, 662–79. Oxford: Oxford University Press.

Dolidze, Ana. 2007. "Inside Track: Georgia's Path to Authoritarianism." *National Interest Online*, August 24.

Donno, Daniela, and Bruce Russett. 2004. "Islam, Authoritarianism, and Female Empowerment: What Are the Linkages?" *World Politics* 56, no. 4 (July): 582–607.

Doyon, Louise. 1988. "El crecimiento sindical bajo el peronismo." In *La formación del sindicalismo peronista*, edited by Juan Carlos Torre, 169–81. Buenos Aires: Legasa.

Drazanova, Lenka. 2019. "Historical Index of Ethnic Fractionalization Dataset (HIEF)." https://doi.org/10.7910/DVN/4JQRCL, Harvard Dataverse, V2, UNF:6:z4J/b/ PKbUpNdIoeEFPvaw== [fileUNF].

Dunn, James. 2003. *East Timor: A Rough Passage to Independence*. New South Wales: Longueville Books.

Durand, Frédéric. 2016. *History of Timor-Leste*. Chiang Mai: Silkworm Books.

ECLAC (Economic Commission for Latin America and the Caribbean). 1985. "Nota sobre la evolución de la economía argentina en 1984." Versión preliminar. Documento de trabajo nro. 15, ECLAC, Buenos Aires. https://repositorio.cepal.org/bitstream/han dle/11362/28507/S8500616_es.pdf.

ECLAC (Economic Commission for Latin America and the Caribbean). 1993. *Social Panorama of Latin America 1993*. Santiago, Chile: ECLAC.

ECLAC (Economic Commission for Latin America and the Caribbean). 2001. *Panorama social de América Latina 2000–2001*. Santiago, Chile: Naciones Unidas.

ECLAC (Economic Commission for Latin America and the Caribbean). 2004. *Social Panorama of Latin America 2002–2003*. Santiago, Chile: ECLAC.

ECLAC (Economic Commission for Latin America and the Caribbean). 2006. *Social Panorama of Latin America 2005*. Santiago, Chile: ECLAC. https://www.cepal.org/en/ publications/1224-social-panorama-latin-america-2005.

ECLAC (Economic Commission for Latin America and the Caribbean). 2021. *Social Panorama of Latin America 2020*. Santiago, Chile: ECLAC.

Emery, Alan. 2006. "Privatization, Neoliberal Development, and the Struggle for Workers' Rights in Post-Apartheid South Africa." *Social Justice* 33, no. 3 (September): 6–19.

Englebert, Pierre. 1996. "Benin: Recent History." In *Africa South of the Sahara 1996*. London: Europa Publications.

Englebert, Pierre. 2002. *State Legitimacy and Development in Africa*. Boulder, CO: Lynne Rienner Publishers.

Epstein, David L., Robert Bates, Jack Goldstone, Ida Kristensen, and Sharyn O'Halloran. 2006. "Democratic Transitions." *American Journal of Political Science* 50, no. 3 (July): 551–69.

Fairbanks, Charles H., Jr. 2004. "Georgia's Rose Revolution." *Journal of Democracy* 15, no. 2: 110–24.

Fairbanks Charles H., Jr., and Alexi Gugushvili. 2013. "A New Chance for Georgian Democracy." *Journal of Democracy* 24, no. 1 (January): 116–27.

FBIS (Foreign Broadcast Information Service). 1992. "Daily Reports, Central Eurasia." FBIS-SOV-92-009, January 14, page 62. Naples, FL: Readex.

FBIS (Foreign Broadcast Information Service). 1994. "Daily Reports, Central Eurasia." August 3, page 38. Naples, FL: Readex.

Fealy, Greg. 2021. "Jokowi in the Covid-19 Era: Repressive Pluralism, Dynasticism, and the Overbearing State." *Bulletin of Indonesian Economic Studies* 56, no. 3 (September): 301–23.

Feijó, Rui Graça. 2016. *Dynamics of Democracy in Timor-Leste: The Birth of a Democratic Nation, 1999–2012*. Amsterdam: Amsterdam University Press.

Feijó, Rui Graça. 2018. "Timor-Leste in 2017: Between a Diplomatic Victory and the Return of 'Belligerent Democracy.'" *Asian Survey* 58, no. 1: 206–12.

Fernandes, Clinton. 2011. *The Independence of East Timor: Multi-dimensional Perspectives—Occupation, Resistance, and International Political Activism*. Portland, OR: Sussex Academic Books.

Figueiredo, Argelina Cheibub, and Fernando Limongi. 1999. *Executivo e Legislativo na Nova Ordem Constitucional*. Rio de Janeiro: Editora FGV.

Fish, M. Steven. 1995. *Democracy from Scratch: Opposition and Regime in the New Russian Revolution*. Princeton, NJ: Princeton University Press.

Fish, M. Steven. 2002. "Islam and Authoritarianism." *World Politics* 55, no. 1 (October): 4–37.

Fish, M. Steven, and Robin S. Brooks. 2004. "Does Diversity Hurt Democracy?" *Journal of Democracy* 15, no. 1 (January): 154–66.

Franco, Marina. 2009. "'Homeland Security' as a State Policy in 1970's Argentina." *Antíteses* 2, no. 4: 887–914.

Freedom House. 2002. *Freedom of the Press: Argentina*. New York: Freedom House.

Freedom House. 2013. *Nations in Transit 2013—Georgia*. New York: Freedom House.

Freedom House. 2014. *Nations in Transit 2014—Georgia*. New York: Freedom House.

Freedom House. 2015. *Nations in Transit 2015—Georgia*. New York: Freedom House.

Freedom House. 2016. *Nations in Transit 2016— Georgia*. New York: Freedom House.

Freedom House. 2017. *Nations in Transit 2017—Georgia*. New York: Freedom House.

Freedom House. 2019a. "Country and Territory Ratings and Statuses, 1973–2019." Accessed July 2019. https://freedomhouse.org/report/freedom-world.

Freedom House. 2019b. *Nations in Transit 2019—Georgia*. New York: Freedom House.

Freedom House. 2020a. "Freedom in the World 2020: Benin." Accessed July 2021. https://freedomhouse.org/country/benin/freedom-world/2020.

Freedom House. 2020b. *Nations in Transit 2020—Georgia*. New York: Freedom House.

Freedom House. 2021a. "Country and Territory Ratings and Statuses, 1973–2021." Accessed April 23, 2021. https://freedomhouse.org/sites/default/files/2021-02/Country_and_Territory_Ratings_and_Statuses_FIW1973-2021.xlsx.

Freedom House. 2021b. *Freedom in the World 2021: Democracy under Siege*. Washington, DC: Freedom House.

Freedom House. n.d. "Global Freedom Scores." Countries and Territories. Accessed October 10, 2021. https://freedomhouse.org/countries/freedom-world/scores?sort=desc&order=Total%20Score%20and%20Status.

Frey, Bruno S., Matthias Benz, and Alois Stutzer. 2004. "Introducing Procedural Utility: Not Only What, but Also How Matters." *Journal of Institutional and Theoretical Economics (JITE)* 160, no. 3 (September): 377–401. https://doi.org/10.1628/0932456041960560.

Friedrich, Carl Joachim. 1939. "Democracy and Dissent." *The Political Quarterly* 10, no. 4 (October): 571–82.

Fuller, Liz. 2005. "Some Georgian Journalists Feel Less Equal than Others." *RFE/RL Report* 5, no. 1 (January 3).

Fumagalli, Matteo. 2014. "The 2013 Presidential Election in the Republic of Georgia." *Electoral Studies* 35 (September): 395–97.

Galston, William. 2018. "The Populist Challenge to Liberal Democracy." *Journal of Democracy* 29, no. 2 (April): 5–19.

Gama, Paulino. 1995. "The War in the Hills, 1975–85: A Fretilin Commander Remembers." In *East Timor at the Crossroads: The Forging of a Nation*, edited by Peter Carey and Carter Bentley, 97–105. Honolulu: University of Hawaii Press.

Gamboa, Laura. 2017. "Opposition at the Margins: Strategies against the Erosion of Democracy in Colombia and Venezuela." *Comparative Politics* 49, no. 4 (July): 457–77.

Garay, Candelaria. 2016. *Social Policy Expansion in Latin America*. New York: Cambridge University Press.

García Lerena, Roberto. 2007. *Saúl Ubaldini: Crónicas de un militante obrero peronista*. Buenos Aires: Ediciones Runa Comunicaciones.

García Vázquez, Enrique. 1994. "La economía durante la presidencia de Illia." *Desarrollo Económico* 34, no. 134: 291–95. https://doi.org/10.2307/3467321.

Garrard, John. 2002. *Democratisation in Britain: Elites, Civil Society and Reform since 1800*. Basingstoke, Hampshire: Palgrave.

Gasiorowski, Mark J. 1995. "Economic Crisis and Political Regime Change: An Event History Analysis." *American Political Science Review* 89, no. 4 (December): 882–97.

Gazibo, Mamoudou. 2005. "Foreign Aid and Democratization: Benin and Niger Compared." *African Studies Review* 48, no. 3: 67–87.

Gazibo, Mamoudou. 2013. "Beyond Electoral Democracy: Foreign Aid and the Challenge of Deepening Democracy in Benin." In *Democratic Trajectories in Africa: Unravelling the Impact of Foreign Aid*, edited by Danielle Resnick and Nicolas van de Walle, 228–55. Oxford: Oxford University Press.

Geddes, Barbara. 1999. "What Do We Know about Democratization after Twenty Years?" *Annual Review of Political Science* 2: 115–44.

Geddes, Barbara, Joseph Wright, and Erica Frantz. 2014. "Autocratic Breakdown and Regime Transitions: A New Data Set." *Perspectives on Politics* 12, no. 2: 313–31.

Gente, Regis. 2013. "Bidzina Ivanishvili, a Man Who Plays According to Russian Rules?" *Caucasus Survey* 1, no. 1 (October): 1–9.

Gerchunoff, Pablo, and Lucas Llach. 2010. *El ciclo de la ilusión y el desencanto. Un siglo de políticas económicas argentinas*. Buenos Aires: Emecé.

Gervasoni, Carlos. 2018. *Hybrid Regimes within Democracies Fiscal Federalism and Subnational Rentier States*. New York: Cambridge University Press.

Gibler, Douglas M., and Kirk A. Randazzo. 2011. "Testing the Effects of Independent Judiciaries on the Likelihood of Democratic Backsliding." *American Journal of Political Science* 55, no. 3 (July): 696–709.

Gibson, Edward L. 1996. Class and Conservative Parties: Argentina in Comparative Perspective. Reprint edition. Baltimore: Johns Hopkins University Press.

Gilbreath, Dustin. 2015. "Are Georgian Politics Boring?" *New Eastern Europe* 1, no. 15: 105–11.

Giliomee, Hermann. 1995. "Democratization in South Africa." *Political Science Quarterly* 110, no. 1: 83–104.

Ginsburg, Tom, and Aziz Z. Huq. 2018. *How to Save a Constitutional Democracy*. Chicago: University of Chicago Press.

Gisselquist, Rachel M. 2008. "Democratic Transition and Democratic Survival in Benin." *Democratization* 15, no. 4: 789–814.

Gleditsch, Kristian Skrede. 2002. *All International Politics Is Local: The Diffusion of Conflict, Integration, and Democratization*. Ann Arbor: University of Michigan Press.

Gleditsch, Kristian Skrede, and Michael D. Ward. 2006. "Diffusion and the International Context of Democratization." *International Organization* 60, no. 4 (October): 911–33.

Godio, Julio. 2002. *Argentina, en la crisis está la solución: la crisis global desde las elecciones de octubre de 2001 hasta la asunción de Duhalde*. Buenos Aires: Editorial Biblos.

Godio, Julio. 2006. *El tiempo de Kirchner. El devenir de una "revolución desde arriba."* Buenos Aires: Ediciones Letra Grifa.

González-Ocantos, Ezequiel. 2016. *Shifting Legal Visions: Judicial Change and Human Rights Trials in Latin America*. New York: Cambridge University Press.

González-Ocantos, Ezequiel A. 2020. *The Politics of Transitional Justice in Latin America: Power, Norms, and Capacity Building*. Elements in politics and society in Latin America. New York: Cambridge University Press.

Graham, Matthew H., and Milan W. Svolik. 2020. "Democracy in America? Partisanship, Polarization, and the Robustness of Support for Democracy in the United States." *American Political Science Review* 114, no. 2 (May): 392–409. https://doi.org/10.1017/S0003055420000052.

Guha, Ramchandra. 2007. *India after Gandhi: The History of the World's Largest Democracy*. New York: HarperCollins.

Guha, Ramachandra. 2017. *India after Gandhi: The History of the World's Largest Democracy*. 10th ed. New Delhi: Picador.

Habib, Adam. 1995. "The Transition to Democracy in South Africa: Developing a Dynamic Model." *Transformation* 27: 50–73.

Habib, Adam, and Vishnu Padayachee. 2000. "Economic Policy and Power Relations in South Africa's Transition to Democracy." *World Development* 28, no. 2 (February): 245–63.

Habib, Adam, Devan Pillay, and Ashwin Desai. 1998. "South Africa and the Global Order: The Structural Conditioning of a Transition to Democracy." *Journal of Contemporary African Studies* 16, no. 1: 95–115. https://doi.org/10.1080/02589000980 8729622.

Haggard, Stephan, and Robert R. Kaufman. 2012. "Inequality and Regime Change: Democratic Transitions and the Stability of Democratic Rule." *American Political Science Review* 106, no. 3 (August): 495–516.

Haggard, Stephan, and Robert R. Kaufman. 2016. *Dictators and Democrats: Masses, Elites, and Regime Change*. Princeton, NJ: Princeton University Press.

Haggard, Stephen, and Robert Kaufmann. 2020. *Democratic Backsliding*. New York: Cambridge University Press.

Hanson, Jonathan K., and Rachel Sigman. 2013. "Leviathan's Latent Dimensions: Measuring State Capacity for Comparative Political Research." September 2013. Paper presented at the APSA 2011 Annual Meeting. https://ssrn.com/abstract=1899933.

Harris, Vandra, and Andrew Goldsmith. 2011. "The Struggle for Independence Was Just the Beginning." In *Security, Development and Nation-Building in Timor-Leste*, edited by Vandra Harris and Andrew Goldsmith, 3–16. London: Routledge.

Harris, Vandra, and Andrew O'Neil. 2011. "Timor-Leste's Future(s): Security and Stability 2010–20." In *Security, Development and Nation-Building in Timor-Leste*, edited by Vandra Harris and Andrew Goldsmith, chapter 13. London: Routledge.

Hashemi, Nader. 2009. *Islam, Secularism, and Liberal Democracy: Toward a Democratic Theory for Muslim Societies*. New York: Oxford University Press.

Heilbrunn, John R. 1993. "Social Origins of National Conferences in Benin and Togo." *Journal of Modern African Studies* 31, no. 2: 277–99.

Helmke, Gretchen. 2005. *Courts under Constraints: Judges, Generals, and Presidents in Argentina*. New York: Cambridge University Press.

Helsinki Watch. 1993. *Human Rights in Moldova: The Turbulent Dniester*. New York: Human Rights Watch.

Herbst, Jeffrey. 2001. "Political Liberalization in Africa after Ten Years." *Comparative Politics* 33, no. 3: 357–75.

Herbst, Jeffrey. 2003. "Analyzing Apartheid: How Accurate Were US Intelligence Estimates of South Africa, 1948–94?" *African Affairs* 102, no. 406: 81–107.

Heribert, Adam, and Kogila Moodley. 1993. *The Opening of the Apartheid Mind: Options for the New South Africa*. Berkeley: University of California Press.

Herring, Ronald J. 1982. *Land to the Tiller*. New Haven, CT: Yale University Press.

Hicks, David. 2016. "Da coligação ao golpe: inevitabilidade e consequência na descolonização do Timor Português." In *Timor-Leste: Colonialismo, Descolonização, Lusotopia*, edited by Rui Graça Feijó, 267–84. Lisboa: Edições Afrontamento.

Hofferbert, Richard I., and Hans-Dieter Klingemann. 1999. "Remembering the Bad Old Days: Human Rights, Economic Conditions, and Democratic Performance in Transitional Regimes." *European Journal of Political Research* 36, no. 2: 155–74. https://doi.org/10.1111/1475-6765.00466.

Hofstadter, Richard. 1969. *The Idea of a Party System: The Rise of Legitimate Opposition in the United States, 1780–1840*. Berkeley: University of California Press.

Hood, Ludovic. 2006. "Security Sector Reform in East Timor, 1999–2004." *International Peacekeeping* 13, no. 1: 60–77.

Horowitz, Donald. 1985. *Ethnic Groups in Conflict*. Berkeley: University of California Press.

Horowitz, Donald. 2000. *Ethnic Groups in Conflict*. Updated edition with a new preface. Berkeley: University of California Press.

Horowitz, Donald. 2013. *Constitutional Change and Democracy in Indonesia*. New York: Cambridge University Press.

Hough, Jerry. 1997. *Democratization and Revolution in the USSR, 1985–1991*. Washington, DC: The Brookings Institution.

Houle, Christian. 2009. "Inequality and Democracy: Why Inequality Harms Consolidation but Does Not Affect Democratization." *World Politics* 61, no. 4 (October): 589–622.

Human Rights Watch. 2015. "Country Summary: Georgia." Human Rights Watch, January 2015. Accessed 2019. https://www.hrw.org/sites/default/files/related_material/georgia_5.pdf.

Human Rights Watch. 2019. *World Report 2019*. Accessed August 11, 2021. https://www.hrw.org/world-report/2019#.

Huntington, Samuel P. 1968. *Political Order in Changing Societies*. New Haven, CT: Yale University Press.

Huntington, Samuel P. 1991. *The Third Wave: Democratization in the Late Twentieth Century*. Norman: University of Oklahoma Press.

IFES (International Foundation for Electoral Systems). 2018. "Election Guide: Democracy Assistance and Election Guide." Accessed 2018. https://www.electionguide.org.

ILO (International Labour Organization). 1975. *ILO Yearbook 1975*. Geneva: ILO.

ILO (International Labour Organization). 2002. *Panorama laboral 2002: América Latina y el Caribe*. Lima: ILO.

Inglehart, Ronald. 1997. *Modernization and Postmodernization: Cultural, Economic, and Political Change in 43 Societies*. Princeton, NJ: Princeton University Press.

Inglehart, Ronald, and Christian Welzel. 2005. *Modernization, Cultural Change, and Democracy: The Human Development Sequence*. New York: Cambridge University Press.

Inglehart, Ronald, and Christian Welzel. 2007. "Mass Beliefs and Democratic Institutions." In *Oxford Handbook of Comparative Politics*, edited by Carles Boix and Susan Stokes, 297–316. New York: Oxford University Press.

Ingram, Sue. 2018. "Parties, Personalities and Political Power: Legacies of Liberal Peace-Building in Timor-Leste." *Conflict, Security and Development* 18, no. 5: 365–86.

Inman, Robert P., and Daniel L. Rubinfeld. 2012a. "Federal Institutions and the Democratic Transition: Learning from South Africa." *Journal of Law, Economics, and Organization* 28, no. 4 (October): 783–817.

Inman, Robert P., and Daniel L. Rubinfeld. 2012b. "Understanding the Democratic Transition in South Africa." NBER Working Paper No. 17799, National Bureau of Economic Research, February 2012. https://doi.org/10.3386/w17799.

International Policy Institute. 2003. *A Review of Peace Operations: The Case for Change*. London: International Policy Institute, King's College London.

Jaffrelot, Christophe, and Narender Kumar, eds. 2018. *Dr. Ambedkar and Democracy: An Anthology*. Delhi: Oxford University Press.

Jaffrelot, Christophe, and Gilles Verniers. 2020, "A New Party System or a New Political System?" *Journal of Contemporary South Asia* 28, no. 2: 141–54.

Jardine, Matthew. 1999. *East Timor: Genocide in Paradise*. Chicago: Odonian Press.

Jaunarena, Horacio. 2011. *La casa está en orden: memoria de la transición*. Buenos Aires: Taeda Editora.

Jayal, Niraja Gopal. 2013. *Citizenship and Its Discontents: An Indian History*. Cambridge: Harvard University Press.

Jensenius, Francesca. 2017. *Social Justice through Inclusion*. New York: Oxford University Press.

Jo, Hyeran. 2015. *Compliant Rebels*. New York: Cambridge University Press.

Jones, Mark P., and Wonjae Hwang. 2005. "Provincial Party Bosses: Keystone of the Argentine Congress." In *Argentine Democracy: The Politics of Institutional Weakness*, edited by Steven Levitsky and Maria Victoria Murillo, 115–38. University Park: Pennsylvania State University Press.

Jones, Mark P., and Juan Pablo Micozzi. 2013. "Argentina's Unrepresentative and Unaccountable Congress under the Kirchners." In *Representation and Effectiveness in Latin American Democracies: Congress, Judiciary and Civil Society*, edited by Moira B. MacKinnon and Ludovico Feoli, 40–74. New York: Routledge.

Jones, Mark P., Sebastian Saiegh, Pablo T. Spiller, and Mariano Tommasi. 2002. "Amateur Legislators–Professional Politicians: The Consequences of Party-Centered Electoral Rules in a Federal System." *American Journal of Political Science* 46, no. 3 (July): 656–69. https://doi.org/10.2307/3088406.

Jowitt, Ken. 1992. *New World Disorder: The Leninist Extinction*. Berkeley: University of California Press.

Kalashnyk, Pavlo. 2021. "A Blow to Political Opponents, a Message for Biden: What Is Behind Zelenskyy's Shutdown of Pro-Russian TV Channels?" Hromadske International, February 16, 2021. https://en.hromadske.ua/posts/a-blow-to-political-opponents-a-message-for-biden-what-is-behind-zelenskyys-shutdown-of-pro-russian-tv-channels.

Kalyvas, Stathis, and Laia Balcells. 2010. "International System and Technologies of Rebellion: How the End of the Cold War Shaped Internal Conflict." *American Political Science Review* 104, no. 3 (August): 415–29.

Kammen, Douglas. 2009. "A Tape Recorder and a Wink? Transcript of the May 29, 1983, Meeting between Governor Carrascalão and Xanana Gusmão." *Indonesia (Ithaca)* 87: 73–102.

Kammen, Douglas. 2011. "The Armed Forces in Timor-Leste: Politicization through Elite Conflict." In *The Political Resurgence of the Military in Southeast Asia*, edited by Marcus Mietzner, 107–26. London: Routledge.

Kammen, Douglas. 2015. *Three Centuries of Conflict in East Timor*. New Brunswick, NJ: Rutgers University Press.

Kapstein, Ethan B., and Nathan Converse. 2008. *The Fate of Young Democracies*. New York: Cambridge University Press.

Karatnycky, Adrian, ed. 2002. *Freedom in the World: The Annual Survey of Political Rights and Civil Liberties, 2001–2002*. New York: Hoepli Editore.

Karl, Terry Lynn. 1990. "Dilemmas of Democratization in Latin America." *Comparative Politics* 23, no. 1 (October): 1–21.

Karumidze, Zurab, and James V. Wertsch, eds. 2005. *Enough! The Rose Revolution in the Republic of Georgia 2003*. New York: Nova Science Publishers.

Kedourie, Elie. 1994. *Democracy and Arab Political Culture*. Second edition with corrections. London: Frank Cass.

Kenney, Charles D. 2004. *Fujimori's Coup and the Breakdown of Democracy in Latin America*. Notre Dame, IN: University of Notre Dame Press.

Khosla, Madhav, ed. 2014. *Letters for a Nation: From Jawaharlal Nehru to His Chief Ministers, 1947–1963*. London: Allen Lane.

Khosla, Madhav. 2020. *India's Founding Moment: The Constitution of a Most Surprising Democracy*. Cambridge, MA: Harvard University Press.

King, Charles. 2000. *The Moldovans: Romania, Russia, and the Politics of Culture*. Palo Alto, CA: Hoover Institution Press.

King, Dwight. 2003. "East Timor's Founding Elections and Emerging Party System." *Asian Survey* 43, no. 5: 745–57.

Kingsbury, Damien. 2014. "Democratic Consolidation in Timor-Leste: Achievements, Problems and Prospects." *Asian Journal of Political Science* 22, no. 2: 181–205.

Kingsbury, Damien. 2018. "Timor-Leste's Challenged Political Process: 2016–17." *Contemporary Southeast Asia* 40, no. 1: 77–100.

Klug, Heinz. 2008. "South Africa's Constitutional Court: Enabling Democracy and Promoting Law in the Transition from Apartheid." University of Wisconsin Law School, Legal Studies Research Paper Series Paper No. 1530, 174–93. https://ssrn.com/abstract=3521504.

Kohli, Atul, ed. 2001. *The Success of India's Democracy*. New York: Cambridge University Press.

Kohnert, Dirk, and Hans-Joachim Preuss. 2019. "Benin's Stealthy Democracide: How Africa's Model Democracy Kills Itself Bit by Bit." *SSRN Electronic Journal*. https://doi.org/10.2139/ssrn.3481325.

Kopstein, Jeffrey S., and David A. Reilly. 2000. "Geographic Diffusion and the Transformation of the Postcommunist World." *World Politics* 53, no. 1: 1–37.

Kothari, Rajni, ed. 1970a. *Caste in Indian Politics*. Delhi: Orient Longman.

Kothari, Rajni. 1970b. *Politics in India*. Boston: Little, Brown and Company.

Kravchuk, Leonid. 2002. *Maemo te, shcho maemo: Spohady i rozdumy*. Kyiv, Ukraine: Stolittia.

Krishnaswamy, Sudhir, and Siddharth Swaminathan. 2019. "Public Trust in the Indian Judiciary: The Power to Transform." In *A Qualified Hope: The Indian Supreme Court and Progressive Social Change*, edited by Gerald N. Rosenberg, Sudhir Krishnaswamy, and Shishir Bail, 123–47. Cambridge: Cambridge University Press.

Kudelia, Serhiy, and Taras Kuzio. 2014. "Nothing Personal: Explaining the Rise and Decline of Political Machines in Ukraine." *Post-Soviet Affairs* 31, no. 3: 250–78. http://dx.doi.org/10.1080/1060586X.2014.920985.

Kuenzi, Michelle, and Gina Lambright. 2001. "Party System Institutionalization in 30 African Countries." *Party Politics* 7, no. 4: 437–68.

Kushnarev, Evgeniy. 2007. *Vybory i vily*. Kyiv: ADEF-Ukraina.

Kvashilava, Bakur. 2019. "The Political Constraints for Civil Service Reform in Georgia: History, Current Affairs, Prospects and Challenges." *Caucasus Survey* 7, no. 3: 214–34.

LABORSTA Labour Statistics Database (Employment by economic activity). Accessed July 2009. http://laborsta.ilo.org/.

Lachapelle, Jean, Steven Levitsky, and Lucan Way. 2020. "Social Revolution and Authoritarian Durability." *World Politics* 72, no. 4: 557–600.

Lang, Matt. 2009. *Lineages of Despotism and Development: British Colonialism and State Power*. Chicago: University of Chicago Press.

Lanusse, Alejandro. 1988. "Entrevista al Tte. Gral. Alejandro Agustín Lanusse por Gregorio A. Caro Figueroa." *Todo Es Historia* 253: 58–63.

Larkins, Christopher. 1998. "The Judiciary and Delegative Democracy in Argentina." *Comparative Politics* 30, no. 4: 423–42. https://doi.org/10.2307/422332.

Leach, Michael. 2016. "FITUN: História preliminar de um movimento de resistência." In *Timor-Leste: Colonialismo, descolonização, lusotopia*, edited by Rui Graça Feijó, 397–412. Lisboa: Edições Afrontamento.

Leach, Michael, and Damien Kingsbury. 2013. *The Politics of Timor-Leste: Democratic Consolidation after Intervention*. Ithaca, NY: Cornell University Press.

Lebanidze, Bidzina. 2014. "What Makes Authoritarian Regimes Sweat? Linkage, Leverage and Democratization in Post-Soviet South Caucasus." *Southeast European and Black Sea Studies* 14, no. 2: 199–218.

Lee, John. 2018. "Understanding Authoritarian Resilience and Countering Autocracy Promotion in Asia." *Asia Policy* 13, no. 4 (October): 99–122.

Lenz, Gabriel S. 2012. *Follow the Leader? How Voters Respond to Politicians' Policies and Performance*. Chicago: University of Chicago Press.

Lepsius, M. Rainer. 1978. "From Fragmented Party Democracy to Government by Emergency Decree and Nazi Takeover." In *The Breakdown of Democratic Regimes: Europe*, edited by Juan J. Linz and Alfred Stepan, 34–79. Baltimore: Johns Hopkins University Press.

Levitsky, Steven, and María Victoria Murillo. 2005. "Building Castles in the Sand? The Politics of Institutional Weakness in Argentina." In *Argentine Democracy: The Politics of Institutional Weakness*, edited by Steven Levitsky and María Victoria Murillo, 21–44. University Park: Pennsylvania State University Press.

Levitsky, Steven, and María Victoria Murillo. 2014. "Building Institutions on Weak Foundations: Lessons from Latin America." In *Reflections on Uneven Democracies: The Legacy of Guillermo O'Donnell*, edited by Daniel Brinks, Marcelo Leiras, and Scott Mainwaring, 189–213. Baltimore: Johns Hopkins University Press.

Levitsky, Steven, and Lucan A. Way. 2010. *Competitive Authoritarianism: Hybrid Regimes after the Cold War*. New York: Cambridge University Press.

Levitsky, Steven, and Lucan A. Way. 2013. "The Durability of Revolutionary Regimes." *Journal of Democracy* 24, no. 3 (July): 5–17.

Levitsky, Steven, and Daniel Ziblatt. 2018. *How Democracies Die*. New York: Penguin Books.

Levitz, Philip, and Grigore Pop-Eleches. 2010. "Why No Backsliding? The EU's Impact on Democracy and Governance Before and After Accession." *Comparative Political Studies* 43, no. 4: 457–85.

Lieberman, Evan S. 2003. *Race and Regionalism in the Politics of Taxation in Brazil and South Africa.* New York: Cambridge University Press.

Lijphart, Arend. 1977. *Democracy in Plural Societies: A Comparative Exploration.* New Haven, CT: Yale University Press.

Lijphart, Arend. 1996. "The Puzzle of Indian Democracy: A Consociational Interpretation." *American Political Science Review* 90, no. 2: 258–68.

Lijphart, Arend. 1999. *Patterns of Democracy: Government Forms and Performance in Thirty-Six Countries.* New Haven: Yale University Press.

Linz, Juan. 1978a. "The Breakdown of Democracy in Spain." In *The Breakdown of Democratic Regimes: Europe,* edited by Juan J. Linz and Alfred Stepan, 142–215. Baltimore: John Hopkins University Press.

Linz, Juan. 1978b. *The Breakdown of Democratic Regimes: Crisis, Breakdown, and Reequilibration.* Baltimore: Johns Hopkins University Press.

Linz, Juan. 1988. "Legitimacy of Democracy and the Socioeconomic System." In *Comparing Pluralist Democracies: Strains on Legitimacy,* edited by Mattéi Dogan, 65–97. Boulder, CO: Westview Press.

Linz, Juan. 1990. "The Perils of Presidentialism." *Journal of Democracy* 1, no. 1: 51–69.

Linz, Juan, and Alfred Stepan. 1989. "Political Crafting of Democratic Consolidation or Destruction: European and South American Comparisons." In *Democracy in the Americas: Stopping the Pendulum,* edited by Robert A. Pastor, 41–61. New York: Holmes & Meier.

Linz, Juan, and Alfred Stepan. 1996. *Problems of Democratic Transition and Consolidation: Southern Europe, South America, and Post-communist Europe.* Baltimore: Johns Hopkins University Press.

Lipset, Seymour Martin. 1959. "Some Social Requisites of Democracy: Economic Development and Political Legitimacy." *American Political Science Review* 53, no. 1 (March): 69–105.

Llanos, Mariana. 1998. "El presidente, el Congreso y la política de privatizaciones en la Argentina (1989–1997)." *Desarrollo Económico* 38, no. 151: 743–70.

Lok Sabha Secretariat. 1949a. "Constituent Assembly Legislative Debates, Volume VII: Tuesday, the 4th January 1949." Delhi: Lok Sabha Secretariat. http://loksabhaph. nic.in/Debates/cadebatefiles/C04011949.html.

Lok Sabha Secretariat. 1949b. "Constituent Assembly Legislative Debates, Volume XI: Wednesday, the 23rd November 1949." Delhi: Lok Sabha Secretariat. http://loksabh aph.nic.in/Debates/cadebatefiles/C23111949.html.

Loney, Hannah. 2018. *In Women's Words: Violence and Everyday Life during the Indonesian Occupation of East Timor, 1975–1999.* Brighton: Sussex Academic Press.

Loxton, James. 2018. "Introduction: Authoritarian Successor Parties Worldwide." In *Life after Dictatorship: Authoritarian Successor Parties Worldwide,* edited by James Loxton and Scott Mainwaring, 1–49. New York: Cambridge University Press.

Loxton, James, and Scott Mainwaring, eds. 2018. *Life after Dictatorship: Authoritarian Successor Parties Worldwide.* New York: Cambridge University Press.

Lührmann, Anna, Nils Düpont, Masaaki Higashijima, Yaman Berker Kavasoglu, Kyle L. Marquardt, Michael Bernhard, Holger Döring, Allen Hicken, Melis Laebens, Staffan I. Lindberg, Juraj Medzihorsky, Anja Neundorf, Ora John Reuter, Saskia Ruth-Lovell,

Keith R. Weghorst, Nina Wiesehomeier, JosephWright, Nazifa Alizada, Paul Bederke, Lisa Gastaldi, Sandra Grahn, Garry Hindle, Nina Ilchenko, Johannes von Römer, Steven Wilson, Daniel Pemstein, Brigitte Seim. 2020. *Varieties of Party Identity and Organization (V-Party) Dataset V1. Varieties of Democracy (V-Dem) Project.* Accessed June 2021. https://doi.org/10.23696/vpartydsv1.

Lührmann, Anna, and Staffan Lindberg. 2019. "A Third Wave of Autocratization Is Here: What Is New About It?" *Democratization* 26, no. 7: 1095–1113.

Lührmann, Anna, Marcus Tannenberg, and Staffan I. Lindberg. 2018. "Regimes of the World (RoW): Opening New Avenues for The Comparative Study of Political Regimes." *Politics and Governance* 6, no. 1: 60–77.

Lundahl, Mats, and Fredrik Sjöholm. 2007. *A Year of Turmoil: Timor-Leste 2006–2007.* Stockholm: Sida Country Economic Report.

Lupu, Noam, and Rachel Beatty Riedl. 2013. "Political Parties and Uncertainty in Developing Democracies." *Comparative Political Studies* 46, no. 11 (November): 1339–65.

Lynch, Gabrielle, and Gordon Crawford. 2011. "Democratization in Africa 1990–2010: An Assessment." *Democratization* 18, no. 2: 275–310.

Lyons, Terrence. 2004. "Post-conflict Elections and the Process of Demilitarizing Politics: The Role of Electoral Administration." *Democratization* 11, no. 3: 36–62.

MacQueen, Norrie. 2015a. "United Nations Integrated Mission in Timor-Leste (UNMIT)." In *Oxford Handbook of United Nations Peacekeeping Operations*, edited by Joachim Koops, Norrie MacQueen, Thierry Tardy, and Paul Williams, 755–66. Oxford: Oxford University Press.

MacQueen, Norrie. 2015b. "United Nations Mission of Support in East Timor (UNMISET)" In *Oxford Handbook of United Nations Peacekeeping Operations*, edited by Joachim Koops, Norrie MacQueen, Thierry Tardy, and Paul Williams, 683–93. Oxford: Oxford University Press.

Madison, James. 1788. Federalist No. 51: "The Structure of the Government Must Furnish the Proper Checks and Balances Between the Different Departments." New York Packet, February 8.

Madrid, Raúl L., and Kurt Weyland. 2019. "Conclusion: Why US Democracy Will Survive Trump." In *When Democracy Trumps Populism: European and Latin American Lessons for the United States*, edited by Kurt Weyland and Raúl L. Madrid, 154–86.: Cambridge University Press.

Magalhães, António Barbedo, Soei Liong Liem, and David Scott. 2007. *Timor-Leste: Interesses internacionais e actores locais.* Porto: Edições Afrontamento.

Magaloni, Beatriz. 2006. *Voting for Autocracy: Hegemonic Party Survival and Its Demise in Mexico.* New York: Cambridge University Press.

Magaloni, Beatriz. 2008. "Credible Power Sharing and the Longevity of Authoritarian Rule." *Comparative Political Studies* 41, nos. 4–5: 715–41.

Magnusson, Bruce A. 1999. "Testing Democracy in Benin: Experiments in Institutional Reform." In *State, Conflict, and Democracy in Africa*, edited by Richard Joseph, 217–37. Boulder, CO: Lynne Rienner Publishers.

Magnusson, Bruce A. 2001. "Democratization and Domestic Insecurity: Navigating the Transition in Benin." *Comparative Politics* 33, no. 2: 211–30.

Magnusson, Bruce A. 2005. "Democratic Legitimacy in Benin: Institutions and Identity in a Regional Context." In *The Fate of Africa's Democratic Experiments: Elites and Institutions*, edited by Leonardo A. Villalón and Peter Von Doepp, 75–95. Bloomington: Indiana University Press.

Magnusson, Bruce A., and John F. Clark. 2005. "Understanding Democratic Survival and Democratic Failure in Africa: Insights from Divergent Democratic Experiments in Benin and Congo (Brazzaville)." *Comparative Studies in Society and History* 47, no. 3: 552–82.

Mainwaring, Scott. 1989. "Transitions to Democracy and Democratic Consolidation: Theoretical and Comparative Issues." Kellogg Institute Working Paper #130, November 1989. https://kell ogg.nd.edu/sites/default/files/old_files/documents/130_0.pdf.

Mainwaring, Scott, and Fernando Bizzarro. 2020. "Outcomes after Transitions in Third Wave Democracies." In *The SAGE Handbook of Political Science*, edited by Dirk Berg-Schlosser, Bertrand Badie and Leonardo Morlino, 1540–57. London: SAGE Publications.

Mainwaring, Scott, and Aníbal Pérez-Liñán. 2013. *Democracies and Dictatorships in Latin America: Emergence, Survival, and Fall*. New York: Cambridge University Press.

Mainwaring, Scott, and Matthew Shugart. 1997. "Juan Linz, Presidentialism and Democracy: A Critical Appraisal." *Comparative Politics* 29, no. 4: 449–71.

Makgetla, Itumeleng, and Ian Shapiro. 2016. "Business and the South African Transition." Unpublished manuscript, Yale University.

Mamdani, Mahmood. 2002. "Amnesty or Impunity? A Preliminary Critique of the Report of the Truth and Reconciliation Commission of South Africa (TRC)." *Diacritics* 32, nos. 3–4: 33–59.

Mamdani, Mahmood. 2018. *Citizen and Subject: Contemporary Africa and the Legacy of Late Colonialism*. Princeton, NJ: Princeton University Press.

Mampilly, Zachariah. 2011. *Rebel Rulers: Insurgent Governance and Civilian Life during War*. Ithaca, NY: Cornell University Press.

Mann, Michael. 1984. "The Autonomous Power of the State: Its Origins, Mechanisms, and Results." Archives Européenes de Sociologie 25: 185–213.

Mann, Michael. 2004. *The Dark Side of Democracy: Explaining Ethnic Cleansing*. New York: Cambridge University Press.

Marais, Nel, and Jo Davies. 2015. "The Role of the Business Elite in South Africa's Democratic Transition: Supporting an Inclusive Political and Economic Transformation." Inclusive Political Settlements Paper no. 8.

March, Andrew. 2011. *Islam and Liberal Citizenship: The Search for an Overlapping Consensus*. New York: Oxford University Press.

March, Luke, and Graeme P. Herd. 2006. "Moldova between Europe and Russia: Inoculating against the Colored Contagion?" *Post-Soviet Affairs* 22, no. 4: 349–79.

Marinov, Nikolay, and Hein Goemans. 2013. "Coups and Democracy." *British Journal of Political Science* 44, no. 4 (October): 799–825.

McFaul, Michael. 1999. "The Perils of a Protracted Transition." *Journal of Democracy* 10, no. 2: 4–18.

Marsh, Christopher. 2005. "Russian Orthodox Christians and Their Orientation toward Church and State." *Journal of Church and State* 47, no. 3 (Summer): 545–61.

Marshall, Monty, Ted Gurr, and Keith Jaggers. 2016. "Polity IV Project: Political Regime Characteristics and Transitions, 1800–2015." Accessed March 2019. http://www.systemicpeace.org/inscrdata.html.

Marshall, Monty, and Keith Jaggers. 2018. "Polity IV Project: Political Regime Characteristics and Transitions, 1800–2017." Accessed April 2019. http://www.system icpeace.org/inscrdata.html.

Marshall, Monty, and Keith Jaggers. 2020. "Polity V Project: Political Regime Characteristics and Transitions, 1800–2018." Center for Systemic Peace. Accessed October 10, 2021. http://www.systemicpeace.org/inscr/p5v2018.xls.

Martin, Ian, and Alexander Mayer-Rieckh. 2005. "The United Nations and East Timor: From Self-Determination to State-Building." *International Peacekeeping* 12, no. 1: 104–20.

Masi, Andrés Alberto. 2014. *Los tiempos de Alfonsín: la construcción de un liderazgo democrático*. Buenos Aires: Capital Intelectual.

Maslin Nir, Sarah. 2019. "It Was a Robust Democracy. Then the New President Took Power." *New York Times*, July 4, 2019. https://www.nytimes.com/2019/07/04/world/afr ica/benin-protests-talon-yayi.html.

McCoy, Jennifer, Tahmina Rahman, and Murat Somer. 2018. "Polarization and the Global Crisis of Democracy: Common Patterns, Dynamics, and Pernicious Consequences for Democratic Polities." *American Behavioral Scientist* 62, no. 1 (January): 16–42.

McFaul, Michael. 1999. "The Perils of a Protracted Transition." *Journal of Democracy* 10, no. 2: 4–18.

McFaul, Michael. 2002. "The Fourth Wave of Democracy and Dictatorship: Noncooperative Transitions in the Postcommunist World." *World Politics* 54, no. 2 (January): 212–44.

McGuire, James W. 1992. "Union Political Tactics and Democratic Consolidation in Alfonsín's Argentina, 1983–1989." *Latin American Research Review* 27, no. 1 (January): 37–74.

McGuire, James W. 1995a. "Interim Government and Democratic Consolidation: Argentina in Comparative Perspective." In *Between States: Interim Governments and Democratic Transitions*, edited by Yossi Shain and Juan Linz, 179–210. New York: Cambridge University Press.

McGuire, James W. 1995b. "Political Parties and Democracy in Argentina." In *Building Democratic Institutions: Party Systems in Latin America*, edited by Scott Mainwaring and Timothy Scully, 200–46. Stanford, CA: Stanford University Press.

McGuire, James W. 1997. *Peronism without Perón: Unions, Parties, and Democracy in Argentina*. Stanford, CA: Stanford University Press.

McMahon, Edward R. 2002. "The Impact of US Democracy and Governance Assistance in Africa: Benin Case Study." Center on Democratic Performance, Working Paper Series no. 118. Department of Political Science, Binghamton University, New York.

McMillan, Alastair, 2010. "The Election Commission." In *The Oxford Companion to Politics in India*, edited by Niraja Gopal Jayal and Pratap Bhanu Mehta, 98–116. Delhi: Oxford University Press.

McWilliams, Andrew. 2008. "Customary Governance in East Timor." In *Democratic Governance in Timor-Leste: Reconciling the Local and the National*, edited by David Mearns and Steven Farram, 129–42. Darwin: Charles Darwin University Press.

Mehta, Pratap Bhanu. 2003. *The Burden of Democracy*. Delhi: Penguin.

Mehta, Pratap Bhanu. 2007. "The Rise of Judicial Sovereignty." *Journal of Democracy* 18, no. 2: 70–83.

Mehta, Pratap Bhanu. 2019. "The Story of Indian Democracy Written in Blood and Betrayal." *The Indian Express*, August 6, 2019. https://indianexpress.com/article/opin ion/columns/jammu-kashmir-article-370-scrapped-special-status-amit-shah-naren dra-modi-bjp-5880797/.

Mehta, Uday Singh. 1999. *Liberalism and Empire: A Study in Nineteenth-Century British Liberal Thought*. Chicago: University of Chicago Press.

Mendes, Nuno Canas. 2005. *A "multidimensionalidade" da construção identitária em Timor-Leste: Nacionalismo, estado e identidade nacional*. Lisboa: Instituto Superior de Ciências Sociais e Políticas.

Mickey, Robert. 2015. *Paths Out of Dixie: The Democratization of Authoritarian Enclaves in America's Deep South, 1944–1972*. Princeton, NJ: Princeton University Press.

Mietzner, Marcus, ed. 2012. *The Political Resurgence of the Military in Southeast Asia: Conflict and Leadership*. London: Routledge.

Mignone, Emilio Fermín. 1986. *Iglesia y dictadura: el papel de la Iglesia a la luz de sus relaciones con el régimen militar*. Buenos Aires: Ediciones del Pensamiento Nacional.

Mill, John Stuart. 1861. *Considerations on Representative Government*. London: Parker, Son, and Bourn.

Mill, John Stuart. (1864) 1975. "Representative Government." In *Three Essays*, by John Stuart Mill, 143–423. Oxford: Oxford University Press.

Millo, Yiftach, and Jon Barnett. 2004. "Educational Development in East Timor." *International Journal of Educational Development* 24, no. 6: 721–37.

Mitchell, Lincoln. 2004. "Georgia's Rose Revolution." *Current History* 103, no. 675: 342–53.

Mitchell, Lincoln. 2013. "What's Next for Georgia? The End of the Rose Revolution." *World Affairs* 175, no. 5 (January/February): 75–82.

Mitchell, Lincoln. 2016. "Rushing Towards Amending the Constitution." *Lincoln Mitchell* (blog). October 23, 2016. http://lincolnmitchell.com/georgia-analysis/2016/10/19/m08m1831no97ojvyutcdzqm6st5jb2?rq=Rushing%20towards%20amending%20the%20constitution.

Modi, Narendra. 2019. "Why India and the World Need Gandhi." *New York Times*, October 2, 2019. https://www.nytimes.com/2019/10/02/opinion/modi-mahatma-gandhi.html.

Montesquieu, Charles de Secondat. (1748) 1900. *The Spirit of the Laws*. Translated by Thomas Nugent. New York: D. Appleton and Company.

Moore Jr, Barrington. 1966. *Social Origins of Dictatorship and Democracy*. Boston: Beacon Press.

Morjé Howard, Lise. 2007. *UN Peacekeeping in Civil Wars*. New York: Cambridge University Press.

Morjé Howard, Lise. 2008. *UN Peacekeeping in Civil Wars*. New York: Cambridge University Press.

Mueller, Sean. 2014. "The Parliamentary and Executive Elections in the Republic of Georgia, 2012." *Electoral Studies* 34: 342–47.

Mukherjee, Aditya. 2015. "Nehru's Legacy: Inclusive Democracy and People's Empowerment." *Economic and Political Weekly* 1, no. 16 (April 18): 38–45.

Müller, Jan-Werner. 2016a. "Protecting Popular Self-Government from the People? New Normative Perspectives on Militant Democracy." *Annual Review of Political Science* 19 (May): 249–65. https://doi.org/10.1146/annurev-polisci-043014-124054.

Müller, Jan-Werner. 2016b. *What Is Populism?* Philadelphia: University of Pennsylvania Press.

Muller, Martin. 2011. "Public Opinion Toward the European Union in Georgia." *Post-Soviet Affairs* 27, no. 1: 64–92.

Munyeka, Wiza. 2014. "The Relationship Between Economic Growth and Inflation in the South African Economy." *Mediterranean Journal of Social Sciences* 5, no. 15: 119–29.

Mustapic, Ana María. 2005. "Inestabilidad sin colapso. La renuncia de los presidentes: Argentina en el año 2001." *Desarrollo Económico* 45, no. 178: 263–80.

Myrttinen, Henri. 2013. "Resistance, Symbolism and the Language of Stateness in Timor-Leste." *Oceania* 83, no. 3: 208–20.

Nash, Andrew. 2002. "Mandela's Democracy." In *Thabo Mbeki's World: The Politics and Ideology of the South African President*, edited by Sean Jacobs and Richard Calland, 243–56. London: Zed Books.

Natalucci, Ana. 2011. "Entre la movilización y la institucionalización: Los dilemas de los movimientos sociales (Argentina, 2001–2010)." *Polis (Santiago)* 10, no. 28: 193–219. https://doi.org/10.4067/S0718-65682011000100012.

Nathan, Laurie. 2004. "Accounting for South Africa's Successful Transition to Democracy." Crisis States Discussion Paper Series DP5, June, London School of Economics, London.

NDI (National Democratic Institute). 2013. "Statement of the NDI Election Observer Delegation to Georgia's 2013 Presidential Election." National Democratic Institute, October 28, 2013. https://cesko.ge/res/docs/StatementonGeorgias2013PresidentialEl ections.pdf.

NDI (National Democratic Institute). 2016. "Statement of the NDI International Observation Mission to Georgia's October 8, 2016 Parliamentary Election." National Democratic Institute, October 8, 2016. https://www.ndi.org/sites/default/files/NDI_ GEO_Parliamentary%20Elections_2016_Statement-ENG.pdf.

Nehru, Jawaharlal. 1942. *Glimpses of World History*. New York: John Day.

Nehru, Jawaharlal. 1946. *The Discovery of India*. New York: John Day.

Neundorf, Anja, Johannes Gerschewski, and Roman-Gabriel Olar. 2019. "How Do Inclusionary and Exclusionary Autocracies Affect Ordinary People?" *Comparative Political Studies* 53, no. 12: 1890–1925. https://doi.org/10.1177/0010414019858958.

Nichols, Jim. 2003. "Coup in Georgia [Republic]: Recent Developments and Implications." Report RS21685. Washington, DC: Congressional Research Service.

Niner, Sara, ed. 2000. *To Resist Is to Win! The Autobiography of Xanana Gusmão*. Victoria: Aurora.

Niner, Sara. 2015. "Women in the Post-conflict Moment in Timor-Leste." In *Security, Development and Nation-Building in Timor-Leste*, edited by Vandra Harris and Andrew Goldsmith, 55–72. London: Routledge.

Nodia, Ghia. 2005. "Georgia 2004." In *Nations in Transit*, edited by Adrian Karatnycky and Alexander J. Motyl, 234–53. New York: Freedom House.

Norden, Deborah L. 1996. *Military Rebellion in Argentina: Between Coups and Consolidation*. Lincoln: University of Nebraska Press.

Norris, Pippa, and Max Grömping. 2019. "Electoral Integrity Worldwide." The Electoral Integrity Project, University of Sydney, May 2019. https://static1.squarespace.com/ static/58533f31bebafbe99c85dc9b/t/5ce60bd6b208fcd93be49430/1558580197717/ Electoral+Integrity+Worldwide.pdf.

Norris, Pippa, and Ronald Inglehart. 2019. *Cultural Backlash: Trump, Brexit, and Authoritarian Populism*. New York: Cambridge University Press.

Novaro, Marcos. 1994. *Pilotos de tormentas: crisis de representación y personalización de la política en Argentina, 1989–1993*. Buenos Aires: Ediciones Letra Buena.

Novaro, Marcos. 2002. "La Alianza, de la gloria del llano a la debacle del gobierno." In *El derrumbe político en el ocaso de la convertibilidad*, edited by Marcos Novaro, 31–105. Buenos Aires: Grupo Editorial Norma.

Novaro, Marcos. 2006. *Historia de la Argentina contemporánea. De Perón a Kirchner*. Buenos Aires: Edhasa.

Novaro, Marcos. 2010. *Historia de la Argentina. 1955–2010*. Buenos Aires: Siglo XXI.

Novaro, Marcos, Alejandro Bonvecchi, and Nicolás Cherny. 2014. *Los límites de la voluntad: los gobiernos de Duhalde, Néstor y Cristina Kirchner*. Buenos Aires: Ariel.

Novaro, Marcos, and Vicente Palermo. 2006. *La dictadura militar*. Buenos Aires: Paidós.

Nwajiaku, Kathryn. 1994. "The National Conferences in Benin and Togo Revisited." *Journal of Modern African Studies* 32, no. 3 (September): 429–47.

Nygaard-Christensen, Maj. 2016. "Timor-Leste in 2015: Petro-Politics or Sustainable Growth." In *Southeast Asian Affairs 2016*, edited by Malcolm Cook and Daljit Singh 347–60. Singapore: ISEAS—Yusof Ishak Institute.

Nzouankeu, Jacques Mariel. 1993. "The Role of the National Conference in the Transition to Democracy in Africa: The Cases of Benin and Mali." *Issue: A Journal of Opinion* 21, nos. 1–2: 44–50.

O'Brien, Thomas. 2017. "Unbuilding from the Inside: Leadership and Democratization in South Africa and South Korea." *Government and Opposition* 52, no. 4 (October): 614–39.

O'Donnell, Guillermo. 1973. *Modernization and Bureaucratic-Authoritarianism: Studies in South American Politics*. Berkeley: Institute for International Studies, University of California.

O'Donnell, Guillermo. 1983. "La cosecha del miedo." *Nexos* 6, no. 6: 51–60. https://www.nexos.com.mx/?p=4147.

O'Donnell, Guillermo. 1986. "Introduction to the Latin American Cases." In *Transitions from Authoritarian Rule: Prospects for Democracy*. Vol. 2, *Latin America*, edited by Guillermo O'Donnell, Philippe Schmitter, and Laurence Whitehead, 3–18. Baltimore: Johns Hopkins University Press.

O'Donnell, Guillermo. 1993. "On the State, Democratization and Some Conceptual Problems: A Latin American View with Glances at Some Postcommunist Countries." *World Development* 21, no. 8 (August): 1355–69.

O'Donnell, Guillermo. 1994. "Delegative Democracy." *Journal of Democracy* 5, no. 1 (January): 55–69.

O'Donnell, Guillermo, and Philippe Schmitter. 1986. *Transitions from Authoritarian Rule*. Baltimore: Johns Hopkins University Press.

O'Flaherty, J. Daniel. 1992. "Holding Together South Africa." *Foreign Affairs* 72, no. 4: 126–36.

ODIHR (Office for Democratic Institutions and Human Rights). 1996. *Presidential Elections in the Republic of Moldova. November 17 and December 1, 1996*. Warsaw: OSCE.

ODIHR (Office for Democratic Institutions and Human Rights). 2001. *Republic of Moldova: Parliamentary Elections, 25 February 2001. Final Report*. Warsaw: OSCE.

ODIHR (Office for Democratic Institutions and Human Rights). 2005. *Moldova: Parliamentary Elections, 6 March 2005, Election Observation Mission Report*. Warsaw: OSCE.

ODIHR (Office for Democratic Institutions and Human Rights). 2006. *Final Report on the 26 March 2006 Parliamentary Elections in Ukraine*. Warsaw: OSCE.

ODIHR (Office for Democratic Institutions and Human Rights). 2007. *Ukraine: Early Parliamentary Elections, 30 September 2007*. Warsaw: OSCE.

ODIHR (Office for Democratic Institutions and Human Rights). 2008. *Georgia: Extraordinary Presidential Election, 5 January 2008, Final Report*. Warsaw: OSCE.

ODIHR (Office for Democratic Institutions and Human Rights). 2010. *Ukraine: Presidential Election, 17 January and 7 February 2010*. Warsaw: OSCE.

ODIHR (Office for Democratic Institutions and Human Rights). 2012. *Georgia: Parliamentary Elections 1 October 2012, OSCE ODIHR Election Observer Mission Final Report*. Warsaw: OSCE.

ODIHR (Office for Democratic Institutions and Human Rights). 2016. *Presidential Election, 30 October and 13 November (second round) 2016*. Warsaw: OSCE.

ODIHR (Office for Democratic Institutions and Human Rights). 2017. *Georgia: Parliamentary Elections, 8 and 30 October 2016*. Warsaw: OSCE.

ODIHR (Office for Democratic Institutions and Human Rights). 2019. *Georgia: Presidential Election 28 October and 28 November 2018, OSCE ODIHR Election Observer Mission Final Report*. Warsaw: OSCE.

Ollier, María Matilde. 2009. *De la revolución a la democracia: Cambios privados, públicos y políticos de la izquierda argentina*. Buenos Aires: Siglo XXI/Universidad Nacional de San Martín.

Ologou, Expedit. 2017. "Constitutional Reform in Benin: Why Did It Fail So Far?" Paper presented at the conference Recent Developments in Constitution-Building in and Beyond Africa, Central European University in cooperation with IDEA and Friedrich Ebert Stiftung, Budapest, July 11, 2017.

Onuch, Olga. 2014. "'It's the Economy, Stupid,' or Is It? The Role of Political Crises in Mass Mobilization: The Case of Argentina in 2001." In *Argentina since the 2001 Crisis: Recovering the Past, Reclaiming the Future*, edited by C. Levey, D. Ozarow, and C. Wylde, 89–113. New York: Palgrave Macmillan.

Orovec, Phillip, and Edward Holland. 2019. "The Georgian Dream? Outcomes from the Summer of Protest." *Demokratizatsiya* 27, no. 2: 249–57.

Oszlak, Oscar. 1984. "Introducción." In *"Proceso," crisis y transición democrática*, edited by Oscar Oszlak, vol. 2:29–42. Buenos Aires: Centro Editor de América Latina.

Palermo, Vicente, and Marcos Novaro. 1996. *Política y poder en el gobierno de Menem*. Buenos Aires: Grupo Editorial Norma.

Palmer, Lisa, and Andrew McWilliam. 2018. "Ambivalent 'Indigeneities' in an Independent Timor-Leste." *Asia Pacific Viewpoint* 59, no. 3: 265–75.

Pepinsky, Tom. 2019. "Religion, Ethnicity, and Indonesia's 2019 Presidential Election." New Mandala, May 28, 2019. https://www.newmandala.org/religion-ethnicity-and-indonesias-2019-presidential-election/.

Pérez Liñán, Aníbal. 2007. *Presidential Impeachment and the New Political Instability in Latin America*. New York: Cambridge University Press.

Pérez-Liñán, Aníbal, and Scott Mainwaring. 2013. "Regime Legacies and Levels of Democracy: Evidence from Latin America." *Comparative Politics* 45, no. 4 (July): 379–97.

Pérez-Liñán, Aníbal, Nicolás Schmidt, and Daniela Vairo. 2019. "Presidential Hegemony and Democratic Backsliding in Latin America, 1925–2016." *Democratization* 26 (4): 606–25.

Peuch, Jean-Christophe. 2004. "Georgia: Critics Say Police Violence, Media Intimidation on the Rise." *Eurasia Insight*, February 20.

Pevehouse, Jon C. 2005. *Democracy from Above? Regional Organizations and Democratization*. New York: Cambridge University Press.

Popescu, Nicu. 2012. "Moldova's Fragile Pluralism." *Russian Politics and Law* 50, no. 4 (July-August): 37–50.

Powles, Anna, 2015. "Local Ownership in the Security Sector Space: Lessons from Timor-Leste and the Solomon Islands." In *United Nations Peacekeeping Challenge*, edited by Anna Powles and Negar Partow, 203–16. London: Ashgate.

Prakash, Gyan. 2018. *Emergency Chronicles: Indira Gandhi and Democracy's Turning Point*. London: Penguin Random House.

Preuss, Hans-Joachim. 2019. "Suicide of a Democracy." *International Politics and Society Journal*, March 5, 2019. https://www.ips-journal.eu/regions/africa/suicide-of-a-democracy-3438/.

Pridham, Geoffrey. 1991. "The Politics of the European Community, Transnational Networks and Democratic Transition in Southern Europe." In *Encouraging Democracy: The International Context of Regime Transition in Southern Europe*, edited by Geoffrey Pridham, 212–45. Leicester, UK: Leicester University Press.

Prodromou, Elizabeth. 2004. "Christianity and Democracy: The Ambivalent Orthodox." *Journal of Democracy* 15, no. 2 (April): 62–75.

Przeworski, Adam. 1991. *Democracy and the Market: Political and Economic Reforms in Eastern Europe and Latin America.* Cambridge: Cambridge University Press.

Przeworski, Adam. 2005. "Democracy as an Equilibrium." *Public Choice* 123, no. 3/4 (June): 253–73.

Przeworski, Adam. 2019. *Crises of Democracy.* New York: Cambridge University Press.

Przeworski, Adam, Michael Alvarez, José Antonio Cheibub, and Fernando Limongi. 2000. *Democracy and Development: Political Institutions and Material Well-Being in the World, 1950–1990.* New York: Cambridge University Press.

Przeworski, Adam, and Fernando Limongi. 1997. "Modernization: Theories and Facts." *World Politics* 49, no. 2 (January): 155–83.

Przeworski, Adam, Susan C. Stokes, and Bernard Manin, eds. 1999. *Democracy, Accountability, and Representation.* Cambridge: Cambridge University Press.

Pucciarelli, Alfredo Raúl. 2006. "La República no tiene ejército. El poder gubernamental y la movilización popular durante el levantamiento militar de Semana Santa." In *Los años de Alfonsín, ¿el poder de la democracia o la democracia del poder?*, edited by Alfredo Raúl Pucciarelli, 115–51. Buenos Aires: Siglo XXI.

Puglisi, Rosaria. 2014. "A Regional Perspective on Post-Maidan Domestic Security." Presentation at the 10th Annual Danyliw Seminar on Ukraine, University of Ottawa.

Putnam, Robert H. 1993. *Making Democracy Work: Civic Traditions in Modern Italy.* Princeton, NJ: Princeton University Press.

Rabushka, Alvin, and Kenneth A. Shepsle. 1972. *Politics in Plural Societies: A Theory of Democratic Instability.* Columbus, OH: Charles E. Merrill.

Rajamani, Lavanya, and Arghya Sengupta. 2010. "The Supreme Court of India: Promise, Reach, and Overreach." In *The Oxford Companion to Politics in India*, edited by Niraja Gopal Jayal and Pratap Bhanu Mehta, 80–97. Delhi: Oxford University Press.

Rajendran, G. 1974. *The Ezhava Community and Kerala Politics.* Trivandrum: Academy of Political Science.

Ramos-Horta, José. 1987. *Funu: The Unfinished Saga of East Timor.* Trenton, NJ: The Red Sea Press.

Ranis, Peter. 1992. *Argentine Workers: Peronism and Contemporary Class Consciousness.* Pittsburgh, PA: University of Pittsburgh Press.

Rantete, Johannes, and Hermann Giliomee. 1992. "Transition to Democracy through Transaction? Bilateral Negotiations between the ANC and NP in South Africa." *African Affairs* 91, no. 365 (October): 515–42.

Reddy, K. Vivek. 2016. "Minority Educational Institutions." In *Oxford Handbook of the Indian Constitution*, edited by Sujit Choudhry, Madhav Khosla, and Pratap Bhanu Mehta, 921–42. Oxford: Oxford University Press.

Reenock, Christopher, Jeffrey Staton, and Marius Radean. 2013. "Legal Institutions and Democratic Survival." *Journal of Politics* 75, no. 2 (April): 491–505.

Remmer, Karen. 1996. "The Sustainability of Political Democracy: Lessons from South America." *Comparative Political Studies* 29, no. 6 (December): 611–34.

Reynolds, Andrew. 2002. *The Architecture of Democracy: Constitutional Design, Conflict Management, and Democracy.* Oxford: Oxford University Press.

Riedl, Rachel Beatty. 2014. *Authoritarian Origins of Democratic Party Systems in Africa.* New York: Cambridge University Press.

Riedl, Rachel Beatty. 2016. "Strong Parties, Weak Parties: Divergent Pathways to Democracy in Sub-Saharan Africa." In *Parties, Movements and Democracy in the Developing World*, edited by Nancy Bermeo and Deborah Yashar, 122–56. New York: Cambridge University Press.

Riedl, Rachel Beatty. 2018. "Authoritarian Successor Parties in Sub-Saharan Africa." In *Life after Dictatorship: Authoritarian Successor Parties Worldwide*, edited by James Loxton and Scott Mainwaring, 175–228. New York: Cambridge University Press.

Riedl, Rachel Beatty, Dan Slater, Joseph Wong, and Daniel Ziblatt. 2020. "Authoritarian-Led Democratization." *Annual Review of Political Science* 23 (May): 315–32.

Roberts, Kenneth M. 1998. *Deepening Democracy? The Modern Left and Social Movements in Chile and Peru*. Stanford, CA: Stanford University Press.

Robinson, Geoffrey. 2010. *"If You Leave Us Here, We Will Die": How Genocide Was Stopped in East Timor*. Princeton, NJ: Princeton University Press.

Roeder, Philip G. 1994. "Varieties of Post-Soviet Authoritarian Regimes." *Post-Soviet Affairs* 10, no. 1: 61–101.

Roll, Kate. 2014. "Inventing the Veteran, Imagining the State: Post-conflict Reintegration and State Consolidation in Timor-Leste." PhD diss., Department of Politics and International Relations, Oxford University.

Roll, Kate. 2018. "Reconsidering Reintegration: Veterans' Benefits as State-Building." In *The Promise of Prosperity: Visions of the Future in Timor-Leste*, edited by Judith Bovensiepen, 139–53. Canberra, Australia: ANU Press.

Romero, Luis Alberto. 2006. "La democracia y la sombra del proceso." In *Argentina 1976–2006. Entre la sombra de la dictadura y el futuro de la democracia*, edited by Hugo Quiroga and César Tcach, 15–30. Rosario: Homo Sapiens.

Ronen, Dov. 1975. *Dahomey: Between Tradition and Modernity*. Ithaca, NY: Cornell University Press.

Roper, Steven D. 2001. "From Semi-presidentialism to Parliamentarism: Constitutional Change in Post-Soviet Moldova." Paper presented at the American Political Science Association meeting, San Francisco.

Rose, Richard, and William Mishler. 1996. "Testing the Churchill Hypothesis: Popular Support for Democracy and Its Alternatives." *Journal of Public Policy* 16, no. 1: 29–58. https://doi.org/10.1017/S0143814X00007856.

Ross, Michael. 2001. "Does Oil Hinder Democracy?" *World Politics* 53, no. 3: 325–61.

Rudolph, Lloyd, and Susanne Rudolph. 1967. *The Modernity of Tradition*. Chicago: University of Chicago Press.

Rueschemeyer, Dietrich, Evelyn Huber Stephens, and John D. Stephens. 1992. *Capitalist Development and Democracy*. Cambridge: Polity Press.

Rustow, Dankwart A. 1970. "Transitions to Democracy: Toward a Dynamic Model." *Comparative Politics* 2, no. 3 (April): 337–63.

Ryan, Alan. 2012. *The Making of Modern Liberalism*. Princeton, NJ: Princeton University Press.

Saunders, Christopher C. 2009. "UN Peacekeeping in Southern Africa: Namibia, Angola and Mozambique." In *From Global Apartheid to Global Village: Africa and the United Nations*, edited by Adekeye Adebajo, 269–81. Scottsville, South Africa: University of KwaZulu-Natal Press.

Scambary, James. 2011. "Anatomy of a Conflict: The 2006–7 Communal Violence in East Timor." In *Security, Development and Nation-Building in Timor-Leste*, edited by Vandra Harris and Andrew Goldsmith, 59–79. London: Routledge.

Schedler, Andreas. 2013. *The Politics of Uncertainty: Sustaining and Subverting Electoral Authoritarianism*. Oxford: Oxford University Press.

Schenoni, Luis L., and Scott Mainwaring. 2019. "US Hegemony and Regime Change in Latin America." *Democratization* 26, no. 2: 269–87. https://doi.org/10.1080/13510 347.2018.1516754.

Schuster, Federico L., Germán J. Pérez, Sebastián Pereyra, Melchor Armesto, Martín Armelino, Analía García, Ana Natalucci, Melina Vázquez, and Patricia Zipcioglu. 2006. "Transformaciones de la protesta social en Argentina 1989–2003." Documentos de Trabajo, Facultad de Ciencias Sociales, Universidad de Buenos Aires, no. 48. https:// dialnet.unirioja.es/servlet/articulo?codigo=1983812.

SEDLAC (CEDLAS and The World Bank). 2018. *Socio-economic Database for Latin America and the Caribbean*. Accessed April 2021. https://www.cedlas.econo.unlp.edu. ar/wp/en/estadisticas/sedlac/.

Seekings, Jeremy. 2009. "South Africa since 1994: Who Holds Power after Apartheid?" In *Turning Points in African Democracy*, edited by Abdul Raufu Mustapha and Lindsay Whitfield, 134–52. Woodbridge: Boydell & Brewer.

Seely, Jennifer 2007. "The Presidential Election in Benin, March 2006." *Electoral Studies* 26: 196–200.

Seely, Jennifer. 2009. *The Legacies of Transition Governments in Africa: The Cases of Benin and Togo*. Basingstoke: Palgrave Macmillan.

Seligson, Mitchell A. 2002. "The Renaissance of Political Culture or the Renaissance of the Ecological Fallacy?" *Comparative Politics* 34, no. 3 (April): 273–92.

Senén González, Santiago, and Fabián Bosoer. 2009. *Breve historia del sindicalismo argentino*. Buenos Aires: El Ateneo.

Seo, Sang-Hyun. 2008. "A Study on Democratic Transition in South Africa: Democratic through Compromise and Institutional Choice." PhD diss., University of South Africa.

Shani, Ornit. 2018. *How India Became Democratic: Citizenship and the Making of Universal Franchise*. New York: Cambridge University Press.

Shaw, Mark. 1997. "State Responses to Organized Crime in South Africa." *Transnational Organized Crime* 3, no. 2 (Summer): 1–19.

Shiosaki, Elfie. 2017. "'We Have Resisted, Now We Must Build': Regionalism and Nation-Building in Timor-Leste." *Journal of Southeast Asian Studies* 48, no. 1: 53–70.

Shoesmith, Dennis. 2003. "Timor-Leste: Divided Leadership in a Semi-Presidential System." *Asian Survey* 43, no. 2: 231–52.

Shoesmith, Dennis. 2013. "Political Parties." In *The Politics of Timor-Leste, Democratic Consolidation after Intervention*, edited by Michael Leach and Damien Kingsbury, 121–43. Ithaca, NY: Cornell University Press.

Sidicaro, Ricardo. 2002. *Los tres peronismos estado y poder económico*. Buenos Aires: Siglo XXI.

Sikkink, Kathryn. 2008. "From Pariah State to Global Protagonist: Argentina and the Struggle for International Human Rights." *Latin American Politics and Society* 50, no. 1: 1–29. https://doi.org/10.1111/j.1548-2456.2008.00002.x.

Sindre, Gyda Marås. 2016. "Internal Party Democracy in Former Rebel Parties." *Party Politics* 22, no. 4: 501–11.

Sing, Ming. 2010. "Explaining Democratic Survival Globally (1946–2002)." *Journal of Politics* 72, no. 2 (April): 438–55.

Slater, Dan. 2015. "Democratic Disarticulation and Its Dangers: Cleavage Formation and Promiscuous Powersharing in Indonesian Party Politics." In *Building Blocs: How*

Parties Organize Society, edited by Cedric de Leon, Manali Desai, and Cihan Tugal, 123–50. Stanford: Stanford University Press.

Slater, Dan. 2018a. "After Democracy." *Foreign Affairs*, November 6, 2018. https://www.for eignaffairs.com/articles/2018-11-06/after-democracy.

Slater, Dan. 2018b. "Party Cartelization, Indonesian-Style: Presidential Power-Sharing and the Contingency of Democratic Opposition." *Journal of East Asian Studies* 18, no. 1 (March): 23–46.

Slater, Dan. 2020. "Violent Origins of Authoritarian Variation: Rebellion Type and Regime Type in Cold War Southeast Asia." *Government and Opposition* 55, no. 1: 21–40.

Slater, Dan, and Erica Simmons. 2013. "Coping by Colluding: Political Uncertainty and Promiscuous Powersharing in Indonesia and Bolivia." *Comparative Political Studies* 46, no. 11 (November): 1366–93.

Slater, Dan, Benjamin Smith, and Gautam Nair. 2014. "Economic Origins of Democratic Breakdown? The Redistributive Model and the Postcolonial State." *Perspectives on Politics* 12, no. 2 (June): 353–74.

Slater, Dan, and Maya Tudor. 2019. "Why Religious Tolerance Won in Indonesia but Lost in India." *Foreign Affairs*, July 3, 2019. https://www.foreignaffairs.com/articles/india/2019-07-03/why-religious-tolerance-won-indonesia-lost-india.

Slater, Dan, and Joseph Wong. 2018. "Game for Democracy: Authoritarian Successor Parties in Developmental Asia." In *Life after Democracy: Authoritarian Successor Parties Worldwide*, edited by James Loxton and Scott Mainwaring, 284–313. New York: Cambridge University Press.

Smith, Anthony. 2004. "East Timor: Elections in the World's Newest Nation." *Journal of Democracy* 15, no. 2 (April): 145–59.

Smith, Benjamin. 2007. *Hard Times in the Lands of Plenty: Oil Politics in Iran and Indonesia*. Ithaca: Cornell University Press.

Snyder, Jack L. 2000. *From Voting to Violence: Democratization and Nationalist Conflict*. New York: Norton.

Socor, Vladimir. 1992. "Moldavia Builds a New State." *RFE/RL Research Report* 1, no. 1 (3 January): 42–45.

Socor, Vladimir. 2013. "Demise of Moldova's Alliance for European Integration Surprises European Union's Leaders." Eurasia Daily Monitor 10, no. 90.

Sousa, Ivo Carneiro de. 2001. "The Portuguese Colonization and the Problem of the East Timorese Nationalism." *Lusotopie* 2001: 183–94.

Southall, Roger. 2001. "Opposition in South Africa: Issues and Problems." *Democratization* 8, no. 1 (September): 1–24.

Southall, Roger. 2018. "Polarization in South Africa: Toward Democratic Deepening or Democratic Decay?" *Annals of the American Academy of Political and Social Science* 681, no. 1 (January): 194–208.

Spiller, Pablo T., and Mariano Tommasi. 2007. *The Institutional Foundations of Public Policy in Argentina: A Transactions Cost Approach*. Cambridge: Cambridge University Press.

Staniland, Paul. 2012. "Organizing Insurgency: Networks, Resources, and Rebellion in South Asia." *International Security* 37, no. 1 (Summer): 142–77.

Steinberg, David A. 2015. *Demanding Devaluation: Exchange Rate Politics in the Developing World*. Ithaca and London: Cornell University Press.

Stepan, Alfred. 1988. *Rethinking Military Politics: Brazil and the Southern Cone*. Princeton, NJ: Princeton University Press.

Stepan, Alfred, Juan Linz, and Yogendra Yadav. 2011. *Crafting State-Nations: India and Other Multinational Democracies*. Baltimore: Johns Hopkins University Press.

Stepan, Alfred C., and Graeme B. Robertson. 2003. "An 'Arab' More than 'Muslim' Democracy Gap." *Journal of Democracy* 14, no. 3 (July): 30–44.

Stepan, Alfred, and Cindy Skach. 1993. "Constitutional Frameworks and Democratic Consolidation: Parliamentarianism versus Presidentialism." *World Politics* 46, no. 1 (October): 1–22.

Steytler, Nico. 2005. "Local Government in South Africa: Entrenching Decentralised Government." In *The Place and Role of Local Government in Federal Systems*, edited by Nico Steytler, 183–211. Johannesburg: Konrad-Adenauer-Stiftung.

Strating, Rebecca. 2016. *Social Democracy in East Timor*. Oxon: Routledge.

Stroh, Alexander. 2018. "Sustaining and Jeopardising a Credible Arbiter: Judicial Networks in Benin's Consolidating Democracy." *International Political Science Review* 39, no. 5: 600–15.

Svampa, Maristella, and Sebastián Pereyra. 2003. *Entre la ruta y el barrio: la experiencia de las organizaciones piqueteras*. Buenos Aires: Editorial Biblos.

Svolik, Milan. 2012. *The Politics of Authoritarian Rule*. New York: Cambridge University Press.

Svolik, Milan. 2015. "Which Democracies Will Last? Coups, Incumbent Takeovers, and the Dynamic of Democratic Consolidation." *British Journal of Political Science* 45, no. 4 (October): 715–38.

Svolik, Milan. 2019. "Polarization versus Democracy." *Journal of Democracy* 30, no. 3 (July): 20–32.

Swenson, Geoffrey. 2018. "Legal Pluralism in Theory and Practice." *International Studies Review* 20, no. 3 (January): 438–62.

Tansey, Oisín. 2009. *Regime-Building: Democratization and International Administration*. Oxford: Oxford University Press.

Tarrow, Sidney. 1996. "States and Opportunities: The Political Structuring of Social Movements." In *Comparative Perspectives on Social Movements*, edited by Doug McAdam, John McCarthy, and Mayer Zald, 41–61. New York: Cambridge University Press.

Taylor, Brian. 2011. *State Building in Putin's Russia: Policing and Coercion after Communism*. New York: Cambridge University Press.

Taylor, John. 1999. *East Timor: The Price of Freedom*. London: Zed Books.

Tcach, César, and Hugo Quiroga, eds. 2006. *Argentina, 1976–2006: entre la sombra de la dictadura y el futuro de la democracia*. Rosario: Homo Sapiens.

Teorell, Jan. 2010. *Determinants of Democratization: Explaining Regime Change in the World, 1972–2006*. New York: Cambridge University Press.

The Economist Intelligence Unit. 2020. *Democracy Index 2019: A Year of Democratic Setbacks and Popular Protest*. London: The Economist Intelligence Unit Limited.

Thiel, Hermann, and Robert B Mattes. 1998. "Consolidation and Public Opinion in South Africa." *Journal of Democracy* 9, no. 1: 95–110. https://doi.org/10.1353/jod.1998.0010.

Tocqueville, Alexis de. 1835. *Democracy in America*, vol. 1., trans. Henry Reeve. London: Saunders and Otley.

Toft, Monica Duffy. 2012. "Self-Determination, Secession, and Civil War." *Terrorism and Political Violence* 24, no. 4: 581–600.

Torre, Juan Carlos. 1983. *Los sindicatos en el gobierno, 1973–1976*. Buenos Aires: Centro Editor de América Latina.

Trochev, Alexei. 2010. "Meddling with Justice: Competitive Politics, Impunity and Distrusted Courts in Post-Orange Ukraine." *Demokratizatsiya* 18, no. 2 (Spring): 122–47.

Trochev, Alexei. 2011. "Editor's Introduction." *Statutes and Decisions* 46, no. 2 (March–April): 4–7.

Tudor, Maya. 2013. *The Promise of Power: The Origins of Democracy in India and Autocracy in Pakistan.* Cambridge: Cambridge University Press.

Tudor, Maya, and Dan Slater. 2016. "The Content of Democracy: Nationalist Parties and Inclusive Ideologies in India and Indonesia." In *Parties, Movements and Democracy in the Developing World*, edited by Nancy Bermeo and Deborah J. Yashar, 28–60. New York: Cambridge University Press.

Tudor, Maya, and Dan Slater. 2020. "Nationalism, Authoritarianism, and Democracy: Historical Lessons from South and Southeast Asia." *Perspectives on Politics* 19, no. 3: 706–22. https://doi.org/10.1017/S153759272000078X.

UCDP/PRIO Armed Conflict Dataset (v.18.1). Accessed August 2019. https://www.prio.org/Data/Armed-Conflict/UCDP-PRIO/.

UNDP (United Nations Development Programme). 2002. *Human Development Report 2002: Deepening Democracy in a Fragmented World.* New York: Oxford University Press.

United Nations. 2006. *Report of the Independent Special Committee of Inquiry for Timor-Leste.* Geneva, October 2. Accessed 2019. https://www.ohchr.org/Documents/Countries/COITimorLeste.pdf.

US Department of State. 2002. *2001 Country Reports on Human Rights Practices: Argentina.* March 4. Accessed July 2021. https://2009-2017.state.gov/j/drl/rls/hrrpt/2001/wha/8278.htm.

V-Dem Institute. 2021. *Autocratization Turns Viral: Democracy Report 2021.* Gothenburg: V-Dem Institute.

Vachudova, Milada Anna. 2005. *Europe Undivided: Democracy, Leverage and Integration after Communism.* Oxford: Oxford University Press.

Vachudova, Milada Anna. 2010. "Democratization in Postcommunist Europe: Illiberal Regimes and the Leverage of the European Union." In *Democracy and Authoritarianism in the Postcommunist World*, edited by Valerie Bunce, Michael McFaul, and Kathryn Stoner-Weiss, 82–104. New York: Cambridge University Press.

Valencia, Fabian, and Luc Laeven. 2012. "Systemic Banking Crises Database; An Update." IMF Working Papers 12/163, International Monetary Fund. https://ideas.repec.org/p/imf/imfwpa/12-163.html.

Van de Walle, Nicolas. 2001. *African Economies and the Politics of Permanent Crisis, 1979–1999.* New York: Cambridge University Press.

Van de Walle, Nicolas. 2003. "Presidentialism and Clientelism in Africa's Emerging Party Systems." *Journal of Modern African Studies* 41, no. 2: 297–321.

van Peski, Caecilia. 2013. "Good Cop, Bad Cop: Georgia's One Hundred Days of a New Democratic Dream." *Security and Human Rights Monitor* 24: 49–100.

Van Wyk, Barry. 2005. *The Balance of Power and the Transition to Democracy in South Africa.* PhD diss., University of Pretoria.

Varshney, Ashutosh. 1995. *Democracy, Development and the Countryside: Urban-Rural Struggles in India.* New York: Cambridge University Press.

Varshney, Ashutosh. 1998. "India Defies the Odds: Why Democracy Survives." *Journal of Democracy* 9, no. 3 (July): 36–50.

Varshney, Ashutosh. 2000. "Is India Becoming More Democratic?" *Journal of Asian Studies* 59, no. 1 (February): 3–25.

Varshney, Ashutosh. 2002. *Ethnic Conflict and Civic Life: Hindus and Muslims in India.* New Haven, CT: Yale University Press.

Varshney, Ashutosh. 2012. "Two Banks of the Same River? Social Orders and Entrepreneurialism in India." In *Anxieties of Democracy: Tocquevillian Reflections on India and the United States*, edited by Partha Chatterjee and Ira Katznelson, 225–56. Delhi: Oxford University Press.

Varshney, Ashutosh. 2013. *Battles Half Won: India's Improbable Democracy*. Gurgaon, Haryana, India: Penguin Books.

Varshney, Ashutosh. 2015. "Asian Democracy through an Indian Prism." *Journal of Asian Studies* 74, no. 4: 917–26.

Varshney, Ashutosh. 2019a. "Democratic Subversion." *The Indian Express*, December 16.

Varshney, Ashutosh. 2019b. "The Emergence of Right-Wing Populism in India." In *Re-Forming India: The Nation Today*, edited by Niraja Gopal Jayal, 327–45. Delhi: Penguin.

Varshney, Ashutosh. 2019c. "Modi Consolidates Power: Electoral Vibrancy, Mounting Liberal Deficits." *Journal of Democracy* 30, no. 4: 63–77.

Verbitsky, Horacio. 1995. *El vuelo*. Buenos Aires: Planeta.

Vom Hau, Matthias. 2008. "State Infrastructural Power and Nationalism: Comparative Lessons from Mexico and Argentina." *Studies in Comparative International Development* 43, nos. 3–4 (December): 334–54.

Walker, Ignacio. 1990. *Socialismo y democracia: Chile y Europa en perspectiva comparada*. Santiago: CIEPLAN/Hachette.

Waters, Trevor. 1996. "Moldova: Continuing Recipe for Instability." *Jane's Intelligence Review* 8, no. 9 (September 18): 398–401.

Way, Lucan. 2002. "Pluralism by Default in Moldova." *Journal of Democracy* 13, no. 4 (October): 127–41.

Way, Lucan. 2015. *Pluralism by Default: Weak Autocrats and the Rise of Competitive Politics*. Baltimore: Johns Hopkins University Press.

Way, Lucan. 2016. "The Authoritarian Threat: Weaknesses of Autocracy Promotion." *Journal of Democracy* 27, no. 1 (January): 64–75.

Way, Lucan. 2019. "Ukraine's Post-Maidan Struggles: Free Speech in a Time of War." *Journal of Democracy* 30, no. 3 (July): 48–60.

Weiner, Myron. 1967. *Party Building in a New Nation: The Indian National Congress*. Chicago: University of Chicago Press.

Weiner, Myron. 1989. *The Indian Paradox: Essays in Indian Politics*. Newbury Park, CA: Sage Publications.

Weiner, Myron. 2001. "The Struggle for Equality: Caste in Indian Politics." In *The Success of India's Democracy*, edited by Atul Kohli, 193–225. New York: Cambridge University Press.

Weldemichael, Awet Tewelde. 2013. *Third World Colonialism and Strategies of Liberation: Eritrea and East Timor Compared*. New York: Cambridge University Press.

Welsh, David. 1993. "Domestic Politics and Ethnic Conflict." *Survival* 35 (1): 63–80.

Welsh, David. 1994. "South Africa's Democratic Transition." *The Brown Journal of World Affairs* 2, no. 1 (Winter): 221–30.

Welsh, David. 2009. *The Rise and Fall of Apartheid*. Charlottesville: University of Virginia Press.

Welt, Cory. 2015. "The Curious Case of Rustavi-2: Protecting Media Freedom and the Rule of Law in Georgia." PONARS Policy Memo 400, November 15.

Welzel, Christian, and Ronald Inglehart. 2009. "Political Culture, Mass Beliefs, and Value Change." In *Democratization*, edited by Christian W. Haerpfer, Christian Welzel, Patrick Bernhagen, and Ronald Inglehart, 126–44. Oxford: Oxford University Press.

Weyland, Kurt. 2013. "Latin America's Authoritarian Drift: The Threat from the Populist Left." *Journal of Democracy* 24, no. 3 (July): 18–32.

Weyland, Kurt. 2020. "Populism's Threat to Democracy: Comparative Lessons for the United States." *Perspectives on Politics* 18, no. 2 (June): 389–406.

Weyland, Kurt, and Raúl Madrid, eds. 2019. *When Democracy Trumps Populism: European and Latin American Lessons for the United States.* New York: Cambridge University Press.

Whitehead, Laurence. 1986. "International Aspects of Democratization." In *Transitions from Authoritarian Rule: Comparative Perspectives*, edited by Guillermo O'Donnell, Philippe C. Schmitter, and Laurence Whitehead, 3–46. Baltimore: Johns Hopkins University Press.

Wibbels, Erik, and Kenneth Roberts. 2010. "The Politics of Economic Crisis in Latin America." *Studies in Comparative International Development* 45, no. 4 (December): 383–409.

Wieczorek, Robert. 2012. "ANC Dominance and Democratic Consolidation in South Africa." *Penn State Journal of International Affairs* 1 (2): 27–38.

Wilkinson, Steven I. 2004. "India, Consociational Theory and Ethnic Violence." In *India and the Politics of Developing Countries: Essays in Memory of Myron Weiner*, edited by Ashutosh Varshney, 150–77. Delhi: Sage Publications.

Wilson, Andrew. 2013. "Filat's Gamble." OpenDemocracy, May 23, 2013. https://www.opendemocracy.net/en/odr/filats-gamble/.

Wilson, Bu V. E. 2012. "The Politics of Security-Sector Reform." In *The Politics of Timor-Leste: Democratic Consolidation after Intervention*, edited by Michael Leach, and Damien Kingsbury, 179–96. Ithaca, NY: Cornell University Press.

Woodberry, Robert D. 2012. "The Missionary Roots of Liberal Democracy." *American Political Science Review* 106, no. 2 (May): 244–74.

World Development Indicators (GDP per capita growth (annual %) [NY.GDP.PCAP.KD.ZG], accessed June 2020 and June 2021; GDP growth (annual %) [NY.GDP.MKTP.KD.ZG], accessed January 2019 and July 2021; GDP per capita (constant 2010 US$) [NY.GDP.PCAP.KD], accessed January 2019, June 2020, and June/July 2021; GDP per capita (current US$) [NY.GDP.PCAP.CD], accessed June 2020; Inflation, GDP deflator (annual %), accessed January 2019 and June 2021 [NY.GDP.DEFL.KD.ZG]; Total natural resources rents (% of GDP) [NY.GDP.TOTL.RT.ZS], accessed August 2015; GNI per capita, PPP (current international $) [NY.GNP.PCAP.PP.CD], accessed August 2021; Gini index (World Bank estimate) [SI.POV.GINI], accessed August 2021; Military expenditure (% of GDP) [MS.MIL.XPND.GD.ZS], accessed January 2019; and Unemployment, total (% of total labor force) (national estimate) [SL.UEM.TOTL.NE.ZS], accessed January 2019). https://databank.worldbank.org/source/world-development-indicators.

Worldwide Governance Indicators (for control of corruption, government effectiveness, and rule of law). Accessed June 2021. https://info.worldbank.org/governance/wgi/.

Wu, Tim. 2020. "What Really Saved the Republic from Trump?" *New York Times*, December 10, 2020. https://www.nytimes.com/2020/12/10/opinion/trump-constitution-norms.html.

Young, Crawford. 2012. *The Postcolonial State in Africa: Fifty Years of Independence, 1960–2010.* Madison: University of Wisconsin Press.

Zakaria, Fareed. 1997. *The Future of Freedom: Illiberal Democracy at Home and Abroad.* New York: W. W. Norton.

Zechmeister, Elizabeth J., and Noam Lupu. 2019. *El pulso de la democracia*. Nashville, TN: LAPOP. https://www.vanderbilt.edu/lapop/ab2018/2018-19_AmericasBarometer_Regional_Report_Spanish_W_03.27.20.pdf.

Ziblatt, Daniel. 2017. *Conservative Parties and the Birth of Democracy*. New York: Cambridge University Press.

Zürcher, Christoph, Carrie L. Manning, Kristie D. Evenson, Rachel Hayman, Sarah Riese, and Nora Roehner. 2013. *Costly Democracy: Peacebuilding and Democratization after War*. Stanford: Stanford University Press.

Index

Printed in the USA/Agawam, MA
June 7, 2022

794009.061